D0849264

THE REPUBLIC OF VIOLENCE

ALSO BY J. D. DICKEY:

American Demagogue:
The Great Awakening and the Rise and Fall of Populism

Rising in Flames:
Sherman's March and the Fight for a New Nation

Empire of Mud:
The Secret History of Washington, DC

THE REPUBLIC OF VIOLENCE

OF

VIOLENCE

The Tormented Rise of Abolition
in Andrew Jackson's America

J. D. DICKEY

PEGASUS BOOKS
NEW YORK LONDON

THE REPUBLIC OF VIOLENCE

Pegasus Books, Ltd.
148 West 37th Street, 13th Floor
New York, NY 10018

Copyright © 2022 by J. D. Dickey

First Pegasus Books edition March 2022

Interior design by Maria Fernandez

Library of Congress Cataloging-in-Publication Data is available.

ISBN: 978-1-64313-928-9

10 9 8 7 6 5 4 3 2 1

Printed in the United States of America
Distributed by Simon & Schuster
www.pegasusbooks.com

To T.C.

CONTENTS

AUTHOR'S NOTE

We can no longer say the movement for the abolition of slavery is overlooked in American culture. The rich legacy of figures like Frederick Douglass is widely discussed and debated; Harriet Tubman may soon make an appearance on American currency; and the names of Sojourner Truth, John Brown, and Charles Sumner are well known to students of history, even in high school. This marks a dramatic change from sixty years ago, when pro-Confederate historians of the Lost Cause maintained that slavery was not the primary cause of the Civil War and that political misunderstandings or economic imperatives led more than a half-million Americans to sacrifice themselves in the greatest conflict in U.S. history.

Though our understanding of nineteenth-century American history may have changed, it does not mean we are anywhere near a full accounting of the nation's role in slavery. And just because abolition is no longer downplayed in popular history, it does not mean we have a complete picture of it. In fact, even today, the early stages of the abolition movement are nearly as clouded in obscurity as they've ever been, with teachers and historians finding it easier to discuss such important names as Douglass and Tubman because their narratives are heroic and inspiring and they lived to celebrate the demise of human bondage. But what of those who came before, and either didn't live to see that victory or were so beaten up by the fight they had to withdraw from it?

The figures of the early movement are no less important because they remain obscure. It might even be argued that without their sacrifices, their endurance under persecution, and their ability to set the strategy that later abolitionists used for their success, the cause might not have achieved the same results. Slavery's demise might have been delayed or compromised. Indeed, their greatest victory may be that they helped the movement survive a brutal and remorseless era—and kept their hope alive.

The current volume focuses on the period 1833–1838, with the abolition movement trying to gain a foothold in the shadow of the hostile administration of Andrew Jackson. A word of warning: it's a tough read for those expecting a happy ending. Instead, it focuses on the way abolitionists learned to use political organizing and social activism to begin to change minds about slavery and racial injustice and persisted despite countless hazards and divisions. The story takes place mostly in the North, which at the time was not a refuge of freedom but a place whose leaders cooperated closely with Southern slaveholders and enflamed mobs to attack Black residents and antislavery activists. Based on primary sources and contemporary resources, the narrative foregrounds the work of Black Americans in the abolition fight, women as well as men, and doesn't assume that William Lloyd Garrison—the one abolitionist of the era known to the layman—was the only one to make a difference. I hope this book will help the reader appreciate, and perhaps celebrate, the less familiar but no less important figures of the time.

J. D. Dickey

INTRODUCTION

t was January 1817, and the African Methodist Episcopal Church in Philadelphia had never seen a crowd this big. Three thousand souls packed into the church for an urgent meeting, having heard reports about a group that claimed to have the solution for America's racial problems. It had the support of major figures like Speaker of the House Henry Clay, former president Thomas Jefferson, current president James Madison, and President-Elect James Monroe. The group had formed just weeks before, and it called itself the American Colonization Society.

The premise of the group was that the racial problems in the United States were too great and enduring to be fixed. Some of these colonizers said free African Americans could not benefit the country because of their presumed limitations or inferiority. Others said the country could not benefit them, and they should emigrate across the Atlantic to a land of plenty, where they could farm and raise families free from the interference of white people. The colonizers encouraged them to depart for Sierra Leone—or later, to Liberia—to leave the only country most had ever known. To leave the place where many had deeper roots than the colonizers themselves.

Trying to gain the acceptance of the Philadelphians were two men: Paul Cuffe, a prominent Black shipbuilder, and Robert Shipley, a white New Jersey minister. They had helped arrange the mass meeting inside the church so local leaders could present the plan for emigration and gain the community's feedback. All they needed to do now was to put matters to a vote. A wealthy Black sailmaker named James Forten polled the crowd for its support. How many were in favor?

Silence.

And how many were against it?

The room erupted with such a thunderous response Forten thought the walls might collapse.

The audience members were so repelled by the proposal, so insulted, they pressed their leaders to pass a resolution describing their feelings. Forten helped write the statement, which did not equivocate.

In response to Henry Clay's claim that Black people were "a dangerous and useless part of the community," the resolution said they were actually "the first successful cultivators of America." Though they had been enslaved and forced to come to the continent, they had made its soil fertile with their sweat and blood. They would refuse any attempt to coerce them to leave their homes, would fight any slander to their name, and would resist being divided: "We never will separate ourselves voluntarily from the slave population in this country; they are our brethren by the ties of consanguinity, of suffering, and of wrong."

As hostility to colonization spread, Forten summed up the popular feeling in a note to Paul Cuffe: "The whole continent seems to be agitated concerning Colonising the People of Colour." From this point on, Black authors, activists, and community leaders stood against the movement to ship them out of the country. In so doing, they also found a new way to speak out against slavery—not in the manner that politicians like Jefferson had, imagining a distant day when human bondage might disappear. Rather, they called for immediate abolition, to end slavery in the South and racial injustice in the North with all due haste. It would take until 1829 for a major white ally, William Lloyd Garrison, to join them in the movement.

By that time, though, the country had changed dramatically. The Philadelphia meeting had occurred during the so-called Era of Good Feelings, when America was still a young nation. Yet by the turn of the 1830s, the nation had entered a difficult adolescence known as the Jacksonian Era. Slavery had expanded into much larger swaths of the continent—even as a small but growing number of Americans looked to fight that expansion. The eight years of the Andrew Jackson presidency would be marked by both the rise of an interracial abolition movement and some of the worst violence the nation has ever seen, often directed against that movement.

To say that Jackson ruled during a time of ferment would be putting it mildly. Even on the day of his first inauguration, March 4, 1829, a riot broke out at the White House when a crowd of up to twenty thousand people imbibed from the tubs and buckets of punch on offer, began destroying the glass and china and other valuables, and nearly waylaid Jackson himself. As a contemporary wrote, he was "*literally* nearly pressed to death and almost suffocated and torn to pieces by the people in their eagerness to shake hands."

The party system he presided over wasn't much more civil: the old Democratic-Republican Party of James Monroe had splintered into pro- and anti-Jackson camps, resulting in disputed elections, an outbreak of conspiracy theories and groups based on them (e.g., the Anti-Masonic Party), and violence and intimidation at the polls. Street crime spiked throughout the country, much of it fueled by liquor. The annual consumption of spirits in 1830 was more than five gallons per person—more than twelve ounces a week—the highest in the country's history. Whiskey, rum, gin, and brandy were the drinks of choice, especially in places where masculine bravado made excessive drinking into sport. Bear baiting and cockfighting were popular forms of gambling, and men battled with pistols, shotguns, and even bowie knives in mortal contests known as duels.

President Jackson carried around bullets in his body from previous duels and had killed at least one man in these contests. Even when he wasn't dueling, he had a bent toward violence. He signed into law the Force Bill, which allowed the use of military power against states like South Carolina that tried to nullify federal law, and he regretted not executing John Calhoun for his role in that attempt, wishing he could hang him "as high as Haman." He enforced the Indian Removal Act against the US Supreme Court's order, which would lead to the expulsion of tens of thousands of Native peoples from their homes on deadly forced marches, later to be called the Trail of Tears. And after a would-be assassin failed to kill him when two of his guns misfired, Jackson beat the man so severely with his cane that bystanders had to intervene to keep the president from bludgeoning him to death.

While Jackson had wide support among his white working-class base, he also faced vigorous opposition from certain mercantile classes and Black Americans. By the time of Jackson's second inauguration, the Whig Party had emerged to take advantage of the animus against him. In 1834 a young Abraham Lincoln joined it, and three years later, he reflected on the era named after Jackson:

> There is even now something of an ill omen amongst us. I mean the increasing disregard for law which pervades the country—the growing disposition to substitute the wild and furious passions in lieu of the sober judgment of the courts, and the worse than savage mobs for the executive ministers of justice . . . Accounts of out-rages committed by mobs form the every-day news of the times.

Lincoln did not exaggerate. The era featured the greatest concentration of rioting in American history, with more than fifty major incidents in two years alone: 1834 and 1835. Indeed, before the Civil War, more than one thousand people died in riots, with untold property damage to homes, churches, schools, and civic institutions. The victims and perpetrators were many: Nativists battling Irish immigrants. Workingmen attacking banks and bankers. Protestants burning Catholic schools and convents. Religious zealots lynching gamblers and torching brothels. Bigots assaulting Mormons. Angry patrons ransacking theaters and beating up actors. More than anything, though, racial hatred fueled the mobs.

Half of the riots targeted free Black people and abolitionists. Both working- and middle-class white men immolated African American churches, schools, assembly halls, even orphanages. They chased Black people in the streets and savaged them in their homes. They beat and stoned abolitionists for the speeches they gave and the literature they distributed. It wasn't just in the South either. The largest cities in the North all saw onslaughts against the opponents of slavery, with guns, knives, bricks, rocks, bludgeons, torches, and tar and feathers as the usual weapons in the rioters' arsenal.

Jackson claimed to disfavor mobs and sent out federal troops on more than one occasion to quash them. But he did so selectively, being careful not to offend the feelings of brick-throwers and torch-carriers who might vote for his party. After the fearsome Snow Riot of 1835, he deployed federal troops to quell the violence of workingmen from the Washington Navy Yard; then he made sure to ask the rioters if there was "anything he could do for them in an honorable way to promote their happiness." And, of course, Jackson's Democratic Party, like the Whig Party, used all manner of tactical violence come election time, from pummeling opposing voters to stealing ballot boxes to brawling outside the polls.

To go along with the turmoil on the streets, the nation found itself riven by upheaval in society and demography. A wave of German and Irish Catholic immigrants challenged the assumptions of Protestant dominance, resulting in battles over religion, politics, and labor relations. People left the countryside for the cities to work in industrial operations, like mills and factories and ropewalks, as those cities expanded to a size never before seen by Americans. Technological innovations, from railways and canals to the telegraph, added to the frenetic sense of change as the republic expanded westward into new territories in the Middle West and the South, bringing slavery in its wake and further conflict with Native peoples.

The upswell of change gave way to an upswell of religious fervor, later called the Second Great Awakening. Evangelical preachers like Charles Grandison Finney and William Miller offered traveling ministries and tent revivals to announce the coming of the Millennium or God's imminent return, sometimes with a schedule for it to happen. Many of these ministers also led reform movements, promoting temperance and prison reform and universal public education and many other causes. The more radical in temperament, like John Humphrey Noyes, announced they had achieved Christian perfection, and self-appointed messiahs blazed the trail for utopian movements that incorporated anything from polygamy to celibacy, socialism to vegetarianism. It made for a crazy quilt of faith healers, wildcat evangelists, and homegrown prophets, and it cemented the United States as one of the most religiously driven societies in the Western world. And out of this society one crusade would emerge that, along with temperance, would dominate the attention of reformers by the mid-1830s: the abolition of slavery.

Slavery had a history in America hundreds of years older than the nation itself. It had been built into the US Constitution. Every president but those named Adams had held human captives, and the system of enslavement reached from the most remote plantations of the South to the commodity markets of Europe. The South may have been synonymous with chattel slavery, but the North wasn't insulated from it and, indeed, profited from it. New York was the nation's chief port for cotton exports, exporting anywhere from $76 to $131 million annually. Its businessmen held stakes in countless textile operations and plantations, and even ownership of slaves themselves. As the *Anti-Slavery Record* put it, "Thousands of northern merchants, manufacturers and others, share with the masters in the unjust gains of slavery. To say that slavery is a sin, touches their pockets almost as directly as those of the slaveholder." Other parts of the East Coast also had a hand in the trade. Shipbuilders made vessels to carry enslaved people from Africa to the Americas. Mill owners used slave-grown commodities in their industrial operations. Mercantile agents sent Southern cotton to the United Kingdom. And Southern planters felt comfortable enough in the North that many brought their captives with them for several months at a time while they took vacations.

All this came at a time when large Northern states were beginning to outlaw human bondage (New York in 1827, Pennsylvania in 1780), even as others, like New Jersey and New Hampshire, were reluctant to follow suit. Overall, legislative progress against slavery in the North was slow and halting. It collapsed not for moral reasons, but due to economic realities: the lack of sprawling plantations, the rise of white factory labor, and so on. In fact, many whites in the region still romanticized the South and enjoyed reading novels, like *Swallow Barn* and *Camden*, that presented plantation life in imaginary splendor—a world away from its actual terrors for Black people. Newspapers reprinted the speeches of ardent defenders of slavery, and performers regularly appeared in black-face on Northern stages, depicting African Americans as grotesque fools and buffoons. T. D. Rice became one of the most popular figures, known by the nickname "Jim Crow."

Even amid Northern sympathies for the South, Black residents pushed back. They held mass meetings in urban centers, created social networks in literary and sewing circles, led campaigns for free produce (not buying slave-grown goods), and published or edited newspapers that helped build the movement. With a burgeoning press they countered the claims of colonizers and proslavery sympathizers—that human bondage couldn't be eradicated without anarchy, that Black and white people could never be equals—and aimed to prove these ideas were lies.

The most important manifesto of this early movement came in 1829, with the publication of David Walker's *Appeal in Four Articles*. As a statement of Black empowerment, it was both a call to reject slavery and racial oppression and, some thought, an inspiration for revolution. Walker's *Appeal* criticized figures like Jefferson, who had promised freedom to all in the Declaration of Independence then denied it to

African Americans; clergymen who endorsed slavery by cherry-picking passages from the Bible; slaveholding politicians like Henry Clay; and all branches of government.

Walker's *Appeal* was an immediate success, going through three printings and bringing its author much attention. Copies circulated through the mail and aboard ships among the free and enslaved, and they also found their way into the South, and possibly into the hands of men and women held in bondage there. Leading politicians of the region demanded the book be suppressed as insurrectionary and passed laws against its circulation, calling it the "diabolical Boston pamphlet."

A year after he published the *Appeal*, Walker died under questionable circumstances—possibly murder. Yet he remained to many Black Americans an inspiration and standard bearer, to others a cautionary example of extremism, and to most whites a militant threat and an anarchist. Some of his words were not likely to be forgotten, none more so than his exhortation to those held captive: "They want us for their slaves, and think nothing of murdering us in order to subject us to that wretched condition—therefore, if there is an attempt made by us, kill or be killed."

William Lloyd Garrison disapproved strongly of the militancy of Walker's *Appeal* and would remain committed to pacifism throughout much of his life. But he also saw it as "one of the most remarkable products of the age," because "a better promoter of insurrection was never sent forth to an oppressed people." Largely because of Walker's *Appeal* and other writings of Black Americans, Garrison dropped his previous support for colonization and came out in favor of immediate abolition.

Most of the key ideas from Garrison's newspaper, *The Liberator*, had been circulating in Black communities for years, but he gave them new and strident voice. He pilloried preachers who sympathized with slaveholders. He lacerated politicians for upholding the trade in human commerce. And he gave colonizers no quarter, spending issue after issue insulting them and imagining how God would punish them for their sins.

His methods brought him a committed group of followers who cheered his words and adopted them as their own.

However, other whites in the movement were much more wary than he. They might accept immediate abolition, but they hesitated about the other parts of the program, especially the push for equal rights and racial justice in the North. For they worried that by taking such a step, and rebuking the ideology of the Colonization Society, they might invite retaliation or worse—especially if Black and white abolitionists worked together to do it. Because working together across racial lines meant accepting "amalgamation," and that would mark them as targets for violence.

Webster's Dictionary of 1828 defined "amalgamation" as "The mixing or blending of different things"—innocuous enough, but when applied to race, it became one of the most loaded words in the English language. Amalgamation could mean Black and white people fraternizing, communing socially, dancing together, working together, worshipping together, becoming friends, sharing a meal, sharing a bed, or getting married. All these things could be subversive, but none more so than interracial sex and marriage, which colonizers called "a principle of repulsion" that was "utterly abhorrent." After all, to propose Black and white people might someday share a life together cut to the heart of their argument that they could never coexist and that the only solution was for Black Americans to be shipped to Africa.

Throughout the era, amalgamation provided the excuse for rioters to run rampant against abolitionists and Black people in cities from Philadelphia and New York to Providence and Cincinnati. Garrison dismissed concerns over amalgamation and chastised whites who cowered in the face of it. He routinely worked in the movement with African Americans, worshipped at their churches, and communed with them in their homes, and he led endeavors and built organizations with them. But though he dismissed amalgamation as just another insult, the colonizers had other accusations just as damning. Perhaps the most potent was the claim that abolitionists meant to encourage slaves to break their fetters and kill those who held them captive. To rise up just as Nat Turner had, in a slave insurrection that shook the nation.

In the late summer of 1831, Turner and a force of up to sixty other slaves took up arms, from guns to broadaxes, to kill fifty-five white people. The slain included men, women, and children, most of them from slaveholding families in Southampton County, Virginia. The violence played out over several days, until a white militia killed or hanged the lot of Turner's men, with the leader himself executed by noose in November. In the hunt for Turner and his men, white mobs and militias attacked an untold number of innocent Black people—killing at least 120 in one day alone, driving them out of their homes, burning them alive, committing numberless atrocities. In the aftermath Southern politicians passed laws against their freedom to speak, assemble, learn, and worship.

In the North, the specter of Turner provided an excuse for authorities to write new laws stifling the liberties and movement of Black citizens, and to rail against abolitionists and accuse them of fomenting chaos with their talk of racial justice. While actual contact between abolitionists and enslaved people was rare, conspiracy theories promoted by colonizers and proslavery men claimed there was a direct link between the Turner revolt and abolitionists who had supposedly encouraged it. They seized on David Walker's work, especially, to make it sound as if abolitionists—most of whom were pacifists—had a secret thirst for bloodshed.

The media amplified these accusations and made activists other than Garrison even more hesitant in what they said and wrote. Aside from papers like *The Liberator*, very few white-published newspapers championed antislavery, and most editors were openly hostile to it, with James Watson Webb's *Courier and Enquirer* being the most powerful. Using the media as a megaphone, proslavery forces could issue threats read by thousands of people—instead of a few dozen by way of a handbill—and enflame mobs to commit even more egregious acts of violence. Indeed, amalgamation, anarchy, and insurrection had become such dangerous charges that many potential converts to abolition refused to support it to avoid being slandered or marked for attack.

—⁓—

Such was the state of affairs in America in 1833, when the narrative of this book begins. The principal figures that follow span the abolition movement in the Northeast, including men and women, both Black and white, with varying degrees of zeal for the cause but a deep commitment to seeing the destruction of human bondage in America and the rest of the Western world.

The most familiar name among them remains Garrison's. For many Americans with limited knowledge of abolition, he *was* the movement, uncompromising and unrelenting in his rhetoric, and always willing to engage in a public fight. Yet Garrison's role in the movement was unique, to say the least. His spiritual beliefs and lifestyle could be as radical as his abolitionism. While he may have been the most combative of white activists, he was paradoxically the most peaceable, and he promoted self-sacrifice in his writings and speeches—even if it led to martyrdom, which almost happened to him more than once. His cavalier attitude toward embracing scandal not only embroiled him in controversy with the supporters of slavery; it alienated him from many of his colleagues. In the end, such internecine warfare would threaten the movement at the moment it was achieving the greatest traction.

Another radical, David Ruggles, put his energies in a different direction. As an African American author, bookseller, and newspaper agent, he maintained a wide network of supporters across the movement, regardless of their ideology. He never forced his allies to choose sides in their degree of loyalty to him, and he championed Black self-empowerment. He was perhaps the bravest of all abolitionists. Against the proslavery contingent he was relentless, lecturing and fundraising and constantly writing and exhorting for the cause. He fought segregation and racial inequality in New York and created new and inventive organizations to assist and defend his fellow Black New Yorkers. The most important of these, the Committee of Vigilance, would be one of the first steps in America toward the creation of the Underground Railroad.

Several Black ministers aided Ruggles in the cause, among them Peter Williams Jr. and Theodore Wright, but none was more important to him than Samuel Cornish. This Presbyterian clergyman did his most important work outside of churches, publishing what may have been the first Black-owned and -edited newspaper in America, *Freedom's Journal*, and leading drives to create schools for Black youth and philanthropic institutions like the Phoenix Society. Though more pacific than Ruggles, he nonetheless provided valuable help to his Committee of Vigilance, using the *Colored American* newspaper to help protect Black New Yorkers and assist fugitives on the run from bounty hunters.

Cornish served as a leader of the American Anti-Slavery Society along with his allies, Arthur and Lewis Tappan. These silk merchants operated a shop in the mercantile district of New York City and generously funded the movement as part of their social gospel of evangelical Christianity. The Tappans would go down in history as the money men behind the movement, but their role was much more pivotal. Arthur's network of abolitionists was one of the most extensive in the nation and helped establish alliances between activists that might not have occurred otherwise. Lewis pioneered a mass mailing campaign that would excite such a furious reaction from the South that the prospect of federal censorship loomed as a real possibility. For all their work, the brothers would find themselves targeted for kidnapping by Southern politicians, their names becoming synonymous with Northern fanaticism, despite their reputation within the movement as conservatives.

Among the Tappans' associates was James Forten, the sailmaker who stood for decades near the forefront of abolition in Pennsylvania. Forten had been present at the creation of the modern movement and later enlisted his family to join him in the crusade, including his wife, Charlotte, and his daughters Margaretta, Harriet, and Sarah. In fact, Sarah Forten may have achieved even greater results than her father for the cause. As one of the founders of the Philadelphia Female Anti-Slavery Society (along with her mother and sisters), she helped organize groundbreaking campaigns like the petition drive to Congress and the building of Pennsylvania Hall, and she ensured that women's role in abolition would be fundamental to it. For their efforts, the Fortens would endure more abuse than any other prominent Black family involved in the cause, and they persisted despite arson, assault, and attempted ambush.

Other figures would also play a major role in the saga of abolition in the 1830s. George Thompson, the British orator who lectured throughout the Northeast at the behest of Garrison, endured scandalous treatment and even riots from hostile crowds. Theodore Weld, known as "the most mobbed man in America," taught field agents to evangelize for abolition throughout the Northeast. And Angelina Grimké, a Quaker and former slaveholder, achieved a striking rise as a speaker on slavery, racial justice, and women's rights. With Garrison as her ally, the question of women in the movement would become one of the most critical issues by the end of the decade, drawing a sharp dividing line between those who wanted to limit the movement to antislavery and those who saw it as a vehicle for addressing all the injustices in American life.

Ultimately, the challenges that lay before these abolitionists were many: they had to engineer strategies never before attempted against a monolith like slavery. They had to forge bonds with each other, resist dissension and division, and rely on their own courage and wits to survive in a perilous landscape. They had to trust in Providence and the power of divine judgment to give them strength against their enemies. And they had to have faith beyond all expectation that eventually their cause would triumph.

Even so, as the struggle began, their numbers were small compared to the number of colonizers and their sympathizers, who didn't just call on God to crush their foes, but were prepared to do it themselves with their fists, torches, clubs, and guns. And that is where the movement found itself in the summer of 1833: at a dangerous crossroads, with William Lloyd Garrison on the run for his life.

★ ONE ★

ROLL, LAVA TIDE

It was a city of a quarter-million people, by far the greatest metropolis in the country, full of sturdy townhouses and rickety wooden slums, raucous theaters and old Dutch churches, docks and warehouses, mansions and hovels, but without enough good places to hide.

William Lloyd Garrison had not come to New York expecting to be kidnapped, but when his associates told him he would be in great danger if he remained, he knew he had to flee. His enemies had already advertised their purpose—$5,000 for the capture of the infamous blackguard and danger to the republic. No less than the legislature of Georgia had put up the reward to punish him for his seditious publications, and if convicted he could be sentenced to death. He had good reason to run for his life.

Learning of the "conspiracy to seize my body by legal writs on false pretenses," Garrison had to move quickly. He escaped New York first by steamboat, then by horsecar, again by steamboat, until he wound up in

Philadelphia. Then he raced by coach to Trenton at a breakneck speed to avoid his abductors—only to have one of the horses nearly plunge off a riverbank and kill him. At last he made it to an artist's garret in New Haven, and he waited there until he could safely rearrange his plans, head back to New York, and from there sail across the Atlantic to Great Britain, where he would find refuge for the summer. Such was the life of an American dissident in 1833.

Even in the northern United States, Garrison was reviled in many quarters as an agent of treason, anarchy, and anti-Americanism. He found himself indicted by grand juries, censured by state legislatures, and condemned by governors and other politicians. As the British author Harriet Martineau would write, "At present he is a marked man," admired by his friends and persons of color, even as "the rest of society jeer, pelt, and execrate him."

He owed this infamy to his support for abolition—*immediate* abolition. In support of the cause, he debuted his Boston-based newspaper, *The Liberator*, on the first day of 1831 and made it into the foremost antislavery newspaper in the United States. Even so, most of his fellow white Americans had little use for his movement, finding slavery either convenient to their needs or worth ignoring when it wasn't. But Garrison refused to let them ignore it any longer, writing in all caps in his debut issue, "I WILL BE HEARD!" And so he was. Within two years, his enemies hated him beyond all reason.

They despised him for the editorials he wrote comparing proslavery politicians to tyrants, for the speeches he gave eviscerating slaveholders for their depravity, and for his brazen attacks on the country's institutions. Southerners repeated his words in their own press as evidence of his wickedness, giving him added attention. The Northern press followed suit, mocking his editorials while quoting at length from them, which helped his message spread widely, well beyond the actual subscription base of his newspaper. So by the time he embarked on his trip to Britain, "Southern resentment had reached a level of hysteria, and Garrison's name was known throughout the North."

This was part of the reason he had gone to the United Kingdom: publicity. He had to capitalize on his notoriety at a critical time, when the movement was just making headway. While it hadn't yet achieved any tangible victories, Garrison's words were so thrillingly vitriolic, so incandescent with moral outrage, that British abolitionists couldn't help but take notice. They thought he might be a useful ally, one who could carry their campaign to abolish slavery across the Atlantic, to the slave empire of America. So they welcomed their new friend with open arms and gave him license to speak in their lecture halls and churches—even if he was quite unlike the zealot they had imagined.

He was, in fact, a bespectacled, balding young man with a soft-spoken manner and an unexpected humility in conversation. Unlike his British counterparts in abolition, he was no heir to inherited wealth or an aristocratic lineage. Instead, he was descended from dirt-poor indentured servants and had labored for years to achieve his fame. At only twenty-seven years of age, Garrison had already experienced enough tumult for an entire life, abandoned by his father as a child, enduring years of deprivation, forced into hard labor, and finally learning a trade as a printer's apprentice, initiating his career. His British hosts found him fascinating: a firebrand whose moral courage had set slave masters and politicians into a frothing rage, but who also looked surprisingly like a file clerk.

They soon learned he came alive on the stump, filling his speeches with the same kind of invective he published in *The Liberator*. The ostensible reason for the speaking tour was to raise money for a manual labor school for free Black youth, but once fired up, he did not confine himself to discussing charitable matters. Instead, he launched into angry stemwinders about everything he found corrupt or indecent in the modern world, from street violence and alcohol consumption to the scourge of slavery. His most prominent opportunity to express his feelings came in a July speech at Exeter Hall.

He billed himself as a man beyond nationality who decried "the narrow boundaries of a selfish patriotism . . . I am in the midst of strangers; but still surrounded by my countrymen." Needless to say, offering this kind of sentiment was risky. To make common cause with a nation millions of Americans still saw as their enemy—just a generation after the last major war—could put Garrison in peril at home, especially when the British were notorious as some of the harshest critics of the United States. They called Andrew Jackson a tyrant supported by "mob-law and pretended self-government," who presided over an uncivilized country littered with knaves and fools. Not all the members of Garrison's audience felt the same way, but if they did, he gave them plenty to work with. He accused America of various sins:

- "giving an open, deliberate and base denial to her boasted Declaration, that 'all men are created equal'"
- "trafficking in the bodies and souls of men"
- "suffering a large portion of her population to be lacerated, starved and plundered, without law and without justification, at the will of petty tyrants"
- "legalizing, on an enormous scale, licentiousness, fraud, cruelty and murder"
- "kidnapping one hundred thousand infants annually, the offspring of slave parents"
- "stealing the liberties of two millions of the creatures of God, and withholding the just recompense of their labor"

In his view, America had engaged in such terrible acts that the nation slept "upon the brink of a volcano which is in full operation, and which threatens to roll its lava tide over the whole land."

His audience applauded his speech with vigor, marveling at the audacity of it. Garrison knew his message would soon be conveyed across the Atlantic, and he would eventually have to answer for it. For now, though, he enjoyed the adulation, even if he felt a bit ambivalent about it.

He wasn't ignorant of the global reach of slavery and knew the British—including many in his audience—had been just as complicit as Americans in the system of slavery, with hundreds of thousands of bondsmen laboring on West Indian sugar plantations and other sites in the sprawling empire. The United Kingdom had taken a worthy first step toward ending the practice when Parliament passed the Slavery Abolition Act, while Garrison was present in the country. But this would occur only after five years and at the cost of awarding twenty million pounds in compensation to British slaveholders, so they might deign to part with the human beings they claimed to own.

In the July 13 edition of *The Liberator*, Garrison blasted the plan as "unsurpassed in the annals of villainy" and demanded such men be rewarded not with payment but with "punishment proportionate to their crimes." Still, he could not force the issue and risk offending those Englishmen who had arranged the deal, men whose alliance he had cultivated for years, and who now had given him entry into their homes and salons to deliver his message. The most important of these was William Wilberforce.

Wilberforce was the hero of abolition, both in Britain and America. Heir to a family fortune, he channeled the zeal of an evangelical Christian into crusades against vice and immorality as well as the much greater juggernaut of slavery. Over five decades, he had devoted such zeal to the cause of abolition that he almost literally drew his last breath from its success: three days after the act passed in Parliament, he was dead. But before he expired, Garrison met him in person.

Wilberforce had such a reputation Garrison expected him to be Olympian in mind and body. But the man he encountered was puny and infirm, of "pygmean dimensions" and so ravaged by disease he could barely hold his head up or keep his back straight. Garrison couldn't get over how tiny he looked, how minuscule compared to his reputation. Nonetheless, he was awestruck. Wilberforce was a man who had battled infamy and won, and who could serve as a model for what Garrison was trying to do in America. So he wasted no time in pitching his ideas.

Foremost of these was convincing Wilberforce to act against the greatest of Garrison's foes, the American Colonization Society. The members of this group claimed as their mission to wind down slavery in the Western world gradually, without threat to the social hierarchy. The ACS was broadly popular among a segment of the white elite, and countless politicians and even former presidents had given it their sanction. However, despite the prestige of the organization, to Garrison it was anathema—not just a competitor in the antislavery field, but an outright menace.

For the previous several years, Garrison had censured the ACS in print and derided its members. He promoted lectures and forums on its failures and solicited funds to undermine it. And when the colonizers didn't pay him enough attention, he condemned them in *The Liberator* and in his 1832 pamphlet, *Thoughts on African Colonization*:

> The Colonization Society is becoming more and more abhorrent to the moral sense of community. The veil has been torn from the brow of the monster, and his gorgon features are seen without disguise. He must die! Already he bleeds— he roars—he shakes the earth—his resistance is mighty—but he is doomed to die!

Garrison's biggest problem with the gorgon was that it wasn't really concerned with ending human enslavement or ensuring equality for Black Americans. Instead, it meant to cajole or, if need be, coerce free Black people into leaving the only country they had known for resettlement along the West Coast of Africa. Describing them as inferior and degraded, the ACS advocated for their removal due to the inability of white people to treat them as equals or to coexist with them—except, perhaps, as their owners.

Garrison despised the overseas agents of the ACS such as Elliott Cresson, who happened to be in Britain at the same time as he. Cresson was a Quaker who had been working to align British abolitionists with American colonizers, claiming they had similar goals. Garrison saw him as a threat to abolition, so he wrote lacerating letters to him, challenged him to debates, attacked him in print, and derided him in public, trying to quash any influence he might have gained in the kingdom. But his most important victory came with the aid of the dying William Wilberforce.

Garrison convinced Wilberforce to sign his name, alongside those of ten other British abolitionists, to a protest against the ACS that he later printed in *The Liberator*. This helped sever cooperation between British abolitionists and American colonizers and gave Garrison a signal triumph over his foes. But they would not soon forget what he had done to them. He would discover this after he returned home.

For now he enjoyed his time in the company of giants in the fight against slavery whom he had long wanted to meet, men like Thomas Clarkson, who had been working against human bondage for as long as Wilberforce and was similarly weakened in health, if not spirit; Daniel O'Connell, that champion of Irish independence who was also a committed abolitionist, known coincidentally as "The Liberator"; and George Thompson, an orator and activist who quickly became a great friend of Garrison's—even to the point of setting up plans for an American speaking tour the following year. His most memorable encounter, though, was with Thomas Buxton, who greeted Garrison with surprise upon meeting him: "Why, my dear sir, I thought you were a black man . . . the black advocate of emancipation from the United States of America!"

Buxton made the assumption not because he was a fool, but because the Americans in Britain who had argued most forcefully against slavery were Black. One such man, Baptist minister Nathaniel Paul, had been in Europe for a full year, touring the country with British abolitionist Charles Stuart and undercutting support for the ACS. In fact, Paul had made such headway in attacking the colonizers that by the time Garrison arrived in the United Kingdom, he had already laid the groundwork. During the summer of 1833, Garrison and Paul toured Britain together, preaching against racism and colonization, with Paul introducing his companion to the key figures he had met during his time abroad. Indeed, Paul had been so effective against the ACS that, upon witnessing his success crippling his organization, Cresson had written cynically to his peers that they needed to find their own Black man to compete with his message.

Even so, Garrison got most of the credit, not only because of the color of his skin, but because his incendiary rhetoric attracted far greater attention in the press. But Garrison knew how critical Paul had been to his work, and in a letter to him asked God to bless him and "abundantly prosper you and your mission, and at last return you in safety to your friends." It turned out Garrison would need such a blessing himself. He later asked Paul for £40 (more than £4,000 in modern currency) to fund his own voyage home, since by the end of summer he was nearly broke.

This wasn't unusual. Black abolitionists in America had already funded a good portion of Garrison's trip to the United Kingdom, from small contributions from subscribers to *The Liberator* to larger investments by businessmen like the sailmaker James Forten. Their support was critical because the Boston publisher certainly couldn't pay his own way and white abolitionists were still hesitant to identify too closely with a man such as he. So Garrison's African American allies stepped into the void to pay for his travels, to promote his speeches and lecture tours, and, most importantly, to let him borrow some of their ideas.

Garrison's arguments against colonization had been developed by Black Americans decades before, from the time colonization emerged with the founding of the ACS in 1816. They attacked it from the pulpit and in public gatherings, printed denunciations of it in pamphlets, and wrote newspaper articles decrying it as a racist ploy. In so doing they also tried to change the minds of potential white allies and persuade them colonization was a pox on moral values and God-given liberties. One of the whites they had to convince was Garrison himself.

It was a part of Garrison's biography that he might have wished to forget. Working in the print trade in the 1820s, he was already imagining ways slavery could be ended—but mostly these involved separating the races and paying or encouraging Black people to sail for Africa. He claimed that funding for the scheme would be as inexhaustible as "the number of applicants for removal" and envisioned colonization societies "in every State, county and town."

Once he began to have actual conversations with Black people, however, he came to understand how nefarious such a plan might actually be. In Boston, he met abolitionists of color who had rejected the scheme and who encouraged him to imagine a solution to racism that wasn't just convenient for white people. While in Baltimore editing a journal called the *Genius of Universal Emancipation*, he met William Watkins, a Black writer, teacher, and minister whose criticism of colonization left such an impression on him that he used many of his arguments in his own writing. All this contributed to Garrison's evolving from a gradualist, who argued slavery could only be ended carefully over the course of decades, to an immediatist, who demanded the practice stop as soon as possible.

Somewhere along the line, Garrison also evolved from a humble printer careful with his words to a slashing propagandist of the first order, an unapologetic radical. Although businessmen like James Forten and ministers like William Watkins had much to lose from appearing too extreme in the fight against injustice—their careers, their legal rights, even their lives—Garrison's pale skin gave him a degree of protection, a privilege he could use to be as scathing as possible.

Almost nothing was out of bounds in his writing. He invoked God's wrath to threaten his adversaries. He said the American government stood on a base of corruption, its politicians were craven opportunists, and its institutions were rotten and immoral. The Founding Fathers had "trampled beneath their own feet their own solemn and heaven attested declaration, that all men are created equal." Even the US Constitution was "a compact by which we have enabled [slaveholders] already to plunder, persecute, and destroy two millions of slaves" and a document "*dripping as it is with human blood.*"

For Black abolitionists, Garrison emerged as that rarest of creatures— a white ally who seemed to understand the stakes not just of slavery's destruction, but of racism and prejudice in general, and was willing to advance unpopular opinions regardless of consequence. So even as he borrowed their ideas, men and women of color rewarded him for his courage. They named organizations after him like the Garrison Literary and Benevolent Society, they attended his lectures and bought his pamphlets, and, most of all, they propped up *The Liberator.*

Garrison's newspaper barely managed to stay in business in the 1830s, with high production costs and few resources, and if it hadn't been for Black abolitionists, the paper would have folded. Three-quarters of its four hundred early subscribers were African American, and they kept it afloat with their donations and testimonials, even as many of Garrison's peers condemned it as extreme and unpatriotic. Reverend Watkins, who had done so much to transform Garrison into an immediatist, endorsed the newspaper as "a FAITHFUL REPRESENTATIVE OF OUR sentiments and interests," and James Forten and the Rev. Theodore Wright compared Garrison's voice and activism to a trumpet call. And now, through Nathaniel Paul, they were also footing the bill for his voyage home.

Ultimately, the trip to Britain had been a worthy investment, a chance for Garrison to make new connections across the Atlantic, to witness abolition's success in person, and to undermine the colonizers in the process. As he wrote in *The Liberator* in October 1833, "The success of my mission seems to have driven [my enemies] to the verge of madness. Those who cannot wield the pen against us, resort to *tar and feathers, and clubs!*" He almost seemed to welcome the clash he knew was coming. But for Nathaniel Paul, such a conflict held no appeal at all.

He wrote to Garrison, disgusted by the contrast between how he was treated in America and how he was regarded in Britain. Namely, in America he had been forced to occupy the segregated "Negro pew" in church, ordered to sit in the outside seat of the coach, and directed to a remote table in a restaurant. But in Britain he had experienced none of these things and was treated like a gentleman worthy of respect, receiving any seat he liked in a church, coach, or restaurant. Considering the difference, he wrote, "My soul is filled with sorrow and indignation. I could weep over the land of my nativity!" But instead, he arrived at a better solution. While he paid for Garrison's trip home, Paul remained in Britain, and he would stay there for years to come.

Once Garrison finally did return to America, in late 1833, he felt transformed. His successful endeavors seemed to justify his strategy of "moral suasion" to advance abolition. It was the idea that slavery and racism were immoral and contrary to Christian teaching, and by appealing to the spiritual ideals of his audience, he could convince them of the need for change. And if that didn't work, he could graphically describe the horrors of captivity and abuse of human dignity experienced by Black people. And if that still didn't work, he could shame his listeners for their indifference and inaction. Such an idea wasn't unique to Garrison, but once he began promoting moral suasion, his name became identified with it.

Inspired by the success of his trip, Garrison became certain that his quest for abolition wasn't just a moral and political goal, but a holy mission approved by God. Even before he had left for the United Kingdom, he had been struck by terrible messianic visions, like something out of the Book of Revelation:

> He imagined Africa with "the flames of a thousand burning villages fearfully reddening the wide heavens, and the shrieks and groans of her enslaved and dying children," after which a heavenly voice commanded, *"Plead for the oppressed!"* Then he saw the corpses of Black men, women and children as "their blood was drenching my garments; and again I hear that voice from Heaven, saying,—*'Plead for the oppressed!'*" And again and again, with visions of slave ships and auction blocks, and millions of slaves abducted, he could "see unborn generations of victims stalking like apparitions before me; and once more I hear that from Heaven, saying, in a tone awful and loud, and with increasing earnestness,—*'Plead for the oppressed!'*"

Language like this convinced his enemies he was a lunatic. But Garrison remained undaunted. No matter how they persecuted him, he would respond with mercy, quoting Jesus—*"Father, forgive them: they know not what they do"*—and vowing to meet his tormentors with serenity. He would thus return to America to meet his fate with a quiet Christian beatitude. Even if he ended up injured or dead, the attacks upon him would benefit his movement and spread the message of abolition beautifully. Yes, he understood it now. He sized up the role of martyr and found he could play it well.

Of course, compared to Black people, Garrison had no real idea of suffering. He could envision himself suffering in the abstract, but when presented with the tangible threat of it, he kept his head down, snuck away to hideouts, sped away in coaches, and sailed across the Atlantic. He therefore had to be careful upon returning to the United States, to judge carefully his actions and separate his friends from his enemies, lest he be kidnapped and strung up in the Georgia woods like a common criminal and hanged for the sin of abolition.

With unfortunate timing, just as Garrison returned from abroad, the press reported his words from Exeter Hall that summer. Using the choicest cuts of his rhetoric—the swipes against the ACS, slaveholders, and the nation generally—press organs like Boston's *Daily Advertiser* and the widely read *Niles' Weekly Register* gave an accounting of Garrison that made him come across, at a minimum, as a breathless fanatic and at worst as an enemy of the nation. Elliott Cresson, too, tried to exact his revenge upon Garrison in New York's *Commercial Advertiser*, saying his nemesis was "endeavoring to crush me, hunt the Colonization Society out of existence, and vilify our national character."

But Garrison's most fearsome opponent spoke in much more aggressive language. James Watson Webb, the publisher of New York's *Courier and Enquirer*, prided himself on his acid tongue and blazing condemnations of anyone who differed with him politically. He had a taste for violence, too: He "caned, kicked, beat, or spat at rival editors on the street, was involved in several libel suits, fought one duel, and was the direct cause of another." He denigrated any group he didn't see as fully American, from Irish immigrants to, especially, Black people. His hulking presence and shock of white hair made him a familiar sight on the streets of New York, and those who crossed him could expect a good pummeling, whether in person or in print.

The *Courier and Enquirer* was no mere news sheet, but nothing less than the most powerful newspaper in America, with its own pony express, to gather news from Washington and major US cities in record time, and a system of bureaus and outlets that enabled it to distribute news quickly throughout the country—and many editors in smaller cities accepted its copy without question. To abolitionists, this meant there was no more menacing press organ in the nation than the *Courier and Enquirer*, and no more dangerous enemy than James Watson Webb.

Regarding abolition, Webb asked his readers, "shall we, by promptly and fearlessly crushing this many-headed Hydra in the bud, expose the weakness as well as the folly, madness, and mischief of these bold and dangerous men?" The question was rhetorical, for Webb had just issued a call to violence to the masses of working- and middle-class white men who read his paper, to counter "the leaders in the crusade against the white people of the United States." If anyone didn't get the message, a "Ghost of Peter the Hermit" also announced in Webb's paper that the abolitionists would bring nothing but slaughter in their wake.

—⁊⁊—

Garrison wasn't the only abolitionist in danger. Also at risk were the silk merchant Arthur Tappan and his brother Lewis, who had emerged as champions of the antislavery cause and supported it generously with their money, time, and reputation. Arthur had known Garrison since 1830, when he learned that the publisher—whom he had never met—had accused a ship owner of trafficking in slaves and ended up losing a libel case brought against him. Garrison languished in a Maryland prison for seven weeks, unable to pay his fine and court costs, until Arthur stepped in and deposited $100 for his release. Garrison left Maryland for Boston soon after, missing the verdict in a second trial, in which he was judged liable for $1,000. Arthur probably would have paid that sum, too, if Garrison had asked him.

The Tappans appreciated the younger man's courage to stand against the colonizers and slave owners. However, in their economics and their attitudes, the Tappans were much more traditional than he, respecting the standard workings of society and never daring to attack the US Constitution or the Founding Fathers. Still, their name was always on the lips of the mob as being in league with Garrison, since the idea of abolition was inherently radical in a society where a considerable number of white people owned or desired to own slaves. This made the Tappans susceptible to charges of sedition and anarchy—just as Garrison was.

It was an absurd charge, because the Tappans would have been among the last people to endorse turmoil and destruction. Arthur was, after all, a successful capitalist, one of the wealthiest importers in the nation, and he and Lewis proclaimed their evangelical faith loudly. They allowed no haggling in their business, housed their employees in strictly controlled boardinghouses, banned them from using alcohol and tobacco, and required proof of regular church attendance. New Yorkers also knew them for endorsing a range of spiritual and moral campaigns that, while unpopular, were certainly no danger to the republic.

They propped up the Society for the Encouragement of Faithful Domestic Servants to keep Irish domestics from abandoning their low-paid jobs and unsettling the labor market and to protect "the calm happiness of domestic life." They created the Magdalen Society to "reform" New York City's ten thousand prostitutes and shame elite brothel owners into giving up their source of lucrative profits—a fruitless task. They pushed for temperance and the search for a "true wine" for communion that wasn't cheap, imported rotgut, and they ended up paying for a cargo of grape juice instead. And they had been early and eager benefactors of various colonization efforts, until they discovered colonizers supported not only sending free Black people to Liberia, but exporting a steady supply of rum there as well. This simply would not do, so they gave up colonization in favor of immediate abolition.

Their crusade for Black education had fared no better than their other campaigns. Two years before, they had tried to create a manual labor school for African American workers in New Haven, near Yale College. They meant to encourage the kind of instruction that was taken for granted in the white world but was uncommon and poorly funded for Black people. Once word of the plan got out in Connecticut, though, local reaction was swift and brutal: a mob protested by hurling garbage at Arthur Tappan's second home, city leaders passed a motion to resist the founding of the school, and citizens in public meetings condemned it in openly racist language. Critics further claimed the education of Black people would lead them to job competition with whites and somehow threaten the fabric of society with "the dangerous mixture of black and white plebeians."

Since then the Tappans had grown wary of the attitude of the majority of whites, but no less committed to their causes. After New Haven, they didn't withdraw to the insular world of the silk trade and instead supported political conventions of Black citizens, funded benevolent societies devoted to Black education and uplift, and helped underwrite abolitionist publications like *The Liberator*—while creating their own, milder version of an antislavery paper, called *The Emancipator*.

They also wanted their own version of an abolition society to match the New England Anti-Slavery Society, the group Garrison backed. That enterprising group sent its agents into the field to speak in lecture halls and churches against slavery, petitioned for the end of the slave trade in Washington, DC, and raised money selling subscriptions to *The Liberator* and other publications. Its membership had swelled to two thousand members, with forty-seven local chapters, more than one hundred clergymen enlisted to preach for immediatism, and the vocal support of figures like John Greenleaf Whittier, who would become one of the country's most famous poets.

New York state had no equivalent, and the Tappans meant to change that. Through their own group, they could support Garrison's society when appropriate, or counterbalance them when moderation was needed.

They looked to create the New York Anti-Slavery Society with Arthur at the helm, with the organizing meeting set for October 2.

Word got out quickly—too quickly. When James Watson Webb learned Arthur Tappan's abolitionists would be organizing in Clinton Hall, he alerted his allies in the Colonization Society, and they put out a handbill. Describing the site and time of the meeting, the flyer was addressed "to all persons from the South" and signed by "MANY SOUTHERNERS." An ominous note at the bottom read, "All citizens who may feel disposed to manifest the *true* feeling of the State on this subject, are requested to attend." Other threats were more direct, claiming the only way to stop Garrison and the Tappans was by "cutting off their heads."

The Southern pitch in the handbill was telling, because Southerners in New York were anything but an abstract presence. Countless planters visited the city and brought their slaves even though human bondage had been outlawed in New York state six years before. The law said bondsmen could obtain their freedom after nine months' presence in the state, but this was routinely ignored, and planters continued to flout the law. Moreover, Southern threats against abolitionists routinely appeared in the Northern press, and white men with a Southern heritage were some of the quickest to turn out to protest or attack abolitionist assemblies and lectures.

More than a few Northern businessmen approved of this kind of violence, since their profits in the banking, shipping, and insurance trades were often linked to the trade in captive human beings. They convinced their employees that labor competition from freed slaves would endanger their jobs, and this, along with racial bigotry, drove many working men to join the ranks of the anti-abolitionists. Webb's *Courier and Enquirer* spoke to both groups, as a mercantile newspaper read by businessmen with economic ties to Southern plantations and their employees who saw Black people as a threat to their livelihood.

So the Many Southerners, joined by Many Northerners, prepared to meet their foes on the evening of October 2. *The Liberator* would later describe these adversaries as "a genuine, drunken, infuriated mob of blackguards of every species, some with good clothes, and the major part the very sweepings of the city," meaning the filth and refuse collected in gutters.

They weren't hard to miss as they made their way to Clinton Hall, shouting, bellowing, and cursing the names of Arthur Tappan and William Lloyd Garrison and chanting "find them, find them." Some vowed to ship Garrison in a box to Georgia, where he could be properly disposed of at the gallows. Others carried bowie knives and pistols, as well as playing cards marked "Alabama," "Georgia," and "South Carolina." As Webb had told them, the Hydra of Garrison and the Tappans would soon be within their grasp, and all they had to do was crush it.

They didn't realize one of the heads of the Hydra was marching alongside them. As Garrison later told the story, he spotted the mob on the move after he returned from his European trip. Not wanting to flee in terror again, he decided to blend in among them as they chanted for his destruction—because while his name was notorious to them, his appearance wasn't. With his bald head, spectacles, and sensible attire, he resembled little more than a middle-class shopkeeper on the march with other enemies of abolition. Thus he escaped his kidnappers once more.

The Tappans, however, did not have the luxury of anonymity. Not only did Arthur Tappan operate a silk shop on Pearl Street—a half-mile south of Clinton Hall—he interacted with buyers regularly and made a keen impression on Manhattanites. Many in the mob knew what he looked like, because some of them purchased the stockings, gloves, hats, and parasols he imported from overseas. But his familiarity wouldn't keep him safe from their violence—and if he had tried Garrison's approach, he might have found himself bound and gagged. The rioters played up the threat by shouting, "Ten thousand dollars for Arthur Tappan!"

Primed by alcohol and anger, the men drew within sight of Clinton Hall. They knew it would be a spirited melee and looked forward to it: "Let us rout them!" However, once they finally reached the hall, they found the building closed and empty. The abolitionists were nowhere in sight.

Abandoning Clinton Hall wasn't a clever strategy, just an accident. Arthur had tried to secure the approval of the hall's Board of Trustees, of which he was one, for the organizational meeting. But the board had rejected the request, seeing abolition as too volatile a subject for consideration. This was an affront to Arthur, since he had helped fund the construction of the building, three years before, to house a mercantile library for the public good. And wasn't abolition also a public good? His peers told him it wasn't.

In response, his brother Lewis argued for the Chatham Street Chapel as a substitute venue for the meeting. It was a former theater and circus complex that Lewis had leased to highlight the evangelist Charles Grandison Finney's sermons. Unfortunately, the building meant for his preaching was no better than a shambling old barn, with no carpeting and plenty of echo. It also stood on the edge of the Five Points slum and kept away many pious middle-class New Yorkers, who didn't want to attend church in the morning near the same gambling halls and brothels that many of their neighbors visited at night. Some even called it the "Devil's Temple." Nonetheless, the chapel survived as an ungainly sort of religious institution, and Lewis didn't need to ask anyone's permission to use it. So his argument carried. The New York Anti-Slavery Society assembled there to organize, with Arthur Tappan as president.

By this time, Webb's mob had adjourned to Tammany Hall for more liquid sustenance and to plot their next move. The hall was the headquarters of the local Democratic Party and the onetime stronghold of Martin Van Buren, former governor and current US vice president. The Democrats allowed the mobsters access to the facility, no doubt realizing Many Southerners would be essential at the polls if Van Buren were to get the nomination for the presidency in the next election. For now, though, it was only a stopover for the rioters. They still had abolitionists to attack.

And attack they did, once they learned their targets would be meeting only four blocks away at Chatham Street Chapel. Within minutes the mob charged out of Tammany Hall and ran to the gates of the chapel. Chanting and yelling, they found the building's iron gates locked, but this only encouraged them to raise their voices to an even more earsplitting clamor. Soon there were two thousand of them in the street, shaking the gates, ready to storm the chapel. But in the end they didn't have to use force to breach the perimeter. A janitor appeared with a key, unlocked the gates, and let the men swarm inside.

They surged into what looked like an old wooden barn, with the lights out, in near darkness.

"Find them! Find them!"

They hunted around for the silk merchant and his brother, and the publisher Garrison, whatever he looked like. They searched under the stage, in alcoves, behind seats and chairs, anywhere to find their quarry. Some in the mob scampered up the stairs to an upper story, where a few stragglers had locked themselves away in a Sunday school room—and would later have to be rescued by the police. After a few minutes passed, they learned Arthur Tappan and most of his allies had escaped through a side door, which again left them empty-handed.

This frustrated the ambition of the rioters. Without anyone to capture, the crowd of thousands dwindled, though some of them still had nervous energy to spare and didn't want to leave. They settled on holding a mock abolition meeting and pretending to be their enemies, and they appointed a lone Black man to play the role of "Arthur Tappan" as a joke.

They called on the man to make a speech. With a surprising amount of courage, the man did so—not joining in their antics but making his own case for liberty: "The Declaration says all men are created equal, and the Bible says God has made us all of one blood. I think, therefore, we are entitled to good treatment, that it is wrong to hold men in slavery, and that—"

This was not what the "Many Southerners" wanted to hear, so they broke up his speech with screaming and profanity. The meeting was over, and they scurried out of the building into the slum outside.

The following day Webb ran a predictable headline:

GREAT PUBLIC MEETING.

THE AGITATORS DEFEATED!

THE CONSTITUTION TRIUMPHANT!

He exalted the Southerners in their attempt to stop "the interference of TAPPAN, GARRISON, & Co. with their slave property." He said it was a promising sign of their ability to crush abolition in the streets before it had the chance to persuade people at the ballot box or anywhere else.

However, the newspaper later had to append a contrary note, mentioning that the New York Anti-Slavery Society had, in fact, organized at Chatham Street Chapel before the mob arrived. It had passed a formal constitution, appointed officers, and set up committees, and it was now in business. The Tappans had met with success in record time and had outwitted Webb's men before they could kidnap them and send them in a box to Georgia. It was a signal triumph in the face of aggression and ensured the fate of the Tappan brothers and William Lloyd Garrison would be tied together for years to come.

★ TWO ★

WEAPONS OF LIGHT AND TRUTH

David Ruggles was a long way from home. The scenery might have been charming and the air clean, but the journey was long and arduous—over the Allegheny Plateau, almost to the Ohio border, and up to the shores of Lake Erie. A traveler could follow the turnpike then go by canals or old Indian trails, even take a short stretch of railroad to get this far, but mostly he went by stagecoach. Hundreds of cramped and uncomfortable miles in a box on wooden wheels, rolling over logs or macadam, just to sell the newspaper of Arthur and Lewis Tappan.

Ruggles didn't even know if the Tappans had ever come this far west. Did they sell their imported silks to people in these villages, or send their stockings and parasols out to these farms? It was doubtful. But they did want to sell abolition to these Pennsylvanians, and he aimed to help them do it.

He had heard the stories, how the backwoods of this state was no place for a Black man. How whites dominated the population and Black people could be kidnapped and sold as fugitive slaves. But David Ruggles never let himself be afraid. As the general agent for *The Emancipator*, he had been traveling through these hinterlands giving talks on slavery and racial equality for weeks, and by the fall of 1833, he felt confident about what he had seen in the town of Pittsburgh.

The townsfolk had established their own abolition society, and he attended several passionate antislavery meetings with them. Most participants were Black, but they were joined by an encouraging number of whites. The message seemed to be spreading throughout the area, even in this gritty working town, known as the "Smoky City" for its growing number of glass factories and ironworks. He thought abolition might have a future here. The trip might end up a success.

He was in good spirits as he rode out of town in a coach with "two ladies, two gentlemen, a two leg[g]ed animal and myself." The darkness in the vehicle was near total, and as the riders became comfortable with each other, they began to express their feelings on slavery, which all of them claimed to oppose. Ruggles offered his thoughts and noticed how agreeably his fellow travelers treated him, so unlike the reception he had gotten from other whites in the state. Of course, inside the unlit coach, none of the riders could see or judge each other by the color of their skin, which allowed one passenger to express his true feelings.

"Madmen! Fanatics! Disorganizers! Amalgamaters!"

The insults issued from the "animal" Ruggles had mentioned, a vehement colonizer who set about condemning abolitionists with every insult he could summon—assuming there were no such troublemakers in the coach.

The man said that to accept Black and white equality was a great offense and that whites should never commingle with Black people ("amalgamation"). Ruggles had heard this before. Words like these were typical from the tongues of ACS men, who claimed to oppose slavery yet said the most scurrilous things about African Americans, especially in private. So Ruggles casually challenged the man and said that he (of unknown race) would happily marry a Black woman if given the chance.

The colonizer exploded. He said no civilized man would prefer a "negress" to a white lady, so he must be an abolitionist! Ruggles admitted that he was. The temperature in the coach rose, the volume increased, and the argument went on until dawn. When daylight finally revealed Ruggles to be Black, the colonizer nearly lost his mind:

"Good heavens! A negro! Why, you are a black man!!"

When the party stopped for breakfast at an inn, the "two-legged beast" tried to send Ruggles away from the place where they all sat, refusing to share the table. But the other travelers intervened to stop him. "I kept my seat; he of course [grunted] and left the room." Later, in a touch of dark humor, he claimed to have seen him wallowing in a pigpen upstate.

Ruggles made light of the situation in a pamphlet he wrote, but the encounter could have easily ended in violence—a fight, a pistol-whipping, or worse—if the other whites in the coach had been as hostile to him as the colonizer. The charge of amalgamation was among the most damning in the lexicon of racism and had been leveled against abolitionists since they had first spoken out against slavery.

Ruggles saw the hypocrisy of it from his home in the Five Points, where many of these same anti-abolitionists growled about Black people and amalgamation during the day but at night weren't above playing faro with them in the same gambling halls, drinking whiskey with them in the same taverns, or soliciting prostitutes with them in the same brothels. In public, though, the colonizers and their allies in the press and in Washington asserted that any relationship with Black people that was open, equal, and unapologetic had the air of immorality, even sedition.

Like most abolitionists, Ruggles shied away from the charge of amalgamation: "I do not wish it, nor does any colored man or woman of my acquaintance." But he also didn't think Black and white intermarriage or relations to be "unnatural" and had seen such pairings up close in his neighborhood, where mixed-race couples appeared on the street, in church, and in their homes. He knew fears over race mixing owed more to prejudice against Black people than any threat against society. But in the end it was all political—amalgamation stirred people up, so the anti-abolition crowd used it as an insult whenever they could.

And now these insults were turning people into beasts. Ruggles saw how brutish the colonizer in the coach appeared, how devoid of empathy, and he wondered how such a man could let himself become so debased. Speaking generally, he wrote, "it is this horror of amalgamation that has frozen up all my brother's charity, all his politeness, all his logic."

Ruggles couldn't afford to be distracted by such miscreants. He had too much work to do. His itinerary on any given day might involve speaking in Black churches and assembly halls, or overseeing the founding of new abolition societies, or receiving pledges for subscriptions, or answering requests from people who wanted him to visit their little towns—places where city folk rarely ventured, and where strangers were uncommon, sometimes unwelcome.

He cut a striking figure on the streets of his hometown of New York City, and it was no different when he was in western Pennsylvania. With his "long double-breasted jacket, white pants, stovepipe hat, a cravat, and thick eyeglasses," he brought a sense of Manhattan style to the country-side, even if it offended local sensibility, or defied how people thought a Black man should dress. Abolitionists already had the reputation of being unusual, so it seemed a minor issue. His enemies hated him no matter what he wore.

His primary foe was the Colonization Society or, as he called it, "the daughter of slavery." The man in the coach had been a member, along with tens of thousands of other white people in the region. For them, embracing colonization was the most socially acceptable way to attack abolition, without making the disreputable move of openly advocating slavery (even though the practical consequences were the same: preserving oppression). So while the ACS had an increasingly checkered image, it was still expanding its member rolls, printing reams of publications, stirring up its followers, and making plans to expatriate Black people to Liberia—which colonizers had praised as a model Black settlement, but which Ruggles said was a trap. In speeches he told his audience the colony was a beleaguered land poor in farmland and commodities but rich in rum and liquor; and liquor, just like slavery, bore the fruit of "licentiousness, misery, and death." The colonizers were nothing more than craven little men, scheming and specious, willing to tell any lie to advance their own fortunes and ruin the lives of Black citizens. Ruggles had no use for them, and neither should his listeners.

The orations of David Ruggles, like those of dozens of other abolitionists on the lecture circuit, made a difference. The colonizers found African Americans hostile to their rhetoric and also found it difficult to secure the allegiance of antislavery whites. They whined about "abolitionist slanders" that sullied the name of their organization. Yet all their complaints did little to help them pay off a deficit of $46,000 that threatened the viability of the group. Garrison delighted in their troubles, writing, "Boston is now fairly redeemed from the thraldom of colonization corruption," while Rev. Henry Ludlow planned a mock "funeral of colonization" to announce their inevitable demise.

Ruggles could not feel so assured. He saw how some in the society had gone from self-described philanthropists to street hooligans "to mob us and our friends with clubs, stones, brick-bats, &c." He compared the society to an "incubus" that preyed on good works in society and said it was "to every coloured American, 'a moral Upas tree,' beneath whose pestiferous shades all intellect must languish and all virtue die." He had seen too much trouble on his travels to assume they would ever relent— and knew that an enemy might disappear for a time, only to emerge later in a new, more dangerous, form.

Ruggles had learned these things from the trials of experience, from eight long years on the move, after leaving home in Norwich, Connecticut, at only fifteen. He'd been a mariner working out of New Bedford, meeting a great range of races and colors and classes of people, some free, some enslaved. He'd met the Black abolitionist Nathan Johnson, who had educated him on the need to immediately help his brothers and sisters held captive and had given him valuable advice on combating slave traffickers. He'd been a grocer, the "butter merchant" who provided goods for a fair price, the sugar dealer who only offered products made by free people, the temperance man who refused to deal in "spiritous liquors." He'd seen his business fail after an intruder broke in and stole $280 and set fire to the building, then he had built another business and watched it flourish. He'd written articles for newspapers and met publishers and benefactors and given speeches throughout the region—and now he sold newspapers.

Although his jobs were often in flux, his ordeals were constant. The coach ride outside of Pittsburgh had ended well for him, but many such encounters did not. In New York, Black people were routinely segregated: made to sit in distant pews in church, assigned to the balconies of theaters, banned from amusement parks, locked out of schools and juries, forced onto the decks of steamboats instead of lodging in private cabins, and ordered to stand or ride on the outside of omnibuses and public transit, even in foul weather.

In an article for *The Emancipator*, Ruggles described how such mistreatment affected him personally on a recent journey in town. Since he preferred not to be wet or sullied, he had paid for a ticket for the inside of a coach and found a seat there. The driver, however, insisted that he ride on the outside—away from the white passengers, to avoid race mixing.

Ruggles erupted in anger. He refused to move and made his stand as he had always done. But the driver was in no mood to discuss it: he charged into the coach and "with his hands like claws tore both clothes, buttons and skin." Then he threw Ruggles from the vehicle, leaving him to walk to his destination. Ruggles was outraged and wrote that the driver had "trampled on my feelings, and he was robbing me of my RIGHTS, my LIBERTY, my ALL." It was encounters like these that made Black men like Nathaniel Paul stay in England.

But David Ruggles refused to move out of his home country, despite the brutal treatment he had endured. If enough brave souls could sit inside the coach, explore the hinterlands, and take on the colonizers, change would come. Violence might come too, but it would expose and humiliate those who waged it, for it meant they had lost the argument. This gave him a strange spirit of optimism. The "daughter of slavery" might bring fear and terror, but as Ruggles saw it, "thanks be to Him who said 'let there be light,' she has been repeatedly defeated, and she must be totally annihilated before slavery can be stabbed to death with the weapons of light and truth."

With such words, Ruggles might have been better suited to work for *The Liberator* than *The Emancipator*. But he wasn't just channeling Garrison in his divine invocations; he had been influenced to a greater degree by Black writers whose work he displayed on his bookshelves in Lower Manhattan—as the creator of the first Black-owned bookstore in the United States.

It was the latest career turn for him, opening a shop at 67 Lispenard Street, in spring 1834, to sell copies of antislavery newspapers, pamphlets, literary and cultural reviews, and the writings of just about every prominent Black author in print, and several much more obscure. One book, however, was by far the most important to Ruggles's own philosophy and to the way the rest of the nation saw abolitionists: *The Appeal in Four Articles* by David Walker.

Ruggles stood among the book's foremost disciples. He had not only borrowed from Walker the impassioned rhetoric that animated his own writing, but he also confronted injustice as Walker had encouraged his readers to do, and he took on the risk that came with it. He was beginning to question the idea of moral suasion, that an appeal to the Christian conscience alone could defeat slavery and racism. At some point fighting back against unjust laws and defending yourself from violence had to take priority. As his biographer said, "Ruggles took the literary defiance of David Walker and married it to quotidian confrontations." As Ruggles himself said, "The pleas of crying soft and sparing never answered the purpose of a reform, and never will."

—⁂—

Arthur and Lewis Tappan, as avowed pacifists, wanted nothing to do with the writings of David Walker or anyone else who might make the cause of abolition seem dangerous. But they got along well with David Ruggles and worked with him regularly. With a skilled agent like him drumming up sales and publicity for *The Emancipator*, the Tappans could remind New Yorkers there was more than one publication fighting slavery in the state, even as Garrison attracted most of the notoriety. That was the idea, anyway.

In reality, Arthur and Lewis needed a newspaper to defend themselves and their cause from all the recent mockery and condemnation directed at them. Lewis knew that "slander always accompanied an unpopular cause," and they felt they had endured the brunt of it. The New York press was among the worst offenders, describing Arthur, in particular, as wantonly mixing the races, stirring up trouble with his Black school experiment in New Haven, and funding all manner of pernicious endeavors.

The Tappans tried to be more pragmatic than Garrison. They couldn't just invoke God's wrath and talk about divine punishment—they tried to create public momentum to convince people abolition was a cause worth supporting, and to do that they needed the support of men in power. So Arthur hatched a plan to distribute 7,600 copies of *The Emancipator* to Northern churchmen and have them promote the cause with his blessing. As evangelical Christians, the Tappans in no way wanted to attack religion or the feelings of ministers who had not yet been convinced of the need for abolition. So Arthur nudged and prodded the clergymen to try to get them on his side—and they stonewalled him. Sect after Protestant sect, be they Baptists, Congregationalists, or even his own Presbyterians, dismissed him and his allies as a band of troublemakers. Some, like a Dutch Reform church journal, even said, "Sinful as slavery is, it is not more so than a plan of emancipation might be made to be."

While the Tappans were dismayed by the disrespect shown to them by their fellow Christians, Garrison wasn't surprised by it. Unlike the brothers, he had no expectation that most men of the cloth would take a turn toward abolition—and he reviled them for it. He would later call them "revilers and false witnesses" and "a corrupt priesthood," made up of imbeciles who spewed "nothing better than drivel." He disdained their hypocrisy for invoking the name of Jesus, the Prince of Peace, in support of the violent captive-labor machine that drove so much of the American economy.

Besides, many of these same holy men were supporters of the Colonization Society. While they might not have borne clubs and bricks in the street, Garrison saw them as obstacles to racial progress as much as anyone, and those who weren't colonizers dabbled in specious ideas and half-truths. One man in particular, the Congregational minister Lyman Beecher, had rankled Garrison's feelings almost from the time they had met, telling him his zeal was misguided: "If you will give up your fanatical notions and be guided by us [the clergy], we will make you the Wilberforce of America." Garrison had no interest in accepting Beecher's bribe, and since then relations with him had only soured. Beecher had even tried to pry the Tappans away from their association with the publisher, saying his behavior was so appalling it drove "decent people" out of the movement. "Get rid of Garrison," he said, "and thousands will join."

It was a clumsy request, but something about the demand lodged in the minds of the Tappan brothers. Garrison did have a streak of zealotry, for better or worse. Arthur came to wonder "whether his 'holy indignation' is always as holy as he appears to think it." Despite this discomfort, though, the Tappans knew they needed Garrison. He attracted attention, drove support in the Black community, and never failed to draw interest from the press. They needed to bring him under their wing, if not to soften his rhetoric, at least to keep closer track of him and guide him toward more productive ends—one in particular.

Almost as soon as the Tappans formed the New York Anti-Slavery Society, Lewis realized they needed to create an even broader organization that could unite the different factions of the movement. An organization that could take the fight to the South, force the North to reckon with its own guilt in funding slavery, and use the print media to create a force that would attract attention across America. Garrison supported the idea, arguing they should form such a group by the end of 1833. Arthur was reluctant, at first, wanting to avoid any more controversy and threats to his life so soon after the last debacle, but in the end he agreed to the timetable. They chose Philadelphia's Adelphi Hall as the site for the founding of their new organization.

On December 3, they began to assemble—carefully. Pennsylvania had a deeply ingrained hostility to abolitionists, as David Ruggles knew, and Philadelphia was no different just because it was the third biggest city in the nation. If anything, the danger was even more acute, between threats issued by hostile editors, the mob activity of wealthy colonizers and the working men who supported them, and the quiet antagonism of politicians in City Hall.

The police encouraged organizers of the new group to meet during the day, because they could not protect them at night. Reports played up how foreign and unusual these abolitionists were, and men of means denounced them as "fanatics, amalgamationists, disorganizers, disturbers of the peace, and dangerous enemies of the country." When they walked along Walnut Street to their meeting, the crowds jeered them with insults and taunts. The police guarded the door of the hall by order of the mayor, as a show of force and to let the activists know how little stood between them and a repeat performance of the Chatham Street Chapel fiasco in October—except with the mob gaining a victory this time.

Upon arriving in the hall, sixty members from ten states gathered and took a deep breath after surviving the gauntlet with their nerves intact. For their troubles, they were rewarded with a snack of cold water and crackers—food considered proper for upright men to sup on, though it left their bellies rumbling for hours on end.

The group would be called the American Anti-Slavery Society, and it marked a daring step forward, because it embraced integration in both its membership and leadership. While Black activists had been at the fore-front of abolition for years, they were almost always denied membership in white-run organizations. In this group, though, African American men would serve alongside Lewis on the executive committee. Arthur would be president and Garrison the secretary for foreign correspondence—an acknowledgment of his success overseas. Garrison also became the author of the Declaration of Sentiments, the mission statement that laid out the purpose of the society in sharp and ringing language, with a nod to the founding document of the United States.

Garrison needed such a boost in his prestige. Subscriptions to *The Liberator* were dwindling, thanks to the competition of *The Emancipator*, which took away some of his readers. And as Garrison wrote to John Vashon, a wealthy Black businessman in Pittsburgh, his newspaper also struggled because "we have printed beyond our means" the various tracts, pamphlets, and books needed to support the cause. Although Garrison remained confident and proud of his progress, he still needed money and asked Vashon to extend a loan and let him repay it when he could. He apologized for the request, since "we are struggling under great embarrassments."

Despite his struggles, Garrison went all out in the Declaration. He lamented "TWO MILLIONS of our people" shackled against their will, abused and tortured, separated from their families, bought and sold like commodities, treated as beasts, all "at the caprice or pleasure of irresponsible tyrants," also known as "MAN-STEALER[S]." He vowed the society would send its agents across the nation, into the churches, across the countryside, using exhortation and rebuke to attack those who upheld the slave trade. For God had given them permission to "overthrow the most execrable system of slavery that has ever been witnessed upon earth." They would either find triumph in the victory over human oppression "or perish untimely as martyrs in this great, benevolent and holy cause."

Except for a minor revision, the delegates approved the Declaration, giving Garrison another victory in his campaign to advance his version of immediate, radical abolition. The mission statement would appear again and again as a founding document of antislavery. Almost as importantly, the newly formed society agreed to purchase a supply of Garrison's publications and bail out *The Liberator* from its growing debts. This gave him the financial boost he needed and helped him pay back his debt to Nathaniel Paul for funding his voyage home from Britain, and it eventually covered his loans from John Vashon and others. Garrison was, at least for the moment, out of the red.

—⁓—

The colonizers were among the first to take notice of, and offense to, the new society. Many of them were vehement that putting Black and white people on the same level undermined the social order and thereby threatened white supremacy. The Jacksonian press greeted the founding of the society with contempt, and some critics, like J. R. Tyson, belittled "new fangled" ideas of immediate abolition as marked by "turbulent invective and acrimonious clamour."

None of this surprised Samuel Cornish, one of the African American men appointed to the society's executive committee. He had been dealing with colonizers for years—reading their arguments about Black inferiority, hearing them claim to be philanthropists, watching them command the loyalty of educated people who should have known better—and he had had enough.

In the 1820s, he'd been one of the first Black leaders to criticize the Colonization Society in print. One of his most famous targets was Francis Scott Key, lyricist of "The Star-Spangled Banner," slaveholder, and cofounder of the ACS. After listening to one of Key's speeches, Cornish wrote, "Prejudice dwelt in his little heart, which cannot be bigger than a cherry." He wondered if he was a true Christian at all. After all, how could men like Key assume that whites would always remain bigoted. They didn't know the mind of the Creator—no one did. But that uncertainty also gave Cornish pause.

He didn't have the surety of David Ruggles, who knew God favored his side and kept driving forward, despite the risk to his own life and livelihood. Cornish liked Ruggles and admired how this young man of twenty-three had achieved so much in only a few years. They had met in 1828, around the time a teenaged Ruggles placed ads for his grocery in a newspaper Cornish published. The year after, when Ruggles no longer sold alcohol and continued to shun slave-grown goods, Cornish commended him in print for his policies and encouraged his readers to patronize his store. In the years after, they crossed paths regularly in abolition circles and supported each other's projects.

Unlike his friend, Cornish wasn't sure this nation would ever see the end of oppression. He also differed from Ruggles in another way: the younger man often saw the most brazen and violent opposers as the biggest threats. Cornish, though, knew the laziness and indifference of common people could be just as destructive to the cause, if not more so. His entire career had made him wary of their empty vows of allegiance, their heartfelt promises masking timid souls.

More than a decade before, Cornish had learned theology in Philadelphia from the founder of the nation's first Black Presbyterian church, John Gloucester, who inspired him to aim his ministry at the free Black citizens of the city, to promote racial uplift and denounce slavery. Cornish succeeded at his mission and, recognizing his value, the Presbyterian hierarchy moved him out of Pennsylvania and into the gritty atmosphere of the Five Points, where the congregation struggled with poverty in a neighborhood full of grog shops and gambling halls. Cornish's work was successful, as he pushed hard for church leaders to devote more attention to the slum and established the First Colored Presbyterian Church south of the neighborhood, two blocks east of City Hall.

It was both a historic achievement and a daunting prospect, for Cornish soon learned the costs of operating such a church could be steep. His ministry soon owed $10,000, or three-quarters of the entire construction cost of the building. Cornish saw no way to continue paying the debt—his Black parishioners could only help so much, and the church elders' promises of support came up empty. The presbytery ultimately sold the building at auction but made Cornish linger for three more years in a pastoral role. He grew frustrated that he had to take the blame for the church's failure and resentful at how hollow all the pledges of assistance had been from those with enough money to help him. But still he moved on after his tenure to look for new opportunities.

He had not originally intended to work in the press while trying to extricate himself from the financial debacle of the Five Points church. But reading editorial after editorial in New York City newspapers against Black citizens, he felt he had no choice. He responded with his own public letters to those papers, until he realized a forum of his own would be much better. So he helped found *Freedom's Journal*, in 1827.

It was the most prominent—possibly the first—African American newspaper in the nation, providing a voice to Black writers, ministers, and activists whose work might otherwise never have appeared in print. The mission statement of *Freedom's Journal* was direct: "We wish to plead our own cause, for too long others have spoken for us." Black businessmen like James Forten and ministers like Nathaniel Paul and Peter Williams Jr. helped support the paper, and the cofounder, John Russwurm, was one of the first Black graduates of an American college (Bowdoin, in Maine). Cornish published the work of various writers, from William Watkins to Phillis Wheatley, the sermons given in Black churches, political commentary, speeches, and even poetry and songs.

As Cornish expected, mainstream newspapers denounced *Freedom's Journal* as a subversive tool to provoke the enslaved to run away from their masters, thus depriving the slave owners of their "property." They claimed its editorials made Black people distrustful of whites and undermined public faith in the "wise and philanthropic men" of the American Colonization Society. But this was Cornish's point: to show how colonization was a failed concept, a blight on philanthropy, and something that no Black person could ever support. Yet he didn't expect that one of the most important colonizers would not only be Black, but the cofounder of his newspaper.

John Russwurm took over as senior editor from Cornish at the same time he was beginning to harbor doubts about Black people staying in America. After some hesitation, Russwurm came out in favor of colonization, claiming they would never be welcome here and might be better off in Liberia. Russwurm felt so strongly about this he quit the newspaper and planned his move to Africa. Feeling betrayed, the paper's subscribers asked for Cornish to reassume control over it, so he did, renaming it *The Rights of All*. But it stood sapped of momentum by Russwurm's decision and ceased publication after six months. This left Cornish once again without a forum, having to fold his newspaper just as he had to fold his church only months before.

As the years passed, Cornish saw others prosper from his pioneering work. The congregation of the First Colored Presbyterian Church relocated, and his ally Theodore Wright took control of the church, which became a center for antislavery activity in the city. Cornish's journalism influenced other Black-run presses, as well as *The Liberator*, with Garrison taking editorial positions that had first appeared in *Freedom's Journal*. And Cornish's brave position against colonization had since been adopted by almost every advocate of immediate abolition.

Despite all this, Cornish was often denied credit for his influential work, and he no longer had a platform of his own. He didn't run a newspaper or a church or have enough money to start his own institution. But he did know abolitionists who did, and foremost among them were the Tappan brothers.

He and the Tappans had several things in common: abolition, temperance, Presbyterianism, and a focus on improper behavior that could be obsessive. They had all been managers of the American Bible Society and took their piety seriously. The Tappans fought against the sex trade, bad communion wine, and wayward domestics, while Samuel Cornish criticized white New Yorkers for their racism and Black New Yorkers for failing to meet his high expectations. He warned them not to smoke in the streets or dress too fancily. He attacked carnivals, theatrical amusements, drinking and carousing, even a festive parade, writing, "Nothing serves more to keep us in our present degraded condition, than these foolish exhibitions of ourselves." The Tappans came away impressed by Cornish's focus on rectitude and soon became his closest white allies, uniting with them on causes both inspiring and hopeless.

The failure came first. Cornish became chief fundraiser for the Tappans' planned manual labor school for Black youth in New Haven. Despite raising sufficient funds, Cornish saw white backlash sink the project before it had a chance to achieve success. The next project, the Phoenix Society, was more successful. It aimed to provide education and enlightenment to Black people in New York, since they had difficulty visiting cultural institutions without being belittled and segregated from other visitors. Cornish, Wright, and the Tappans proposed raising $10,000 for a library and reading room that could host lectures on everything from the liberal arts to vocational training. Cornish would run the institution as its librarian, giving him a chance to reestablish his name as a critical figure in the movement despite the recent setbacks.

In short order, the society raised the funds it needed; Arthur Tappan, as treasurer, paid his salary; and within a year it was hosting scientific lectures that drew up to five hundred people and establishing branches throughout the city. Months later, the Tappans pushed for Cornish to join the executive committee of the American Anti-Slavery Society (along with Theodore Wright and Peter Williams Jr.). This ensured Cornish would once again have a platform as one of the most prominent abolitionists in New York.

Shortly after these triumphs, Cornish felt confident enough in his relationship with Arthur Tappan to accept his invitation to sit with him in church. This should not have been unusual. Samuel Cornish was a Presbyterian minister, Arthur was a fellow member of the sect, and the two men had become friends in recent years. However, since Cornish was Black and the church was white, this mixture was enough to create an uproar in the house of the Lord.

The minister of Laight Street Presbyterian Church, Samuel H. Cox, wanted to break the ugly tradition of segregation and racism in the North. But one of those traditions was present in his own church—the Negro pew—that forlorn section at the back or in the balcony of white churches where Black parishioners were forced to sit. According to custom, Reverend Cornish, despite being an officer of the church, would have to sit there as well. But on this morning, upon Arthur's invitation, he chose not to.

Scores of churchgoers were outraged that Arthur and Cornish had amalgamated within sight of God. After the service, they reprimanded both men and warned them against committing the same transgression again. With the controversy growing, Reverend Cox tried to persuade his flock to change their views. He had previously criticized color lines in church, including his own, and told his listeners to rise above bigotry and reject segregation. They might as well ask "how white must the complexion of the Saviour be, were he now on earth, in order for us to tolerate his person or endure his presence."

This set off yet another furor. Immediately, James Watson Webb vented his spleen against Arthur Tappan and Reverends Cornish and Cox in his *Courier and Enquirer.* He had already blistered abolitionists for impeding the work of colonizers to expel Black people from America, and now he condemned Cox for being in favor of race mixing, attacking him for supposedly saying "the Saviour of mankind is a negro." He and other news editors later amplified the attack to involve Arthur Tappan, claiming he had divorced his wife to marry a Black woman and that he and other abolitionists favored interracial marriages—including for their own daughters.

Arthur scrambled to contain the damage. It had been only a few months since the American Anti-Slavery Society had formed, and the church scandal threatened to draw attention from the society's good works and, once again, damage his reputation. For Cornish the episode just confirmed what he had already feared about the hostility of his white neighbors. That his mere presence in a church sitting next to Arthur could upend local society was a depressing commentary on how similar New Yorkers were to Southerners and how much work remained to change their minds about abolition and racial equality. Struggling with these issues, he again faced a question he couldn't answer: Would God reward the side of righteousness, or would he reward the men with hearts as small as cherries?

By this time, the spring of 1834, it certainly appeared that men with the smallest hearts, and greatest weapons, held the advantage. For at this moment, as Cornish and the Tappans struggled to defend their reputations, an election riot erupted that would serve as a model for attacks on them and their allies just months later. Indeed, the story of the riot was daunting for any abolitionist with a sense of omen:

New York City, April 8–10, Sixth Ward

It was the first direct election in the city's history, a contest between the Democrats and their enemies the Whigs. The rules were simple: A voter didn't have to register in advance, he didn't need identification, and he might try to vote multiple times without anyone stopping him. The only thing he needed was to be a white man with a strong spine, and perhaps a large club. Black men could try to vote if they had $250 in property, but caution kept even well-heeled black voters at home, because of the danger they knew was coming—the mob that would soon rule the streets.

James Watson Webb helped light the fuse for the riot. He had once been a firm ally of Andrew Jackson's Democrats, but differences over trade and monetary policy had, in just two years, made him into their implacable enemy. He now vilified the Democratic Party at every turn and "declared open war on the Jacksonian administration." This was more than figurative. When Webb published a damning article in the Courier and Enquirer *against the Irish immigrants who voted for the Democrats en masse, they erupted in a rage and vowed to meet the insult with violence. But Webb's Whigs had already planned out the battle ahead.*

The Whigs hoisted the U.S. flag and built a boat called the Constitution and rolled it through the streets, sang patriotic songs, drank whiskey to excess, and yelled their huzzahs until the lot of them grew to the thousands. The Democrats met them with their own boat called "Veto," named after the favorite tool of their hero in the White House. The sides converged on the Five Points: the

Democratic slum-stronghold of the Sixth Ward, and the site of Lewis Tappan's Chatham Street Chapel.

The Whigs' invasion splintered when they met a force of immigrants who drove them back with a volley of paving stones. Webb quickly recruited 300 volunteers as his own private army, swore them into service and assembled them to march to Democratic polling places. The Democrats surprised him by counter-attacking the offices of his newspaper and forcing him to defend his garrison. He assembled a barricade in front of the building, then gathered thirty volunteers, 70 muskets, 100 pistols and six loads of paving stones. He climbed up to the roof with a musket and aimed it at the crowd, warning that anyone who marched on his office would be shot. His defense of the newspaper fortress worked.

Other Democrats and Whigs faced off in city polling rooms. At one, twenty Whigs "stretched bleeding and maimed on the floor; one so badly wounded that he was carried out lifeless." Their foes ripped down campaign banners, shredded the ballots, and moved on to the next polling site. Thousands of Whigs assembled for revenge, warned of "a state of anarchy" and pledged to be "conservators of the peace." They spread out to the polls, across the city wards, grabbed whatever weapons they could muster, and what they couldn't muster they raided from gun shops and stole from an arsenal.

Crowds poured out into Duane and Pearl streets and around the spokes of the Five Points, and beat each other in an animal frenzy, "howling and screaming in a savage manner." Webb sent his volunteers into the decrepit neighborhood armed with newly acquired weapons, looking for Irishmen to attack or whoever seemed to be in league with them. The Democrats assailed the rolling Constitution in a sea of drunken rioters, and the violence spread to envelop more of the city. Near City Hall, the mayor demanded the combatants put down their weapons, but the crowd savaged 15 of his watchmen, beat them bloody or unconscious, and left the mayor helpless, struck down by a rioter, while his guards were hobbled with skull fractures, broken ribs and bloody faces.

Overwhelmed by three days of mayhem, the mayor finally called it an insurrection. The US Navy dispatched Marines, infantry, and squadrons of cavalry with bayonets, sabers and guns, and they quelled the violence. The ballot boxes were closed up, the votes counted, and the results announced. Andrew Jackson's party had triumphed by a margin of 180 votes, a victory hard earned in the arena of urban combat.

For James Watson Webb the brutality was a practice run. He had done well with his assembly of troops and arsenal, had mounted a vigorous defense, and burnished his reputation as a committed foe of the Jacksonians. He had earlier claimed credit for inventing the insult "King Andrew" for the president and could stir feelings of rage in his readers like few others. And he still had boundless energy left after the election—which he now directed at abolitionists.

In the weeks after the riot, Webb wasted no time in reminding his readers of the recent controversy in Samuel Cox's church and just how scurrilous race mixers were, and he invented a new insult for them: "amalgamists." The *Courier and Enquirer* ran articles denouncing them as threats to the nation and worthy of nothing but scorn. Inspired by Webb, other white supremacists composed pamphlets that condemned abolitionists as apostles of interracial sex. Dr. David Reese wrote "no white person would consent to marry a negro, without having previously forfeited all character with the whites; and that even *profligate* sexual intercourse between the races [is] the most despicable form of licentiousness."

This hysteria fed new charges and rumors and fantasies in the press: that abolitionists presided over secret mixed marriages, that amalgamated groups of men and women discussed obscene matters in public, that Black men on horseback had paraded through the city looking for white brides, and that antislavery supporters had "entered into a conspiracy against the human species" by indulging in race mixing. By June even casual readers of the New York press could only assume that anyone who spoke out against slavery was part of some cabal to destroy the white race. Observing this charged atmosphere on a trip to America, the British abolitionist Edward Abdy was shocked: "A silly cry of 'amalgamation' had exasperated the public mind; and so completely obstructed the perception of truth . . . Never did pride, and prejudice, and presumption gain more thorough mastery over the heart and the intellect. It makes one blush for the inhumanity and folly of mankind."

Garrison could scarcely contain his contempt for Webb and his fellow travelers in the press, like the pro-colonization editor of the *Commercial Advertiser*, William Stone. Garrison told his readers that both men were "throwing all manner of filth upon abolitionists." But he knew that merely cleaning up that filth wouldn't be enough—the charges were so absurd that any thinking reader of *The Liberator* would immediately recognize their falsity. So Garrison ran Webb's editorial—over three columns—on the front page of his May 31 edition, to show just how much poison he had injected into the body politic.

Webb accused abolitionists of laying the foundation for war and dissolving the Union, because emancipation was an idea "no rational, humane white man can anticipate without shuddering." He condemned those who attacked the Colonization Society and worked to undermine slavery, thereby inciting revolution and racial anarchy. He conjured conspiracies about his enemies, imagining them as zealots from the Middle Ages—"a new race of monks and fanatics"—who would debauch the schools with integration and upend society. In short, these "mad malignant hypocrites" were nothing more than "robbers and murderers" who would "prepare the way for the earthquake" that would shatter the nation.

Webb's invective was only the first in a series of salvos he directed against abolitionists in the spring and early summer, attacks that were copied and printed in other publications across the country. Indeed, the *Courier and Enquirer* influenced other journals to adopt a similarly vicious tone against abolitionists, referring to them as rogues who had to be stopped before they ripped apart the fabric of society.

Lewis Tappan was not content to sit back and allow Webb and his cohorts to smear the reputation of his colleagues. He and his allies took a public stand to defend themselves and went ahead with the "funeral of colonization" that would celebrate the financial demise of their foes. Lewis also helped organize an antislavery week in May that would present discussions and lectures about the designs of the ACS and the need for immediate abolition, as well as reports on the harrowing conditions in Liberia for those who had been sent there. On the day of the event, at Chatham Street Chapel, a carpenter named Thomas Brown answered questions about rampant slave trading, intemperance, blasphemy, and poor health in the colony, before a mostly sympathetic audience of opponents of slavery. But suddenly—angry white men broke into the meeting.

They interrupted Brown and Lewis with shouting. Then taunting, then threats of violence. The meeting broke up in chaos, and the colonizers celebrated a victory by stifling any discussion of colonization and its true purpose.

Webb trumpeted the moment in the *Courier and Enquirer* and encouraged his readers to interrupt proceedings of the abolitionists wherever they found them, to give voice to their feelings at full volume and push the emancipation cause backward. And he offered an ominous warning to anyone who resisted him:

> There is a point beyond which the patience and endurance of the public will not be carried. And if these few infatuated men should attempt again to hold a public meeting, and force themselves and their opinions and principles on the community in despite of public opinion, we should much fear the consequences to the abolitionists themselves.

Garrison didn't have to be reminded of the danger. He was already worried about the threat to the movement. And now, with his and the Tappans' heightened reputation and their new antislavery society, Webb had found his next target. Garrison, usually so sanguine in his feelings of martyrdom, started to fear for his health and safety. He wrote to his ally George Benson, "Let us not deceive ourselves. Although our cause is certainly advancing with a mighty stride, yet the opposition still to be encountered is truly formidable. This is no time for repose; and if we exult, it must be with our weapons in our hands, ready to meet the combined powers of earth and hell."

★ THREE ★

THE OTHER CONFEDERACY

The nexus of New York abolition was Arthur Tappan and Company—122 Pearl Street, in Lower Manhattan. The three-story granite edifice was both a bulwark of the importing and dry goods trade and an unmistakable symbol of the Tappans' wealth channeled into their moral crusades. Accordingly, James Watson Webb and other editors took care to remind their readers of the brothers' prominent location near Wall Street and how easy it was for any would-be patriots to chastise them by force.

From his upper-story office, Arthur understood just how exposed he and his business were to the ever-shifting, ever-threatening tides of public opinion. But he had defied popular feeling before and, by the summer of 1834, had grown callous to the threats of his enemies. God had given him the strength to undertake his campaign of moral reform, and he knew his divinely guided cause would prevail. Besides, many of his enemies were also his clients.

Among them were a fair number of Southerners, whether vacationers in New York or planters and merchants from below the Mason-Dixon Line. Arthur relied on their desire for his product to keep his business profitable and, ironically, the antislavery movement well funded. His customers may have considered him a race traitor and their state leaders might have put out rewards for his capture, but they still paid well for his exquisite goods. Of course, they also requested that the customary "From A. Tappan and Co." not be marked on the boxes, to keep their affections hidden. It was the worst of bad marriages, each party despising each other but in too deep to do anything about it.

Arthur and Lewis ended up working together in the building out of financial necessity—namely Lewis's. A few years before, he had fallen on hard times, at least in comparison to the style he was accustomed to. He had tried to be a venture capitalist, but he had entered the game at the wrong time, after a recession in the mid-1820s, and found himself mired in red ink from speculating in cotton and woolen mills. His brother rescued him from drowning in debt by giving him a job in the silk trade. In the late 1820s, they worked out an agreement: after an allowance for his family's needs, Lewis would invest half his salary back into the business and use the other half to pay down his debts. Since then Lewis had become essential to the Tappan operation, managing teams of draymen, overseeing clerks and bookkeepers, and receiving crates of silk imports from places like France, Italy, and India.

Lewis, in fact, was more the face of the business than Arthur, though his familiarity didn't make him any more popular among New Yorkers. Indeed, the Tappans were among the most unpopular men in the city, their campaign against vice only giving them a reputation as rigid moralists in a town where sin had the upper hand. Arthur supposedly never said a profane word in his life, and the brothers not only railed against prostitution and alcohol; they tried to shut down post offices on Sunday for violating the Sabbath and operated "Christian spy cells to watch tavern-keepers and other dispensers of pleasure" for violation of city codes. So in combining their unpopular campaign against vice with the even more unpopular campaign against slavery, the brothers were loathed among large segments of the white working class.

Their activities weren't limited to patrolling the behavior of white people. They had long been wary of how Black New Yorkers celebrated Emancipation Day—marking the end of slavery in the state—which took place on the same day as the Fourth of July. It had been a spirited event for the previous seven years, with lively music, parades, drinking, and other festivities that were as clamorous as they were joyous. The Tappans, of course, did not approve of such merriment, nor did Samuel Cornish and other ministers in the American Anti-Slavery Society, who saw it as "scandalous and disheartening."

As an alternative, they proposed a pious commemoration that would remove the rum and whiskey, mirth and pleasure, and replace it with solemn odes to liberty and hymns to God (and perhaps cold water and crackers for snacks). It would take place at Chatham Street Chapel and feature Black and white parishioners singing hymns together and sitting side by side, in defiance of the warnings over amalgamation. John Greenleaf Whittier would compose a poem for the occasion, speakers would read from the Declaration of Independence as well as Garrison's Declaration of Sentiments, and the entire effect would be peaceful and ennobling.

But weeks before the event, word got out. The culprit was William Stone, the publisher whom Garrison called a "murderous hypocrite." Stone let his readers know abolitionists would gather on Independence Day, and sure enough, menacing handbills began appearing on the streets: "The friends of the union and of the South are requested to attend the anti-slavery meeting at Chatham Street Chapel," the principal topic of which would be "the disunion of the states." Just like the previous October, when a flyer signed by "MANY SOUTHERNERS" had circulated, the new one was signed by "MANY FRIENDS OF THE COUNTRY." They both served the same function: to incite a mob.

The Tappan brothers, Cornish, and their colleagues knew this kind of agitation might occur, but they went forward with the event anyway. Cornish, in particular, had spent three months keeping his head down after the fracas with Arthur at Samuel Cox's church, and he had no desire to retreat any longer from public view. Lewis and Arthur agreed, since the commemoration had already been planned and had such a dignified purpose, to honor both revolution and emancipation.

And so the day began. First, a chorus of Black and white singers sang of God's mercy and the promise of freedom from oppression. Then an orator read Whittier's poem, speaking of God's power to crush human bondage—"When smitten as with fire from heaven, the captive's chain shall sink in dust"—after which "a solemn address was offered to the Throne of Grace." A reading of the Declaration of Independence stirred the emotions further and set the stage for Garrison's Declaration of Sentiments. The recital of that mission statement of abolition would mark the climax of the event, but before the speaker had even begun to read from the text, a vulgar cacophony echoed through the church.

The Many Friends of the Country had arrived.

Led by a city alderman, hundreds of anti-abolitionists infiltrated the chapel, hooting and screaming and stomping, pounding the floorboards of the building to drown out the words the speaker tried to offer. They yelled "Treason! Treason!" and "Hurrah for the Union!" The audience sat stunned, the choir now silent. A group of city watchmen soon arrived and chased the blustering men out of the chapel, but those men weren't finished yet. They went on to attack a group of Black people in a nearby city park until the police drove them off a second time.

The Independence Day commemoration broke up in confusion, fulfilling the worst fears of the Tappans and Cornish. For William Stone, though, it was a success. His *Commercial Advertiser* crowed about how a group of patriotic New Yorkers had prevented treason, overthrown villainy, and so on. Webb joined in by mocking the abolitionists in the *Courier and Enquirer* and blaming them for the disruption, claiming the intruders were only defending America with their screams.

In the wake of the disruption, the American Anti-Slavery Society postponed the event three days, until July 7, when African Americans would finally get their chance to honor emancipation in the state. They gathered once again at Chatham Street Chapel, with a program of solemn hymns and speeches, pleas for divine guidance and support, and vows to remain resolute in the face of injustice. They also added a few more guards, to keep out any horde of self-proclaimed patriots.

The ceremony began and proceeded without interruption, until the vice president of the New York Sacred Music Society, William Rockwell, arrived. His group regularly met here to rehearse their chorus and orchestra, known for renditions of Handel's *Messiah*, Beethoven's "Hallelujah to the Father and the Son of God," and other spiritual favorites. He had not come, however, to add the voices of his choir to the ceremony. Instead, "finding the house occupied by colored people . . . [he] undertook to disturb the meeting by ordering the House to be cleared."

It turned out Rockwell was mistaken: the president of the music society had given up the space for the night, and Rockwell hadn't been informed. But that didn't stop him and a group of fifteen other musicians from shouting down the Black choir and drowning out their hymns. But the abolitionists refused to leave the space, so the Sacred Music Society men attacked them, shattering lamps and breaking chairs and beating them with their canes. The chaos enveloped the sanctuary and overwhelmed the guards. After someone threw open the chapel doors, passersby poured in from the Five Points, clambering up to the balconies to wreck whatever they could get their hands on and hurling church pews down to the main floor. The police eventually arrived and broke up the melee, but they also locked up the church and forced the Black parishioners to vacate the building—once again denying them their chance to have a celebration of freedom.

Webb had little to do with starting this latest outbreak of turmoil, but he could not resist rewriting the story and inventing a new version of the event, based not on what actually had happened but on what would most upset his readers. Under the title "Negro Riot" he wrote, "The white citizens present were there with no disposition to disturb the blacks . . . and when they mildly insisted on their clear rights, they were beaten—yes, beaten, fellow-citizens, by the bludgeons of an infuriated and an *encouraged* negro mob!" The *Commercial Advertiser* embellished the story further, reporting that Black people had assailed Rockwell and the pious musicians "with canes loaded with leaden bullets on the head [and] knocked some down and injured others severely . . . The scene was one of deep and dark disgrace, and many an innocent white man suffered to appease the negro wrath." Abolitionists, who knew the truth of the riot, were once again stunned, with Garrison writing in *The Liberator*, "The Colonization men have let loose a Legion of fiends; and now they are untamable, and where this thing is to end, no mortal knows or can foresee."

Witnessing this latest round of violence, Lewis Tappan knew the methods of his adversaries had changed. Webb and Stone had always twisted and exaggerated the beliefs of abolitionists, but never had they been so blatant in their lies. Now readers of their newspapers—and lesser papers that parroted their editorial line—learned of events that were entirely imaginary. For anyone who thought about it for a moment, such a tale made no sense (Why would abolitionists in the chapel ransack their own building?), but appeals to logic were never the strong suit of Stone and Webb. With more than a little gall, Webb wrote, "In the name of the country, in the name of heaven, how much more are we to bear from Arthur Tappan's mad intemperance?"

The Tappans could now feel the hostility on the streets, the nasty looks and the hateful comments. *The Liberator* reported that proslavery businessmen in town had ordered their employees to accost Lewis "expressly to tar and feather." He had escaped that fate so far, but after the melee with the Sacred Music Society, he knew the mob would make some attempt to assault him. As he left the chapel and walked down the street, a small crowd began to gather behind him, closely following his footsteps. The crowd grew larger as he left the Five Points, becoming more and more vocal until they were hooting and yelling. And when he reached his house on Rose Street, they were making "a tremendous noise [with] mingled groans, hisses and execrations."

This made quite a clamor in the neighborhood, an otherwise placid area where mechanics and merchants lived side by side, with a Quaker meetinghouse across the street. Lewis hurried inside his house, as his hired guards tried to control the crowd. They kept up the noise, demanding to get their hands on him, and threw rocks at his windows. Looking out at the fury of these men, Lewis knew this wouldn't be their last attempt to storm his house. The next day, he moved his wife and children up to the then-village of Harlem for their own safety and kept a guard behind to secure his property.

Five days had now passed since the first strike against the antislavery activists on Independence Day, and Webb saw no reason to relent. On July 9, in an article titled "The Fanatics," he advertised that another meeting in favor of abolition would occur at Chatham Street Chapel, and "we caution the colored people of this city against it." That evening a mob duly assembled, expecting to find the Tappans, Garrison, and a mixed crowd of worshippers. They stormed the chapel with tempers high and voices raised—only to find an empty building, without an amalgamist in sight.

That didn't deter the men from holding their own ad hoc meeting, in which some gave speeches in favor of colonization and expelling Black people from America. Others "struck up a Jim Crow chorus" in the style of T. D. "Daddy" Rice, whose act drew large crowds to watch him caper about in blackface. The mob wasn't satisfied with such mockeries, though, and charged out of the building to assault any target they could find.

They headed to the Bowery Theatre, where the *New York Sun* had reported that the English performer George Farren had punched a butcher who had protested his remark, "damn the Yankees, they are a damn set of jack-asses, and fit to be gulled." *The Sun* raged about the insult, writing, "When the character of our country is assailed by foreigners," violence is justified. "This will teach English play actors a lesson they will long remember."

The mob took the *Sun*'s message to heart and aimed to find Farren and give him a rough lesson in American justice. But Farren had already fled the city in terror, never to return to New York. So when the mob arrived, they found legendary actor Edwin Forrest on stage and broke up his performance instead. Charging inside, the rioters sent the actors and the audience fleeing toward the wings of the stage, as they smashed benches and broke the theater's windows. With a good measure of bravery, Forrest emerged from backstage to try to calm the crowd. He managed to stall them just long enough for fifty watchmen to arrive with clubs to pummel the invaders. This result not being to the *Sun*'s liking, the paper presented an alternate version of the event the next day—claiming the crowd had been pacified by the theater manager waving American flags and leading them in a rousing rendition of the minstrel song "Zip Coon."

While the Bowery Theatre was under siege, another, larger, group of rioters marched to Lewis Tappan's house. He and his family, however, had already vacated their home, leaving only a crew of guards to fend off a mob that was building toward the hundreds. The guards stood no chance against them and fled. In minutes, men wielding clubs and bricks smashed open the doors, broke the windows, and hurled the family's elegant early American furniture into the street—sofas, tables, mirrors, beds, anything they could grab. The rioters set a great bonfire to the furniture pile, which burned brightly enough to illuminate the entire street.

Unlike the usual reports of the mob comprising "the sweepings of the city," eyewitnesses would characterize these rioters as a particularly top-shelf assortment: "men of excellent standing, among whom were sundry members of churches, and particularly one deacon." Most of the mob's heavy lifting, though, was done by two gangs—the Battenders and Huge Paws—with merchants and wealthier men watching with approval from the sidewalk. Finally, at 2:00 A.M., with the flames dying and the crowd shrinking, a group of watchmen chased off the remainder of the rioters, who left shouting cheers for James Watson Webb.

Those who sacked the house of Lewis Tappan did not realize that Arthur had watched the event from across the street, knowing that his business was probably next on the mob's list. He had little doubt that his shop would make a tempting target, since all the silk parasols, hats, scarves, and other dainty items would burn well in the hands of rioters, as would his entire business. "$10,000 for Arthur Tappan . . . find him, find him," they had chanted in October. "Away to Arthur Tappan's!" they chanted in July.

It was as essential to protect the business as it was to protect himself. With every batch of imports he sold, he funded the causes synonymous with antislavery: charitable groups like the African Improvement Society and the Phoenix Society, conventions of people of color, educational projects and schools for Black youth, newspapers like *The Liberator* and *The Emancipator*, and activist groups like the New York Anti-Slavery Society and the American Anti-Slavery Society. Lewis Tappan's house, the chapel on Chatham Street, Clinton Hall—all those sites could be destroyed with less consequence, but if Arthur Tappan's business were ruined, abolition in New York would suffer a crippling blow. And the crowd that gathered that night knew it.

The mobsters arrived on cue, many of them drunk. They began with hurling rocks and other missiles at the building's windows. The mayor refused to protect the building from the attackers, so Arthur secured the presence of 15–20 watchmen to defend it. But when these watchmen tried to arrest some of the offenders, the crowd surged upon them "and handled them so roughly that they were compelled to take refuge in flight"—running in terror just as others had fled from his brother's house. The mob then shattered the windows on the lower level and tried to break down the front door with an awning post. In the turmoil they wounded city alderman John Labagh, but he turned out to be the rare authority figure who refused to run, and instead he cursed his assailants: "Break open the doors if you dare! The store is filled with armed men, who will blow your brains out the moment the door gives way!"

The alderman wasn't bluffing. Arthur Tappan was nominally a pacifist, but he was also a realist who had no interest in sacrificing himself as a martyr to a bunch of whiskey-fueled hooligans. So from his redoubt behind granite walls, Arthur acted as field general. According to one report:

> The oldest clerks were put on guard; thirty-six stand of arms were bought at Hinton's, in Broadway, and five hundred ball cartridges . . . Some thirty or forty of us were ready behind the door, Mr. Arthur Tappan himself in command. Every moment we expected the door to give way. "Steady, boys," says Mr. Tappan. "Fire low. Shoot them in the legs, then they can't run!"

They were now fully under siege. The mob stamped on the wooden sidewalks of Pearl Street and pounded the doors with their clubs and awning posts. But Arthur's small army held firm, and as the night passed, the mob's zeal gave way to fatigue and the need for another drink.

Still, while Arthur had secured his building for the night, his fears did not abate, nor did those of his colleagues on Pearl Street. Some of them became chilled at the prospect of further unrest: "Moneyed men were exceedingly frightened at the apparent strength and violence of the mob." Because if the fortress of Arthur Tappan and Company could be laid under siege, any less well-protected trading house or bank might be ransacked, looted, and burned.

Lewis was alarmed at the risk Arthur was taking, sticking his neck out at a time when a reward for his capture was still on offer and, it was rumored, a ship waited in the harbor to deliver him to the South. Lewis implored him to escape the city just as he had, to leave behind an armed guard to secure the building, and to trust in God to keep his business from being destroyed. It took some persuading, but Arthur agreed. The brothers left for a weekend sojourn in Poughkeepsie.

The Tappans had no desire to learn more about the composition of the mob. But if they had, they would have discovered a crazy quilt of skilled and unskilled workers, merchants and laborers, Catholics and Protestants, Irish and native-born citizens, Whigs and Democrats, and men with no interest in politics whatsoever. They worked in a broad array of occupations: hatter, shoemaker, butcher, sailor, stevedore, thief, mason, clerk, blacksmith, vagrant, and tavern owner, among many others. But one thing the men had in common was they were almost all white and most of their targets were Black.

Although reports would later call the mayhem spontaneous, for the most part, it was anything but. The armed men communicated across wards and neighborhoods to decide on their targets, splitting themselves into small, mobile units to travel across the city and regrouping into larger forces for the attack. Once confronted, shorter and weaker men formed the core of the group, wielding rocks and missiles, while the larger men— often from gangs—would patrol the outside bearing clubs loaded with lead or other metal to make them more deadly. Faced with such tactics, watchmen found it hard to fight them, and when the men blocked off entire streets with chained carts and wagons and barrels and ladders, the riot zone appeared almost impenetrable, the rioters unstoppable.

Ultimately, nothing like this level of violence had ever been seen in New York. For the mob wasn't just burning and ransacking due to the scheming of newspaper editors like Webb and Stone. It was on the attack because it hated abolitionists and Black people. Not surprisingly, it saved the worst of its destruction for the Five Points.

The slum was notorious as a lodgment for penniless immigrants from Ireland and a segregated zone for Black people kept out of other, whiter neighborhoods. Homes and hovels were scattered between grog shops and gambling halls, with theaters, churches, and merchant shops in between. As part of the city's poorest ward, the Sixth, it had already seen partial destruction in the election riot in April, and most of that damage hadn't been repaired. And now, once again, into this beleaguered neighborhood came two to three thousand men bearing clubs, bricks, knives, and muskets.

They charged into the Five Points via Orange, Mulberry, Elm, and Centre streets, plundering houses, burning and tearing apart furniture, and savaging the people inside. Black cultural and religious institutions faced the brunt of the damage, with bordellos and taverns only lightly affected. The mob spread news around the neighborhood that white homeowners should place candles in their windows to identify themselves, and they would be spared. Black homeowners were not informed, and their homes faced vandalism, robbery, and incineration. Rioters also demolished the African School on Orange Street, beat up a barber who had a shop nearby, and assaulted anyone else whose complexion wasn't white: "Whenever a colored person appeared, it was signal of combat, fight and riot." Finally, they went after the men that Webb and Stone despised the most: antislavery ministers.

Samuel Cox knew he would be among the first targeted. It was in his Laight Street church where Samuel Cornish had refused to sit in a segregated pew, and where Webb had claimed Cox preached that Jesus was Black. For weeks newspapers had been threatening him with lurid punishments: "A coat of tar and feathers might be of service to this man; HE RICHLY DESERVES SUCH A DRESS."

Cox asked the mayor, in a letter, to protect his house and his church, but assuming he wouldn't, he packed up and left the city. The mob, as expected, descended on his home, ripping apart fence posts to use as clubs, barricading the street with carts, and breaking windows and doors. They then moved on to his church, where a small group of watchmen took a volley of rocks and missiles head-on and fled for their lives. The attackers smashed the windows, shouting racial slurs, and almost burst into the nave before a group of police on horseback drove them off. They promptly moved on to Henry Ludlow's Spring Street church, their fury fueled by a rumor in the press that he had presided over an interracial marriage. This time they penetrated the building, demolished the pulpit and pews, and even ripped down the galleries. Some in the mob continued to Reverend Ludlow's house on Thompson Street. They threw paving stones into the parlor; sliced up the carpets; piled portraits, furniture, and a chandelier into a great shambles; and littered the house with graffiti. They would have burned the house, too, had watchmen not come in time to stop them.

However, no timely appearance of the authorities could save Peter Williams Jr.'s St. Philip's African Episcopal Church. He was New York's first Black Episcopal priest and for fifteen years had been shepherding his middle-class congregation. More cautious than some of his peers, he served with Cornish and Theodore Wright on the executive committee of the American Anti-Slavery Society and allied with them on many projects for racial equality. This made him the subject of rumors, namely that he had officiated at a wedding with a Black groom and a white bride. The consequence: "It is next to impossible to describe the scene; hundreds of infuriated devils were shouting, hallooing, and busily employed in tearing out the doors and windows, the interior of the Church, and whatever they could lay their hands on, and throwing it into the street."

For two hours, uninterrupted, they savaged the church, even obliterating the organ, until they rendered it unfit to be a place of worship. The windows were shattered, the pews damaged and heaved about, and the adjoining rectory demolished, leaving Williams without a home. The mobsters also descended upon three other Black-owned homes nearby, smashing windows and doors and terrifying the residents. It all made for the riot's worst violence in and around a church, but city officials didn't come to the rescue. For unlike ministers Cox and Ludlow, Reverend Williams was Black, and they had no interest in defending him or his neighbors.

In fact, city authorities protected almost none of the Black-owned homes and businesses of the Five Points. Mayor Cornelius Lawrence—freshly elected by the mob in the April election riot—dithered while an outnumbered crew of city watchmen and private guards tried to fight the mob for days without success. Only when the violence spread into more "respectable" districts did Lawrence finally do something about it, when he heard a rumor that the masses of working-class men were now about to ransack Wall Street.

At this point Lawrence suddenly became very interested in stopping the mayhem, to keep the masses from attacking the banks, the vaults, the concentration of wealth at the southern end of Manhattan Island. He vowed to quash disorder and justified his belated action by slandering abolitionists. In a proclamation he wrote, "however repugnant to the good sense of the community are the doctrines and measures of a few misguided individuals . . . their conduct affords no justification for popular commotion."

Mayor Lawrence called up the 27th Regiment of the National Guard, sending it into the streets armed with muskets and bayonets, to break apart the mob's barricades and advance in columns against the rock-throwing and club-wielding masses. The soldiers rallied with volunteer fire companies and militias to secure the streets and arrest whatever ringleaders of the mob they could find—locking up 150 men to await trial. Many of the other rioters simply disappeared into the streets and alleys, to be heard from again in future melees, while the bolder among them shouted at the troops in defiance, praising the name of their hero: "Three cheers for James Watson Webb, of the Courier!"

Garrison, in *The Liberator*, made it clear he had no doubt about the key figures behind the violence: "the *Newspapers*; especially Webb, with his Courier, and Stone, with his Commercial Advertiser. These two are the most criminal." (Garrison also wrote, "If any man ever deserved to be sent to the Penitentiary or State Prison for life, Stone is that man.") He also accused merchants and lawyers associated with the Colonization Society of playing a prominent role in "the other confederacy [that] includes those who have instigated the riots."

Residents were shocked at the scale of destruction and how unceasing it was, lasting for an entire week. They questioned how long abolition could persist in the face of such violence. Others, mainly in the press, asked antislavery activists to repent, or to make amends to colonizers and find common ground, and let slavery and injustice go on as they always had, unimpeded. But for many abolitionists, the violence only steeled their commitment; it made them realize the cause was more critical than ever.

In one memorable letter from a "Colored Baltimorean," a man wrote to Garrison's newspaper with a call to arms. He said the time to support "deeply injured abolitionists was . . . *now*, while their lives and all they hold dear in life are at the tender mercies of infuriated mobs:—*now*, while they are threatened with assassination, and ruthlessly assailed in their persons—their houses pillaged, and their property given to the devouring flames."

Due to widespread press coverage and copycat violence, the flames weren't confined to New York. In the days after, the mere sight of a Black man at a church in Newark led a mob to destroy lanterns, the pulpit, and pews and shatter all the glass in the building. In Norwich, Connecticut, men grabbed an antislavery minister during his sermon and forced him to leave town. Other disorders in the house of God erupted in New Britain, Connecticut, and Concord, New Hampshire—the common element being rage against Black people, abolitionists, or both.

Neither Stone nor Webb showed the least amount of remorse for their actions. Instead, Webb announced, during the riots, that when antislavery advocates push "doctrines which outrage public feelings, they have no right to demand protection from the people they thus insult." After the violence he was even more brazen, celebrating the attack on "wicked and absurd doctrines" that he loathed. "If we have been instrumental in producing this desirable state of public feeling, we take pride in it." Webb may have even coordinated some of the mayhem, as he did in the election riot. If so, the authorities had no interest in finding out to what degree.

While Webb and Stone boasted about their actions, other papers weren't so charitable to them. Rival editors were hardly sympathetic to abolitionists—and blamed them equally for the chaos—but they made sure to condemn the press barons. The *New-York Sentinel* said, "we have styled them 'Colonization riots' because they were instigated by colonization papers, particularly the Courier and Enquirer," while the *Journal of Commerce* wrote, "It is ridiculous to talk about respect for the laws, and at the same time to encourage their violation."

Some of the most radical abolitionists were not touched by the violence. William Lloyd Garrison was visiting the village of Brooklyn in Connecticut, enjoying a pristine landscape where "the perfume of the flowers is wafted upon every breeze" and the fields and hills were "beauti-fully luxuriant." More surprisingly, David Ruggles eluded the clutches of the mob, even though his house was only a short distance from Arthur Tappan's and his bookstore sold some of the most outspoken tracts in the city. This was likely more of an oversight than a conscious decision by the men with bricks and torches, who despised Ruggles as much as any other abolitionist in the city, if not more so for his skin color.

Arthur and Lewis Tappan attracted most of the attention for their sacrifices, but countless Black ministers and parishioners suffered much more, with ruined sanctuaries and damage to buildings beyond repair—and no financial security to weather the storm. Samuel Cornish escaped the violence, lacking a congregation and living well north of the chaos, and Theodore Wright's church was spared, though standing a short distance from Lewis's house. For Peter Williams Jr., though, the mob did its worst.

Episcopal Bishop of New York Benjamin Onderdonk presented Williams with an ultimatum: he could continue his work with abolitionists or he could lose his ministry. In a letter to him, Onderdonk had hardly expressed his condolences for Williams's home and church being wrecked when he wrote, "Let me advise you to resign, at once, your connexion, in every department, with the Anti-Slavery Society, and to make public your resignation." The bishop refused to offer his reasons but simply told Williams to embrace "meekness, order, and self-sacrifice to common good, and the peace of the community." In other words, to bow before those who had destroyed his life's work.

Williams published his response in the press, detailing his good works with the Phoenix Society and other philanthropic causes but also expressing regret at some of the actions of the Anti-Slavery Society, since "it is a most difficult matter to avoid extremes on subjects of great public excitement." He defended himself for speaking out against the colonizers, but he also said he had assisted any Black person willing to emigrate. In sum, he said he would have resigned sooner if he had thought he could have made a difference and prevented some of the turmoil that had occurred.

Regardless of the words he used, Williams felt he had no choice but to accept Onderdonk's demand. He quit the abolition society, lowered his profile, and withdrew into the diocese. Although he kept his position as rector and sometimes ventured out to support philanthropic causes, his career as an abolitionist would be the most prominent casualty of the riot.

By contrast, in the days after the violence, the Tappans remained unrepentant, even defiant. *The Emancipator* printed a rallying cry that echoed the style of Garrison's radiant Christian fury:

> NON-RESISTANCE!—PATIENCE!!—FORBEARANCE!!!
>
> If thine enemy hunger, feed him.
>
> If a man smite thee on the one cheek, turn to him the other also.
>
> Be these the watch-words of abolitionists. Fear God, and fear none else. If our opponents think it for their credit and ultimate advantage, to silence us by strength of lungs and by brute force, let them try the experiment. Whenever they see fit to reason with us, we are ready for them.

Left unstated was the fact that Arthur had not turned the other cheek but had planned to greet his tormentors with a volley of musket fire if they had successfully invaded his shop. And Lewis had hardly been meek or sheepish. Instead, he had felt emboldened enough to confront his enemies face to face.

He resolved to leave his wrecked house unrepaired for the entire summer, as an open rebuke to those who had attacked him, and as a "silent anti-slavery preacher to the crowds who will flock to see it." He also visited the offices of the *Commercial Advertiser* to demand that William Stone stop publishing libelous material about him, and instead publish his statement of defense. Stone refused to do so, Lewis refused to leave until he did, and Stone threw him out of the office. When the press heard of the dust-up, it couldn't resist the irony of Stone claiming to be a pacifist when he also "shove[d] a man out doors who came into his office just to tell him that he must stop writing any more lies about him."

Yet Lewis's boldness could only get him so far in the face of hostile public attitudes, as lies about the brothers had a habit of persisting, even multiplying, in the days after the riot. The press once again picked up its drumbeat of animus against them, with *The American* demanding a grand jury "indict Dr. Cox, Mr. Tappan, and their associates as PUBLIC NUISANCES." Other papers rehashed the old stories about their alleged lack of patriotism, seditious intent, and zeal for amalgamation. The more responsible papers played down the rumors, but they still held the Tappans responsible for promoting the dangerous idea that Black and white people might one day coexist without threat to the republic.

So the brothers and their allies felt forced to retreat. Arthur and an associate, John Rankin, put out a handbill titled "DISCLAIMER." In it, they disavowed "any desire to promote or encourage intermarriages" and promised to do nothing to undermine any laws, or to "dissolve the Union, or to violate the constitution and laws of the country, or to ask of Congress any act transcending their constitutional powers." Days later, the executives of the American Anti-Slavery Society, including Lewis and Samuel Cornish, sent a letter to Mayor Lawrence. They built upon Arthur's statement and defended themselves, "as patriots, as Christians, as friends of the Union," against the slurs made against them. While they said they would still fight against slavery, they fiercely resisted the charge of amalgamation and the rumors they supported "individuals adopting colored children, ministers uniting white and colored people in marriage, abolitionists encouraging intermarriages, exciting the colored people to assume airs, &c."

The letter proved that the mob had won the battle. The rioters had set the terms of the debate and forced a disclaimer from the biggest names in New York abolition, making them retreat to protect themselves from any further trouble. But few were happy about it. Foreign critics, especially British abolitionists, called it outrageous that such a statement even had to be made and claimed that such "groveling" did the movement no favors. But the Tappans felt they had no choice: they stood little chance against the masses with their torches and clubs, and no one but the men in power could protect them. All the brothers could do was humbly ask the mayor for relief from their miseries, in hopes that this man—a product of mob violence—would indulge them and grant them protection from their enemies.

They were wrong. Mayor Lawrence forwarded the letter to city aldermen, who forwarded it to their clerk "with instructions to send it right back where it came from, with no reply."

★ FOUR ★

TRIED AS BY FIRE

As the New York riots unfolded, William Lloyd Garrison remained well away from the violence, but he felt as if the mob had attacked him personally. The depravity of the rioters astounded him, and he could not believe that good and decent people protesting slavery "are branded by the daily press as outlaws, and declared to be unworthy of the least protection from the murderous designs of a lawless mob!"

He printed the outrages of the mobsters in *The Liberator*, but the riots were far from the only thing on his mind. He had also been courting George Benson's daughter, Helen, for a number of months and wrote to her regularly with his thoughts on the movement and his growing ardor for her. Even amid the terrible reports coming out of New York, he still had time for romance, and he was giddy about their upcoming marriage: "O, but love is a naughty thing! How it becomes a part of our person, following us like our shadow, wherever we move, over hill and dale, in tumult and in solitude, by day and by night!"

However, his thoughts were also occupied by another woman, someone whom rumors had once said he would marry and to whom he had devoted a great deal of attention in his newspaper: a Quaker schoolteacher named Prudence Crandall. Long before the events in New York, her story had warned abolitionists of the danger of mass violence, and the threat that could imperil anyone with a mind to do something about racial inequality. Garrison fired off letters to associates like Samuel May concerning her upcoming trial, which had "such momentous consequences to a large portion of our countrymen—implicating so deeply the character of this great nation." As any reader of *The Liberator* knew, that trial was both literal and figurative, and many abolitionists had become fixated on it, even obsessed with it.

The controversy began in spring 1833 when Crandall decided to admit a Black girl to her school in Canterbury, Connecticut. Once word got out, the townsfolk became furious at the prospect of race mixing in their hamlet. Garrison heard about her story and wrote to George Benson that "all true friends of the cause—must make this a common concern."

She visited him in Boston to get his advice on the next steps to counter her neighbors in town, and to get his opinion on whether she should go further and establish an entire school for young Black women. Garrison told her to go ahead, even at risk to her safety. She agreed and soon received assistance from Black ministers and others who could help her find a promising group of students. Samuel Cornish became one of her sponsors, and James Forten took an interest in Crandall's project too. He was happy to act as an adviser and to suggest pupils who might benefit from her tutelage.

Soon after, Crandall opened her doors to twenty young women of color. In response, the white folk in town heaped insults upon her and threatened her with violence; they threw manure down her well and spread rumors she wanted to make the region into "the Liberia of America"; they put pressure on the town druggist and doctor to refuse her medical care; they barred her from attending church; they attacked her house and broke its windows; and they slit the throat of a cat and hung it over her schoolhouse door as a warning. Still, despite the persecution, she persisted in her plans.

Local politicians led by Andrew Judson—later a congressman and federal judge—held a public meeting at which Crandall's name and reputation were defiled. Witnesses issued one accusation after another about her, which Samuel May tried to rebut to no avail. Finally, an angry Judson spoke to May and removed any ambiguity about why he opposed Crandall: "The colored people never can rise from their menial condition in our country; they ought not to be permitted to rise here. They are an inferior race of beings, and never can or ought to be recognized as the equals of the whites. Africa is the place for them." Not surprisingly Judson was a stalwart of the Colonization Society who had earlier helped destroy Arthur Tappan's plans for a Black school in New Haven.

Judson did even more against Crandall. He cajoled the Connecticut legislature into passing a "Black Law" against schools for students of color. She defied the law and kept her school open, then faced two trials for breaking the statute; the first ended in a mistrial, the second in her conviction. However, she was freed on appeal and, by this time, Garrison had been trumpeting her cause for more than a year. He made good use of the publicity her case attracted, at one point writing, after she spent an evening in jail, "Savage Barbarity! Miss Crandall Imprisoned!!! The persecutors of Miss Crandall have placed an indelible seal upon infamy! They have cast her into prison! Yes, into the very cell [once] occupied by WATKINS the MURDERER!!"

For Garrison the story was a publicity coup, as he promised his readers Crandall would keep teaching Black students regardless of the danger. She duly continued her work and, in April 1834, visited Boston. Local abolitionists feted her and painted her portrait, stunned to have a chance to see her face, in the manner of a living saint. They showered her with praise, and she received letters of support and gifts from around the world. But her actual Black students were less famous—harassed, insulted, even arrested and threatened with whipping, just for trying to obtain an education.

The episode was all part of Garrison's strategy for spreading the message of abolition. Allowing Crandall to lodge in jail overnight (though her bond could have been paid) and showcasing her persecution, Garrison created a martyr out of the young schoolmarm—just as he meant to sacrifice himself one day for the cause. He expected the persecution of good Christian men and women would enflame the passions of his readers and persuade them to support the cause. This strategy, however, left no room for political action, and it didn't account for another threat that the Tappans had learned in New York: their enemies might eventually grow so strong they would become overwhelming—and exhaust whatever supply of martyrs Garrison had left.

Months after Crandall appealed her conviction, the Court of Errors finally produced a ruling, on July 22, that reversed the judgment and allowed her school to stay open, though on a technicality. The court based its ruling on the legality of her license, not on her abuse by the legal system or the errancy of the Black Law. Indeed, the court said, "It would be a perversion of terms and the well-known rule of construction to say that slaves, free Blacks, or Indians were citizens within the meaning of that term as used in the constitution." It was not quite the result Garrison wanted: Crandall had won her case, but the movement for racial equality had lost.

Nonetheless, Prudence Crandall stood as a worthy symbol of abolition and a testament to the power of antislavery activists—women in particular. Unlike the Tappan brothers and ministers like Cornish and Wright, Garrison had no hesitation about backing women in the struggle against slavery. He supported their role in the public arena and teamed with them to advance even the most controversial ideas. He also promoted the works of the essayist Lydia Maria Child, including *An Appeal in Favor of that Class of Americans Called Africans*, one of the first books by an American woman to argue for immediate abolition.

In *The Liberator* Garrison presented a regular "Ladies' Department" column with updates on women's activities in the movement, as well as their essays, editorials, and poems. He often paired the column with an image of an enslaved woman praying in chains under the heading "Am I not a woman and a sister?" Abolitionists sold commemorative coins, cameos, ceramics, stationery, and even textiles and needlework with the image, which supported both the cause and his struggling newspaper. But Garrison didn't just use African Americans as symbols; he published their work in his newspaper, becoming one of the first white newsmen— perhaps the only one—to present the art and argument of Black women. One who made the most regular appearances called herself Ada.

Her real name was Sarah Forten, the daughter of James, and Garrison had been publishing her verse for three and a half years. He had printed her first poem, "The Grave of the Slave," under her pseudonym, in one of the very first issues of *The Liberator*: "Poor slave! Shall we sorrow that death was thy friend, the last, and the kindest, that heaven could send? The grave to the weary is welcomed and blest; and death, to the captive, is freedom and rest." She was all of sixteen at the time.

At first, James Forten didn't even realize Sarah was Ada, or that he shared space with her in Garrison's paper, since he had written for *The Liberator*, *Freedom's Journal*, and other publications for many years. Sarah kept her submissions from him, perhaps believing her writing would be disallowed at a time when wealthy young ladies of color were expected to be quiet, even decorative, in the home. One book of the era warned Black girls with "purity of mind and strict moral worth" to keep to themselves and avoid social contact with outsiders, under threat of having their reputations ruined. But she needn't have worried that her father would restrict her: Garrison told James the identity of Ada, and he approved of his daughter's work. He could have hardly done otherwise: he and his wife, Charlotte, had raised Sarah and their other children to be themselves, in an atmosphere where they could think and speak their minds freely.

They had sheltered her from the worst and most bestial elements in America. In their home, they enjoyed the comforts of genteel living, employed several servants, and hosted apprentices from the maritime trade. Sarah knew other young Black men and women from moneyed families, along with a smattering of whites, but for the most part lived in a social bubble. She recited her poetry at family gatherings, among literature clubs, at church events, and within sewing circles, always allowing room for discussion and sometimes debate.

It made for a cozy world of gracious parties, creative pursuits, and intellectual gab sessions, all of it far removed from the streets, from the working world most Black Philadelphians knew. Still, she knew she had been privileged by her isolation in the upper class of freemen. As she would later write, "We never travel far from home and seldom go into public places unless quite sure that admission is free to all, therefore we meet with none of those mortifications which might otherwise ensue."

Sarah's ancestry was wide-ranging—African, Dutch, and Native American of the Delaware Valley. Her intellectual interests were just as varied. She'd been involved in literary circles and lyceum lectures for years and had learned music, art, and the French language from tutors hired by her father. Still, with the assortment of visitors in the Forten home, she hardly needed those tutors—an evening's dinner provided an education all its own. Guests appeared like the founder of the African Methodist Episcopal Church, Richard Allen; British activists like Harriet Martineau and George Thompson; and abolitionists like Samuel May and the Tappan brothers. John Greenleaf Whittier honored her and her siblings with a poem titled "To the Daughters of James Forten." She also met artists and musicians, one of whom would later set "The Grave of the Slave" to music, enabling her verses to be played and sung at abolitionist rallies across the region. More than any other guest, though, Garrison left the strongest impression.

The family had known him since the time he copublished *The Genius of Universal Emancipation*, and when Garrison founded *The Liberator*, they spread the word among fellow Philadelphians that the Bostonian's words were worth reading. Few other white abolitionists said things like "I never rise to address a colored audience, without feeling ashamed of my own color; ashamed of being identified with a race of men who have done you so much injustice." More than guilt, though, rage motivated Garrison to fight slavery, and he had expressed his feelings in lectures in major cities like Philadelphia with people like the Fortens either in the audience or on the dais alongside him.

In the third issue of *The Liberator*, James Forten offered his strongest endorsement of Garrison's work: "I am astonished that any man should be so prejudiced against his fellow man; but we pray for the aid of the Almighty to take the scales from their eyes; and that the Liberator may be one of the instruments in commencing the work." The family aided Garrison's newspaper with their donations and encouraged other Black Philadelphians to buy subscriptions.

Sarah admired Garrison just as her father did. Upon his trip to the United Kingdom, Sarah wrote "To the Hibernia," commending him, as he sailed to Britain, as "the Champion of the slave." More importantly, her verses began to echo the fiery style of *The Liberator*. In one poem, "My Country," she asked:

> Can the name of "MY COUNTRY"—the deeds which we
>   sing—
> Be honored—revered—'midst pollution and sin?
> Can the names of our fathers who perished in fight,
> Be hallowed in story, midst slavery's blight?
>
> When America's standard is floating so far,
> I blush that the impress of falsehood is there;
> That oppression and mockery dim the high fame,
> That seeks from all nations a patriot's name.
>
> Speak not of "my country," unless she shall be,
> In truth, the bright home of the "brave and the free!"
> Till the dark stain of slavery is washed from her hand,
> A tribute of homage she cannot command.

This went a step beyond what her father believed. James had always held to the promise of America, to the ideals of the founders, yet Sarah wrote that those ideals had been corrupted from the start. Slavery, colonization, racial injustice, violence, mob rule—it all made for a poisonous brew that, as the years passed, only became more corrosive to the spirit. She confronted it the only way she could, writing under a pen name from behind the walls of her home.

By contrast, James did not have the option of withdrawing from the public arena like his daughter. His business was too important, his profile too prominent, to retreat into anonymity. He wasn't naive, of course: he saw the same daunting landscape Sarah did. He simply trusted in the promise of freedom embodied in the Declaration of Independence—and had been working for decades to make the country's leaders honor it.

—m—

James remembered how, as a child, he had stood near the Pennsylvania state house and heard the Declaration read aloud for the first time. Five years later he fought in the revolution, working on a privateer, and was captured by the British and spent seven months in jail. His captors gave him the opportunity to return with them to Britain, but he turned them down. He had an opportunity to escape, but he let another captive flee instead. At last he was exchanged in a prisoner swap near the end of the war.

He read the words of the nation's founders and took them to heart. "It cannot be that the authors of our Constitution intended to exclude us from its benefits," he wrote. "They acknowledged us as men, and found that many an honest heart beat beneath a dusky bosom." He carried the hope that slavery would soon be abolished. But with every step forward came a step or two back, until not only was human bondage firmly entrenched on American soil, but free Black citizens of America like himself saw their own liberties jeopardized, ever in peril.

James worried over the persistence of racism and what it meant for his family. Northern state governments regularly targeted African Americans through restrictions that hampered their movements, speech, ability to own property, ability to enter into contracts, and common behavior in society. And if they managed not to fall afoul of these rules, vagrancy laws gave officials another excuse to arrest them. Even Pennsylvania, which had begun outlawing slavery in 1780, was no different in the severity of its laws against minorities. James had written *Letters from a Man of Colour*, in 1813, against a bill that would bar Black people from the state. The bill failed, but other proposals against the Black community followed, including one that James had once actually supported, though, in retrospect, he was embarrassed to have ever considered it.

In 1816, his associate in the shipping trade, Paul Cuffe, had tried to convince him white Americans would always be so resolute in their racism that expatriation might be the only solution. James had his doubts, but he was willing to help Cuffe find Black individuals willing to relocate to Africa. Then white politicians formed the Colonization Society and followed a similar plan, and Black Philadelphians held their church meeting in reaction to it.

James led that meeting from the platform, and whatever ambivalence he had about colonization disappeared when three thousand of his friends and neighbors overwhelmingly rejected it. In later months he would emerge as a committed opponent of the scheme, writing, "to separate the blacks from the whites is as impossible, as to bail out the Delaware [River] with a bucket." But still he wondered whether the behavior of the colonizers didn't prove their point about the persistence of bigotry.

Ever since then, he had ripped into the American Colonization Society in print, calling the organization unworthy of trust or support, since its object was to "get rid of the free people of colour." In return the colonizers issued threats against him. Violence was becoming one of their most powerful weapons, and James was exposed in a way few other Philadelphians were—his home, his family, his business, all offering tempting targets for the mob. He hadn't been attacked yet but realized it might have been a matter of luck. Philadelphia had witnessed its most recent race riot in November 1829, with white men attacking Black churches, homes, schools, even an orphanage. The colonizers did nothing to stop this kind of violence and sometimes even encouraged it.

Despite the threat, James couldn't withdraw from his public role. He had made too many public stands and supported too many causes to back down. He had funded and written for abolitionist newspapers, inaugurated conventions for people of color that cultivated Black leadership, steered self-improvement societies, and even allied with white officials and businessmen. Black Philadelphians depended on him, too, as the largest minority community in any Northern city, reaching fifteen thousand in 1830—a jump of nearly a third within a decade. Yet even with their greater numbers, the freemen of Philadelphia were always under siege.

Unlike the Irish immigrants, who immediately became candidates for recruitment into Andrew Jackson's Democratic Party, residents of color mostly could not vote, and state laws treated them as second-class citizens. White legislators had no incentive to seek their favor and used them as straw men to take the blame for everything from crime to immorality to amalgamation to slave insurrections. The latest outrage was House Bill 446, which would create a color bar at the state border, demand Black visitors pay a $500 bond, and force Black residents to carry registration papers on penalty of being arrested as fugitives. James could not believe he had to fight another attempt to quash the civil rights of Black Pennsylvanians—some twenty years after the first one. With his allies William Whipper and Robert Purvis (husband to James's daughter Harriet), he submitted a statement to the state senate denouncing the plan and defending the presence of Black people in the state:

> Why are [the state's] borders to be surrounded by a wall of iron, against freemen, whose complexions fall below the wavering and uncertain shades of white? . . . It is not to be asked, is he brave—is he honest—is he just—is he free from the stain of crime—but is he black—is he brown—is he yellow—is he other than white?

Due in part to his words, the politicians in the House tabled the bill, but they kept it alive for future sessions. The result did not surprise him: when it came to race, there was no such thing as a complete triumph over a terrible idea. He would settle for a half-victory for now and continue to lobby the legislature whenever draconian laws were proposed. It was how he maintained a guarded sense of optimism and kept his faith in the progress of history. "Mankind are becoming more enlightened," he wrote, "and all tyrants, and the tyrants of this country, must tremble."

Sarah may not have shared her father's hopes, but she knew she couldn't afford to be cynical. She had been one of the few Black people in the city to be born into a world of comfort and could never take it for granted. After all, the violence on the streets grew worse every day, and isolation could protect her family from turmoil for only so long. Even the Tappan brothers, with all their wealth and privilege, had been hounded and threatened by mobs, with a price put on their heads. How could the Fortens be any different?

By the end of 1833, Sarah felt she had little choice but to emerge from her well-crafted anonymity, stepping into the public arena to join her father. His cause would be hers, in practice as in poetry. As she later put it, "I am wholly indebted to the Abolition cause for arousing me from apathy and indifference, shedding light into a Mind which has been too long wrapt in selfish darkness."

─᚜᚛─

In early December, James Forten watched as many of his friends and allies founded the American Anti-Slavery Society in his hometown, and the following year he became its vice president. Just three days after that event, in the same city, twenty-one women, including Sarah Forten, assembled in the schoolroom of Catharine McDermott to create the Philadelphia Female Anti-Slavery Society. The setting was much more sedate than the one for the men's group. There was no shouting in the streets as the delegates filed past, no angry harangues by colonizers, and only a fraction of the people present, but this society would prove to be just as historic.

One-third of the members were Black—a step forward since almost every other women's group was segregated, with African Americans forced to take a lesser role or no role at all. Here, though, women of both races ran the organization. Along with Sarah, her mother Charlotte and her sisters Harriet and Margaretta were among the founders, with Margaretta one of the leaders and drafters of the charter. They were joined by their friends Grace Douglass and her daughter Sarah (no relation to Frederick), who had emerged as one of the most compelling spokeswomen for racial equality, operating a well-regarded liberal arts academy for Black students. Most of the rest of the delegates were white Quaker women.

The leader among the Quakers was Lucretia Mott, a "Hicksite" reformer and minister who questioned the elders in her church, as well as their indifference to abolition, and pushed for social change, even at the risk of being shunned. The city was still abuzz with stories of how, three days before, Mott and three of her allies had to sit in the balcony of Adelphi Hall watching the American Anti-Slavery Society take shape. Mott, despite being barely five feet tall and a hundred pounds, had a commanding presence, rising up repeatedly to offer changes to the founding documents and make suggestions. This was unheard of at the time. Men dominated the proceedings, no woman was allowed to sign the society's constitution, and the weight of tradition pressured Mott and her allies to keep silent. But she did not. At one point, after the men worried over the absence of some delegates with sizable reputations, she reminded them "right principles are stronger than great names. If our principles are right, why should we be cowards?"

Sarah Forten knew Lucretia and her husband, James, from their appearances in the family home. Mott, in turn, opened her home to Black women like the Fortens to develop plans for the society, and attended Black churches to get the perspective of women of color on how to run the group. It soon became clear that the society would not be an organization where the African American presence would be symbolic or ornamental. Instead, it would be fundamental.

With Mott and her associate Esther Moore in charge, along with Margaretta Forten, Sarah felt confident the group would do good work. It officially pledged to battle against slavery, to tackle racial injustice, and to reject slave-grown goods such as sugar and cotton. The constitution of the group spelled it out clearly: "We deem it our duty, as professing Christians, to manifest our abhorrence of the flagrant injustice and deep sin of slavery, by united and vigorous exertions for its speedy removal, and for the restoration of the people of color, to their inalienable rights."

The backlash came quickly. Once word got out about the creation of the Philadelphia Female Anti-Slavery Society, critics in the press lit into them. They called their work frivolous and mocked them as having nothing better to do than advocate for a hopeless cause like slave liberation, instead of properly attending to their domestic duties. Others accused them of undermining society with their race mixing, or acting in ways threatening to men, or using abolition as a springboard for women's equality—a particularly shocking notion at the time.

Such a radical prospect had deterred many abolitionist men from supporting women's role in antislavery, claiming they "should not debase themselves by engaging in public work." But William Lloyd Garrison once again rejected such arguments, seeing women's groups as a potent force in the movement, and women's rights as parallel to the rights of Black Americans. In return for Garrison's support, the Philadelphia society bought subscriptions to both *The Liberator* and *The Emancipator* and purchased a library of abolitionist works, some by Garrison himself. Not only did this help prop up his finances; it made his paper core reading material for activist women, who would come to purchase twice as many subscriptions as men did.

Sarah relied on Garrison to publish her work and to stand against attempts to diminish the group. But she knew white Americans saw her color first, always before her sex. And many of the abolitionist men who derided women's role in the movement also claimed, even in *The Liberator*, that Black people needed to be improved or redeemed from their "degraded" condition—instead of just being treated equally by law and society. Authors who had composed valuable works could lapse into naked racism, too, as when Lydia Child wrote that abolitionists "have not the slightest wish to do violence to the distinctions of society by forcing the rude and illiterate into the presence of the learned and refined," and their aim was to bring Black people up to the status of "the lowest and most ignorant white man."

Sarah had heard language like this more than once, and after a certain point it became exhausting to hear how her race forever needed to be reconstructed, lifted up, transformed, or otherwise tinkered with. As Sarah later wrote to a friend, "No doubt but there has always existed the same amount of prejudice in the minds of Americans toward the descendants of Africa. Even our professed friends have not yet rid themselves of it. To some it clings like a dark mantle obscuring and choking up the avenues of higher and nobler sentiments."

She now understood the pressure her father felt on many levels: to work with allies but rebut their claims of Black inferiority, to take risks but also be a role model, to challenge the foundation of society but avoid being seen as seditious. She had just begun her work in abolition, but already the balance seemed difficult, at times impossible.

She questioned just how much work she could take on. Her father, with all his money and his network of allies, had struggled to counter the tide of anti-Black legislation in the state—how could she do any better? The ideal of womanhood demanded a certain reserve, a domestic withdrawal from public affairs, but this work would require civic action, public activism, everything custom said women should not do. Someone like Lucretia Mott, as a major figure in her church and a galvanizing presence, could dismiss tradition and stand up to pressure, but Sarah was a generation younger, still only nineteen and living at home with her parents. Could she summon the same spirit and, if so, at what cost?

Sarah knew her immediate foes were the same as her father's. The Colonization Society had many women supporters, with no fewer than eighty auxiliaries in Pennsylvania. White women could be just as zealous in trying to send Black people to Africa as their male counterparts, and they greatly outnumbered the female advocates of abolition. Their influence had to be matched and then rebutted to keep the public's mind open to the message of antislavery.

The range of women they had to persuade in the region was kaleidoscopic: from Black seamstresses to white mill workers, from farm wives in remote towns to urban sophisticates, and the full range of working- and middle-class women in between. The message had to reach them, to impress upon them the need for immediate abolition and the rejection of racial injustice. So Sarah did what she had done for years—she wrote a poem about it.

First appearing in the *Lowell Observer*, and later reprinted in *The Liberator*, Sarah Forten's "An Appeal to Woman" addressed the problem of female bigotry and made an attempt to cross the color line with a plea for sisterhood.

> Oh, woman, woman, in thy brightest hour
> Of conscious worth, of pride, of conscious power,
> Oh, nobly dare to act a Christian's part,
> That well befits a lovely woman's heart.
> Dare to be good, as thou canst dare be great
> Despise the taunts of envy, scorn and hate
> Our "skins may differ," but from thee we claim
> A sister's privilege, in a sister's name.

The poem became a great success and would be used as an ode by a number of women's antislavery groups. It was popular enough to inspire other women to write abolitionist poems under the pseudonym "Ada" in her honor and to invite responses, in rhyme, to her work. But some of that verse was critical, coming from men who felt Sarah had been too strident in her tone, too lacking in Christian mercy.

She faced again the impossible balance, between being outspoken enough to make a difference and dealing with the backlash that would surely follow. The trap had ensnared more than a few women writers. Few had forgotten the example of Maria Stewart, who had been driven out of the movement just months before. The widely read Sarah was almost certainly familiar with her writings and speeches. Stewart left an indelible mark, for no American woman of any color had ever done what she had, making her both an inspiration and a warning of the dangers to come.

—⁓—

Stewart was an African American widow who had, in 1831, come to Garrison's Boston office with a manuscript titled "Religion and the Pure Principles of Morality." Garrison was so impressed by it he set it to type before her eyes. It was an Old Testament–style jeremiad, not only decrying slavery as a sin against God, but also calling for women's liberation:

> How long shall the fair daughters of Africa be compelled to bury their minds and talents beneath a load of iron pots and kettles? Until union, knowledge and love begin to flow among us. How long shall a mean set of men flatter us with their smiles, and enrich themselves with our hard earnings, their wives' fingers sparkling with rings, and they themselves laughing at our folly?

Published in *The Liberator*, her words caused a stir, as did her subsequent pamphlets and essays. She soon stepped outside the world of print and became the nation's first woman lecturer—at Franklin Hall in Boston on September 21, 1832. Stewart told her listeners God had great compassion for the suffering of African Americans and encouraged them to defend one another from injustice, using force if needed. She castigated the white men who owned slaves and enforced racial oppression, and also their wives, the "fairer sisters, whose hands are never soiled, whose nerves are never strained." She commanded them to "go learn by experience!" to find out the miseries Black women went through in their daily lives. More surprisingly, she also criticized the behavior of Black men for their supposed timidity, asking, "Have the sons of Africa no soul? Have they no ambitious desires? . . . Where is the man that has distinguished himself in these modern days by acting wholly in the defense of African rights and liberty?"

Stewart called back to the Book of Revelation to offer an apocalyptic vision of divine punishment against America. She borrowed from the style of David Walker, whom she had known in Boston before his death, and imagined violent revolution as a prospect. She even made Walker's threat of violence more explicit, claiming that if Black citizens were denied their rights, "they will spread horror and devastation around."

Stewart received a reaction as great as could be expected for the early 1830s, but great was not to say good. White critics and Black ministers condemned Stewart over the course of her one-year speaking tour, and she even received opposition from abolitionists, especially for chastising Black men for drinking, gambling, and other vices, even though Samuel Cornish had said the same things in his writing. In the end, the wave of opposition drove her to leave Boston: "I find it is no use for me, as an individual, to try to make myself useful among my color in this city . . . Thus far my life has been almost a life of complete disappointment. God has tried me as by fire." She retired from the lecture circuit and never again spoke in a public forum.

Maria Stewart had been brave beyond measure, but she had crossed that elusive boundary that separated women's "sphere of influence" from forbidden behavior that led to banishment. Prudence Crandall had crossed it, too, and had faced insult and injury in Canterbury, her neighbors threatening her life and livelihood. And now Sarah Forten would face the same dilemma, for having the nerve to try to make change in a world hostile to it.

The danger first emerged in the press. With subtle reference to the Fortens, the *Pennsylvania Inquirer*, in July 1834, warned abolitionists not to call a meeting—the weather was too hot, the social climate too explosive—and if such an event was planned, the authorities should use force to prevent it. Benjamin Lundy, Garrison's old associate, wrote about how men in power had made "certain arrangements . . . to get up a MOB in this city," just as they had in New York earlier that summer. At the same time, hundreds of petitions circulated to the legislature demanding an end to the migration of Black people into Pennsylvania, and for them to be driven out of the state. And if the legislature wouldn't do it, gang members and criminals in Philadelphia might just try.

They carried names like the Rats, the Bouncers, and the Blood Tubs and regularly marched through the city yelling, swearing, and hunting for Black people to attack in neighborhoods like Moyamensing and Southwark. The gangs recruited from the ranks of young white working men who shacked up in boardinghouses, spent their pay in gambling halls and brothels, and, after a day's work, "were turned loose upon the street at night." Many sported bowie knives or pistols or dirks to make short work of their enemies, and they had no use or respect for the law.

The gangsters weren't alone. They forged alliances with the city's volunteer fire companies, who not only fought fires but battled each other over neighborhood turf. The firemen put up obstacles to Black men integrating with them or forming their own engine companies. Together the gangs and the fire companies made discreet pacts with city officials, who corralled their violence for political purposes and to influence voting. This made their lawlessness a menace to civic order, and increasingly difficult to curtail when social conflict rose to a boil.

Adding to the trouble, resentment of the Fortens had been building for years among working-class whites, not only for James's prominent role in abolition, but also for his money. Chronic unemployment and a lingering recession had made them restless, eager to cast blame for their miseries on minorities. Cartoons circulating in print viciously parodied the small number of wealthy Black Philadelphians, deriding their taste in fashion, music, art, and learning languages. One historian of the time mocked "dressy blacks and dandy coloured beaux and belles," whose "aspirings and little vanities have been growing since they got those separate churches"—meaning the Black churches that attracted them because they lacked Negro pews and other signs of segregation.

The Fortens also received scorn for their material possessions. Along with a townhouse, they owned a country estate and a carriage and rental property occupied by whites. The Colonization Society made sure to circulate rumors as well that James had accumulated undeserved wealth and was so ambitious, "he coveted to wed his daughter to a whiter species at some sacrifice of his fortune." In other words, he aspired to amalgamate. With such rumors swirling, the family tried to keep a low profile over the summer and not to venture into uncertain territory—places like the carousel of the Flying Horses.

It was well outside the social world of the Fortens, a brash and noisy carnival near the diverse neighborhood of Moyamensing, attracting men and women of different races to commingle for pleasure and entertainment. It also attracted criticism as a vulgar amusement, where brutal conflicts broke out between white gangsters on the hunt and Black men trying to defend themselves.

On August 8, at the Flying Horses, a group of Black youth made off with the hose of the Fairmount Engine Company. This was no mere tool for fighting fires, but an emblem of their strength and virility, so the theft of their equipment enraged them and sent them into the streets looking for the culprit. They formed a group of up to sixty men wearing similar outfits—blue jackets and trousers, with low-crowned straw hats—so people could see them coming.

The next day they surged into neighborhoods where middle-class and a few upper-class Black people lived, looking for any excuse to use their cudgels—short, thick clubs that had wrecked churches and entire neighborhoods in the Five Points just weeks before. It wasn't a random hunt. They had the names of "Yorkers" they were after: abolitionists like the Tappans in New York, but who were Black activists in Philadelphia. Two nights before, they had come to the south part of the city looking for their targets, and on the afternoon of August 9, they struck.

They spotted a fifteen-year-old Black boy out on an errand and went after him. They cornered him quickly. One gangster beat him with his club, nearly knocking him out. Once the boy was down, the other gangsters set upon him. They were so eager to pummel him, to dash his brains out, they crossed their sticks in the melee. In the confusion, the boy stumbled up and ran off. They chased after him but couldn't catch him.

The boy ran home to his parents. They opened the door to see Thomas, bruised and terrified. Sarah's brother.

James Forten was stunned but moved fast. He sent out word to the mayor, Jonathan Swift, and the mayor responded, sending a force of constables to the place where the gangsters had beaten Thomas. They took seven of the men into custody, including one with a bludgeon. The gang put out word this was only the beginning. An eyewitness heard them talking, saying they would scatter for now but would reassemble soon: "We will then attack the niggers."

The Fortens' lives were in danger. The city sent out armed men, including a horse patrol, to guard their house from the mob still on the prowl—the mob that had attacked Thomas and would soon attack all of Black Philadelphia. Sarah, her siblings, and her mother and father prayed for God to protect them and save the lives of their friends and neighbors.

God answered sooner than expected. The constables arrested some men lurking right outside their home—catching them just before they ambushed the family. It was a narrow escape for the Fortens. But Sarah knew they were no longer safe from harm, no longer isolated by their wealth. The violence had reached their door.

★ FIVE ★

THE INCUBUS

The mob had been held at bay, for the moment. They had attacked the Black teen Thomas Forten but had been kept from murder by their own zeal for it. The police had checked their violent ambitions further by protecting the rest of the Fortens. And now some of them found themselves in jail, held on a bond of $300 each, with their confederates on the street monitored closely by a complement of constables and watchmen. With the city now fortified over the weekend, they would have to find something else to do than burn, loot, and maim.

The gangs despised the mayor for his clampdown, but they could afford to wait. They spent their time trading lurid stories about the neighborhood around the Flying Horses, at Seventh and South streets. They repeated tales of white women seen in the company of Black men, ginned up each other's fury over race mixing, and cursed the city's Black residents and the authorities who, at least for the moment, guarded them. They stewed over Saturday, fumed on Sunday, and waited until Monday, August 12, to strike.

Five hundred of them descended on the Flying Horses with clubs, bricks, and paving stones to smash the building and tear apart the carousel. The Black people riding the horses were shocked at the mob's appearance and tried to fight back, but the invaders overwhelmed them. They ripped apart the wooden planks and beams of the building—turning them into sticks and bludgeons, weapons for their march into Moyamensing.

Moyamensing didn't need the trouble. South of the Flying Horses, it was Philadelphia's version of the Five Points: a small district just outside the city limits, packed with around ten thousand people, with a core group of Black residents. The authorities usually ignored the area and did little to help its residents, who faced high levels of illness and poverty, but on this night, they had to pay attention to it. The mob was on its way, bearing fresh weapons and a desire to use them. The only thing in their way was a group of constables, night watchmen, and sheriff's deputies who saw them coming.

The gangsters charged, pounding against police lines with their posts and beams, but the authorities held their ground, pushed them back, and arrested dozens. A city alderman battled hooligans with a pistol in each hand. Men waged war over control of a brothel. Chaos unfolded for hours. Finally, enough of the mob was under arrest that the rest scurried back into the shadows, the night's combat ended.

The next day the rioters were back, assembling quietly this time. The lawmen guarded the streets near the southern border of Philadelphia with increased numbers, a show of force to ward off the miscreants. But those miscreants knew the schedule of the police and waited until many of them had ended their shifts, at eleven o' clock. Then, the number of lawmen on patrol diminished as the number of rioters expanded: perhaps two hundred, or five hundred, different reports said. Once they had the numbers they needed, the mob shoved past the skeleton crew of police and started their march down Seventh Street—into the heart of Black Philadelphia.

The mobsters flooded into Moyamensing and found house after house occupied by working- and middle-class Black people—brick apartments, townhouses, little wooden frame homes. Fired up by a weekend's worth of rage, the rioters wasted no time in destroying them. They pummeled the walls with their clubs and shattered the windows with their bricks. They dragged out their inhabitants, screaming at them, savaging them, beating them with abandon. They stole silverware, watches, and pocketbooks; trashed family heirlooms; and ruined antiques. Less valuable things they pulled out into the street, the bedding and furniture, the chairs and lamps and rugs—and made a great pile in front of each home and set it burning. Soon the entire area around Seventh Street was illuminated with the wreckage of Black families' possessions and treasures.

The rioters had told white people to leave candles burning in their windows—just as in the New York riot—to protect them from arson, so they could focus on burning out the Black residents. Many of those residents had fled the city before the mob could reach them. Some ended up in the woods and clearings outside town, choosing to be homeless rather than see their houses destroyed while they were beaten in the street. Stories later described the people left behind: a dead child left beside its bed, a person hurled from a window, a corpse thrown out of its coffin.

The mob held sway over South Philadelphia for at least one hour, possibly two, until the city and county gathered their forces once more and the watchmen and constables gave chase. The authorities arrested only twenty or so hoodlums, with the rest disappearing into the darkness, waiting for their next chance to unleash terror on the city.

When the next day dawned, the streets were "covered with feathers torn from beds, mahogany sideboards, tables, looking glasses, China ware, chairs, and other household furniture shattered to pieces and lying about in heaps," marking the mob's footprints over Black Philadelphia. Several churches and three dozen homes had been obliterated, while others were unfit for habitation. In his own house, Mayor Swift sheltered a dozen Black people fleeing the mob, but many others had fled the city, crossing the Delaware River to camp in the fields near Camden, New Jersey. Of those who remained, the picture was of shock and desolation: "Their little property is totally lost, and many were driven from their dwellings, with their children, almost without a rag of clothing; their persons lacerated by the violence of the bloodhounds."

The landscape recalled war, insurrection. The sheriff surveyed the wreckage and knew he needed greater numbers to stop the army of criminals who had laid waste to the neighborhood and would strike again that night. So he assembled a posse comitatus and swore them into service: three hundred constables, a mounted militia armed with muskets, and a military force called the Washington Greys, held in reserve in case the mob became overwhelming.

Night fell. The mob gathered once more, and the sheriff deployed his posse. The mobsters hissed and cursed the authorities, refusing to disperse and looking ready to fight. But the rioters were outnumbered this time, and they withdrew. They drifted into other parts of the city and found new targets, tearing down a church near Wharton Market, tenements on Vernon Street, and a Masonic Hall built by and for African Americans. They also damaged the First African Presbyterian Church, founded by John Gloucester, the onetime spiritual mentor to Samuel Cornish. This followed the pattern of the mob violence in New York: destroying the homes of Black people first, followed by their churches.

The violence simmered and occasionally boiled over the next few days, the rioters attacking several buildings here and there, even returning to the wreckage of the carousel to stir up more trouble. But the residents now took the opportunity to arm themselves to fight back. A group of sixty Black men, part of the Benezet Society brotherhood, used swords and clubs for defense against the mob gathered outside their meeting place, Benezet Hall. The mobsters began hurling rocks and bricks, but the Black brotherhood charged at them and drove them off with their sabers. The mob later returned, but the authorities negotiated a cease-fire, and the battle ended. The charge of the swordsmen had saved the Hall and the people inside it. Black Philadelphians would not forget the lesson.

In the end the race riot in Philadelphia exacted a shocking toll, with a steep but unknown number of injuries, a few deaths, dozens of buildings damaged or destroyed, and a carousel pulverized. Only ten men ever appeared in court, but none was punished for his role in the riot. This judicial injustice, along with the devastation on the streets, made for an atrocity in America's third-largest city, coming only a month after the other atrocity in America's largest one.

The mob made sure to target the small but significant number of upper-class Black people. The community had been one of the most established in the Northeast, one of the fastest growing, the strongest and most stable—and for that the rioters savaged them with a special ferocity. James Forten received death threats, and the armed guard around his home held criminals at bay to keep them from invading it. It wasn't hard to see why the mob had singled him out. An observer explained that "a man of wealth and great respectability," likely referring to him, "was told afterwards by a white, that he would not have been molested, if he had not, by refusing to go to Liberia, prevented others from leaving the country."

Such threats had the fingerprints of the Colonization Society all over them. And their involvement in the violence may not have stopped there. Reports came out of men of "high and honorable office" threatening police officers with revenge for enforcing the law too vigorously, and hampering investigating committees from discovering the names of those who had plotted the riot. The evidence was clear: this was no spontaneous burst of mass anger. The rioters were well organized, used key words and whistles to communicate, assigned guards to watch for police, and carefully planned what would be destroyed and where.

While the most brutal men with clubs and bricks found themselves in handcuffs, the men of means who had sparked the mayhem stood in the shadows, their names never divulged, their identities well concealed. The investigators may not have determined the key culprits behind the riot, but local abolitionists did. The Pennsylvania Abolition Society created its own report that said what opponents of slavery had long known: the colonizers had driven the violence with their rhetoric and their public actions, and their plotting and coordination behind the scenes. They hadn't found a way to intimidate Black people into leaving the city, so they burned them out of their homes and neighborhoods instead.

James Forten's hopes for the enlightenment of white Americans had been fully immolated, as the mid-1830s became one of the worst times in US history for free Black citizens of the North. Whatever hope he had held for the promise of the Revolution now dissolved into the reality that achieving racial equality would be a monumental task and would outlast him and members of his family. His daughter Sarah had suspected as much, expressed in her poem "My Country," and now this bleak vision of America seemed ever more accurate with each burned-out house and bonfire of furniture, in Philadelphia and beyond.

—⁂—

An epidemic of violence was consuming America, and it started at the top. Andrew Jackson's empowerment of white working men had uplifted them in voting rights and economic mobility, but it also tacitly gave them the license to attack any minorities they despised. Jackson himself worried that the "spirit of mob-law is becoming too common and must be checked . . . or we will soon have no safety under our happy Government of laws." He suspected a secret plan by the aristocratic class to thwart his populist designs and blame his party for the mass rioting, to prove Americans were not capable of self-government. But Jackson's Democratic Party had profited, not suffered, from the chaos. Its men had organized at Tammany Hall to try to crush the New York Anti-Slavery Society in the streets; its partisans had rioted against Whigs over ballot boxes and secured the election of a mayor; and its allies had demonized abolitionists in the press, posted inflammatory handbills on public streets, and allowed them to do their bloody business with little fear of punishment. Jackson might wag his finger against mob violence, but when it came to results in the real world, his party had gained greatly from it.

Yet the turmoil would not be so easily contained. As each frenetic month passed, the list of the mob's targets grew longer—including members of Jackson's own party. Black people and abolitionists were still the main focus of their attacks, but beyond them were Democratic and Whig poll workers, urban bankers, landlords, Mormons, Irish laborers, Catholic nuns, industrial workers, riverboat gamblers, brothel owners, even hot-air balloonists. In the face of such pandemonium, publisher Hezekiah Niles would write, "The state of society is awful. Brute force has superseded the law, at many places, and violence has become the 'order of the day.' The time predicted seems rapidly approaching when the mob shall rule."

William Lloyd Garrison had no doubt about who was to blame for most of the violence in society, especially against his colleagues. He saw the press and the Colonization Society as the most culpable, but he also indicted public officials for being complicit. However, he had developed a strategy for dealing with this violence, as part of his commitment to moral suasion. He wrote, "If we are to be hunted as wild beasts, by a ferocious mob—let it be plainly declared by those who are in authority, and we will prepare ourselves for the consequences." By which he meant, prepare for martyrdom.

Not all abolitionists were with him on the theme of self-sacrifice. David Ruggles, for one, had no interest in laying down his life to people he hated. He had fought off his persecutors more than once—wrestling with a coachman to remain in his seat on a coach, keeping his grocery in business in the face of threats, confronting people in small towns over their racial attitudes. A mob of street criminals hadn't deterred him from going about his business in July, and he kept up his work no matter what barbarity he encountered.

Selling books on abolition at his store on Lispenard Street had given Ruggles fresh energy and purpose. Even after the New York and Philadelphia riots, he advertised his wares in *The Liberator* under "ANTI-SLAVERY BOOK STORE," offering abolitionist "publications of every description, wholesale and retail," along with school texts, stationery, print jobs, and picture framing. He sold "likenesses of Wilberforce and Garrison" and hosted a circulating library of works on slavery and colonization, which readers could check out for the cost of $2 per year. The store became a gathering spot for a new wave of activists, where they could not just read books, but meet and plan new strategies for advancing the movement and protecting it from violence.

Among the books he had on offer were several by Maria Stewart, who, even after she had been forced to end her public speaking career, still appealed to radical abolitionists. Ruggles was especially taken with Stewart's attempt to change the minds of white Northern women, and to keep them from identifying with proslavery Southern women. He wrote a pamphlet, called *The Abrogation of the Seventh Commandment*, that encouraged these women to reject fellowship with those who benefited from slavery, in hopes that eventually "not an evangelical church north of the Ohio and the Pennsylvania line would own as a disciple of Jesus any Slave Driver." Ruggles also saw how Black women's activism could be a powerful weapon to fight human bondage. He spoke before groups like the African Dorcas Society and Colored Ladies Literary Society, raised funds for them, and encouraged them to raise their voices in abolition campaigns.

For his various activities, the press labeled him an insurrectionist. In response he called James Watson Webb and William Stone "the editors of the most filthy prints in the country" and schemers who tried to silence abolitionists with violence—because men used force when they couldn't appeal to reason. He singled out the enemies of the movement whose arguments were gaining traction. One of them, David Reese, had gained acclaim from the anti-abolition press for denouncing the work of the American Anti-Slavery Society and its members. Reese called Garrison's Declaration of Sentiments "sophistical, dangerous, and Anti-American," and he revised the history of the July riots to make it appear abolitionists had instigated them with their rhetoric. If history could be so easily rewritten, that would enable every riot to be blamed on its victims. Ruggles knew Reese had to be challenged.

In response Ruggles published *The "Extinguisher" Extinguished! Or David M. Reese, M.D. "Used Up"*—one of the first works written and published by a Black American (after Walker's *Appeal*). He claimed the doctor was "choking the truth" and castigated Reese for claiming that whites were superior to Blacks and using the Bible to justify white supremacy. Ruggles's salvo against a powerful white man did not go unnoticed and brought further attention to himself and his writings. He would go on to satirize Reese in another pamphlet, under a pseudonym, and dissect his racism in articles in *The Emancipator*. But as the months passed, a menace much worse than a hypocritical doctor attracted his attention. It was the kind of menace that didn't just argue that Black people should be forced to leave their homes but actually did it, using stealth and brutality. These were the kidnappers, the slave catchers, the man-stealers.

Empowered by a 1793 federal law, the agents of slaveholders operated freely in the North and routinely abducted Black men, women, and children they claimed had escaped from bondage. They had nearly free rein to haul in actual fugitives, but they had also been known to kidnap people who had purchased their freedom, and people who had always been free. The burden of proof lay with those who had been seized to prove they were freemen, which was often difficult. Courts of law were unsympathetic to Black plaintiffs, since the majority of judges were pro-Southern and skittish about doing anything to interfere with the traffic in human property. Other times, captives might be spirited away to the South without recourse to the legal system at all. It made for a terrifying situation, with Black Americans fearful of coming into contact with strange white people, who might take them away from their homes and families, possibly forever.

Ruggles knew there were many man-stealers active in New York, and how they cooperated with businessmen with a stake in the slave trade to track down fugitives and sweep up other Black people as well. The kidnappers known as "black-birders" were especially ruthless in the Five Points, near where he lived, and he didn't have to go far to hear stories of the latest man seized on the street, or woman dragged from her home. As he learned more about these episodes, he discovered new outrages perpetrated by "kidnapping clubs" to seize African Americans, sometimes with the aid of Black accomplices, and to imprison them on Southern plantations.

While groups like the Manumission Society and Pennsylvania Abolition Society waged court battles to prevent people from being abducted, those organizations didn't challenge the premise that slaveholders had a legal right to their human property—they could only raise questions of legal procedure. And in any case, Black citizens weren't invited to join these groups. They were almost all run by whites.

Ruggles aimed to change this. He knew abolitionists needed to be stronger and more active to take on the slaveholders. Speaking out against them wasn't enough; writing pamphlets wasn't enough; selling *The Emancipator* wasn't enough. He had to break the system at its foundation and help make New York a free state in practice and not just in theory. On March 25, 1834, in *The Emancipator*, he published a notice of his intent to help Black people kidnapped into slavery, and to break the power of the man-stealers and the black-birders. In future years, it would be this struggle that would most define David Ruggles—severing the bonds of slavery in the North, by making sure that if a man came to him as a slave, he would leave as a free man.

—ɯ—

The long reach of the South into the Northeast wasn't confined to human abductions or wanton destruction of Black homes and possessions. It even extended to freedom of expression, and the desire by Southern politicians to make speech just as fraught with danger as it was in their home region. There, publishing tracts against slavery was usually illegal, and the weight of white public opinion was so severe that anyone, of any color, questioning human bondage was marked for punishment. Vigilance committees drew up mobs to attack people who spoke out about slavery, state law suppressed the mails, and slaveholders made threats against anyone suspected of sympathy to emancipation. The authorities felt their system worked well enough that they insisted Northern politicians suppress the same speech they found seditious. Some even demanded that abolitionists be extradited to their states and punished as they saw fit. South Carolina representative, and later governor, James Hammond proposed that Northern governors hand over such activists for retribution, writing, "These men can be silenced in but one way—*Terror*—*death* . . . This is the only remedy."

For the most famous abolitionists, there were bounties. In New Orleans, $20,000 was on offer "as a reward to be paid for the delivery of Arthur Tappan, the celebrated agitator, upon the levee of that city. Tappan will soon find that even his extreme wealth will not enable him to repose in quiet." Lewis Tappan, too, with his heightened profile after the July mob attacks, became a target for kidnapping, and ministers accused of amalgamation received similar threats. Black abolitionists, if caught, could expect treatment much worse than that of whites— not held for trial, not given a lawyer, but whipped and tortured and, if not killed outright, then sold into slavery. David Walker, many suspected, had been executed just for writing his *Appeal*, and countless other less famous figures had been jailed for questioning slavery or saying it was not divinely sanctioned. In some Southern cities, those suspected of trafficking in abolitionist literature could be marked for extermination. In Clinton, Mississippi, a civic resolution stated that anyone who circulated such material "is justly worthy, in the sight of God and man, of immediate death." Similarly, the *Augusta Chronicle* said, "The cry of the whole South should be death—instant death—wherever he is caught." The *Richmond Enquirer* summed it up: "We again warn the Fanatics of the north, the Tappans, the Garrisons, the Coxes, to beware . . . for, if they once undertake to interfere with these delicate relations [i.e., slavery], the consequences must be fatal beyond calculation."

Garrison continued to worry about being kidnapped and sent to Georgia, in a box or otherwise. The bounty that hung over his head was worth $5,000, and he had little doubt that any number of ruffians along the Eastern Seaboard would be happy to receive such a sum if they could capture him. Even his followers in the South, what few there were, had been marked for death. One man found with copies of *The Liberator* faced a mob surrounding his house, which then "dragged him out, tarred and feathered him. After that they poured oil on his head and set him afire. Still recalcitrant, he was tied to a rail and ducked in the river. What had survived of him was then returned to a post and whipped." Garrison could expect worse if he were ever caught.

Yet thoughts of kidnapping and torture were not the only things on his mind. He also found time for a measure of happiness, delighting in his new life as a married man and writing jubilant letters to his wife, the former Helen Benson. She was his friend and love partner, the daughter of his great ally George Benson, and someone to whom he could expose his private hopes and longings. He effused so strongly in his letters that he seemed not to have any other cares, as he wrote elaborate odes to marital bliss and the union of their souls under God.

But then reality crept in, and he remembered: a mob had terrorized his allies in New York, rioters had destroyed Black houses and lives in Philadelphia, and a sizable bounty still hung over his head. The dangers swirled in his mind, tormenting him once again and interfering with his odes to love. In one letter to Helen, he wrote, "Our joy will spring from fountains of affection" and then just a few paragraphs later: "It is somewhat difficult to decide who are most hated, or who are most in jeopardy, abolitionists or Black people. Neither of them can claim popularity or safety; and there is a spirit abroad that would sacrifice them all in one great bloody hecatomb."

Garrison had little doubt mass murder was a possibility if things worsened, but he knew he couldn't relent. Too many people had been inspired by his words, and he could no sooner abandon his strategy of moral suasion than he could turn away from abolition itself. Yet the casualties of the fight continued to mount, and not just in the major cities. Even in the smallest towns there were sacrifices—places like Canterbury, Connecticut, and people like Prudence Crandall.

Garrison had thought that, with Crandall's triumphant visit to Boston and her successful court case, she might set a precedent for Black education in the rural North, having survived her trials and persisting in her mission. But he was wrong: the mob had beaten her spirit too. On September 9, a team of men with weighted clubs and iron bars smashed panes of glass in her house; then her school fell under assault—the windows smashed, several of the rooms battered and wrecked, and the site left "hardly tenantable." The Black girls who attended and lodged at the school were accosted by the townsfolk and coerced into leaving with not-so-veiled threats. As Samuel May described the scene, "I have never before felt so sensible of the uncalled for, cruel persecution which has been carried on in this New England village against a family of defenceless females . . . I felt ashamed of Canterbury, ashamed of Connecticut, ashamed of my Country."

Costs related to Prudence Crandall weighed upon Garrison. While her school no longer existed, five different libel suits against him did. One of them had been entered by Andrew Judson, one of Crandall's prosecutors, who had been offended by what Garrison had to say about him and his associates in a March 1833 issue of *The Liberator*. Garrison had printed "Shame, shame, shame to those men who had no more honor" and said that their names were as "black as the infamy which will attach to them as long as there exists any recollection of the wrongs of the colored race." The suits had dragged on for two years, with Garrison burdened by ever greater attorneys' fees as the months passed, until the charges were finally dropped by mutual agreement in early 1835. What had begun as a fight for moral victory ended with a stack of legal bills.

In the years hence, *The Liberator* carried no more news of Crandall, except to occasionally recount her trials. She married, sold her house, and left Canterbury, and the young Black women returned to their families. Garrison had spent considerable energy, and many issues of *The Liberator*, building her up as a secular saint. But, in the end, even she had to retreat from the violence. This presented a problem for his strategy: it didn't seem to matter whether the town was small, like Canterbury, or huge, like New York. Violence could be employed on any scale, and every time its perpetrators had waged a campaign of terror, they had won. Crandall had shut down her school, the Tappans and Cornish had written their humble disclaimer, and Black people in Philadelphia had to flee the city.

Martyrdom obviously had its limits. Aside from pity, it gained the opponents of slavery nothing in the press and did little for the movement politically. After a full year of being the victims of riots, antislavery activists were no further along in their mission than they had been before the turmoil. If anything, the only lessons they could draw were that Black men at Benezet Hall could drive off their attackers with swords, and three dozen men armed with muskets could protect Arthur Tappan and Company. Despite this, Garrison refused to bend to David Walker's ideas of self-defense, or meet violence with violence. He redoubled his commitment to pacifism and moral suasion, with the addition of a more hectoring tone and a louder voice. A voice with an English accent.

On September 27, Garrison informed his readers that the "distinguished philanthropist and most eloquent orator arrived in the ship Champlain, in New-York, on Saturday last." The man in question was George Thompson, who had become one of Garrison's bosom friends on his trek through the United Kingdom the year before. On that fabled journey, Thompson had shared a dais with him to preach against injustice, traveled with him as he met Wilberforce, and helped him taunt colonizers and expose them to ridicule. Garrison could only imagine what a treat it would be for this fiery British freedom fighter to come to America to challenge the Yanks to do their part to end the scourge of slavery.

Garrison wrote columns of hype in advance of Thompson's travels. He said no greater British abolitionist existed and claimed his work in America would be as substantial as Marquis de Lafayette's in the Revolutionary War. He said later that, in all the important ways, Thompson had "the identical mission of the Son of God." With his booming voice and dramatic gestures, the English orator certainly played the part of a preacher of God, if not quite the Messiah. Garrison felt sure that after hearing this majestic figure from overseas, audiences would have little choice but to submit to his arguments and his charisma.

Thompson had just returned from Scotland, where he had lectured against the Colonization Society and received gifts for Prudence Crandall's school: silver plate and a collection of books. He arrived after the school had shut down, but he remained committed to the cause. America seemed like fertile ground for the blossoming of immediate abolition, and if it could succeed in the United Kingdom, it could surely take root in the former colonies. Feeling confident in his mission, the Glasgow Ladies' Emancipation Society sponsored his trip and billed him as the "Philanthropist of the World." He received the title because he had rejected nationalism and spoke to his listeners as a fellow brother in the fight for human freedom—the gospel of universal emancipation.

Yet when he arrived in New York, he learned his gospel had preceded him. Even before he got to his hotel, he was told that "numerous lodgers held a meeting and notified the landlord that Mr. Thompson must quit the premises, or that they would . . . The people do not like foreign interferences in their domestic affairs." In fact, the guests had passed resolutions against him and any other "foreign incendiaries" who tried to visit the United States and lecture people on their morals. Chucked out of his hotel, Thompson had to find new lodging. He wrote to Garrison in confusion, saying he had been "somewhat curiously received by the other dwellers." This was putting it mildly. They knew exactly who he was, and they didn't want him anywhere near them. The reason: the press had been drumming up hatred against him for weeks.

The chief culprits were, as usual, James Watson Webb's *Courier and Enquirer* and William Stone's *Commercial Advertiser*. They claimed the British abolitionist had come to undermine American society, to rip it apart at the behest of Garrison and other fanatics, and it was essential this strange man not be given an audience, to prevent his anti-American message from insulting patriots everywhere. In the South, Thompson was already a pariah. The *Richmond Enquirer* reported on his arrival and "welcomed" him in a certain fashion: "We of the south are prepared to give him a *warm reception*. If he crosses the Potomac, he may rue it the longest day he lives."

The hostile reaction created a problem for Garrison. Thompson was one of his major projects for this year and the next, and his tour needed to be a success so abolition could gain momentum after all the recent setbacks. The movement could ill afford another abolitionist of renown to be attacked and abused, and the nation humiliated by its bigotry. Garrison addressed the threat with a flash of defiance in *The Liberator*, writing, "Well may the enemies of liberty tremble in view of his contemplated labors in this country!" But he also worried in private, knowing foreign visitors could spark the most intense hatreds.

Lecturers from abroad found traveling in America difficult, especially if they came to critique the country or offer their helpful hints on how such a backwoods nation could grow more civilized. Many English critics printed caustic reviews of the violent and primitive character of life in the United States, the unruly culture and lack of order, the scant regard for high art and literature, the ongoing abuse of Native Americans, and the corruption that permeated its politics. Some writers, like Frances Trollope, had a field day mocking the crudities of life here, notably in her ironically titled book *Domestic Manners of the Americans*, and more sympathetic writers also criticized some of what they saw. The early feminist and antislavery advocate Harriett Martineau ventured to the South to tell residents their support for slavery was "inconsistent with the law of God." They gave her a prompt response: "They would hang me. They would cut my tongue out, and cast it on a dunghill."

From the beginning, Garrison had known Thompson would inspire some rancor, and he had told his British hosts as much during his tour of the United Kingdom in 1833. He said Thompson "would undoubtedly stir up the bile of all those who were opposed to the abolition of slavery; that he might expect to encounter severe ridicule and bitter denunciation" among other unpleasantries. But despite the challenges, Garrison still banked on his success. He needed Thompson to excite a frenzy for emancipation, and also to help bail out his struggling business.

The financial health of *The Liberator* had once again declined precipitously, and its expenses threatened to overwhelm him. Beyond paid subscribers, of which there were never enough, Garrison needed to find new sources of revenue. James Forten had already loaned a significant amount of money to him, and he certainly couldn't ask him for more. So he pleaded with the American Anti-Slavery Society to buy more of his books, signed on to a plan for the New England Anti-Slavery Society to make *The Liberator* its official news source, and contemplated touring the countryside to raise funds. But his best source of hope was George Thompson.

Garrison told Thompson his tales of financial woe before the Englishman began his lecture tour, and Thompson was sufficiently taken with Garrison's problems that he agreed to help. On his tour, he solicited donations to keep *The Liberator* in business and pitched the sales of more than 1,500 unsold copies of the newspaper. He implored activists like Robert Purvis to help, writing that the paper must not succumb to its debts: "There are few things which would pain me more than the downfall of The Liberator . . . No. It must not—it shall not sink." And he worried over the health of Garrison and his increasing miseries: "Let us determine to relieve him from a weight of care and apprehension which like an incubus oppresses and paralyzes him."

As the tour began, Thompson was slated to deliver hundreds of antislavery stem-winders, mainly in the Northeast, in towns large and small. He spent considerable time in Maine, addressing antislavery groups and preaching in all-Black churches—which he had never encountered in Britain. In Portland he lectured in an "Abyssinian church" and asked himself whether "any feelings of prejudice or dislike were called forth. I can with truth declare, that I experienced none."

He journeyed between Augusta and Brunswick, then west to Plymouth, New Hampshire, and south to Pawtucket, Rhode Island, each time greeting adoring audiences, as well as more dubious townsfolk who politely but firmly asked him to leave, on the grounds "that I was regarded as a foreign emissary, an officious intermeddler." The press dogged him the entire time. The *Boston Centinel* derided "the *silly women* who squandered their money for his support," while Webb's *Courier and Enquirer* attacked the "Glasgow seamstresses" and "canting old women" who sent him to America to preach blasphemy and sedition. Webb also said Thompson was such an instigator of "treason, robbery and massacre" that he should be expelled from America and consigned to Bridewell prison as a lunatic and an enemy of society.

Most of the charges Webb and other publishers leveled against Thompson were absurd, but one stuck because it had an element of truth to it. Five years prior, Thompson had embezzled eighty pounds from his employer, and he had slowly been paying back the purloined sum. It was especially embarrassing since abolitionists prided themselves on their piety, and Thompson had acted like a common thief. Moreover, British antislavery groups knew this when they sent him to America, hoping Thompson's transgression would stay hidden. But it did not.

When the story leaked out, Garrison and his allies tried to change the subject or to say nothing at all—a hopeless strategy since the Colonization Society press was already making Thompson out to be a criminal of epic proportions. Garrison couldn't deny the charges against him, which only made Thompson's troubles worse when he came to lecture in a new town, and the only thing the residents heard was that a smug Englishman with a flair for robbery had come to lecture them on proper morals.

Things got even worse in early December, when Thompson lectured in Lowell, Massachusetts. Although he had spoken with great eloquence, "the lecture was interrupted by hideous noises from certain brutes and reptiles, and by a shower of missiles, one of which came into the window before which Mr. [Thompson] was speaking, very narrowly missing his head: the blow would unquestionably have proved mortal." The attack roused the interest of pro-Southerners in town, who posted a notice to the "freeborn sons of America" asking "Shall Lowell be the first place to suffer an Englishman to disturb the peace and harmony of our country? Do you wish instruction from an Englishman?"

Thompson's subsequent lecture was called off out of fear for his safety, and a small group of townsfolk took possession of the hall where he had nearly been brained with a brick. They passed resolutions against abolition and advised against any further agitation from foreign emissaries. Thompson would pick up his lecturing afterward, but the precedent had now been set: he was a target as much as any native abolitionist, and the object of even more contempt for being foreign.

Garrison was aghast at how close the Englishman had come to being martyred, but he was determined to showcase it. At the offices of the New England Anti-Slavery Society, he exhibited the brick that had nearly struck Thompson, with a note attached that "this deadly missile was hurled with tremendous force at his head by one of the Citizens of Low(h)ell." He worried over Thompson's safety and wondered what, if anything, could be done to improve it. The threats and violence had scared away some audience members, and though Thompson persisted through the abuse, Garrison wondered how much stamina remained in him.

He also fretted over the continuing problems with his finances. In January 1835 he complained to George Benson about "the non-payment of our numerous subscribers, and the faithlessness of a majority of our agents." His strategies for keeping *The Liberator* in business were sputtering. He faced $2,000 in unpaid subscriptions, issues were printed late and irregularly, and Thompson had failed to be an effective fundraiser while fearing for his life. Garrison thought about shutting down the newspaper.

At the same time the colonizers had developed a powerful new weapon against him called the American Union for the Relief and Improvement of the Colored Race. Its aim was to drive a wedge between radical abolitionists like himself and more moderate antislavery men—namely those with money and influence. Garrison wasted no time in thrashing the group in print, calling it defective, corrupt, deceitful, wretched, and doomed, and later he labeled it an "ANTI-GARRISON SOCIETY." This wasn't far from the truth: the Congregational churchmen who founded the American Union were resolutely hostile to him and considered him little better than a rabble-rousing atheist. An observer saw that they "hate Garrison more than they detest slavery" and would hang him in spirit if they could. The new organization would indeed be his gallows, if it could splinter the immediate abolitionists and persuade the moderates to abandon the radicals. Such a project would take time, but they committed their resources to it.

Arthur Tappan fell for it. Not completely, but just enough to do damage to the cause. Answering questions put to him by the American Union organizers, he allowed that Garrison's greatest fault was his "severe and denunciatory language with which he often assails his opponents and repels their attacks." He hoped his ally would correct his errors "and that argument will take the place of invective." This was exactly what the colonizers in the American Union had in mind for their wedge. The proslavery press played up his critical comments and predicted an imminent split between the factions—the moneyed New Yorkers finally wising up to the fanatics and denouncing the chief madman of their tribe.

Garrison held his tongue, at least in *The Liberator*. He could not afford to alienate Arthur, even if he had been goaded into answering loaded questions. Garrison had too much on his mind—the troubles of George Thompson, the danger of more mass violence, the financial health of his newspaper, even his ability to provide for his wife and (soon to be) children. With such challenges, 1835 threatened to be even more of a struggle than the year before. He had already beseeched God so many times he wondered if the Creator would continue to indulge him.

He also looked to Thompson for inspiration. His fellow traveler had confidence in the success of the mission and had lifted Garrison's spirit more than once when he found it flagging. The men journeyed together to towns large and small, preaching emancipation to audiences both supportive and wary. They lodged together and exchanged hopes and ideas. They appeared in churches and lecture halls, and they rarely clashed or found themselves in heated disagreement. Thompson had proved to be just as much the bosom friend as before, even if circumstances had changed since their trek through Britain and the devil had placed obstacles in their path.

Garrison looked forward to traveling with Thompson, his brother-in-law Henry Benson, and several allies to Philadelphia, where people of color had begun rebuilding their homes after the August horror. Garrison would meet with friends in the movement, and he would introduce them to Thompson's orations. The trip would, in short, offer a respite from all the challenges of recent weeks, in the company of supporters who could provide solace from his torments.

Yet on the steamboat to Philadelphia, they had barely begun their trip when reality broke the mood. They were cornered by a group of passengers that included slaveholders. "Some writhed and gnashed upon us; some sneered; some ridiculed; some threatened; and some laughed." Vigorous debate followed, and Garrison and Thompson defended themselves from all directions, using logic and quoting scripture. The abolitionists argued well enough to quiet their interrogators and reduce the tension, and to keep themselves out of danger. But in writing to Helen after the episode, Garrison was left feeling uncertain of how much progress they had made in changing people's minds. The experience left him feeling dour and concerned that his fellow citizens were becoming uncivilized, even blasphemous. He tried not to dwell on it, but the more he thought about these reprobates, the more they upset him. His anger welled up.

They had rejected him—they had rejected the Holy Spirit—they had rejected faith and providence and divine revelation. In fact, "the American people have no fear of God before their eyes. They assume the eternal prerogatives of Jehovah, and despise his law, and rebel against his authority. Miserable nation!"

SIX

THE TORCH OF DISAFFECTIONS

William Lloyd Garrison and George Thompson arrived in the City of Brotherly Love after yet another explosion of hatred. In an election riot the previous October, Whigs and Democrats had battled in the streets of Moyamensing and turned it into a war zone. The Jackson men had begun the fracas by attacking a tavern owned by the Whigs, smashing lanterns and tearing up campaign handbills, before invading the tavern, assaulting the inhabitants, and building a bonfire of furniture in the street. A gun battle erupted, the entire building took flame, and firemen were threatened with beatings "if they put a drop of water on the fire." Ultimately an entire city block was incinerated and became yet another eyesore in South Philadelphia, already littered with the carbonized hulks of homes and churches. Mob rule had once again held sway, with constables and watchmen too exhausted and outnumbered to do anything to stop it.

Garrison had seen this kind of destruction before, in the Five Points in the aftermath of the New York riots. But no matter how much he condemned such barbarity in the pages of *The Liberator*, the rioters only grew bolder and spread their carnage to more American cities. It didn't bode well for the safety of his friends and colleagues, or for the protection of George Thompson, his traveling companion, for whom mobs had a special affection.

Despite the threats, local abolitionists had expressed great interest in hearing Thompson speak, and he did not disappoint, lecturing to a crowd of a thousand in a Presbyterian church, and another three thousand in Bethel Church—that citadel of Black Methodism whose members had denounced colonization in 1817. Garrison's associate Arnold Buffum witnessed the spellbinding performance of Thompson and saw how he captivated his listeners: "He pleads with Christians of every name, to arouse from their lethargy . . . to vindicate the right of man to be free."

Thompson's lectures met with wide approval, especially among the members of the Philadelphia Female Anti-Slavery Society, who invited the Englishman and his fellow travelers into their homes. Garrison was happy to stay in the house of the Motts and stood in awe of Lucretia, whom he had seen in Adelphi Hall speaking before the delegates of the American Anti-Slavery Society. He wrote she was "one of the most remarkable women I ever saw. She is a bold and fearless thinker." Thompson stayed the night with a different Quaker, Abraham Pennock, while Henry Benson lodged with Robert and Harriet Purvis, the latter the sister of Sarah Forten.

The Fortens had survived the tumult of the previous August and remained in the city, even as so many others in the community had been forced to leave after the destruction of their homes. The Fortens' wealth and the presence of an armed guard had protected them, but they knew they were just as vulnerable to the rising of a crowd as the poorer residents of Moyamensing. And every day they heard of new threats against people of color and rumors of mobs assembling with the approval of those in power.

Despite the threats, Sarah continued her work with the Philadelphia society and, if anything, became more devoted to the cause. She saw Thompson as a worthy vessel to spread the message of abolition, quite far from the foreign devil depicted in the anti-abolition press: "his eloquence surpasses any thing ever before heard." She was quite taken with him personally too: "I find him a most delightful and companionable person. He is witty—full of anecdote,—and very lively . . . we really loved him—not only for his greatness—but for his goodness." Sarah sat through four of his lectures and spent hours afterward with her friends discussing them.

She wasn't alone. Thompson was adored to the point of peril. So many people crowded into one church where he spoke that the gallery almost collapsed: "the alarm was excessive—and the meeting adjourned in great confusion." This was both regrettable and encouraging, because rarely had he been so esteemed. He felt humbled to be the object of such acclaim, and he told Garrison that if he could have chosen the place of his birth, it would not have been Britain but Boston or New York or this city. To have Philadelphia love him back gave him energy for the difficult road ahead.

—⁂—

Thompson's visit was only the latest of the increasing ties between domestic and foreign activists. Robert Purvis had recently returned from Britain to meet the Glasgow women's group that sponsored Thompson. Garrison had maintained his transatlantic contacts after his tour of the United Kingdom, and Sarah Forten communicated with British abolitionists to share stories and strategies. Sometimes she didn't even have to write to them—guests like Harriet Martineau and Edward Abdy attended the Fortens' dinner table and provided enlightening conversation and anecdotes from overseas.

From these conversations, Sarah learned that women abolitionists in Britain had been particularly successful in their campaign against West

Indian slavery. The Tappans knew this as well, and in an executive committee report for the American Anti-Slavery Society, they spelled out just how critical they had been: "Female Societies probably did more for the abolition of slavery, in Great Britain, than those of the other sex . . . They made the matter a topic of conversation on almost all occasions."

The report encouraged women's societies in America to do the same, but the Philadelphians hardly needed the advice. They had already built a school for Black children and supported other antislavery societies in the state, and, through the new Anti-Slavery Sewing Societies, they planned to sell handicrafts to fund the cause. The group was still buying copies of *The Liberator* and *The Emancipator*, helping keep both newspapers in business, and purchasing enough antislavery books and pamphlets to create their own library. They had even more projects in the works, including a new plan based on the work of Lucretia Mott.

More than three years before, Mott had circulated a petition against slavery that she sent to Congress. She did so without the approval of the hierarchy of her church or any formal organization, since the Philadelphia society hadn't been formed yet. Her petition failed to gain traction, but since then she had kept the idea alive and looked for new possibilities to mount a similar campaign. The opportunity came when the Philadelphia society decided to send Congress the signed names of Pennsylvanians who demanded an end to slavery in Washington, DC.

Needless to say, congressmen had not been receptive to the petitions they had already received from other groups. In February, a representative from New York had presented the names of eight hundred women who pushed for abolition in the capital. The House tabled the petition, but more kept coming, from Ohio, Maine, and Massachusetts. This annoyed the congressmen greatly—that they had to deal with the pleas of citizens who cared more about the welfare of slaves than the peace and comfort of themselves. They preferred to run their fiefdom free of complaint and not be constantly shamed for the scenes they allowed to persist in the District: the chain gangs driven through the streets, the auction blocks where human beings were treated like cattle, the captives held for transport to

Southern plantations. They could not bring themselves to care about these things because no one, Black or white, could vote for federal office in the District anyway, so the question to them seemed . . . moot.

Henry Clay, Kentucky senator and cofounder of the American Colonization Society, was particularly aggrieved that the petitions from the New York women and other meddlers had distressed his duties. He said in Congress that no enlightened citizen of the North and border states could support such agitation. "It was confined to a few fanatics urged and guided by the Garrisons, the Tappans, and others." In fact, these zealots "were ready to light the torch of disaffections and civil discord through the country."

Whigs and Democrats both charged that the women who had mounted such a campaign had stepped outside of their proper duties, and sacrificed "all that delicacy and maternal tenderness which are among the highest charms of woman." Others worried that by entering into the political domain, women might disavow their femininity and somehow become mannish or reject the needs of their children. And ministers constantly reminded women of the admonition of the apostle Paul, in 1 Corinthians, that women must stay silent in church and submit to men's authority, and they said this rule applied in society as well.

Few of these charges mattered to the members of the Philadelphia Female Anti-Slavery Society. Lucretia Mott had been scolded by those in her church for so long that she dismissed the barbs as irrelevant. For Sarah Forten, the criticism was bracing, but it didn't deter her. The backlash to her later poems, the near ambush of her family's house, the ongoing state of urban violence—all of it had hardened her to the perils of activism and steeled her against the critics. Surrounded by friends and relatives who faced many of the same challenges, she saw no reason to change her course.

In organizing the upcoming campaign, Sarah and the other Philadelphians worked out a plan in concert with women's groups in Boston and New York. She would be one of the principals, preparing documents to send to Congress for the September opening of the fall legislative session and in November for the winter session. This meant her group had to quickly find enough canvassers to solicit people's signatures and keep those canvassers on task, armed with persuasive information and protected against assault or intimidation. It was an especially daunting project to arrange at a time when a spark of controversy could ignite a firestorm of violence—a time like the summer of 1835, when Philadelphia once again exploded into riot.

—⁂—

The latest tumult began with a story of an enslaved man who had attacked his owner. The press hyped up the report, calling it an outrage, even though the man had been hit first and had only injured, not killed, his captor. Nonetheless, the press ginned up the anger of readers and enflamed the still-high racial tensions in town. On the evening of July 13, a white mob assembled to march down Sixth, Seventh, and Eighth streets into the heart of Black Philadelphia, just as it had less than a year before. Despite the presence of a hundred constables, the rioters grew to 1,500 people and attacked nine houses of African Americans along what was called "Red Row." They hacked them apart with axes and assaulted anyone they found inside, including shooting and stabbing people in the kneecaps. One man tried to hide in his chimney, which encouraged the mob to set fire to his house with him in it.

City firemen rushed to prevent the blazes from spreading through the neighborhood and quickly became the next target for the gangs. Trying to fight off the mob, the firefighters battled in the streets for hours over their hose and apparatus, even as the rioters raced to other houses to light them up and savage the residents. Some of the Black people inside fought back, armed with axes or guns, while others succumbed to the onslaught. Those attacked raced across rooftops to escape, and they were shot at when they tried to run. The mayor made a citizen's arrest and received a flying brick for his effort. The mob ruled South Philadelphia until 2:00 A.M., when enough constables, watchmen, and sheriff's deputies gathered to put the criminals down and restore some order to the neighborhood—with homes still burning and the streets littered with ransacked furniture and other property. The color line determined the extent of suffering: white residents evaded violence by, once again, placing candles in their windows, while Black residents suffered most of the damage.

In the end thirty houses owned by Black people had been burned, countless Black men and boys had been beaten and injured, and the rioters escaped any charges or punishment. Garrison, in *The Liberator*, called the riot diabolical and the press's treatment of it "cold-blooded, incendiary, *smoothly* ruffian, and *hypocritically* cruel." He blamed "sinful prejudice in the high and educated classes" for allowing the destruction to take place and politically benefiting from it.

The violence put abolitionists in a precarious spot. Political speech now seemed to require a small arsenal to defend it, but most abolitionists didn't assert a right to use violence, even to protect themselves. Moreover, a new trend had sent antislavery activists in a completely different direction—to argue that the true answer to social change lay not in confrontation, but in changing the hearts of individuals.

This notion went back to the idea of "lifting up" Black people from what white colonizers, white abolitionists, and some Black abolitionists called "a degraded state." James Forten, Samuel Cornish, and Lewis and Arthur Tappan promoted the idea of Black men improving their lot so they could achieve success in business and society. Garrison, too, felt that a commitment to pacifism, temperance, and piety would put African Americans on a superior moral plane above white people. It all added up to "moral reform," which ultimately put the burden on African Americans to prove they were worthy of being treated with dignity and respect.

Behind it lay a distaste for the lower classes. Samuel Cornish had already spilled much ink in *Freedom's Journal* attacking working-class Black people who drank and gambled, held lively celebrations, and marched in parades. Moral reformers derided such behavior as a distraction from their goal of making African Americans into model citizens who had no acquaintance with "grog houses, cellar bistros, theaters, and lottery stalls." They said such places were dangerous not only because they encouraged illicit behavior, but because they involved mixing with the lowest sorts of white people—which might inhibit the uplift of Black society.

Philadelphia became a center of this trend, with James Forten's allies Robert Purvis and William Whipper the prime advocates. Whipper helped create the American Moral Reform Society to promote Black self-improvement and to fight racial hostility, which he saw as rooted in "the depravity of our morals." Whipper and his associates thought that with enough effort, Black citizens might set an example of rectitude and inspire whites to help them fight prejudice. "We are unable to conceive of any better method by which we can aid the cause of human liberty, than by improving our general character." They had high hopes for the success of their crusade, and "we do most cordially hope that a moral fabric may be reared, that will promote the cause of righteousness and justice throughout the universe."

But such utopian pronouncements were at odds with reality, as Whipper knew by reading any newspaper. Figures of authority such as bankers, lawyers, and politicians had no use for moral reform or the uplift of Black people—respectable or not. Many of them wanted African Americans to leave the country and denounced those who attempted to put the races on an equal footing. The Forten family, perhaps the greatest example of working-class Black people rising to unprecedented wealth and status, had, for all their efforts, seen their son attacked and themselves nearly ambushed. And the same was true of others in South Philadelphia, in Lower Manhattan, and wherever else white people had rampaged in recent years.

Moral reform also made targets of abolitionists. The activists who had fought so hard to create literary societies, lecture halls, libraries, schools, and churches saw their efforts ridiculed, their institutions attacked and burned, their names defiled in print. The social fabric that Whipper and his reformers tried to sew up was already rent and in tatters, and it didn't take a radical abolitionist to understand the problem. Having seen the cruelty and violence of New York's riots, even Samuel Cornish had to backtrack from some of his ideas of respectability conquering all. He would come to call Whipper's moral reformers "vague, wild, indefinite and confused in their views. They created shadows, fought the wind, and bayed the moon."

—⁓—

This left a dilemma. If Whipper's moral reform did nothing to stop mass violence, and Garrison's moral suasion had been equally ineffective, what other choices did abolitionists have to protect themselves? Lewis had seen how thirty-six gunmen could defend his brother's silk shop, but that was no strategy to fend off a much greater horde of rioters who reveled in barbarism and were armed to the teeth. Moreover, as he saw it, the argument for armed defense defied logic and common sense. What could they do, raise an army to fight the Blood Tubs and Huge Paws? Lay siege to the Courier and Enquirer building? Garrison and Webb at twenty paces? The idea was as absurd as it was impossible, when so many abolitionists were pacifists whose only acquaintance with guns was being the target of them.

Lewis began to realize that all of these arguments missed the point. Abolitionists were in danger because there were too few of them. As long as their enemies outnumbered them, they would always be helpless against them in the press, in the courts, and on the streets. The only solution was a political one: keeping the movement together as a unified front, persuading a larger group of Americans to join the cause, and growing the ranks to achieve social momentum. The power of law and custom would follow, and eventually lead to the end of violence. However, the first step was the most important—keeping the movement together at a critical time.

Arthur had made a grave error in falling into the trap set by the ministers of the American Union. For by speaking ill of Garrison, he had injured the movement and raised the threat of schism. Unfortunately,

Arthur's skills in business hadn't translated well into social activism, and Lewis knew he would have to be the one to mend the damage, even if it meant contradicting his brother in public. So he joined Garrison's attack on the American Union.

In a letter that appeared in *The Liberator*, Lewis borrowed Garrison's words and called it "AN ANTI-GARRISON SOCIETY." He praised Garrison for his "decision and courage," and said "I feel thankful to God for your steadfastness at the post which His providence has assigned you. Go on and prosper, thou friend of the oppressed! The Lord will be thy shield and thy buckler."

This went far beyond what Garrison could have hoped for, and he found himself doubly rewarded when Arthur—under pressure from Lewis and others—backed down and gave up the fight. He disavowed the American Union in a meeting of the Anti-Slavery Society, gave the Society one thousand dollars, and even helped Garrison with his outstanding debts. Garrison took it as a blessing from God for his mission, though Lewis had quietly arranged it.

Lewis had, by this point, learned how to influence his more prosperous brother, and to push the more conservative Arthur in directions he might not have gone if left to his own devices. One such direction was to confront the South and to sever it from the sympathies of the North. The Tappans couldn't use bricks and bludgeons like their enemies did, but they could use words as fearsome as any weapons.

They had to act quickly, because there was an opportunity in the aftermath of the recent urban violence, as more people read about abolitionists and what they stood for. The great majority of Americans still disapproved of the movement, to be sure, but a small but growing minority found it worth considering. In the last two years, hundreds of new antislavery groups had formed in the Northeast and out to the Great Lakes—from Augusta, Maine, to Windham, Ohio—run by men and women, Black and white, laity and clergy, moderates and radicals.

These groups had been fueled by their abhorrence of plantation slavery, but to maintain their momentum, Lewis needed to show them proof that abolition had gained traction, or at least attracted attention. The secretary of the American Anti-Slavery Society, Elizur Wright, provided him with a tempting opportunity: for an economical cost, they could flood the South with pamphlets and newspapers against slavery, inciting a reaction that would generate publicity and spread the word of abolition further than it had ever gone. Lewis endorsed the plan, but he knew the Society's publications would have to be more readable and compelling for it to succeed. So he took over as the chairman of publications, revamped the newspapers, and targeted new recipients. They would include:

- A monthly *Emancipator* with more uncompromising rhetoric, in the style of its general agent, David Ruggles
- A children's antislavery magazine, *The Slave's Friend*, which Lewis would edit himself, with sentimental stories mixed with stories of injustice
- *The Anti-Slavery Record*, a bracing publication meant for fundraising, rich with woodcuts and advocacy against slavery and racial inequality
- *Human Rights*, featuring the strongest and most aggressive articles against slaveholders, almost as if Garrison had written them

Lewis set a goal of raising $30,000 to fund the publications for national distribution—to send them to every corner of the United States, but especially the South, by printing 25,000 to 50,000 copies a week. The Society set about raising the money for the campaign and enlisting volunteers to research the names and addresses of potential recipients: politicians, ministers, businessmen, and other key figures.

Through his earlier experience with printing evangelical tracts, Lewis knew something about mass distribution, so he employed cheap steampress printing and the national network of the US postal system to send 175,000 copies of materials out of New York alone. The Society sent off more than a million pieces of mail for the four publications, making it the largest persuasion campaign abolitionists had ever mounted.

The publications were visually striking, with images that illustrated the depravity and cruelty of the plantation system. Even *The Slave's Friend*, aimed at children, used images of Black people in chains being whipped and abused. The copy that went along with such images was meant to provoke readers to take a stand on what they read, describing Black women freezing to death rather than submit to whipping, entire families broken apart at the auction block, and myriad other horrors.

Lewis's mailers followed a recent trend in the North of depicting slavery in all its brutality. Preacher George Bourne's controversial *Picture of Slavery in the United States of America* spent 120 pages focusing on the physical and emotional toll of human bondage for Black women, showing them flogged, sold at auction, "exchanged for a ram and sheep," and other outrages. Bourne used language in his work that echoed other abolitionists like Garrison, as he called the South "one vast brothel, in which multiform incests, polygamy, adultery, and other uncleannesses are constantly perpetrated." The Tappans' associate David Ruggles had said much the same thing, decrying rape and sexual abuse that he said only the depraved could fully imagine. Even less radical writers, like Lydia Child, drove the point that violations of the body weren't just a by-product of slavery; they were a key element, a means for masters to gratify their bestial compulsions at the expense of Black women's human rights—and to produce children whom they could also claim as their "property."

Like all the publications that pushed the boundary of what could be printed in America, the Society's publications that Lewis oversaw addressed the most notorious subjects head-on. They even touched on amalgamation, a topic abolitionists usually wished to avoid, by turning the argument against those who usually raised it. Papers like the *Anti-Slavery Record* reminded their audience that rape by plantation masters was the ultimate form of race mixing, as "slavery produces amalgamation at the most rapid rate possible"—a charge the planters found hard to deny in a world where sexual violence was the norm.

Lewis knew the mailings would be explosive, but he saw them as a way for abolitionists to take the offensive against their opponents instead of just taking their punishment. Such words and images would be among the most arresting things abolitionists had ever printed, with rhetoric in the style of *The Liberator*, but aimed at a much bigger audience. By taking the risk of sending out such material, Lewis outdid even the most brazen column Garrison had ever written, and he provoked a reaction in the South far greater than any abolitionist ever had.

On July 27, 1835, the *Norfolk Herald* announced that thirty copies of *Human Rights* had been found on a steamship docked in Virginia. It said the controversial literature was designed to "excite sedition among the colored population of the south, and overturn the existing social and political relations of the country." A few days later, the *Charleston Mercury* enflamed the anger of its readers about this "most scandalous and seditious" material. "We give this information in order to put our southern friends on their guard, and to warn them of the insidious measures now in a course of execution for their destruction." The *Charleston Southern Patriot* went further, demanding the suppression of "the moral poison with which these publications are drugged." If the post office would not suppress the mail, then the states "must take the law into their own hands. Extreme cases require extreme remedies."

The steamship *Columbia* arrived in Charleston on the night of July 29, bearing mailbags loaded with pamphlets sent by the American Anti-Slavery Society. The bags were conveyed to the post office, after which the locals, having heard news of the delivery, intercepted them. They broke in through a window and carried off all the mail they could grab. The next day the white townsfolk held a meeting and, with the clergy's blessing, resolved to burn all mail concerning abolition. They rifled through the sacks picking out newspapers that looked suspicious and gathered to dispose of them that night.

When darkness fell, three thousand Charlestonians assembled at the parade ground and threw a bonfire to incinerate the literature. It was a festive affair, with a balloon ascending to the sky and effigies of Arthur

Tappan, William Lloyd Garrison, and Samuel Cox hanging by the neck, to burn along with the newspapers below their feet. The city council justified the burning of newspapers by claiming they "would be likely to produce incalculable evil" if people could read them and begin to question the slave-labor system the region was built upon.

A former governor and four other men formed a committee to inspect steamships for offending literature, reserving the right to burn whatever they found objectionable. In response, the Charleston postmaster asked the postmaster general, Amos Kendall, what he should do in the face of the mob action. Kendall told him to use his own judgment, because "We owe an obligation to the laws, but we owe a higher one to the communities in which we live." Censoring the mail might just be necessary.

Following the riot, reports appeared in the Southern press that the abolition papers were turning up everywhere—discovered in Mobile, Alabama, at a post office; trundled into Virginia by an antislavery agent; received en masse in Savannah; found along a roadside in Enfield, North Carolina. The stories grew ever more alarmist as the days passed: that secret subversives had penetrated the South and littered it with their mail, that free and enslaved Black people had received and read the literature to plot insurrections, and that steamboats carried dangerous pamphlets that were shoved into the pockets of unwary travelers.

Vigilance committees formed to suppress the mail, to track down stray copies of the material, and to threaten those who possessed it. Those suspected of sympathizing with abolition were publicly defamed, put on trial, or expelled from their communities—even jailed, assaulted, or murdered. A committee found a man in Nashville, Amos Dresser, with a few copies of the Tappans' literature, interrogated him, and sentenced him to twenty lashes on his bare back, after which he was forced out of the city. Torchlight parades and protest meetings erupted with demagogues decrying the propaganda from the North and vowing to prosecute those who had sent it. The vigilance committees, with virtually unlimited power outside of the law, swept into the quarters of Black citizens, charging them as potential accomplices, and hunted through post offices, stagecoaches, and steamships for evidence of sedition. Several white people found guilty of "association with Negroes" were executed in South Carolina and Georgia.

Increasingly fanciful conspiracy theories credited Northern abolitionists with powers far beyond their means, from seeding the South with agents to inspire slave revolts to secretly preparing the ground for civil war. Planters, ministers, and common workers held mass meetings at which they vented their hatred of interlopers who dared to question slavery. They launched into diatribes about white Southerners' supposed constitutional right to own Black human beings, and biblical justifications for slavery. They vowed to take the fight to the North and demand that governors and legislatures censor any literature that offended the South. The *National Intelligencer* spoke for many whites in the region by claiming the distribution of the papers was "a crime of so deep a dye, in comparison with which murder and midnight incendiarism are acts of white robed innocence, there ought to be some adequate punishment." Those most targeted for this punishment were Arthur and Lewis Tappan and William Lloyd Garrison.

The Southern press said the Tappans were capable of causing havoc anywhere, at any time, and lay in wait to strike with cold-blooded cunning. The *Washington Telegraph* bizarrely compared the sending of inflammatory pamphlets to Arthur Tappan "hiring an assassin to go to Georgia to murder the governor." Fresh bounties were offered, including one from a Norfolk rally that promised $50,000 for the silk merchant's delivery to Virginia, dead or alive. A state grand jury indicted the entire membership of the American Anti-Slavery Society, with hopes of seeing them extradited to receive their punishment. Rumors of a pilot boat from Savannah waiting in New York Harbor to kidnap Arthur and other abolitionists frightened some activists, while Lydia Child described assassins lurking in the city to stab him, "like the times of the French Revolution, when no man dared trust his neighbor." In the pages of the *Courier and Enquirer*, James Watson Webb warned of civil war, "with all its kindred horrors of rape, sack, and slaughter," and he issued a special message to his adversary: "Keep a look out, Arthur—a large reward is offered for you—before you are aware, you may be boxed."

Southern businessmen took action to boycott Arthur Tappan and Company, refusing to buy products from the notorious friend of Black people. The boycott expanded from South Carolina to Tennessee and Virginia, with pressure groups demanding that Southerners stop buying or importing their delicate parasols, gloves, hats, and other niceties from such "fanatics," admonishing fellow citizens, "It is you who have enriched these miscreants."

Scores of bankers and merchants on Pearl and Wall Streets began to fear the reprisals. They urged the Tappans to tamp down their support for abolition, lest the entire trading economy of New York suffer. But Arthur was unswayed, since his brother's bold publishing gambit had made national headlines and drawn more attention to the cause than it had ever received. Arthur answered his critics with uncharacteristic fury: "You demand that I shall cease my anti-slavery labors, give up my connection with the Anti-Slavery Society, or make some apology or recantation—I WILL BE HUNG FIRST!" Lewis spoke more peaceably but just as defiantly. In a letter to a South Carolina Vigilance Committee, he wrote, "We will persevere, come life or death, if any fall by the hand of violence, others will continue the blessed work."

Ironically, the storm of mostly negative publicity provided Arthur Tappan and Company with some of its largest profits in August and September. He could barely keep the controversial newspapers and pamphlets in stock at the store, and he sold dozens of goods that advertised the cause—silk prints with "The Poor Slave" embroidered on them, wax seals and handkerchiefs with antislavery pledges attached, plaster mannequins of enslaved men and women, and other figurines and emblems and knick-knacks. It helped to offset any loss of income from the Southern boycotts and keep the company financially secure, at least for the moment.

The American Anti-Slavery Society also profited by the campaign. It had already expanded its membership with chapters throughout the United States—now 215 affiliates in thirteen states—and publicity from the mass mailing spread the word further, even with mail being suppressed. In small cities and towns in the North, sympathetic ministers, women from literary societies, and philanthropists joined the cause, subscribing to *The Liberator* and *The Emancipator* and reading stories that would never have appeared in the pro-Southern and pro-colonization press in their hometowns. They signed petitions to demand an end to slavery and injustice, contributed money to help fund the effort, and encouraged their friends and neighbors to support the cause.

Feeling confident in their progress, the executive committee of the Society submitted a public statement that, unlike the disclaimer after the New York riots, did not equivocate and raised the rhetorical stakes. The committee men defended their mail campaign and condemned Washington, DC, as "the great slavemart of the American continent." They warned of the demands of Southerners to suppress the mails with "ten thousand censors of the press," who might inspect every pamphlet and newspaper for material they found offensive. And if such action did occur, "the days of our republic are numbered, and that although abolitionists may be the first, they will not be the last victims offered at the shrine of arbitrary power."

Lewis Tappan and the Anti-Slavery Society had forced the issue upon the North, but the full federal response was yet to come. Postmaster General Kendall took advantage of the outrage in the white South to argue that all local postmasters, not just the one in Charleston, should take it upon themselves to personally censor the mail and strip it of any abolitionist literature, should it offend local (white) sensibilities. Even though Kendall admitted federal law did not allow him to order the confiscation, he suggested local mail chiefs were under no such obligation.

Southern postmasters responded to his advisory with enthusiasm, as did several in Northern states. One of them was New York's postmaster, Samuel Gouvernor. He at first tried to persuade the executive committee of the American Anti-Slavery Society to desist in their mailings, but they refused to comply. So Gouvernor, to aid in "preserving the public peace," took to censoring abolition pamphlets by his own authority and refused to let them be mailed out of New York post offices.

This cut off the main distribution point for the literature. The Anti-Slavery Society scrambled to come up with an alternate means of distribution, while many observers—even those hostile to abolitionists—found it hard to believe de facto mail suppression could be so easily achieved. The diarist Philip Hone said Kendall had given sanction to mob violence and that "the people are to be governed by the law just so long as it pleases them . . . substituting 'Lynch's law' for the written law of the land." Various New York newspapers joined in the criticism, charging that Kendall's edict made it much easier for federal law to be violated at the whim of popular uprisings, and that the postmaster general was wrongheaded, ill-advised, or lying about his motives. Even William Stone's fearsomely proslavery *Commercial Advertiser* saw nothing worthwhile in his approach.

As that newspaper suspected, quietly standing behind Kendall's strategy was none other than President Andrew Jackson. While he claimed not to approve of mob violence, Jackson suggested it may have been inevitable once white Southerners were provoked. As for a strategy, he initially thought that shaming the subscribers to the newspapers would be enough to stifle the mailings, telling Kendall that local postmasters ought to record the names of recipients "and have them exposed thro the publik journals as subscribers to this wicked plan of exciting the negroes to insurrection and to massacre." But Jackson didn't realize that most of the papers had been received unawares, and that no one in the white South wanted to be a subscriber—and thus be at the mercy of the vigilance committees. As an alternative, the president endorsed the idea of local censorship, and as for the abolitionists, "they ought to be made to atone for this wicked attempt, with their lives."

But Arthur and Lewis weren't ready to hang just yet, and they redoubled their efforts. In response to the suppression in New York, the Anti-Slavery Society sent out its mail from other cities, like Philadelphia, and hid the newspapers in boxes along with merchandise like dry goods.

The persistence of the abolitionists drove pro-Southern businessmen and colonizers in the North into fits of rage, as they warned of "CIVIL AND SERVILE WAR" and other apocalyptic outcomes if the newsprint continued to flow southward.

Looking to solve the abolition problem, Kendall argued for a national censorship policy that could stifle any offending literature. Having been a slaveholder in Kentucky, he had no interest in seeing his behavior questioned, and he took it personally that the antislavery campaign presented men like himself as monsters. In his autobiography, he forcefully defended human bondage, writing, "There are some features in Southern slavery which are humanity itself compared with the factory system carried to its perfection as in England."

He worked out his postal strategy throughout the fall and, in December, issued a report claiming that the federal government must obey any state laws that suppressed the mail and that it had no right or obligation to circulate papers "calculated to produce domestic violence." Andrew Jackson went one step further, and a week later he asked Congress to pass a federal censorship law to "prohibit, under severe penalties, the circulation in the southern States, through the mail, of incendiary publications intended to instigate the slaves to insurrection." His request ended up in front of a special Senate committee headed by John Calhoun, the former vice president and current senator from South Carolina.

Calhoun, just three years before, had encouraged the nullification of any federal law that offended the South, and he was known for crafting elaborate defenses of white supremacy and slavery (calling it a "positive good") and owning dozens of human beings. He represented a state whose voters were the most aggrieved in the country over abolition, and he would now be in charge of determining what kind of national legislation to pursue to keep the nemesis of the white South—the American Anti-Slavery Society—silent, stifled, and suppressed.

Mob law now stood on the cusp of becoming federal law.

SEVEN

LAYING ON VIOLENT HANDS

By the late summer of 1835, the practice of mob law was flourishing in America. *Niles' Weekly Register* reported so many riots and insurrections it was hard to keep track of them all: three hundred Irish laborers battling on the Wabash and Erie Canal—anti-Irish attacks in Rochester, New York—lynchings of Blacks and whites in the South—vigilante murders of gamblers in Mississippi—anti-Catholic mobs made up of "the wildest classes of the community"—and assorted outrages in Nashville, Norfolk, Philadelphia, Worcester, Augusta, and Baltimore. And all this appeared in one issue, on August 22.

Even Washington, DC, got caught up in mob fury. It started after police arrested Reuben Crandall, the brother of Prudence Crandall, for having abolitionist newspapers in his trunk. Unlike his sister, Reuben was not an abolitionist and was only using the papers as packing material. Nonetheless, district attorney Francis Scott Key ordered his arrest for sedition and had constables spirit him away to jail before a growing mob could get its hands on him. Their bloodlust thwarted, the mobsters instead decided to attack the business of a Black restaurateur, Beverly Snow. A riot against Black Washington ensued, with a score of homes ransacked or destroyed, churches and schools plundered, and citizens like Snow having to flee for their lives. In the end, Andrew Jackson had to call out federal troops to restore order, but he made sure to ask the rioters if there was "anything he could do for them in an honorable way to promote their happiness." He also vowed that "by Eternal God in this City," if any Black Washingtonians "had violated any law whatever, they shall be tried in court and punish[ed] severely."

Garrison wasn't surprised by the riots, which he ascribed to "the progress of Misrule in the City of Washington." He would have to wait until the following year, though, to defend the cause of Reuben Crandall—who languished in jail for eight months before his trial—and was disturbed to see that even the family members of abolitionists were now fair game for prosecutors like Key and targets for mob violence. The demons had the run of the country.

Garrison had been unsettled to the point of nausea in recent months. On one hand, he had achieved several victories. Arthur Tappan had helped him with his debts from *The Liberator*, and Lewis had helped him expose the American Union as a shadow group for colonizers. In February, as a gesture of allegiance, Garrison placed his New England Anti-Slavery Society under the umbrella of the American Anti-Slavery Society (renaming it the Massachusetts Anti-Slavery Society), ceding some of his authority to the Tappans. It had been a successful three-year run for the New Englanders, as they gained thousands of members and inspired the creation of forty-seven local branches in ten states. But it was time to consolidate abolitionists under one banner, to expand their power nationwide—a prospect that gave Garrison hope for the ultimate success of their mission. In his personal life, too, he couldn't have been happier, writing passionate odes about his wife: "How wise, how benevolent, how invaluable is the institution of marriage!"

He knew that if he could just concentrate on his domestic life, his friends, and his mission, he could keep his fears at bay. But trouble always lurked outside in the wider world. In the same letter to Helen in which he praised their marriage, he also wrote of Sodom and Gomorrah, and how only marriage could close "the floodgates of pollution" where sin and misery dwelled. But those floodgates now barely held back the torrent of terrible news.

Again, his life had been threatened. He wrote, "I have just received a letter written evidently by a friendly hand, in which I am apprised that 'my life is sought after, and a reward of $20,000 has been offered for my head by six Mississippians.'" Yet another group of Southerners had marked him for death, and potential assassins no longer bothered to conceal their aims. But Garrison had greater concerns than his own peril. What especially galled him was the shocking treatment of his friend George Thompson.

Garrison had spilled ink over dozens of issues of *The Liberator* praising Thompson's tour of America, offering editorials and testimony about the Englishman's noble bearing and oratory. Yet few beyond abolitionists seemed to agree with him. The Fortens of Philadelphia may have lauded him, but in Concord he faced flying rocks and eggs that broke up a women's assembly. In Lynn, Massachusetts, he encountered the same missiles at a different women's gathering and, according to a snide report in *Niles' Weekly Register*, "probably escaped under the protection of a petticoat." Even people mistaken for him could face a shower of rocks and mud, as when John Greenleaf Whittier encountered an angry crowd who thought he resembled Thompson. Garrison's associate Samuel May witnessed much of the chaos in person:

> During the last six months of his stay here the persecution of
> him was continuous. The newspapers, from Maine to Georgia,
> with a few most honorable exceptions, denounced him daily,

and called for his punishment as an enemy, or his expulsion from the country . . . He was often insulted in the streets. Meetings to which he spoke, or at which he was expected to speak, were broken up by mobs. Rewards were offered for his person or his life. Twice I assisted to help him escape from the hands of hired ruffians.

Thompson found himself the target of twenty major mobs over the course of a year, and to Garrison the tumult he endured went far beyond his worst fears of American xenophobia. He described his friend in almost saintly terms and condemned those who persecuted him. Yet no amount of passion Garrison could summon in *The Liberator* seemed to have any effect on the public reaction to Thompson. The conditions were only getting worse for the lecturer as he traveled through the region, making a few friends and a much larger group of enemies.

But who was to blame for these outrages? Politicians, colonizers, and the press stood among the worst offenders, but Garrison increasingly faulted the working-class white men from whose ranks he had risen, and whom he had come to distrust. He saw these workers and mechanics as a danger to the country, having elected the arch-slaver Andrew Jackson to the White House and now waging violence against good-hearted people like Thompson. Garrison especially feared the Irish and wrote in response to one attack, "many of the rabble were foreigners of the *lowest* grade, who assembled to put down a foreigner of the *highest!* It shows what sort of animals are opposed to abolitionists, and furnishes good proof of the excellency of the anti-slavery cause." And yet even a foreigner of the highest grade could be blamed for some of the backlash, as Thompson hurt himself with one self-inflicted wound after another.

For one, Thompson rarely moderated his tone in his speeches, which some listeners found smug and self-righteous. He also made claims about American religion that his listeners found jolting, indicting their denominations for aiding oppression. More shocking were Thompson's insults to members of his audience who didn't share his views. At Andover

Theological Seminary he attacked the faculty as well as students to incite a debate on slavery. Critics called it a "demoniacal assault" that plunged Thompson "to the lowest mire of degradation." The *Commercial Advertiser* even reported a rumor that he had advocated slitting the throats of his enemies "distinctly" and "repeatedly," thus beginning a battle of words in print over what he said and how he said it—with Thompson rebutting the sworn testimony of a seminarian and three of his professors.

Even more ill-advised was Thompson's attack on a Baptist minister from London, Dr. F. A. Cox, who was in America as a member of the Agency Society for the Universal Abolition of Negro Slavery. Cox, like Thompson, had come to New York to attend the anniversary of the American Anti-Slavery Society's founding. But he had also received a warning from a Southern colonizer that, should he speak at the event, his life might be endangered. Cox withdrew out of caution, but Thompson, who had received the same warning, did not.

Thompson spoke at the meeting and wasted no time in mocking the minister, saying that by slavery's "torpedo power a man has been struck dumb" and claiming Cox had deserted his principles out of cowardice, and for that "I denounce, I abjure him." The crowd was stunned and interrupted Thompson's words with an outbreak of hissing and stamping. The Society's own report admitted, "Expressions of much dissatisfaction were now heard in various parts of the house" as people yelled, "We want to hear no foreigners lecture us!" among other outbursts.

Critics seized on this "tiger-like malice" in Thompson's character to cast him as a villain. He had insulted America, they said, and now had even defamed a peaceful ally from his own country. A storm of derision soon followed Thompson almost anywhere he went, making it difficult for other abolitionists to defend him—just as they had remained tight-lipped over the story of his embezzlement a year before.

Garrison knew his friend had made a grievous error, but he defended his conduct in *The Liberator* and cast doubt on the motives of Dr. Cox. However, he must have known his readers didn't buy his argument, because in a later print edition of his friend's speeches, he quietly removed the offensive oratory from the transcript, as if it had never happened. But by this point, not even careful editing could help Thompson's case, as the mass reaction to abolition grew ever more venomous.

In New Hampshire Samuel Noyes deeded land for a school for Black youth, with the endorsement of Dartmouth College. But just as the first fourteen students were set to take their classes, a mob led by the sheriff destroyed the schoolhouse, with a team of oxen to pull it down, and shot at the students as they fled. In Haverhill, Massachusetts, Samuel May tried to lecture in a Baptist church, only to be swarmed by a rock-throwing mob that injured some of the women parishioners, all to the sound of "the most hideous outcries, yells, from a crowd of men" about to burst inside. Even in Rutland and Montpelier, Vermont, May's appearances met with violence and bloodthirsty demands: "Down with him!" "Throw him over!" "Choke him!"

Yet the most pressing danger came from a peaceable assembly that, nonetheless, stirred up a fury against anyone who dared to question slavery. In August, Boston's Faneuil Hall—that famed holdover from revolutionary days—hosted some 1,500 people to listen to speakers denouncing those who called for immediate abolition. Although former Senator Peleg Sprague attracted much of the attention, the key speech belonged to Harrison Gray Otis, former Massachusetts senator and representative and onetime mayor of Boston.

Otis indicted abolitionists with the charge of trying to upend American government and society. Unlike the sandblasting harangues of James Watson Webb or William Stone, Otis used polished oratory and detailed arguments. He praised the country's founders who had also been slaveholders, and proclaimed the harmony of North and South, and the compromise between regions under law and tradition—at least until the abolitionists came along. Otis said they "eviscerated" the holy scriptures to support their cause, and he denounced their inflammatory words and images. In his view, they were almost like a cult, ready to overthrow the government:

All men are invited to join in this holy crusade. The ladies are invoked to turn their sewing parties into abolition clubs, and the little children when they meet to eat sugar plumbs or at the Sunday schools are to be taught that A B stands for abolition . . . men, women and children are stimulated, flattered and frightened in order to swell their numbers. This picture of the society fully supports my assertion that it is revolutionary.

Otis's speech attracted nationwide attention in the press. *Niles' Weekly Register* said, "It is the language of the heart—simple, but strong; and . . . truly sublime in the flow of its eloquence." It was reprinted and lauded in regional papers, too, and cited as proof of how the nation's founders would have despised Garrison and his cronies for their treachery.

Garrison wasted no time fulminating against the meeting in *The Liberator*, spending issue after issue picking apart Otis's speech (as well as Sprague's) and using the strongest rhetoric he could summon: "pollution and disgrace" for the meeting, the "COFFIN OF LIBERTY" for Faneuil Hall, "utter degeneracy" for Bostonians, and Satan, demons, corpse-selling drunkards, incestuous perverts, and parent-murdering thieves for various other enemies—and all this in a single column. But privately, Garrison knew that simply printing the strongest words he could think of would have little effect against the swell of hatred growing against him and his movement.

George Thompson again faced the brunt of the abuse. Even residents of the smallest hamlet he visited now greeted him with a hail of brickbats, vicious oaths, or rotten eggs. He took the brutal treatment in stride, but Garrison realized his journey had reached a dangerous point. After hearing of Thompson surviving yet another close call on the stump, Garrison wrote to Henry Benson that "we had better not attempt to lecture," given the current state of unrest. Writing to George Benson, Garrison was even more resigned—"That some of us will be assassinated or abducted, seems more than probable."

It was around this time that Garrison received a letter from an unknown woman, almost as if Providence had deposited it in his mailbox. Her name was Angelina Grimké, and she was the sister of the better known, and recently deceased, lawyer and colonizer Thomas Grimké. Yet this Grimké was a fervent advocate of immediate abolition, along with her sister Sarah. In her letter, she dissected the violence that had plagued the abolition movement in recent years, writing, "Religious prosecution always begins with *mobs*" made up of "a lawless band of unprincipled men" who received support from "a large majority of those who are too high in *Church* and State to *condescend* to mingle with them, tho' they secretly approve and rejoice over their violent measures."

Angelina reminded him that abolitionists must not fear martyrdom— "Yes! LET IT COME"—because "If persecution can abolish slavery, it will also purify the Church." She flattered Garrison by writing "The ground upon which you stand is holy ground: never—never surrender it," for they were fighting a war of the spirit, mortal combat in which the antislavery army must prevail. "Let us endeavor, then, to put on the *whole* armor of God, and, having done all, to stand ready for whatever is before us." The ideas in the letter so impressed Garrison that he resolved to publish it in *The Liberator*. He called it a "soul-thrilling epistle . . . with a spirit worthy of the best days of martyrdom."

And yet—the thought of death at the hands of his enemies grew ever more repellent to him the more immediate it became. On September 10, those enemies left a reminder of his vulnerability on the doorstep of his house: a nine-foot-high gallows cut from maple wood and draped in seaweed, with a threatening note from "Judge Lynch" and two nooses attached—one for him and the other for Thompson. Garrison passed word of the threat to his friends and allies, writing to Henry Benson, "pray, be very careful all of you, especially about venturing out at night. I yearn to see dear Thompson, and beseech him to look well to his movements for the present."

Garrison took his own advice to lie low, at least for several weeks. But he would soon have to venture out once more. For the Boston Female

Anti-Slavery Society had set their annual meeting for October 21, to be headlined by none other than George Thompson.

This bold action was not unusual for the women's society. They had already led the petition campaign to Congress, setting the template for the strategy now undertaken by other women's groups in Philadelphia and New York, and remained the most assertive and uncompromising of all abolition societies. One of their leaders was Maria Weston Chapman, the corresponding secretary of the group, who knew Garrison through the New England Anti-Slavery Society and helped him develop some of his thinking on the role of women in the movement. With him, Chapman and her allies fought back repeated attempts to limit their autonomy, and they trusted him fully: "Mr. Garrison is regarded as a brother by every one of us."

They had proposed to book Thompson for the speech near the height of his infamy in America, thinking it would attract attention to the cause and drive further interest in the Society's campaigns. But the blowback in the press and on the streets was sudden and unrelenting. The newspapers, most of them proslavery, warned Thompson that he wouldn't be able to hide under ladies' petticoats again and would be properly punished for his misdeeds. Other press organs mocked Chapman's group and said they belonged in "their proper sphere—the domestic fireside." Boston's merchants were especially appalled that the incendiary Englishman might make an appearance in their town—and threaten their trade with the South. They worked with the editor of the *Commercial Gazette* to print a handbill and distribute it all over town, to inflame public feeling beyond its already blazing temperature:

THOMPSON—THE ABOLITIONIST. That infamous foreign scoundrel THOMPSON, will hold forth this afternoon, at the Liberator office, No. 48, Washington street. The present is a fair opportunity for the friends of the union to *snake Thompson out!* It will be a contest between the abolitionists and the friends of the union. A purse of $100 has been raised by a number of patriotic citizens to reward the individual who shall first lay violent hands on Thompson, so that he may be brought to the tar kettle before dark! Friends of the union, be vigilant!

But Thompson was not even in the city, having wisely decided to keep his distance this time. And the meeting would not be held at the offices of *The Liberator*, but in the adjoining rooms of Anti-Slavery Hall (also known as Stacy Hall), the venue for Chapman's group. The discrepancies didn't matter, though. The message of the handbill ensured people would fill the streets when Chapman's group held its meeting and would be filled with rage. As one budding mobster told them, "You will be killed as sure as fate, if you show your heads at that hall." Yet despite the threats, the women stuck with their plan, seeing that "The greater the opposition to a right action, the stronger the necessity for its performance."

Chapman remained wary of the potential danger. She asked Boston mayor Theodore Lyman for a security detail to keep any invaders out of their building. The mayor blithely responded, "You give us a great deal of trouble," and added no constables for their protection. So on the day of the event, the twenty-five women of the society arrived at the hall to find it unguarded. Almost as soon as they entered the auditorium, a score of interlopers did too.

Fresh off the streets, a wayward group of men scuttled through the hallways of the building while the society tried to hold its meeting, even as hundreds of others gathered outside to protest it. Unlike Garrison's idea that workers and mechanics caused the trouble, this crowd was thick with "a great multitude of neatly dressed young men . . . merchants' clerks"—as well as their bosses. In the words of Samuel Sewall, one of Garrison's allies on site, "The merchants connected by business with the South were undoubtedly the chief instigators of the movement." Many had also attended the Faneuil Hall meeting two months before.

The trespassers in the building didn't accost the women, but they did find abolition tracts and pamphlets that looked suspicious, and they tossed them out the window down to the street, where the crowd shredded them. Around this time Garrison arrived at the hall, and the crowd spotted him. But he eluded their grasp and made his way inside. He asked Chapman's group if he should offer an address to substitute for Thompson. Worried over his safety, they politely declined.

With Garrison was an abolitionist named C. C. Burleigh, who was among the strangest people in the movement. Burleigh had a reputation as a fantastic orator but prided himself on his lack of grooming, shaving, and even basic hygiene. In Samuel May's words, "the peculiar dress of his hair and beard has given offence to many," while Henry Stanton put it more plainly: "He dressed like a tramp." But Garrison trusted him, and on a day like today, that was enough. They both headed up to his newspaper office on the second story.

Garrison pushed past the interlopers in the corridors, reminding them this was a women's gathering and they had no business there. His words convinced none of them to leave. When he and Burleigh reached the office, they locked the door and looked out the window. The crowd had swelled to more than a thousand people, many of them chanting his name and Thompson's.

Suddenly—a boot from the hallway kicked open the lower panel of the office door.

The men were trying to burst into the office to assault Garrison or hand him over to the crowd. Burleigh acted fast; he slipped into the hallway and created a distraction. He drew some of the men away from the office, giving Garrison just enough time to decide what to do next.

By this time, Mayor Lyman had come into the auditorium to implore Chapman and her group to leave the building, considering the growing danger outside. Some of the women debated whether to unlock the doors and confront the invaders directly, saying to Lyman, "if it was necessary to die in that cause, [we] might as well die there and then." But Chapman was sardonic, asking the mayor if he might use his influence with the crowd since many of his "personal friends are the instigators of this mob." Lyman rebuffed her question and said if they would all leave now, he would order the constables to protect them; if they delayed, they would have to face the mob on their own.

So the Boston Female Anti-Slavery Society left Anti-Slavery Hall. Black and white women walked arm in arm, to the outrage of the crowd that surrounded them. Chapman could barely contain her contempt for the men—merchants and traders whom she knew, many with families. She wrote, "These men are fathers; they have daughters just coming forward into womanhood. Yet they can find it in their hearts to heap insult and outrage on the daughters of their townsmen." And those insults were terrifying: "The tumult continually increased, with horrible execrations, howling, stamping, and finally shrieking with rage."

She and the rest of the Society would retire to her house to continue the meeting, but Garrison—unbeknownst to them—remained inside the building, squirreled away in his upper-story office. Chapman learned of Garrison's vulnerability hours later, to her horror, and "we could only find relief and composure under this shock, in fervent prayer for his life."

After the women's society departed, the mayor appeared out front to try to calm down the crowd, which had swelled to two thousand people. The chants were loud and incessant: "Thompson! Thompson! Garrison! Where is Thompson? Where is Garrison?"

Mayor Lyman knew Garrison was inside, having briefly spoken to him. Yet outside, Lyman told the crowd he wasn't present and they should disperse. But they refused to go, and instead pulled down a sign marked FEMALE ABOLITION SOCIETY ROOM and hurled it to the ground, where people stomped on it.

It was at this point Garrison chose to leave the office. Samuel Sewall had been scouting around the building to help him find an escape route, and he located one through a back window on the second story. It looked a bit shaky, requiring a descent over boxes onto a shed roof, but there were few other options that didn't involve confronting the mob. Once Sewall returned to the *Liberator* office to let Garrison know about the escape path, he found the publisher mortified by fear: "He seemed more agitated than I had ever seen him." Still, with the mobsters now racing through the corridors of the Anti-Slavery Hall, Garrison had no time to waste.

Outside, the chanting crowd grew louder: "We must have Garrison! Out with him! Lynch him!"

The window was twenty-five feet above the ground. Garrison lowered himself out the window and balanced unsteadily onto the first box; then he tried to descend to the shed roof. But his footing gave way and he tumbled onto the roof, then a dozen feet to the ground.

In the clamor, the mob spotted him. But instead of giving himself up, Garrison ran for his life.

A young abolitionist named Campbell helped him into the shop of a friendly carpenter. The workman hid Garrison on the second floor under some planks and wood shavings. But the crowd was already onto the scent and surged inside. They pummeled Campbell to learn where Garrison was, and soon uncovered him, covered in wood and sawdust.

Now they had him. They quickly wrapped a rope around Garrison's body three times. Instead of hanging him then and there, they pushed him out a window and lowered him to the ground. His expression was blank, making for all manner of interpretations. Some abolitionists claimed he showed a quiet Christian serenity, but at least one newspaper report said he was "convulsed with terror."

The mob swarmed around the publisher, hounding him, screaming for his death. They debated where and how to kill him—by a rope around his neck or in a kettle of boiling tar. They decided to lead him toward Boston Common, where British soldiers had killed five Americans sixty years before, and where another sacrifice now seemed imminent, just as—

Four hands grabbed Garrison.

They belonged to Daniel and Buff Cooley, two wagoners who had been milling in the crowd as spectators. They were just the kind of workers Garrison had come to distrust, but on this day they came to his rescue, fighting off a band of rioters. They were soon overwhelmed by the mass of people pressing in around them.

The mobsters tore at Garrison's clothes and shattered his eyeglasses. One of them whipped out a club and nearly brained Garrison with it before the Cooleys deflected the blow. The brothers tightened their grip on the publisher, yelling, "Don't hurt him! He's an American!"

Mayor Lyman, leaving Anti-Slavery Hall, saw the mob on the move and heard some people saying, "They are going to hang him; for God's sake, save him!" He led a small team of police around the corner to see a battle erupting in the streets—a brutal fight to gain control of a thin, balding man wrapped in a rope.

The Cooleys delayed the lynch mob long enough for Mayor Lyman and ten constables to drive the crowd back and to take control of Garrison and hustle him into City Hall across the street.

This was not, however, a place of safety. The constables were undermanned, the building poorly secured, and the mob of thousands nearly unstoppable. The mayor was alarmed to see Garrison's clothing reduced to rags and his body beaten. He found a spare coat, hat, and pants for him to wear, but his charity couldn't go much further than that. Garrison could not stay in the building.

The city records and post office were housed in City Hall, and the mayor knew the mob might burn down or ransack the building if the turmoil went on much longer. So he worked out a plan: he would have the sheriff issue a warrant for Garrison's arrest on a technicality, so they could convey him to the city jail a mile away—a much better stronghold against the mob. Garrison agreed as long as the jail stint wouldn't result in a fine or other expense. Meanwhile, the mayor would address the crowd while a coach arrived to pick up Garrison and take him to safety.

On the other side of the building, a second coach appeared as a feint to draw away the crowd's attention, but the ruse didn't work. The main coach arrived, and the rioters ran toward it. Garrison hurried down the steps of City Hall protected by two lines of up to forty constables. The crowd charged at him.

The mobsters pressed against the police to break their lines. The constables shoved Garrison into the coach, but the masses surrounded it and blocked it from leaving. Samuel Sewall saw the coach wedged in, trapped by the bodies around it, "in the hands of wild beasts." Men grabbed at the wheels, tried to open the doors, and heaved against the vehicle to overturn it. Other rioters tried to cut the reins and untether the horses so they could strand the coach and pry it open and seize the valuable cargo inside. In response the coach driver used his whip furiously, striking both the horses and the heads of the rioters.

Eventually, the wheels turned. The coach moved and picked up speed. But the crowd did not disperse—when the horses turned a corner, the rioters lunged toward them, to slow them down or grind them to a halt.

Finally, with enough effort, the coach made its way to the jail. Several hundred people in the mob arrived with it, but another line of officers held them back as the coach door opened and "Garrison seemed to bound from the carriage to the jail door with a single leap."

Garrison found his way to a cell for safekeeping. Sewall visited him and found him to be in lively spirits, overjoyed to be alive, in the company of two friends: "a good conscience and a cheerful mind." Other friends visited him in his cell and offered their prayers and support, thanking God for preserving his life from the forces of evil. After a while, he put the episode in perspective and stirred with thoughts of what the story of the riot might do to advance the cause of abolition. He wrote down some of his feelings on the walls of the cell.

Garrison's mood soured the next day when he learned the technical charge for which he had lodged in jail was a real one: disturbing the peace. He protested this show of bad faith by the authorities, and a judge promptly released him from custody. But the judge also strongly recommended that, since Garrison's life was under threat, and to preserve civic order, he should leave town for a while. Garrison agreed and departed for Brooklyn, Connecticut.

In his absence almost every press organ tore into him and other abolitionists for bringing the violence upon themselves. The *Evening Transcript* announced, "Riot Caused by the Abolitionists," while the *Boston Centinel* said the people of Boston had "expressed their decisive reprobation, of the outrageous perseverance of fanatics, in disturbing the public peace." But the *Boston Gazette* printed the most memorable line, which would be used to describe the enemies of abolition for years afterward. It called the riotous assembly "a meeting of gentlemen of property and standing from all parts of the city" who merely wanted "to preserve the peace of the city from all domestic incendiaries, as well as to protect the union against foreign interference."

Garrison wasn't surprised that so many pressmen lauded the rioters instead of condemning them. In *The Liberator*, he asked, "WHO ARE THE AUTHORS OF THIS RIOT? The Daily Press of the city." They had been provoking public opinion since the meeting at Faneuil Hall and had riled up the masses almost to the point of murdering him. He wrote, "If this country is ultimately and totally ruined, it will be by the profligacy of the Press. Our fears are terrible."

In the following weeks, abolitionist journals and pamphlets tried to change the narrative by printing their own version of the story. They attacked the "gentlemen of property and standing" who had made up the horde and described Garrison as a hero for his principles. Garrison offered a personal account of what it was like to be abducted and abused at the hands of the mob, imagining himself as a Christian martyr, though with the added benefit of still being alive. He wrote that throughout the ordeal, "I felt perfectly calm, nay very happy. It seemed to me that it was indeed a blessed privilege thus to suffer in the cause of Christ."

While Samuel Sewall's and other accounts had described Garrison as terrified, the revised narrative depicted him at peace with his tormentors. Garrison published the verses he had written on the jailhouse walls, with no small parallel to the Gospels:

Confine me as a prisoner—but bind me not as a slave.
Punish me as a criminal—but hold me not as a chattel.
Torture me as a man—but drive me not like a beast.
Doubt my sanity—but acknowledge my immortality.

Garrison's nemesis, James Watson Webb, understood the publicity value of his near murder and was appalled by it. In the *Courier and Enquirer*, he accused Garrison and his allies of stirring up a violent reaction in society, to encourage "the hue and cry of 'persecution' raised in their favor! . . . The villain who expiates a murder upon the gallows, always becomes a saint about the time he is hanged."

The lynching attempt had an electric effect on Garrison and the movement—the first time moral suasion had actually made a difference. In the months that followed, sales of *The Liberator* increased markedly and notable figures like Wendell Phillips endorsed immediate abolition after witnessing the riot in person. But that stroke of fortune, while it made Garrison's name more famous, did nothing to help George Thompson.

The American Anti-Slavery Society and those who had sponsored his trip realized that if Thompson had been present in Boston instead of Garrison, the result would have been fatal: the mayor would not have acted to protect him; no wagoners would have shielded him; no constables would have surrounded him; no coach would have driven him away. Thompson also understood the tempers that had been unleashed were now too hot to be contained. He wrote to Garrison, "my life was sought. I believe many were prepared to take it—many more prepared to rejoice over the deed, and I . . . [had] the conviction that I could not go abroad without the almost certain prospect of death."

Garrison understood Thompson had to leave, but it didn't make him any less resentful about it. He wrote to Helen, "My heart swells with sorrow, my cheeks burn with indignation, when I think of the treatment which Thompson has received at the hands of the people of this country. If he were a murderer, or parricide, he could not be treated more shamefully than he has been."

After planning his return to Great Britain by way of New Brunswick, Thompson bid his farewell to Garrison and hid quietly in the city until the moment was right to escape. Then he rowed a small boat out of Boston Harbor to a waiting brig named *Satisfaction* and sailed for home.

Thompson's trip would not soon be forgotten by the enemies of abolition—the most important of whom was the president of the United States. In his December message to Congress, Andrew Jackson praised those Americans in the North who had defended slaveholders in the South against the supposed menace of abolitionists, "and especially against the emissaries from foreign parts who have dared to interfere in this matter."

As a practical matter, Thompson's trip to America had been a failure for all the negative attention it attracted. But he had also generated enough interest to draw hundreds, sometimes thousands, of sympathetic listeners to his lectures and had raised funds for the American Anti-Slavery Society and chapters from Pennsylvania to Maine. He had been as loved and admired in some quarters as he was hated and reviled in others. It was just that his enemies always had the louder voices, and the more active fists.

—⁂—

Lewis Tappan took heart that Thompson's approach to abolition had not foundered; only the man himself had failed. Indeed, other antislavery activists had found success using a similar strategy of stump speaking and fundraising around the region. Some of the greatest progress had come in the rolling hills and small towns of the Middle West—a region much more inhospitable to abolition than anywhere Thompson had visited. Cincinnati, for example, remained notorious for its brutal 1829 race riots, in which mobs of whites attacked Black homes, churches, businesses, and schools, driving two thousand African Americans into Canada rather than remain as targets for racial violence. Yet even here, abolition could take root.

Lewis had learned this through the parallel experience of an agent hired by the American Anti-Slavery Society, Theodore Weld. Like Thompson, Weld spoke of God's wrath upon slaveholders and made a heartfelt plea for liberation and a demand for racial equality. Unlike

Thompson, Weld was an American, a good listener, a convincing debater, and only occasionally smug or arrogant.

In recent years Weld had achieved a stunning rise, his reputation familiar to every abolitionist. Most famously, he had led a series of debates over slavery and colonization at Lane Theological Seminary in Cincinnati, convincing the student body to support immediate abolition against the wishes of the faculty. Weld lectured and taught among the Black community in the city and devised plans for a women's school to go along with the men's institution. For these activities, the press condemned him, locals threatened him, and the leaders of the school tried to stifle his activities. Yet still he persisted as long as he could.

Ultimately, the board of trustees and the president, Lyman Beecher— Garrison's longtime nemesis—forbade any more discussion of abolition among the students. The students responded with a mass walkout, thus becoming the "Lane Rebels," causing a sensation and crippling the viability of the school. Arthur Tappan sent financial assistance to help the students in their protest and promoted an alternative school for them in Cincinnati. But many of the rebels transferred to fledgling Oberlin College or hit the road to spread the message of abolition, as Weld did.

Lewis and the rest of the executive committee followed Weld's successes throughout 1835, impressed by his magnetism and ability to connect with people, as he went from one village to another in the Ohio countryside building support for the movement. Weld founded the Ohio Anti-Slavery Society and convinced thousands of his listeners that immediate abolition was the only proper way to fight slavery, and colonization was an ungodly and fiendish pursuit.

Weld faced the same angry mobs Thompson had. In many little towns the residents threw eggs and rocks at him, and in Circleville a large stone smashed through a church window and knocked him on the head. He brushed off the incident, but he admitted, "for a few days I had frequent turns of dizziness." In Elyria, a sizable crowd assembled "with tin horns, sleigh bells, drums, etc., and ding dong'd like bedlam broke loose." Other indignities included ruffians mobbing his audience, hecklers interrupting his speeches, and insults targeting him in the press and in handbills. All this clamor and rock throwing would have given any abolitionist pause, but Weld, perhaps alone among his peers, had devised a useful strategy to deal with it.

Namely, he waited out the trouble. By persisting through the initial violence and insults, he spent days making his case in speeches and discussions that went on for hours, even debating his opponents if that helped convince them to change their minds. As he spent days in a town, at first only a few accepted his arguments, then dozens, and later more than a hundred. Once convinced, these listeners persuaded their friends to give him a hearing, until by the end of his visit, a good portion of the townsfolk had become converts to the cause. Then he moved on to the next town and started the cycle anew.

This was the kind of strategy against mass violence that the movement had been lacking, and Weld was convinced it worked best in the rural heartland. He had no use for evangelizing in the cities of the East Coast, which he saw as deaf to the call to justice. Weld vowed to stay committed to the frontier and to keep his distance from urban life, which he saw as riddled with corruption and immorality. But Elizur Wright and Lewis Tappan could not accept this from Weld. They thought his talents were much better spent in large cities, where he might convert thousands at a time, instead of dozens. They asked him to move east, to bring his strategy to New York, where it could help grow the movement and inspire new people to join it. Weld ignored their pleas.

Wright and Lewis refused to give up so easily, though, and as the months passed, they became increasingly adamant that the proper place for Weld was on the East Coast. He could be the tool that abolitionists needed to expand the cause throughout the nation, to achieve victories both spiritual and political and turn the tables on their adversaries.

They nudged and cajoled Weld at first, but failing that, resorted to hectoring him. He must come east while the movement was gearing up for some of its most important work—new agents to train, new societies to fund, new campaigns to unleash. Wright told him the executive committee was "most decidedly and unanimously in favor of your coming to New York this winter—and soon . . . If we need you ever, we need you *now*."

Wright and Lewis wanted him to attend the organizing convention of a new statewide antislavery organization, to harness the energy of abolitionists in New York. It would not be founded in New York City, but somewhere closer to the center of the state. Somewhere like Utica, a growing industrial town of cotton mills and furniture and textile manufacturing, linked to the South through its economy but receptive to the appeals of Northern activists.

Utica also happened to be just four miles from the site of the Oneida Institute, the favorite of several western colleges that the Tappans funded and a school close to Weld's heart—where he and three dozen of his peers had studied before departing for the Lane Seminary. It was a place that admitted Black and white students equally, and it had established the kind of model for interracial education that the Tappans had hoped, but failed, to create at New Haven and Canterbury. Here, though, they had succeeded, and one of the vice presidents of the American Anti-Slavery Society, Rev. Beriah Green, ran the school as president.

The signs had been promising for the convention in Utica. Through the efforts of Green and the Tappans and other organizers, the town's Common Council allowed the event to be held at the Academy building, an esteemed site for such a historic assembly. Hundreds of supporters in the region pledged to be there, as well as noteworthy men like Gerrit Smith, a land baron who had lavishly funded the Colonization Society in recent years and whom abolitionists had been trying to persuade to join their side. But one notable name was still missing: Theodore Weld.

Beriah Green wrote to Weld pleading that he attend the event, asking to "see the face, and grasp the hand, and hear the voice, and sympathize in the spirit, of our own dear, persecuted, triumphant brother in the best of causes . . . Dear brother, *come*, COME, if you can." Other abolitionists wrote too, begging Weld to attend, perhaps hoping that he might bring some magical charm to ward off the trouble they knew was coming.

Despite their entreaties, Weld demurred. And sure enough, the trouble followed. Once news of the convention got out, anti-abolition meetings denounced the event in strong and bitter language, and the local press condemned it, warning of "disorderly fanatics" who would "degrade the city." Colonizers had already taken aim at Green, burning him in effigy just two years earlier and nearly indicting him for treason. Now they resurrected the old charge that he was undermining American society with his plans and had to be stopped. James Watson Webb joined the denunciation from New York City and openly called for violence. He wrote, if the convention could not be suppressed by legal means, then "the law of Judge Lynch" should prevail. Congressman Samuel Beardsley, who represented the area, even announced "it would be better to have Utica razed to its foundations, or to have it destroyed like Sodom and Gomorrah, than to have the Convention meet here."

Speeches like Beardsley's met with applause in the anti-abolition meetings. The most enthusiastic came from the same kind of "gentlemen of property and standing" who had attacked Garrison in Boston. They passed resolutions praising the South and excoriated those who did not, calling them fanatics and traitors. Although an opposing meeting of "respectable mechanics" came out in favor of the convention, the gentlemen's voices were the loudest. Led by Beardsley, they successfully got the Common Council to revoke its permission to hold the event at the Academy. It would take place at the Second Presbyterian Church instead.

Inauspiciously, the convention would be held on October 21, the same day Garrison was being attacked on the streets of Boston. In Utica, some seven hundred abolitionists from all around New York arrived in town, taking the risk of being targeted for their beliefs just as Theodore Weld had been, though without the benefit of his strategy to deal with it.

In the Presbyterian church, the conventioneers arrived. They planned to pray for God's mercy and assistance, then discuss resolutions and pass a constitution. Outside the church, a mob of a few hundred people gathered. A city alderman tried to keep them from entering the building, only to be pummeled and have his clothing ripped apart. They shouted, "Open the way! Break down the doors! Damn the fanatics! Knock them down!"

Lewis Tappan was reading out the Declaration of Sentiments, defining just what the new society stood for, when a "Committee of 25"—leading a horde of angry whites—burst into the church and ground the proceedings to a halt. Amazingly, the abolitionists gave them a hearing, though they outnumbered the interlopers by more than four to one. Congressman Beardsley and his allies spouted insults and made accusations of sedition and treason. "They belched forth blasphemies and foamed like the troubled sea," heaping a volley of "abusive, profane and obscene epithets" upon ministers and pacifists who were at first too shocked to respond.

The Beardsley mob was in high spirits from the grog shops in the neighborhood that had offered them free drink in the hours before. But those spirits turned to rage when the convention answered the mob's abuse by downvoting their resolutions and ordering them to leave. But instead of departing, Beardsley's men ransacked the church.

"Give us Tappan! Hustle them out of the house!"

"Clear out! Clear out! Disperse the fanatics!"

The mob tore down banners and ripped up papers. They shoved their way to the front of the church and manhandled the presiding minister, Oliver Wetmore, who kept the minutes of the meeting and refused to give them up. One of the gentlemen in the mob shouted over him, "God damn you! Give the papers up, or I will knock you on the head!"

Collared around the throat with a cane brandished over his skull, Reverend Wetmore complied. Hooligans tore apart the papers and littered them throughout the church. The meeting adjourned and the mob poured into the streets to celebrate its victory—by destroying the offices of the one newspaper in town that had endorsed the convention's right to assemble.

And yet what had appeared to be a victory for the rioters ended in defeat. While the abolitionists were chased out of the Presbyterian church and had to leave Utica altogether, they reassembled twenty-five miles away and finished their business. In the town of Peterboro, they met at the estate of Gerrit Smith, the man they had been trying to persuade to reject the Colonization Society. He had always refused them, until he witnessed the violence of his fellow colonizers in person. Now he changed his mind and became their ally.

Smith offered a speech expressing his new feelings, which were bracing, even a touch militant: "It is not to be disguised, that a war has broken out between the north and the south . . . True, permanent peace can never be restored, until slavery, the occasion of the war, has ceased. The sword, which is now drawn, can never be returned to its scabbard, until victory, entire, decisive victory is ours or theirs."

Smith was the most important convert to the cause yet. He had given the Colonization Society up to $10,000 in recent years, and now his largesse would help fund their enemies. At his estate, the New York State Anti-Slavery Society came into being, and with his assistance it raised $1,200—a promising sum after the most tumultuous day in the history of the movement.

With the events in Boston and Utica, the face of mob violence changed. Whereas the property destruction and attacks on Black citizens in Philadelphia and New York City had hampered the movement, almost crippling it for a time, the riots on October 21 had a galvanizing effect. No one died, no one was maimed, no furniture was burned in the street, and no churches were torched. But the near-lynching of William Lloyd Garrison and the debacle in Utica had, nonetheless, inspired revulsion in enough onlookers that the ranks of abolition swelled further. High-profile figures like Gerrit Smith and Wendell Phillips now allied with the movement and used their own charisma, money, and publicity to give it greater momentum, while Theodore Weld and other agents drove the cause ever deeper into the heartland.

And unlike what Garrison had always assumed, it didn't take a single martyr to accomplish this feat. The strongest, most powerful voices were always better off alive than dead, better off organizing and petitioning and publishing than being sacrificed to their enemies. Besides, there were already enough casualties in a country where violence could erupt on any corner, and mayhem was now so common as to seem unremarkable.

★ EIGHT ★

TROJAN WARS

A mong the delegates chased out of Utica was David Ruggles. He had been to this part of upstate New York before, knew it wasn't friendly territory for abolitionists, and attended the antislavery convention anyway. And it was worth it, for when the inevitable riot came, it proved to be underwhelming. The mobsters made a clamor but left no broken bones or burned houses in their wake, unlike the more seasoned maniacs of New York City.

In Utica, Ruggles met dozens of new contacts to help him broaden his network across the region, from obscure burgs near Lake Erie to the major cities of New England. One of them was Gerrit Smith, who had just rejected colonization and seemed interested in funding Ruggles's projects for Black equality and uplift. Ruggles also continued to keep close company with Lewis Tappan, sharing with him a passionate belief in Christian reformation and spiritual renewal. He could also sympathize with Lewis's plight after his house had been ransacked by rioters—since Ruggles, too, had been the victim of a recent mob attack.

That episode began, as usual, with an anonymous handbill, which circulated in the summer of 1835. It was from one of Ruggles's anonymous enemies, likely a slaveholder or colonizer:

> Take Notice!—There is an incendiary depot at the corner of Broadway and Lispenard street, where the notorious Garrison's incendiary Liberator is received and distributed through the city by David Ruggles, a black amalgamator, who lately married a white wife! Let him be Lynched!—A VOICE FROM THE SOUTH.

Ruggles's life had been threatened countless times, so the call to assassination was nothing new. But the charge of amalgamation required a rebuttal, so he printed one in *The Liberator*, reminding readers he had never married anyone, Black or white. He also stood up for selling Garrison's newspaper, calling it "a herald of light and truth—and a balm for the lacerated bodies of two and a half millions of my countrymen."

But no explanation would satisfy the mob, which assembled in mid-September outside his business to chant and yell for his punishment. They knew he lived in the same building and threatened to smoke him out or ransack his home or worse. In the end they settled for destroying his business, with an unknown arsonist immolating the store one evening. Afterward, Ruggles offered a $50 reward for information on the crime, but no one answered him. Faced with heavy losses, he had no choice but to move his bookshop to a less desirable address. But he refused to relocate his home—so the intimidation continued and kept Ruggles under threat.

The white New Yorkers who menaced him didn't do so just because he sold *The Liberator*. What really infuriated them was how he had repeatedly called them out for cooperating with the slave traders and the man-stealers. In *The Emancipator* and in his pamphlets and public lectures, Ruggles continued to tear into the "kidnapping clubs" that made life hell for Black New Yorkers. In a speech in October 1835, Ruggles accused several Black New Yorkers by name of cooperating with the kidnappers and betraying their brothers and sisters in chains. When the meeting concluded, he and several of his allies took to the streets and went looking for one such informant to "bring him justice."

A month later Ruggles helped create the New York Committee of Vigilance, his boldest stroke yet against the bounty hunters. At the inaugural meeting—held by the "Friends of Human Rights"—the committee vowed to protect the rights of Black people, whether they were fugitives threatened with a return to slavery or free people abducted into captivity. Ruggles made it clear the destruction of his business had done nothing to stop him from investigating the illicit slave trade and those who profited from it.

Most of the press organs of the city quickly took note of the new organization and vilified it. The pressmen worried the group might alienate the white South or make New York City unfriendly to slave commerce. The *New York Express* fretted over the possibility of the committee hampering free trade, while the *New York Gazette* denounced any cooperation between the races and execrated "Negroes with a white skin" who aided the work of activists like Ruggles.

The new organization grew quickly and developed a workable infrastructure that aided its mission. At the ground level, up to a hundred men and women made up an Effective Committee. They monitored neighborhoods like the Five Points where man-stealers had operated with near impunity. Beyond them, more than a thousand people—10 percent of the Black population of the city—chipped in small amounts of money and provided the resources needed to hire lawyers, fight cases in court, and pay salaries and other costs.

At the top was an Executive Committee, all Black men who had been active in antislavery causes and had experience dealing with issues of civil rights and the judicial system. Several among them were full-time abolitionists, and others included a grocer and a restaurateur and men from the middle class. Most notable were minister Theodore Wright and his longtime ally Samuel Cornish.

—∞—

By this point Cornish had become restless, even agitated, over the glacial progress of abolition. There was far too much talk of eventual emancipation, and not enough action in the here and now. He had faith in his friends the Tappans and Gerrit Smith to follow through with their commitments, but other whites vexed him. Garrison, of course, had shown scant deference to men of the cloth like himself, and many of his fellow churchmen promised to rid the world of slavery while also fraternizing with colonizers who only wanted to rid America of Black people. Whites with wealth and influence might decry slavery, but they feared to associate with abolitionists, terrified of being called amalgamators and subversives. They put distance between themselves and people of color. *Distance that weakened the movement.*

Even worse was the persistence of church hierarchies in not hiring Black ministers. Cornish couldn't get a Presbyterian congregation assigned to him, and he had been "without charge" ever since he had seen his own church founder. Such disrespect rankled him, along with all the other indignities heaped upon him: the inability to get his children into a quality school after they had aged out of the schools for Black youth, the prejudice that forced him to walk the streets of New York because he might be refused admission to a segregated streetcar, the spiritual insult of the Negro pews, and so many other violations and transgressions that his mind reeled from a full accounting of them.

The weight of these stresses made it fraught just to live in America, let alone practice religion. How many times had he gone to church and, because he would not sit in a segregated seat, had to stand up for the service with his wife and family, and heard his child ask, "Why do the white people hate us so?" Cornish would later write that the American church was the "STRONGHOLD of an unholy prejudice against color, more *oppressive* and *fatal* in its results than any other sin."

In the face of all this hostility came David Ruggles, who had advertised in *Freedom's Journal* as a grocer and whom Cornish had praised in his newspaper. Cornish might not have had the fortitude of Ruggles—who did?—but he felt stronger and more resilient just by working with him. Cornish would soon become essential to the Committee of Vigilance, helping it raise money and publicize its drives for operating cash. He identified and called out the mercenaries who plagued his community. He announced court cases and the hearings where Black people's fates were determined. And he let readers know about his own successes and exploits as he drove the Committee of Vigilance forward. Even though Ruggles was far more radical than he, Cornish respected how he took action to combat oppression and had repeatedly suffered the consequences, instead of merely talking about it and congratulating himself for doing so.

Ruggles's official position with the Committee was secretary, though in reality his duties were much greater. He oversaw teams of agents recording accounts of abductions, uncovering cases of illegal slave labor, helping kidnapping victims take their cases to court, identifying informants who had been aiding the slaveholders and, increasingly, finding a home for fugitives in Canada.

He received encouragement from Lewis Tappan, who at one meeting proposed a resolution that "it is the privilege and should be esteemed the duty of every abolitionist, to aid the New York Committee of Vigilance by liberal contributions." Despite the support, Ruggles was determined to preserve the independence of his committee. In the first report of the organization, he said it had a separate purpose from the American Anti-Slavery Society—a different philosophy, group of donors, and mission. Whereas that group was mostly run by white men like Lewis with strong ties to evangelical circles, the Committee of Vigilance was mostly run by Black people, with membership open to both men and women. Ruggles was particularly determined to bring women activists into the group, and he championed their participation, while other reformers, like the Tappans and Cornish, shunned them. He wrote that "women's rights are as sacred as men's rights" and used the Committee to aid both in the cause of liberty.

The people served by the Committee included a wide swath of New York City's Black population. Among them were freed bondsmen from the South who had come to the city with little money, food, or clothing and needed assistance settling down. Black people arrested on false charges, who needed a legal defense to prove their free status. Slaves forced to transit north with their owners and illegally hired out, even though New York was supposedly a free state. Fugitives from plantations in the South who had made their way here and needed help to flee farther north. And those who had been kidnapped and sent to the South on slave ships, and now needed to be emancipated in court—the most difficult task of all.

All of this was perilous work, but Ruggles's own duties were perhaps the most hair-raising of all. He literally went to the doors of white employers of Black working-class people to inquire whether they were being held against their will, and he faced resistance and threats in return. He also tracked down slaveholders to determine the status of their bondsmen, sometimes by boarding ocean-bound ships to inspect them for illegally abducted citizens. When he found a person whose status seemed unclear, he took the case to court and offered whatever aid the Committee could provide.

This work was a brave step for someone who had just been the target of rioters, but Ruggles felt he had no choice: God had invested him with the power to help his community, and he could not turn away from that duty. As he wrote, "let us in every case of oppression and wrong, inflicted on our brethren, prove our sincerity, by alleviating their sufferings, affording them protection, giving them counsel, and thus in our individual spheres of action, prove ourselves practical abolitionists."

At the same time he battled against a hostile press and judiciary. Among his greatest foes was the city recorder, Richard Riker, who sometimes acted as a judge in kidnapping cases. He scarcely tried to be objective and privileged the testimony of whites over Blacks, allowed the arrest of Black people on the thinnest of evidence, sent them into captivity in lieu of a fair trial, and forced the separation of spouses and families. His associate, the constable Tobias Boudinot, worked with Riker to ensure that most Black New Yorkers who appeared before them would be sentenced to slavery and shipped off to the South. Ruggles condemned both men for empowering the kidnapping club by legal means, saying that the constable went "pouncing on an innocent person and dragging him before the Recorder who is ever ready to sacrifice him upon the altar of slavery."

Faced with the antagonism of such officials, Ruggles and the Committee of Vigilance took the defense of their clients as far as it could go in the legal system. And sometimes they took it a step further. As he wrote, "Let a remedy be prescribed to protect us from slavery. Whatever necessity requires, let that remedy be applied. Come what may, anything is better than slavery."

Ruggles put this philosophy into practice the following December, when he learned that the slave ship *Brillante* had docked in the harbor after transporting a dozen or so Africans across the Atlantic. He surmised the boat was the property of a high official in Rio de Janeiro and, like other slave ships, this one had come to port either to outfit for an upcoming journey or to sell its human cargo to a visiting Southerner. It might even abduct Black residents to boost its profits. These activities were strictly illegal, but with the connivance of authorities at the port, in the legal system, and in law enforcement, this kind of activity made New York a key stopover in the international shipment of enslaved people.

Wasting no time, Ruggles alerted the *New York Evening Post* to the presence of the slave ship and convinced the editor the story was worth publishing. Ruggles followed it up by getting the *New York Sun* to publish a disturbing account of conditions on board the "floating sepulchre," rife with disease and squalor, "men's bones and all uncleanness." The report generated enough attention to force city authorities to arrest the captain, Joas de Souza, and take into custody the Africans held captive.

De Souza claimed that he was no slave trader and that he had been unfairly targeted, since his arrest was illegal under a decade-old trade pact. He said the Black people on board were "bona fide seamen" who were able crew members. Proslavery papers like the *Courier and Enquirer*—which Ruggles saw as a "moral and political cancer"—came to de Souza's defense, making the captain appear to be the victim of an unfair legal system. A judge summarily released the captain from custody, after determining that "no bringing in, no holding, and no selling" had taken place. He kept the enslaved men in prison on a technicality then ordered constables to return them to de Souza's ship.

This aroused fury in the Black community. The evidence of slave dealing had been convincing, de Souza's defense had been paltry, and the proof of his guilt had been clear, but still the judge ruled in his favor. Ruggles's deposition was rejected on technical grounds, which prevented additional evidence from being considered and ensured the trial would become a textbook travesty of justice. Ruggles stood shocked by the outcome, knowing the slave ship would, "on future voyages, follow the same inhuman traffic with perfect impunity."

On Christmas Eve, a handful of Black New Yorkers took action to correct the outrage. Armed with pistols, they clambered on board the *Brillante*, overpowered the crew, and freed two of the five slaves on board. They returned later to pick up the remaining three, but this time the crew was ready for them. After a violent fight for control, they repulsed the liberators.

The press responded with indignation, calling the rescue a "Negro riot!" or "Assault." Proslavery editors blamed abolitionists generally, and Ruggles particularly, for stirring the tempers that emboldened Black New Yorkers to attack the *Brillante*. They also suggested he may have been one of the gunmen who stormed the ship. In his rebuttal, Ruggles refused to accept blame, or credit, for the rescue, though he insisted African Americans had every right to self-defense.

This was all too much for the slave traders and their mercenaries to bear. A few days later, they paid a visit to Ruggles. Arriving at the door of his house, around 2:00 A.M. on December 28, they tried to force their way in. This tactic failed, so they demanded he open the door, on the excuse of having "some private business" with him. Ruggles, though, knew exactly why they had come and refused to let them in. They would surely bind him and haul him to the *Brillante* or another slave ship, where he would be whipped and beaten and, if not hanged, sold to a Southern plantation.

The invaders kept yelling and demanding Ruggles answer them. They pounded and shoved against the door, until one of them finally burst through it, as "others of his clan made a rush up to my room like hungry dogs." They couldn't find their target though. Ruggles had escaped his room and found a hiding place in the building.

Incensed by his escape, the men descended on his landlady with clubs, guns, and knives, insisting she inform them of his whereabouts. One held a dagger to her neck, vowing "I will strike you down!" if she didn't give him up. She resisted their threats just long enough for a team of watchmen to arrive. They arrested the would-be kidnappers and took them into custody. On his way to jail, one of the men confirmed Ruggles's worst fears, saying, "I would soon have put an end to his existence: he would never interfere with Brazilians again."

The next day, Ruggles went to City Hall to press charges against his attempted abductors. Yet as soon as he appeared in the building, constable Boudinot arrested him on a flimsy charge and put him in prison, with plans to ship him South. Boudinot said, "We have got him now, he shall have no quarters, we will learn him to publish us as kidnappers!"—the irony escaping him that an act of kidnapping was a poor way to demonstrate that he was not a kidnapper.

Boudinot claimed he had a warrant from the governor, which he had been using for at least three years, enabling him to freely arrest Black people and send them off to captivity. Ruggles, however, was not only smarter than Boudinot; he knew his way around the legal system and realized the case against him was so thin as to be nonexistent. A judge had no choice but to release him from prison and to dismiss Boudinot's fanciful charges.

Having survived this brush with abduction and death, Ruggles published an account of the dramatic events in the *New York American*, with a message to his fellow Black New Yorkers:

> Now, I thank Heaven that I am still permitted to live, and take fresh courage in warning my endangered brethren against a gang of kidnappers, which continues to infest our city and the country, to kidnap men, women and children, and carry them to the South . . . Our houses may be broken open at night by northern or southern or Portuguese slave catchers; we may be assaulted and threatened with clubs, pistols or dirks, and handcuffed and gagged, and carried away to the South, while HUMANITY and JUSTICE continue to sleep!

Yet this frightening episode, instead of chastening him, only encouraged him to be bolder against the practice of New York slavery. Through his daring work, he was quickly becoming one of the most esteemed abolitionists in the state, and a model for what resistance against human bondage could do in the face of a legal and political system stacked against anyone of African heritage, and anyone who tried to help them.

—⁓—

Ruggles carried out his action against the slavers without much help from his colleagues the Tappans, who might otherwise have financially assisted him. It wasn't that the Tappans were indifferent to his plight; they were consumed with their own troubles. And foremost among them was that the firm of Arthur Tappan and Company had burned to the ground.

It was a bleak night in mid-December 1835 when the Tappans and the rest of the executive committee of the American Anti-Slavery Committee sat in session trying to figure out how to respond to President Jackson's fiery message to Congress—the one in which he condemned the "unconstitutional and wicked" designs of domestic fanatics and foreign agitators. They knew the battle over the mails and the petition campaign would only be heating up in 1836.

Just then, word arrived that an inferno had erupted in Lower Manhattan near their silk shop.

Lewis and Arthur hurried to Pearl Street, where flames had already engulfed structures on both sides of their granite building. Clothing and merchandise sat in piles in the street, and panic had broken out among the merchants trying to save anything they could from the blaze. But in this scene of destruction, one thing was missing: a violent mob.

The fire had ignited by accident in a dry goods warehouse and spread quickly despite the frigid temperatures. Worst affected was the area north of Wall Street—the heart of New York's mercantile district, with millions of dollars' worth of inventory on site. City authorities did all they could to protect the businesses there, but the ramshackle system of leather buckets, water drawn from wells, horse-drawn wagons, and uncoordinated volunteers proved to be no match for the wall of flames. When the water in firemen's hoses turned to ice, the fire easily devoured any buildings in its path, many of them made of combustible wood.

Some merchants piled their goods in Hanover Square to keep them away from the fire, but embers from the inferno ignited them anyway. The Tappans summoned their employees and rushed to remove as many goods as possible from their store, as the dainty silk parasols and hats and gloves were already starting to carbonize from the heat. They felt the urgency—their valuable inventory wasn't just the key to their business; it was the linchpin of the New York abolition movement.

The store's sturdy granite construction gave them a bit of time. As Lewis and his crew hauled products out of the business, Arthur removed a half-million dollars of promissory notes from the company safe, since everything inside the vault stood at risk of being incinerated. But the heat soon rose to near-scorching temperatures, and the granite walls and the iron shutters over the windows couldn't hold back the inferno much longer. With men still grabbing silk goods from the shelves, the flames invaded the store and annihilated it.

The Tappans and the volunteers saved two-thirds of the stock, with the loss amounting to nearly $50,000. Other merchants lost much more, up to $20 million, as the fire consumed twenty-three square blocks of Lower Manhattan and ruined seven hundred buildings. Afterward, a detachment of US Marines and sailors secured the streets against looting, while volunteer infantry and cavalry units patrolled the district, which looked like a war zone. The *Courier and Enquirer*, which otherwise delighted in the Tappans' misfortunes, somberly reported the toll of the devastation, block by block, describing the ruin of "our largest shipping and wholesale dry goods merchants, and filled with the richest products of every portion of the globe."

The Tappans were lucky to be spared the worst of the damage. To ensure the confidence of his clients, Arthur announced that he and his business were financially strong and ready to rebuild. He put a notice in the newspapers stating the business would move into a "new and commodious warehouse, No. 25 Beaver-street" and the proprietors "will be happy to see their friends and customers, until their store in Pearl-street shall be rebuilt, for which they have made arrangements."

Yet the truth was more troubling. Many insurance companies had failed in the disaster, and the Tappans couldn't get fully reimbursed for their losses; some goods they thought they had saved actually belonged to other businesses; and Southern boycotts continued to hamper the firm's profits and worsen the effect of their losses. The business had to extend credit repeatedly to its remaining clients, forcing it to take out loans to remain solvent—at rates of up to 30 percent.

So by the beginning of 1836, even as Lower Manhattan looked to rebuild and the Tappans made a public show of leading the way, their finances had never been more dire. The bruising effect of public controversies, the attacks by mobs, and now an unexpected inferno—all of it combined to force Arthur to limit his largesse for the antislavery movement and retrench just to stay in business. To underscore the misery, it was at this moment that Theodore Weld wrote to the brothers to tell them the fire that had destroyed their business was nothing less than divine punishment.

In a Christmastime letter Weld warned Lewis of "The terrors of God!" and wrote, "My brother I can't resist the conviction that this terrible rebuke is but a single herald sent in advance to announce the coming of a host. The Land is full of blood. It will . . . cover the slain. The groans of slaughtered thousands go up to heaven from the dust where they welter." Weld went on for several paragraphs like this, prophesying "disshevelled hair and streaming tears and lamentation and wailing" and other horrors right out of the pages of Revelation.

But Lewis Tappan had no interest in listening to another jeremiad about the end of the world. He already heard enough of that from Garrison. He needed Weld to think practically about his work on the lecture circuit—not to gnash his teeth and rend his garments, but to imagine how his mission could move forward, and how he could publicize his successful effort to bring abolition to Ohio. Weld could be the greatest inspiration the antislavery movement had yet seen. All they needed was for this most obstinate of Lane Rebels to take advantage of his success.

Weld balked. He didn't want to build himself up as a hero or be celebrated in *The Emancipator* or be lauded to excess—all that smacked of egotism and vanity. His philosophy required that he live humbly, free of vainglory . . . and in the outback like a rustic. It was a subject on which he had seemed to only grow more stubborn in recent months. In one example, after Anne Weston asked him to lecture in Massachusetts, he responded like Daniel Boone: "I am a *Backwoodsman untamed*. My bearish proportions have never been licked into *City Shape*, and are quite too uncombed and shaggy for 'Boston notions' . . . A stump is my throne, my parish my home."

Weld's intransigence frustrated Lewis and reminded him how difficult star orators could be. Who could forget how George Thompson had driven the passion of his audience but couldn't resist casting petty insults at those who offended him? Or how Garrison could fully engage his listeners but inevitably wasted his energy on picking fights with clergymen? And now the silver-tongued Weld had converted much of rural Ohio, and might do even better in the Northeast, but continued to style himself as a wood-chopping bumpkin.

In response, Lewis lashed out in frustration and scolded Weld over his methods. Not only did he cast doubt on his claim to be a frontiersman; he questioned his commitment to racial equality. Lewis had already needled Weld over an episode in which he refused to walk down the street alongside a Black woman, and he now added to the charge a rumor that he had disallowed Black delegates from attending the convention for the antislavery society in Ohio. Did Weld not understand how hypocritical this made him appear, that he preached equality but neglected to practice it in his own life? Lewis and the Anti-Slavery Society had expected better of him than that.

Weld responded with rage—"Really, after so long a time I must forsooth solemnly avow my principles on this subject!! Has it come to this!!" He claimed he would freely walk alongside any Black American who desired it, as long as he didn't put that person in jeopardy by his presence. To do so would be to invite violence, all for the sake of his own "*blustering bravado defiance.*" Furthermore, he had tried to get Black Ohioans to attend the convention, but most were too afraid of being attacked by white mobs to risk it. And how dare Lewis Tappan accuse him of shying away from his oppressed brothers and sisters in Christ! During his time in Cincinnati alone, "If I ate in the City it was at *their* tables. If I slept in the City it was at *their* homes. If I attended parties, it was *theirs—weddings—theirs—funerals—theirs—religious meetings—theirs—*Sabbath schools—Bible classes—theirs."

He charged Lewis and his colleagues with being the real hypocrites for congratulating themselves on their charity to Black Americans *while resolutely keeping their distance from them.* They had apologized for race mixing and temporized over racial equality, all because of their fear of white mobs—which Weld faced every day on his own! He demanded that more be done to aid Black people with better opportunities for education and housing and jobs and all the other aspects of a just existence that were routinely denied them. If Lewis and his friends would not seek racial equality with the proper amount of vigor, abolitionists were no better than colonizers, paying lip service to ridding the world of slavery but offering no useful prescription for doing it.

To twist the knife, in another letter, Weld told Lewis that he would not be attending the upcoming anniversary meeting of the American Anti-Slavery Society to which he had been invited. He condemned the "stateliness and Pomp and Circumstance of an anniversary I loathe in my inmost soul. It seems so like [an] ostentatious display, a mere make believe and mouthing, a sham and show off. It is an element I was never made to move in." And once again he insisted, "I am a Backwoodsman—can grub up stumps and roll logs and burn brush and break green sward. Let me keep about my *own* business and stay in my *own* place."

Lewis did not respond in kind. He knew he had offended Weld and provoked his arrogance, which could be formidable. Years before he had written, "a man like Weld thinks the center of the world is where he acts." But the Anti-Slavery Society needed him on the stump—really needed him. Without him the movement would be most identified with the still-notorious George Thompson and the outbursts of William Lloyd Garrison. Weld *had* to occupy the role of popular evangelist, for there was no one else who could do it with as much skill and confidence. They could not afford to risk his quitting over strategy, or because he felt insulted. So Lewis and Elizur Wright went back to making gentle suggestions and nudging him toward their goals by using flattery and subtle persuasion. This method worked better than nitpicking.

By early 1836 they had prevailed upon Weld to finish his Ohio mission and head to rural Pennsylvania and New York—to break new ground there and grub up stumps or roll logs or do whatever it took to attract people to the movement. Their ultimate goal was to bring Weld to New York City, but they realized it might take time to convince him, so in the meantime they kept him busy in the backwoods closer to home.

In Pennsylvania Weld picked up where he had left off in Ohio. He settled into small towns and waysides, making his case, and found his listeners much more amenable to his ideas than they had been in the Middle West. At Pittsburgh he reaped a new harvest of converts to abolition, and everywhere else the doors opened for him, and people seemed ready to follow where he led them. "Churches competed for the honor of entertaining him, and the daily papers reported his words. Never before had such success attended his efforts."

All of this ground had, of course, been treaded by David Ruggles just two years before, when he was the general agent for *The Emancipator*. Ruggles had spoken on the stump, had preached in churches, had engaged with audiences of all colors, and had overseen the growth of new abolition societies across remote farmland and villages. He had also faced hostility, mobs, and angry encounters in stagecoaches, but still he persisted and seeded the ground for abolition. Because of those groundbreaking efforts, Weld had a much easier time of bringing his message of liberation to the Keystone State, without risking an egg to the face or a brick to the skull. Yet Ruggles rarely got any credit for his earlier efforts—that public acclaim now went to Weld.

After Pennsylvania, Weld traveled to New York, in February 1836, and spent a month in Utica, which had been a bugbear for abolitionists just four months before. Weld boldly chose to deliver sixteen lectures there, mostly in the Presbyterian church where proslavery rioters had heckled and stamped and chased away the men they called fanatics. Weld knew this history and was determined to make Utica into a bastion of antislavery.

He employed all his standard techniques—delivering spellbinding speeches, arguing with naysayers, using the Bible to make his case, and out-talking and out-debating anyone with a mind to challenge him. By the end of the month, he had achieved a great success. In this former hotbed of anti-abolition, the crowds now overflowed for his oratory, with up to 500 people turned away at a time, plus 600 new members joining the rolls of the local antislavery society, and 1,200 voters putting their names on a petition to Congress against the capital's slave trade.

The next stop was Rochester, the homeland of the Burned-Over District and the Second Great Awakening, where just a few years earlier, evangelical religion had flourished. The area still retained a zeal for piety and moral reform, recalling the influence of Charles Grandison Finney, the charismatic preacher and friend to abolition who was also an ally of Weld's. It was the perfect setting for anyone who preached of providence and the extermination of worldly evil. Weld gave his audience what it wanted to hear, speaking to rapt crowds and inspiring up to nine hundred people to join the local antislavery society.

Moving on, Weld encountered greater opposition in the village of Lockport, where the Irish canal workers and mechanics resident to the town interfered with his lectures and tried to keep him from speaking. With his usual persistence, though, he waited out the resistance. By the time he left, 440 locals had signed the constitution of a new antislavery society—membership that would quadruple in only a year's time. Propelled by this hard-fought victory, Weld ventured on to Buffalo and Apulia before targeting Troy for his next conquest.

Emboldened by his recent successes, Weld wrote to Lewis Tappan arguing for the adoption of his backcountry strategy. He had tramped through dozens of waysides and villages, from distant farms to county seats, and his listeners had followed the call. He proclaimed "our Cause is *work*, *work*, boneing down to it" in rural America, and Lewis and the Anti-Slavery Society should "Let the great cities alone." They must sidestep places like New York, Philadelphia, and Boston and allow their efforts to "be poured upon the *country*—the *country*—the villages—and the smaller cities in the interior." How could Lewis even argue now that Weld had chalked up one success after another across the heartland of three different states?

This time, Lewis had no mind to disagree, because his mind was on more important matters than Theodore Weld. The fate of Arthur Tappan and Company had grown bleaker by the month. British lenders who funded the company set increasingly strict terms for their loans, just as many of its clients could no longer afford to pay for the goods they had ordered. More and more businesses in the mercantile and financial quarter failed in New York City, with bankruptcies becoming legion in Lower Manhattan and on Wall Street. Arthur and Lewis needed an infusion of cash desperately to keep the silk shop in business.

Lewis headed to Philadelphia to meet with Nicholas Biddle, the president of the Bank of the United States and one of Andrew Jackson's greatest enemies. Biddle and Jackson had warred over economic policy for years, and the president had finally ended the bank's federal charter by refusing to renew it. This ratcheted up volatility in the American economy, which only made it harder for businessmen like the Tappans to stay solvent.

Lewis crossed paths with Biddle just as he was trying to charter the bank anew under Pennsylvania law. He talked him into loaning the firm $150,000 and returned to New York to announce the happy news to Arthur. But his brother told him the firm needed far more than that to stay afloat for the long term, so they would have to keep scrambling for loans and greatly cut back on expenses. Just as they realized the depth of their problems, they discovered a thief had stolen $3,500 from one of their clerks. Even worse, amid these troubles came disturbing news from Weld, now settled into Troy.

—m—

It seems this city of fifteen thousand souls, located 150 miles up the Hudson from New York City, had put an abrupt end to his victory tour of the state. The reason: the gentlemen of property and standing had been preparing for months in advance of his visit. Proslavery legislators and merchants had spread rumors that he had been chased out of Ohio in disgrace, that he consorted with Black women and advocated race mixing, that he meant to incite slaves to rebellion, and that he looked to shred the fabric of the union. The anti-abolitionists printed handbills and editorials making their false claims and convinced a sizable chunk of the population that a fanatical seditionist was on his way to destroy their little hamlet.

Weld arrived in late May and lectured several times in town, but each time the reaction grew nastier, the threats more intimidating. At some churches he faced brick-throwing mobs that intimidated anyone who dared to attend his lectures. He kept trying to speak in different venues, convinced he could change people's minds, if only they could hear him above the chants and screams. But the mobs refused to listen to a word from him, and they grew more brazen in their violence, more unrestrained by police or the authorities. He had never seen anything like it:

> The Mayor and the City officers were with a few exceptions totally inefficient, and pursued such a course as to embolden rather than to intimidate the mob. One of the City leaders was openly a leader of the mob. Twice a rush was made up the aisles [of a church] to drag me from the pulpit. Stones, pieces of bricks, eggs, cents, sticks, etc. were thrown at me while speaking.

It didn't get any better when Weld tried to exit the church. Several thousand people swarmed around him, hurling stones and trying to pummel him. His friends and allies helped him make it through the gauntlet alive, but the mob shadowed him to his lodgings and kept up their angry threats well into the night. Following the violence, the mayor made sure to blame Weld for causing the commotion through his "dangerous activities."

Weld vowed not to let the mob win. He wrote defiant letters in which he said he would sacrifice himself for the greater good—recalling the rack, the gallows, the stake—like a true Christian martyr. He promised to stand firm against the violence and to stay in town until he won over a fair measure of those who now hunted him for sport.

To Lewis Tappan and Elizur Wright, Weld's behavior in Troy made no sense. Why had he let himself be distracted by such thuggery? Wouldn't it have been easier just to leave the town alone until tempers cooled? Troy was no more important than any other midsized city, and Weld could have accomplished more—at much less risk—by moving on while he still had the strength and energy. Not every town required vanquishing, at least not in one lecture tour.

Wright wrote to Weld to let him know that Troy was much less critical to abolition than a new danger that had arisen in Rhode Island, where the state legislature was considering legislation to cripple the activities of abolitionists under the charge of inciting slaves to insurrection—to placate Southerners offended by the recent mail campaign. Simeon Jocelyn and the Rhode Island Anti-Slavery Society separately wrote letters imploring Weld to visit and convince lawmakers to table their proposal, which could serve as a model for crushing abolition in the North under the power of law. But Weld dug in his heels and promised to visit Rhode Island only if conditions improved in Troy. He was determined that his mission must succeed in the riverside village.

Lewis and others on the executive committee were stunned. How could Weld invest so much time and energy in such a dreadful little place? Garrison entered the fray as well, writing that it was "very unfortunate" that Weld wouldn't be heading to Rhode Island, especially at this perilous time for the movement. After all, he had a good excuse for abandoning the town, and besides, "what is Troy compared to the nation?"

To Weld it had become everything. As the weeks pushed further into June, he tried to speak and get a hearing before the public in Troy, but he was met each time with stamping and hissing and shouting, and a volley of stones and bricks—with the missiles increasing by the day. He had to be escorted to his lodgings nightly by police and faced insults and threats along the way, and according to one report, "not a day passed during which he was not stoned."

At last the mayor demanded he leave the city or face arrest if he didn't. Weld protested, but the mayor could no longer offer him any sanctuary whatsoever and just wanted to be rid of him. And so Weld, who had invested so much labor and publicity into converting this village to the movement, now stood defeated by it. The anti-abolition press played up Weld's failure, marking it as a victory for patriotism over zealotry and madness.

Weld spent a few more weeks lecturing in various small towns, then he gave in and attended a meeting of the executive committee of the American Anti-Slavery Society on July 6. What should have been a moment of triumph became a scene of resignation. Some who met him were surprised at how beleaguered he looked, despite his legend and all the successes he had achieved. Others saw him as "permanently shaken" by the Troy experience, with his vocal cords strained after all his attempts to be heard above the clamor. So at least for a while, "he was forced to stop public speaking lest he lose his voice altogether."

Lewis recognized the opportunity in Weld's humbled state. He and Elizur Wright told him that, from here on, he would work out of the New York City office. Weld had little choice but to agree and to make peace with them. He would step away from the lecture circuit and instead train field agents to spread the message of abolition—for what the movement needed now were hundreds of Theodore Welds traversing the nation, not just one. And he would get to work tracking down legislation about the slave trade and the history of petitioning the government. Because by the summer of 1836, the focus of abolitionists had gone well beyond changing hearts in the countryside. They were now petitioning Congress en masse and battling the growing threat of federal censorship.

★ NINE ★

THE WHOLE ARMOR
OF GOD

On April 14, 1836, James Forten spoke before the Philadelphia Female
Anti-Slavery Society. In his audience were some of his dearest friends
and family members, who had been shaken by all the recent turmoil.
The moment was fraught for the movement—attacked by mobs for three
years, threatened by government with punitive legislation, condemned
by most newspapers, and targeted by vigilantes with death threats. Not
surprisingly, he had come to warn his allies of a long, brutal fight to come.
He reminded them where they stood in the eyes of other Americans:

> You are called fanatics. Well, what if you are? Ought you to
> shrink from this name? God forbid. There is an eloquence
> in such fanaticism, for it whispers hope to the slave; there is
> sanctity in it, for it contains the consecrated spirit of religion

. . . Then flinch not from your high duty; continue to warn
the South of the awful volcano they are recklessly sleeping
over; and bid them remember, too, that the drops of blood
which trickle down the lacerated back of the slave, will not
sink into the barren soil. No, they will rise to the common
God of nature and humanity, and cry aloud for vengeance on
his destroyer's head.

It was as bracing a statement as James Forten had yet made—all the
more because it came not from a radical like David Ruggles or William
Lloyd Garrison, but from a prosperous sailmaker who had much at risk
financially. Still, having seen his son attacked and his neighbors' homes
destroyed, he had come to realize moderation had its limits. So he channeled the word of God and told his audience, "Vengeance is mine, and
I will repay."

The women of the Philadelphia society appreciated that James had
maintained his passion and commitment to the cause, especially in this
moment of crisis, when other abolitionists had faltered. James implored
them not to "surrender your pure and unsullied principles into the hands
of a vicious and perverted portion of the community"—the portion that
wielded immense power, from hostile pressmen and colonizers, all the
way to the president of the United States.

Since the previous winter, Andrew Jackson had demanded Congress
prohibit "under severe penalties" the distribution of abolitionist mail to
the South, using the pretense of preventing insurrections among the
enslaved. He said antislavery literature must be curbed, his postmasters
given the enforcement power of censorship, and prosecutors made to
subdue the fanatics once and for all. While such legislation would abro-
gate the right to free speech and a free press, Jackson and his Democratic
allies saw it as a necessity to preserve the peace of mind of the slaveholders
and the unity of the nation behind them.

The strategy had two pincers: the national government would silence
by law the antislavery activists in their mass mailings, while street-side

ruffians would silence them by violence when they spoke in public forums. The approach had already worked in the South, where censorship had stifled their writings with confiscation and bonfires, as mobs savaged them in person with vigilante squads, kangaroo courts, and whippings and hangings. In reaction to the threat that such tactics might be used nationwide, James Forten said, "the desperate struggle has commenced between *freedom* and *despotism—light* and *darkness.*"

Southern politicians now pressured Northern legislators to not only muzzle the agitators, but to enforce the punishment Southern prosecutors had arranged. County officials passed laws against them, grand juries indicted them in absentia, and state governors demanded their extradition. In one case, the governor of Alabama insisted his New York counterpart hand over one antislavery activist for trial even though the man had never set foot in the state.

Politicians of the North also felt pressure from their constituents. Public meetings in places like Portsmouth, New Haven, and Bangor, "attended by the best people of the town," called for the suppression of abolitionist literature and the suppression of the abolitionists, too, if possible. One mass meeting in Cincinnati featured vehement calls for the protection of Southern interests and a crackdown on antislavery speech—a startling turn in a place where Theodore Weld had made his name preaching toleration and racial justice.

Doing the South's bidding, lawmakers from New England to New York and Pennsylvania began writing measures to clamp down on antislavery speech, and to stymie those who delivered it. After Weld's failure to visit Rhode Island, that state's legislature moved toward labeling abolitionists as public enemies, claiming, in Garrison's words, "we were endeavoring to excite the slaves to insurrection, bloodshed" and other imagined terrors. He quoted the *Richmond Whig* in saying the South "wants the Northern States to PUNISH their incendiary citizens, who are disturbing her peace, and to prevent a repetition of the wrong. The people of the North must go to HANGING these fanatical wretches."

The first step toward controlling them was censorship. The man helming these efforts in the US Senate was the unapologetic white supremacist John Calhoun, newly appointed as the head of a select Senate committee made up mostly of slaveholders like himself. Through his committee, he claimed radical zealots had mounted a warlike campaign against the South, despite international laws that disallowed propaganda against sovereign nations, thus depicting abolitionists as foreign aggressors who waged battles by illicit means.

In his committee's report, Calhoun warned that a conspiracy of these zealots planned to violate the rights of slaveholders and sever them from the sympathies of the nation. Such radicals would create "convulsions that would devastate the country, burst asunder the bonds of the Union, and ingulf, in a sea of blood, the institutions of the country." But his bill would remedy the danger, because "by its passage the evil would be cured."

The bill shot holes through the First Amendment and, at a time when the US Supreme Court hadn't struck down a federal law since 1803, the censorship law would likely survive judicial review and allow politicians to control the speech of abolitionists at every level. But in a curious twist, Calhoun didn't trust the federal government or his nemesis, Andrew Jackson, to decide how they would be targeted by the law. If the president had that power, Calhoun worried he might use it against the sovereign interests of the South. So instead, his bill would make the federal government the enforcer of local censorship laws, with severe penalties for postmasters who didn't comply with them.

Abolitionists worried the new censorship codes, once established, might be expanded beyond slavery to include topics like racial equality, religious unorthodoxy, and the legitimacy of politicians' actions. Garrison would later eviscerate the legislation in *The Liberator*, shocked at how it stood logic on its head and made victims out of the worst villains. He said the ability to shut the mouths of abolitionists was only the first step toward the nation curbing the rights of anyone who spoke out against oppression—and this censorship would set a precedent to crush the movement by law, just as the mobs had tried to do by force.

But Calhoun had no patience for the argument of his enemies, and certainly not for the likes of Garrison. He pushed his censorship bill through his committee and set up votes in the Senate to pass the measure, with hopes of eventually putting President Jackson's signature on it. Calhoun's bill faced three consecutive tie votes, until Martin Van Buren finally broke the tie as vice president—part of his strategy to be elected president in November with the help of slaveholders, and to disprove any rumors that he had once been friendly to abolitionists.

Such were the conditions in America when James Forten gave his speech to the activists in Philadelphia. Whatever faith he had in the nation's leaders to do the right thing—to uphold virtue and the promise of revolutionary change for all citizens—he saw dissipating in a fog of moral blindness.

> The recent scenes in Congress are a specimen of the evil times we live in, the corrupted atmosphere we breathe. There, behold the Constitution of the United States . . . rights which should be the pride and boast of a republic, are trampled under foot, scoffed at by statesmen and senators, and the gag and Lynch law held up as a model of the glorious march of *Virtue*, *Liberty*, and *Independence*.

James's audience knew intimately of these issues, because they had spent months fighting Washington—not just in battling the proposed censorship law, but in trying to force the federal government to acknowledge its role in the slave trade. At the heart of this campaign was his daughter Sarah.

As one of the managers of the Philadelphia society, Sarah Forten had been working for months to help draft and circulate petitions that denounced slavery in the District of Columbia. She had met women leaders throughout her state, as well as new friends across the region. One of them was Elizabeth Whittier (sister of the poet John), a member of the Boston Female Anti-Slavery Society who had worked on some of that group's most important campaigns. Unfortunately, Elizabeth often found herself confined to sick bed, but she valued Sarah as a wise and thoughtful correspondent. As she wrote in her journal, "Oh! I know I should love that girl—wonder if I shall ever see her."

Through Elizabeth, Sarah made valuable contacts and learned new strategies for advancing the movement. Black and white women worked together in the Boston society, just as they did in Philadelphia, and Sarah found much to admire about them. They had devised many of the strategies now used by women's groups across the region: house-to-house canvassing, developing a precinct system to distribute petitions, and building a network to reach an entire state. As one of their reports said, "Let us know no rest till we have done our utmost to convince the mind, and to obtain the testimony of every woman, in every town, in every county of our Commonwealth."

For their efforts the Bostonians received the usual mockery and insults, and threats to finish the violent work begun by the mob outside their headquarters in October. In answer they wrote, "We shall never, therefore, be intimidated by the threats of the violent, or impeded by the scoffs of those who think it beneath them to raise up the bowed down . . . We are accused of going too fast; of feeling too deeply. Aye!"

Elizabeth had seen some of the worst violence in person. In August 1835, she watched a mob descend upon Samuel May in Haverhill. She took his hand and escorted him through the gauntlet, in hopes that the crowd wouldn't attack a woman—a risky but successful gambit. She had also been present during the October riot and had seen the crowd invading their building, tearing down their sign, and accosting Garrison before nearly hanging him. The assault had left a deep mark on Elizabeth as she saw the workings of hatred on the minds of merchants and common people, and the brutality that inevitably followed.

Sarah discussed the riot with Elizabeth, shocked that she and Garrison could have faced such abuse. With forty other abolitionists, Sarah put her name on a resolution that praised him for his "moral courage and devotion to the cause of the oppressed colored American . . . we tender him our approbation of his services, and our heartfelt sympathy for his sufferings." But privately she was more critical.

She told Elizabeth how disappointed she was that Garrison had fled Boston after the tumult, "as the enemies of our cause will have room to accuse him of cowardice—I woman as I am—would never yield an inch in the prosecution of what I considered my duty." Sarah had read all his paeans to martyrdom and wondered why he had escaped the city, instead of continuing to stand up to his tormentors. By contrast, her brother Thomas had been beaten on the street by a criminal gang, the mob had tried to burst into their home, and her father had endured vile threats and abuse. But still they had never fled, remaining in their city even as it burned around them.

The last two years had been a trying time for Sarah, and not only because of the rash of violence around her. When she began her work in abolition, she wrote poems that gave voice to enslaved people who had been silenced in popular culture, and to the ghosts of past horrors that haunted the nation. But she now had less time for her poetry and had to devote her efforts to writing for the Philadelphia society—working with other authors to change public beliefs about emancipation, and to counter the corrosive spleen printed in the daily newspapers.

She and her colleagues had penned an *Address to the Women of Pennsylvania*, which spelled out the aims of the petition campaign and called out Northerners for profiting from slavery. It said the prisons in the nation's capital that held slaves "are built with *Northern*, as well as with Southern money," and even in Philadelphia "there is a regularly organized system of kidnapping" to put Black people into the clutches of slave traders. The *Address* said that trade in DC was a moral obscenity, and "the centre of our American republic is now a slave market, presenting to the whole world the disgusting anomaly of the seat of government of a proud republic being the very heart of the most horrible system of abject slavery the world ever knew."

She and the other authors asked women to venture out of their sphere, and to challenge the norms of how they should act—"is it a time for *us* to keep silence? Is it a time for *woman* to shrink from her duty as a citizen of the United States?" The abolition of slavery required mass action despite the risk, and any Christian woman with a conscience had no other choice than to act: "Let *us* then go up, year after year, and year after year, to our proud Capitol with the faith of an Esther . . . to break the fetters which bind 7,000 of the inhabitants of the District of Columbia." For any readers inspired by these words, the *Address* also included a sample petition that provided the text they could use when soliciting signatures for the upcoming campaign.

Sarah's allies in Philadelphia worked closely with Bostonians like Lydia Child and Maria Chapman to drive the effort across the region. Their work was matched by other abolition groups that contributed their labor and financial support, among them the American Anti-Slavery Society, which also relied on women petitioners, in a network of five hundred abolition societies that would grow to around a hundred thousand members.

Still, even within such a massive organization, women had to gather the signatures one by one. They went door to door, home to home, farm to farm, ranging from places that gave support and comfort to abolitionists, to streets where mobs had recently rampaged. They visited "stores, banks, and barber shops . . . at hustings, at church fairs, at log-rollings and camp-meetings." They reached planters and mechanics, shopkeepers and clerks, wagoners and tradesmen. Sometimes they met with success, sometimes hostility. But their creed remained "Let no frown deter, no repulses baffle. Explain, discuss, argue, persuade."

Sometimes men snapped at petitioners, saying they had no right to engage in public affairs, or accusing them of advocating sedition, or making other claims that took time and patience to answer. A later report from a women's antislavery convention called the job "weary work. We have deeply felt the difficulties and trials that attend it. We know how painful it is to endure the scornful gaze, or rude repulses of strangers," but persistence was essential, to endure in the face of obstacles. Many canvassers soon realized they weren't only confronting slavery, but "we may also overthrow the injurious prejudices relative to the real duties and responsibilities of women."

The burden of meeting opposition didn't always fall upon experienced campaigners who could respond with a verse from the Bible or a quick rejoinder. Some of the canvassers were only in their teens, with no experience navigating the wider world, and they found that world alien and intimidating. In a few cases, girls as young as eleven went out into the field to ask strangers for their signatures, often without the aid of a parent for support. Among these adolescents was the obscure sixteen-year-old daughter of a cotton mill manager in Battenville, New York, who would later become more widely known as Susan B. Anthony.

No matter what their age, the petitioners had to memorize a script and be able to answer questions about slavery and why it was disallowed by Scripture. The Philadelphians focused on the slave trade in Washington, DC, but other societies acted against human bondage in territories across the West, or interstate slave commerce, or admitting Texas and Florida to the Union as slave states. The boldest petitions accused slaveholders of being rapists and sexually torturing Black women. They said such actions "fill us with horror" as predatory plantation owners "sundered all the sacred ties of domestic life . . . for the gratification of avarice."

Regardless of its content, each petition was created with one signature at a time, each scrawl the product of minutes of persuasion or hours of argument. With their effort in soliciting these names, girls and women across the North achieved momentum for the cause. New antislavery societies emerged and drafted their own petitions that spoke to local conditions, and they inspired their neighbors to spread the word and solicit more signatures, until those signatures filled up papers with hundreds of names, and those hundreds became thousands, until—

The names found their way to Congress.

Assisting the abolition groups, Pennsylvania senator Samuel McKean and representative James Harper presented the petitions to Congress in early 1836. This was no moment of celebration, however, for the politicians worried about the effect they might have on their colleagues.

McKean thought the campaign might incite such a baleful reaction it would turn people against abolition, which he otherwise supported. And both knew how defensive congressmen could be when questioned about their role in protecting slavery.

Their guess was right. Southern politicians immediately attacked the women's societies for hassling them about a topic they felt to be a settled matter. They called the women "old maids" whose chatter was only good for putting men to sleep, and claimed the movement was propped up by "hoydenish women, effeminate men, and uppity blacks." Future president John Tyler was particularly incensed, writing that due to the petition campaign, "woman is to be made the instrument of destroying our political paradise . . . She is to be converted into a fiend to rejoice over the conflagration of our dwellings, and the murder of our people." Others added to the charge by calling petitioners harlots or potential murderers. New York representative Francis Granger even said, "Woman in the parlor, woman in her proper sphere, is the ornament and comfort of man; but out of the parlor, out of her sphere, if there is a devil on earth, when she is a devil, woman is a devil incarnate!"

The contempt didn't come only from men. Proslavery women and "moderates" indifferent to abolition piled on women petitioners with charges like those of the Southerners. Author and educator Catharine Beecher proved to be as much a foe of immediate abolition as her preacher father, Lyman, Garrison's longtime adversary. She decried the campaign for thrusting women into the realm of politics and said it would worsen slavery by making slaveholders defend it more vigorously. Women participating in the petition drive might even appear "obtrusive, indecorous, and unwise" and would "increase, rather than diminish the evil which it is wished to remove."

—✳—

Garrison, of course, enthusiastically supported women's activism and the mass petition drive and announced his full-throated support in

The Liberator. It was one bright spot for him amid the bad news of recent months. He had nearly been hanged the previous October, forced to flee to Connecticut, and now suffered from a "scrofulous affection" throughout his body and a leg wound that put him in constant pain, after he tried to leap from a garden wall and ended up with a deep gash that wouldn't heal. Along with these troubles, he was distracted by the birth of his first child in February, perpetually stressed for money, and still waging battles with his many foes in print. But instead of redoubling his efforts, as he had in previous years, he chose this moment to withdraw from public view. Despite the entreaties of those in the American Anti-Slavery Society that he should take a more active role at a critical time for the movement, he mostly stayed home, tried to heal his mind and body, and spent his time writing letters—for nine months, until the end of September.

He occasionally went to Providence to drum up resistance to the Rhode Island legislature's plan to curb antislavery speech. That city was also a place where he acquired medicine for the "catarrh in the head almost entirely destroying the sense of smell!" and other maladies. He found a doctor to prescribe a bottled medicine "to benefit my blood" and "a white powder to take in pinches as snuff," and he would also "snuffle up a red liquid, to cleanse my head." While he was taking the mysterious potions, he planned to meet a young Quaker who wanted to meet him in person.

That Quaker was Angelina Grimké, the woman who had written him a letter in praise of martyrdom just before he was almost martyred. Her note had thrilled him so much that he published it in *The Liberator*, and it had since been published and republished in abolition journals and the *New York Evangelist* newspaper. Some called her "the new light of the movement," who had done more in a single letter to drum up enthusiasm than years of effort by more well-known figures. However, she had never meant the letter for public reading, fearing it would make her a target of criticism. For the woman Garrison was about to meet wasn't just an abolitionist—she was a daughter of South Carolina, born to a family of slaveholders.

The Grimkés were upper crust in the low country, judges and law-yers who owned a Charleston estate with a household of enslaved people. Even at a young age, Angelina and her sister Sarah reacted with horror to their mother's brutal treatment of slaves and the violent condi-tions African Americans suffered in the region. The sisters became alienated from the plantation world around them. The younger Ange-lina drifted from the family's Episcopalian beliefs—even refusing confirmation at thirteen—until, like her sister, she became a Quaker. Also like her sister, she left for Philadelphia once she came of age and rejected her family's slave-owning legacy. Once she departed Charleston, she never saw the city or her mother again.

Sarah and Angelina became committed abolitionists, but they found that Philadelphia, despite its reputation for radicalism, also fueled some of the most vicious white backlash in the North. Most of its churches resisted the call to emancipation, including their own Society of Friends. The Quaker hierarchy, in fact, tried to suppress discussion of slavery altogether, and many meetinghouses maintained the Negro pew and social segregation. Sarah and Angelina disputed these practices but were met with resistance by the church elders, including white women leaders who refused to discuss it. In response the sisters took to sitting among Black members of their church whenever they could.

Lucretia Mott soon provided a way for them to remain loyal to the faith while rejecting the backward views of the hierarchy. She guided them toward a better understanding of God and faith and justice and likely encouraged them to join the Philadelphia Female Anti-Slavery Society. After they became members, they met Black women leaders of the group who gave them a much wider perspective on race and inequality—figures like Grace and Sarah Douglass, and Charlotte Forten and her daughters Harriet, Margaretta, and, of course, Sarah. Galvanizing them further was the spring 1835 visit of George Thompson, when the crowds were so dense and eager to hear his orations, a church nearly collapsed under their weight.

Angelina threw herself into the work of the Philadelphia society. She worked on many of its projects and assisted in the preparation of its petitions to Congress and reached out to other abolitionists with her ideas. All this activity led to the publication of her letter to Garrison, and the swell of fame that she now labored under.

By early 1836 the Quaker elite pushed back against her display of political activism, and her accusations about churchmen being in league with slaveholders. The father of her former fiancée erupted in fury and brandished the copy of *The Liberator* that contained her letter. He and other church elders demanded she retract her statement and beg forgiveness for her transgressions. The conflict made her physically ill, plagued by guilt from "the extreme pain of extravagant praise to be held up as a saint in a public newspaper before thousands of people when I felt I was the chief of sinners . . . the name of Grimké associated with that of the despised Garrison . . . I cannot describe the anguish of my soul." Despite her torment, though, she refused to relent or ask for a retraction of her letter.

The negative reaction among church elders put her at a distance from other Quakers and seemed to quash any chance she might have had of becoming a minister in the church like Lucretia Mott. Worse, the controversies gave her few options for earning income after rejecting the slavery-tainted wealth of her family. Her friends sent her a small amount of money to live on every month, but she remained mired in poverty, with scant hopes of finding a teaching job or any decent work and feeling increasingly distant from her Philadelphia home. By contrast, it was a joyful release to visit a place like Rhode Island, which was less hierarchical, less segregated, and more welcoming than the City of Brotherly Love.

Garrison was delighted to finally cross paths with Angelina in Providence, feeling some pride in helping launch the career of the woman who had demanded he "put on the whole armor of God" in service of the cause. He wrote, "it was an hour that went pleasantly, profitably, rapidly." She revealed to him her current activities in the free produce movement, boycotting slave-grown produce and trying to encourage farmers and businessmen to support crops like cotton being grown with unforced labor. She had other plans as well, but she kept quiet about what would become her most important project yet: writing a pamphlet addressing the white women of the South, calling on them to accept responsibility for their role in slavery and reject it completely. While she would not be the first to make such an address (Black writers like Maria Stewart and David Ruggles had said the same thing years before), she would be the first product of a white plantation family to make the argument—and to direct it at her old friends and relatives.

—m—

While Angelina prepared her next salvo against human bondage, her peers in Philadelphia were sending boxes of signed papers on the subject to Congress. As this tide of petitions rolled in, Southern politicians and the press became ever more offended by them. South Carolina representative James Hammond—the same man who said abolitionists should be punished with *"terror—death"*—was the first to demand Congress reject any more petitions on slavery, since they would "subvert the institutions of the South . . . and dissolve in blood the bonds of this confederacy." He and his colleagues argued for tabling the petitions, instead of actually reading them or referring them to a committee. While in previous years, Americans had submitted petitions on banking, Indian policy, currency, and tariffs, those mailings had been intermittent. But slavery as a topic of debate would not go away—the activists had ensured that with their flood of petitions. So the members of Congress ensured they would not read them.

John Calhoun became as committed to stopping the petitions from abolitionists as he was to censoring their mail. He and his fellow South Carolina senator, William Preston, denounced the surge of unwanted papers, with Preston claiming they had made the "bosom of society heave with new and violent emotions." Many Northern politicians agreed with the South Carolinians that the zealots had once again become a nuisance and prevented them from exercising their rightful duties. There were, however, a few notable exceptions. One of them was John Quincy Adams, the former president, who had lost reelection to Andrew Jackson in 1828, and had since rebuilt his career as a Massachusetts representative. Adams called the attempt to stifle the mailings a "direct violation of the constitution of the United States, the rules of this House, and the rights of my constituents." It wouldn't be the last word he said on the subject.

However, another representative held more sway. Charles Pinckney, from South Carolina, worked out a compromise, with the support of Martin Van Buren, to require all petitions about slavery to be tabled without any further action. Congressmen on one key committee supported the idea, saying that abolitionists "threaten to bring the citizens of the different states into collision, and to overthrow the whole system of civil society itself." Their verdict against the petitions was severe: the House would not read them, discuss them, or refer them to committees. It was as if they didn't exist. The measure passed overwhelmingly, and the "gag law" was tied in place.

Yet while the congressmen had freed their desks from an onslaught of paper, they did not make the debate over slavery go away. Instead, the gag law became a source of controversy. Although the rule did not apply in the Senate, its presence in the House made it seem that Congress had rejected any discussion of slavery—and thus was deaf to the pleas of citizens. Women in the Philadelphia Female Anti-Slavery Society and other groups used the gag law as a recruitment tool, a rallying cry against politicians' attempts to curb abolitionists' freedom to petition, just as they tried to curb their freedom of speech. In reaction, more women joined the antislavery societies to canvass for the cause, those societies gathered more names to send to Congress, and Congress rejected ever more of their petitions.

But even as Calhoun's colleagues in the House easily passed the gag law, the South Carolina senator met with more resistance over his censorship law. Through agitation in the press and on the streets, abolitionists had aroused enough concern over the infringement on Americans' constitutional liberties that even their adversaries began to share their worries. The *Evening Post* was one of the first to break from the orthodoxy of the New York press, warning that if the government could decide what kind of speech was safe or dangerous, then "farewell, a long farewell to our freedom." A few other major papers agreed with the *Evening Post*, making sure to pair their praise for constitutional freedoms with bitter denunciations of fanatics, zealots, subversives, and the like.

The timing was fortuitous, because just as the question of censorship came to a head in Congress, debates in Northern legislatures were heating up over whether to control the speech of abolitionists or otherwise punish them for their agitation. Garrison's allies were especially vigorous in Massachusetts, trying to keep the legislature from passing laws against them. Committee hearings broke down into shouting matches between politicians and witnesses, insults flew back and forth, and chaos marked the debate at its fiercest moments. Samuel May sarcastically remarked, "The Constitution secures to us the freedom of speech, but we cannot enjoy the immunities of the Constitution as citizens, unless we shut our mouths!"

Yet despite their frustrations, abolitionists swayed the debate just enough to maintain their liberties. Leaders of Massachusetts and New York and other Northern states took pains to condemn antislavery activists, but they did not outlaw their speech or enact penalties against them. By the beginning of summer, attempts to silence them had faltered in one Northern state after another, from Maine to Pennsylvania. In a letter, Garrison recited a roll call of failed attempts to muzzle his friends and allies, feeling especially proud that the politicians of Rhode Island had tabled their measures to clamp down on speech. Garrison could only wonder, "What will the South say now?"

On June 8, John Calhoun's censorship bill failed in the Senate by six votes. Aside from the grasping attempts of Martin Van Buren to curry favor with the South, a diminishing number of New Yorkers and Pennsylvanians felt comfortable openly doing the bidding of plantation bosses. Younger politicians saw the danger of their interference in state politics much more clearly than the old guard did. One of them, future governor

William Seward, wrote in a letter that "no honorable, or high-minded, or reputable man, in the North, even in the very excitement of mass meetings, will lend his sanction to the monstrous claims of the South."

Surprisingly, in just a few months, the public mood had shifted so dramatically that in July both houses of Congress passed a bill reorganizing the post office that included a measure preventing any postmaster from interfering with, hampering, or censoring the mail, regardless of subject matter. Violators would be subject to a $500 fine and up to six months in jail. However, though the law was a blow against censorship, it was less of a triumph than it seemed. Andrew Jackson may have signed the bill, but he refused to enforce it. So abolitionists had the freedom by law to send anything they might wish, but Southern postmasters had the freedom in practice to destroy those mailings. To their frustration, abolitionists learned once again that laws were no good unless they were enforced, and could end up as dead as the paper they were printed on.

—⁊⁊—

One activist, however, thought she might be able to bypass the Southern blockade. Angelina Grimké felt confident she could reach an audience in her former home state of South Carolina and other parts of the South, where the white women might pay more attention to the words of a native daughter than a meddling Northerner.

At the beginning of August, she sent her *Appeal to the Christian Women of the South* to Elizur Wright at the American Anti-Slavery Society, with hopes he would help get it published. Wright was delighted by her thirty-six-page pamphlet, writing that it had made him tear up, and "Oh that it could be rained down into every parlor in our land." He agreed that the words of someone from the slave empire would carry more weight than those of a Northern author, male or female.

In the *Appeal*, Angelina spoke bluntly to her readers, reminding them how much they had profited by forced labor, even though many claimed to be powerless over its existence. "I know you do not make the laws, but

I also know that *you are the wives and mothers, the sisters and daughters, of those who do*; and if you really suppose that *you* can do nothing to overthrow slavery, you are greatly mistaken." For a start, her readers could liberate any people in bondage their families owned, and provide them with education and opportunity, and learn more about the cruelties of slavery, speak out against it, and pray for its extermination. She implored her audience to imagine what it would be like to be enchained, treated as property rather than a child of God: "Are you willing to enslave *your* children? You start back with horror and indignation at such a question. But why, if slavery is *no wrong* to those upon whom it is imposed?"

She knew her way around the Bible and quoted liberally from it in making her case, drawing parallels between Black slaves and the Jews of Exodus, and emphasizing how Scripture did not allow human bondage, but provided a reason to reject it. Then she turned to the North and described how businessmen of the region had made their profits from Southern forced labor, how the white public stood "dreadfully afraid of Amalgamation," and how they had fought against fair treatment in education and jobs for their Black neighbors. "Prejudice against colour is the most powerful enemy we have to fight with at the North."

She made no apologies for being a religious activist, knowing people would see her as a zealot. But she had no choice. She would violate the law to help the enslaved, even if it meant going to jail. "If a law commands me to *sin, I will break it*; if it calls me to *suffer*, I will take its course unresistingly. The doctrine of blind obedience and unqualified submission to *any human* power, whether civil or ecclesiastical, is the doctrine of despotism, and ought to have no place among Republicans and Christians." Thus she advocated not just sacrifice, but civil disobedience against tyranny—a dozen years before Thoreau said the same thing.

Needless to say, the reaction to Angelina's pamphlet in the white South was not favorable. The newly emboldened postmasters of the Jackson administration stripped copies of the book from the mail stream, and when some copies did arrive in Charleston, the townsfolk burned them. The pamphlet was also censored in cities from New Orleans to

Richmond, even though the new postal law forbade such a practice. And it was all done with the support and encouragement of the Southern public, women as well as men. For in their eyes, Angelina had given up her claim to be a daughter of the South; she was now a Yankee. And as such, the mayor of Charleston said she was forbidden to enter the city—and if she ever tried, she would be arrested and sent on the first boat back to the North. The pamphlet also worsened the rift with her family members, who continued to profit by slavery and live in comfort, while Angelina maintained her principles and lived in poverty, seven hundred miles away.

Despite the rejection by its intended audience, Angelina's *Appeal* did produce a galvanic reaction in the North. Here, the pamphlet found its way into the salons and parlors of middle-class women and their literary and sewing circles, and it became essential reading among all abolitionists. Angelina provided marching orders for a crusade against not just slavery but racial inequality as a whole, and she put women at the center of the fight. "Have not *women* stood up in all the dignity and strength of moral courage to be the leaders of the people, and to bear a faithful testimony for the truth whenever the providence of God has called them to do so?"

Angelina's pamphlet also found its way into the hands of Sarah Forten, who couldn't have been happier to see that one of her friends in the Philadelphia society had achieved such renown. With her background of wealth and privilege, Angelina seemed to understand more about the lies and moral compromises white people lived by, and Black people suffered under, than most of her peers. Sarah wrote to Elizabeth Whittier that the pamphlet was "an admirable work . . . full of holy zeal—powerful reasoning—and affectionate remonstrance."

Recognizing the powerful effect this former Southerner could have on the minds of Northern women, Sarah agreed with Elizur Wright's plan to arrange a lecture tour for Angelina and personally endorsed it. She and her mother, Charlotte, as managers of the Philadelphia society, signed a certificate of recommendation so Angelina could hit the speaking circuit and give voice to all the stirring things she had written. They hoped that this once-obscure Quaker from Charleston might be introduced into the homes of women throughout the North—and that their movement would finally emerge from its defensive crouch after years of attacks, and mount its greatest assault yet against the juggernaut of slavery.

★ TEN ★

STAGGER THEM GREATLY

Theodore Weld was exhausted. It was his third day in transit from New York City, and he found himself in a place called Hollidaysburg, along the ridge of the Allegheny Mountains in Pennsylvania. He had come by railcar to Columbia, arriving at 2:00 A.M., and boarded a canal boat for a leisurely—too slow—ride across central Pennsylvania, only to be dropped here in this village, where he'd have to take a railcar to Johnstown then another canal trip to his destination. He would miss the Sabbath in Pittsburgh, and he was already behind in his schedule, with people to meet, speeches to be given, and funds to be raised. He also had to write letters to Lewis Tappan and others explaining how he was spending his time and what good works he had accomplished. His body should have given out long before, but still his mind kept working, churning, deliberating, and of course he spoke constantly to all who would listen.

This was not the ideal way to raise an army to take down slavery. But he had no choice; this was the course he had set for himself, beginning in the summer of 1836, and now it was October and he had to finish his plan. He had to find a collection of young men in training for the ministry who would volunteer to go into training as lecturer–field-agent–revivalists for the American Anti-Slavery Society. Weld would teach them, and over the next year, they would have to give speeches and face down mobs and transform souls and endure abuse and do all the things the followers of Jesus had once done in the ancient world. Just as those worthy men had impassioned their listeners to accept Christ as their savior and toppled the pagan religion of the Roman empire, Weld wanted his men to do the same thing against the slave empire. As Luke 10:1–3 put it, "the Lord appointed other seventy also, and sent them two and two before his face into every city and place, whither he himself would come . . . Behold, I send you forth as lambs among wolves." Weld was in search of new, modern lambs—which he called "The Seventy."

He traveled through the backcountry with Henry Stanton and John Whittier, visiting seminaries and colleges in New York, Ohio, and New England. To draw attention and potential converts, Weld lectured on racial injustice and oppression, holding sway over his listeners and rekindling the missionary fire that had ignited his reputation. He offered appeals to the heart and the spirit, speeches and conversations and personal transformations . . . one by one, town by town, county by county. Elizabeth Whitter watched him in action in Boston, stunned by this "thunderer of the West" who showed a "God like and expanded soul" in his orations, while James Thome of the Anti-Slavery Society witnessed the mesmerizing effect he had over his audience, "to *stagger them greatly* in their new notions."

Weld had such charisma that he seemed to some almost like a messiah in his own right, as he took his message into quarters both friendly and hostile. Once, on a canal boat, Weld faced off against colonizers and slaveholders from Alabama, New Orleans, Vicksburg, and St. Louis—the same kind of men who had incited mobs in Northern cities. However, it wasn't long before he forced them to withdraw from the debate, overwhelmed by the force of his argument. As Weld humbly put it, "The Lord sent confusion into their councils and discomfiture into their ranks."

Yet his impassioned rhetoric and brilliant performances came at a cost. His energies flagged, and his health suffered, with his voice weakening as the four-month trip dragged on across an array of towns and villages separated by long stretches of canals and railways and turnpikes and country lanes. Most of the time, he struggled to find enough young men who were suited to work for the cause. Some had full hearts and noble intentions but lacked any experience with the wider world. Others had the proper experience but no cash on hand. Weld was reduced to writing to Lewis Tappan asking him to put as little as $5 in the pockets of the men he had chosen, because "Most of them are entirely out of money and cannot get to their fields of labor without five to fifteen dollars apiece." Weld promised to pay back the total—one hundred dollars—when he returned to New York.

In response, Elizur Wright wrote to Weld telling him that a credit squeeze had hampered the Tappans' ability to fund his mission. While they had once showered thousands of dollars on worthy causes, now a fraction of that seemed too much. "The Wall Street fever is terrible, and has siezed [*sic*] some of our committee. A. Tappan especially was afraid to go ahead any more till he could see where the funds were to come from." In short, there would be no money until the next society meeting at the earliest, and until then Weld would have to "*drive* on until you hear from us."

This just added to Weld's dilemma. He was now in Oberlin, Ohio, his small but growing collection of field agents was desperate for money, and the Tappans had chosen the worst possible time to be tightfisted. In just weeks Weld would be expected to bring all his young men to New York City for the training sessions, and he would have to convince them to work through their penury in hopes of . . . what? Greater penury?

And then, piled upon his other duties for the Anti-Slavery Society, Weld had to moderate an ugly little dispute between the Tappans and the famed revivalist who ran Oberlin College, Charles Grandison Finney. It seems Finney had begun separating Black and white students at Oberlin and was doing the same in church services at Chatham Street Chapel by insisting on a Negro pew for Black parishioners. Lewis became particularly incensed by such practices, and now Weld had to poll the students on their feelings and convince Finney that segregation was contrary to God's plan—and Finney was an abolitionist, no less!

There was simply no time for Weld to solve all these problems. They had mounted and multiplied in his absence, and the scant few weeks he had in Ohio would not be enough time for him to resolve them. And then there was Cincinnati.

Here, in this town where Weld had made his reputation as a rebel from the nearby Lane Seminary, he had changed the heart of the Kentucky slaveholder James Birney, who published a pro-colonization newspaper called *African Repository*. With Weld's encouragement, Birney freed his bondsmen, directed his money and labor toward abolition, and founded *The Philanthropist*, a journal demanding the immediate, unconditional end of slavery. It became the official paper of the Ohio Anti-Slavery Society, with a circulation of 1,700 subscribers.

Birney proved to be a tenacious publisher, despite being threatened in mass meetings and shouted down by hooligans. Over the summer, a mob broke into a building housing his news office and damaged some of the equipment, and weeks later, they destroyed the office and dragged his printing press through the streets and tossed it into the Ohio River. Afterward the rioters went hunting for Birney carrying tar and feathers, invading the houses of his friends and family members demanding information on his whereabouts. But Birney went into hiding, so the mob redirected its hatred to the Black community—causing a riot that made national headlines.

Led by gentlemen of property and standing, they surged into the part of town known as The Swamp and invaded brothels rumored to host liaisons between Black and white customers. They dragged out those they found inside and beat them in the street, also smashing and vandalizing the buildings. From there they moved on to a half-dozen homes owned by Black citizens, wrecking the furniture, shooting at the owners, and menacing them for hours. In the aftermath, local officials tried to pin blame for the violence on its victims, and they passed a resolution claiming "the recent outrages were caused by the establishment of the abolition press."

The terrible fallout from the violence continued for some time afterward, and to his alarm Weld received letters from allies warning of "bloodthirsty men—mayor and chief men at their head" who had allowed the rampage to take place. "Dangers are thickening about them and dangers are coming like a whirlwind." Aware of just how vulnerable his African American friends were, Weld wrote to them, imploring them to keep their distance from meetings of white abolitionists, lest they be further attacked by the mob. This made for a depressing coda, to realize that despite his years of effort to promote racial integration and understanding, all that work could burn down in a single evening, at the hands of men whose behavior only grew more brazen and bestial.

Weld finished his journey across the Middle West and Northeast in November, having gathered far fewer than the seventy men he had imagined. The total came to thirty-nine, and the Anti-Slavery Society promptly sent them to New York, where they could be instructed in the proper ways of abolition as Weld understood them—making haste since the year 1837 would be the busiest yet, with a vigorous schedule of fundraising, petitioning, lecturing, and evangelizing. To provide the proper inspiration for the trainees, the guest speakers included Charles Stuart, an English activist known as the less incendiary version of George Thompson; Weld's fellow Lane Rebel Henry Stanton; Arthur and Lewis Tappan; and Beriah Green from Utica. But of course most of the young men were here for the sake of Weld, and he did not disappoint.

Blasting out what remained of his ragged voice, Weld demanded they devote their lives in service to God under the banner of antislavery, and sacrifice themselves if needed. He told them about the evils of slavery, the glories of emancipation, the lies of the colonizers, the nature of the Southern plantation system, the prospect of racial equality and justice, and the need to compensate slaves for the sins of their masters. Even though he struggled with a cold, Weld oversaw most of the thrice-daily sessions, speaking continually and working to prepare and arrange the next day's events until two or three in the morning. Attending the event, William Lloyd Garrison stood in awe of his talents, writing, "Weld was the central luminary, around which they all revolved." Another observer wrote, "He was the master spirit, the principal speaker in that assembly. His labors were intense . . . Human nature could not endure it." Nor could the human larynx. By the end of the training sessions, Weld could not talk above a whisper. It would be the last time he ever spoke at length in a public forum.

Lewis Tappan watched the dissipation of Weld's talents with concern. He had long worried that the great orator was working himself to death, and now he saw it in person. How many times had the executive committee warned him about this? Last year, after an exhausting stretch for Weld on the stump, Elizur Wright had written to him, "How can you stand *fourteen such* lectures as you give in succession? Remember that the hopes of millions, under God, hang on you, and therefore economise your strength." But the hopes of millions were not Weld's concern at the moment, only the training of thirty-nine young men, and by inspiring them to new heights, he also sacrificed his own ability. The worst part was that no gentlemen mobsters had destroyed Weld's speaking career—only Weld himself.

Weld's ill health meant that his disciples—those green, dewy-eyed seminarians—would now have to carry the torch of abolition for their master. And that torch would have to light the way for the entire Anti-Slavery Society, whose leaders had recently decided, under pressure from Weld, to focus their energies on evangelizing in the hinterlands . . . exactly what Lewis had fought against for months. To support them, Lewis would have to collect funds from state affiliates, most of whom wanted to keep their money to themselves. But the society could not afford to let any dollar go uncollected, even if Lewis had to ride herd over them to get it.

Lewis felt the urgency of the situation. The pressures were great within the organization—to spend, to fundraise, to uplift, to convert, to deliver—yet it always teetered on the edge of disaster. The greatest peril was financial, as Weld had discovered when he asked for money to put in the pockets of his field agents, and the situation had hardly improved since then. It was now an open question whether the Tappans could continue funding the group at all.

Earlier in the year, he and Arthur had constructed a new building for their shop, erected in Maine marble like the old structure, with sturdy iron shutters to resist mobs and vandals. They proclaimed their confidence in the mercantile trade rebounding and made a show to convince their clients that their business stood on firm ground. But in private Arthur was using whatever resources he could to stay afloat, selling his silken goods for cash in lieu of credit and trying to find new customers to make up for those lost in boycotts. Still, he could only do so much, as the economic policies of the Jackson administration had begun to harm the entire economy.

Conditions had become so volatile in the financial world that waves of farmers and merchants defaulted on their debts, their creditors sustained millions of dollars in losses, and the public, out of fear, pulled their money from the banking system. Credit soon dried up for many firms, and the Tappans found it hard to borrow money when so many of their customers were in default. They tried to secure a second loan from Nicholas Biddle and his rechartered bank in Pennsylvania, but the answer this time was no. That kept their coffers bare and their worries high. The brothers had never stood this close to the edge.

Beyond their livelihoods, the Tappans also stood in danger of losing their lives, as did so many other abolitionists at this time of hazard. The most recent report of the Anti-Slavery Society spelled it out, with twenty pages of "BRUTAL AND ARBITRARY INFLICTIONS" upon those who spoke up against slavery. There were vigilante attacks, whippings with cow skins, illegal detentions, public hangings, mobs and insurrections, "plentiful showers of bludgeons and brickbats," hateful charges in the press, frenzied town meetings, kangaroo courts, unjust convictions, and constant threats, violence, and intimidation against enslaved and free Black people in the North and South. And throughout it all, these outrages took place with the connivance of Northern politicians, businessmen, and ministers, which especially infuriated Lewis. He wrote, "Never did the church give evidence of more fearful corruption, never was the awful power of religion more dangerously perverted" than when churchmen who should have known better gave sanction to human bondage. To an evangelical Christian like himself, this may have been the greatest sin—twisting the word of God to achieve an unholy end.

Even ministers who claimed a commitment to the cause, like Charles Finney, vexed him, as did the clerics on his own executive committee. Among them, prejudice had made a resurgence, as the mob violence convinced them they should distance themselves from their Black colleagues and strictly avoid African American churches, lest a cry of amalgamation be raised against them. This made no sense to Lewis, who invited Samuel Cornish to dine at his home and regularly attended Black churches. But the other whites in the society would not follow his example.

In the most egregious case, Lewis moved to have the Reverend Theodore Wright make a keynote address at a meeting, but the majority of the committee rejected the idea—despite Wright being a member of that committee. As Lewis wrote in his diary, race continued to be an incendiary topic, and "if ever there is a split in our ranks it will arise from collision on this point." But as much trouble as the reactionaries and backsliders gave him, Lewis always found the radicals in the move-ment to be the hardest to manage, and the chief troublemaker among them was Garrison.

Lewis was aghast at his latest antics, which not only threatened to divide the movement, but made antislavery activists appear blasphemous and sacrilegious. For what else could you call an attack on Christian dogma?

The conflict started when the nettlesome Lyman Beecher aroused Garrison's temper by holding a meeting, in Pittsburgh, in which he proclaimed the Sabbath as "the great sun of the moral world," and those who violated it to be sinful. In response, Garrison fired off a rebuttal in *The Liberator* in which he claimed the Sabbath was no more exalted than any other day of the week, and hypocrites like Beecher had long been proclaiming the glories of the day while allowing moral outrages to take place during it. He reminded readers of the seventeenth-century Puritans, who kept the Sabbath "with more rigor and exactness, probably, than will ever be seen again," yet banished Baptists from the Massachusetts Bay Colony, hanged pacifist Quakers, and waged wars of extermination against Native people. "What a strange and horrible paradox!"

As Lewis had feared, the proslavery press pounced. They called Garrison a menace to the nation, a heretic at war with God's own words—at war with an actual Commandment!—and forced all abolitionists to account for the claims of their brother madman . . . knowing most of them would remain silent or change the subject. Lewis worried the controversy had damaged the movement, alienated the wider public, and made activists look like cartoon extremists. In his view they could achieve *nothing* by waging fruitless wars over doctrine. The goal was to build a strong and unified movement, not to wage a purity crusade.

Yet Garrison would not relent in his criticism, and he spent edition after edition of *The Liberator* reinforcing his points and calling Beecher a knave and a miscreant.

Lewis had no choice but to weigh in on the controversy in Garrison's own newspaper, claiming the publisher had been the source of "animosity and contention among brethren" by assailing the Sabbath, and would only divide abolitionists at a time when the movement needed unity. He didn't stop there: he paid Garrison's way to New York for the training meeting of Weld's agents and took him aside to have words with him, and to pepper him with questions about his conduct. Was he trying to subvert the good works of the movement? Did he not understand the perils of division and playing into their enemies' hands? An argument followed and ended without resolution. As Garrison put it, "we harmoniously agreed to differ."

The Sabbath story, and Lewis's angry reaction to it, spread well beyond churchmen and abolition leaders. Fears over Garrison's conduct affected the seminarians at Weld's training session, and some openly worried about being in the company of such a dangerous individual. At one point Garrison realized how easily he could become "a great stumbling block in the way of the people," so he took pains to meet all of them individually, using charm and deference to calm their fears. In the end they greeted him like "a brother beloved," even if they distrusted what he said about the rudiments of Christian doctrine.

Lewis knew he was outmatched in strategy against Garrison. His plans and calculations only allowed for influencing the behavior of orthodox, churchgoing Christians, people who prayed weekly to the risen God and had at least a vague sense of the power of divine judgment. But here was someone who defied the truth of Exodus, who opposed family prayer, who dogged clergymen as his enemies, who refused membership in any church, and who resisted being reborn in Christ. Lewis could not fathom it. Was this man even a Christian, and if not, why had God made him so important to the movement?

There was more for Lewis to chew over: Garrison had blasted the Constitution, calling it "wet with human blood," and questioned the principles upon which the country was founded and mocked the leaders who ruled it. He delighted in conflict and maintained an unhealthy paranoia that men in robes were out to destroy him. ("I am conscious that a mighty sectarian conspiracy is forming to crush me, and it will probably succeed, to some extent.") And then there was his behavior—it was odd! He dabbled in "Thompsonian medicine" by regularly checking into an infirmary where he would "first drink a 'coffee' laced with lobelia and cayenne to induce sweating and vomiting and then relax in a perpendicular steaming box." He even explored Sylvester Graham's health regimen, which combined vegetarianism with sleeping on hard mattresses, exercising, wearing loose-fitting clothing, and eating a curious cracker made of coarse ground wheat.

Yet even Garrison's close attention to his physical condition couldn't prevent a bevy of ailments affecting him. In November he wrote, "I have not been very well. There is something wrong about my system, which needs to be radically affected." Between bouts of scrofula and mysterious swellings, abscesses in his ears, and a chronic wound on his leg, Garrison never seemed free of malady. He spent months homebound, absent from field work at a critical time, when Lewis felt he should be lecturing and raising funds and encouraging petitioners, instead of firing off hateful editorials against the latest minister who had offended him. After all, if Garrison was going to incite people to action, the least he could do was show up in person to do it.

For all these reasons, Garrison chafed and frustrated Lewis. But the worst part of all was that Lewis actually liked him, thought him good company, a fine speaker, and a committed ally. But the man's flaws were becoming harder to bear, and Lewis and his colleagues in the movement could no longer answer for them.

And yet—

Just days later, on a December night in New York City, when the new United Anti-Slavery Society held its first meeting—before an audience "completely electrified"—there stood David Ruggles, hallowing the name of William Lloyd Garrison for all he had done against slavery while other white men stood idly by. Ruggles knew that Garrison was controversial and divisive and could stand a bit of praise even as so many of his friends disavowed him. So Ruggles went all in for the Boston publisher.

He reminded his audience that, only a few years before, white elites who claimed to be against slavery were possessed by the fever of colonization, the *spirit of expatriation*, eager to ship Black people out of their homes and on to Africa. They didn't seem to care that the Black community stood appalled at the prospect and protested the scheme. "The American press universally cried, 'away with them'—'away with them!'

The tide of feeling designed to sweep the free colored population across the Atlantic, rose higher and higher, with tearful aspect." But one white man did not follow the tide.

Instead, Garrison and his *Liberator* had eviscerated the colonizers, denouncing their aims as well as their character—and it had made a difference. "Oh! it was at this crisis *The Liberator* nobly came to the rescue of the abused and oppressed, and its voice was heard in 'trumpet tones' throughout the land. That voice shook this nation to the very centre." Ruggles had not forgotten his ally "in this mighty conflict between light and darkness; between heaven and hell. I ask, sir, can we forget the Liberator? No, sir, we cannot—we cannot, but with the most base ingratitude."

The room exploded with emotion, for in the crowd were people recently freed from bondage, members of families that had been ripped apart, and those who feared for the sake of relatives who remained imprisoned and "writhing under the bloody lash." Ruggles spoke with the passion and authority of a minister, and the ministers in the crowd—Samuel Cornish, Charles Ray, John Miter, and others—recognized his power. They too would honor Garrison and laud his newspaper, but in so doing they were also honoring Ruggles, for at this moment he had done more to strike at the juggernaut of slavery than any other New Yorker.

His Committee of Vigilance was now a year old and had obtained the freedom of 335 Black citizens and spent more than $1,200 on court costs and funding to help fugitive slaves make their way to freedom. The group took on one new case a day, with one thousand members and associates acting as the grassroots power behind the committee: as witnesses to highlight cases of injustice, as informants to bring kidnappers to trial, and as fundraisers to keep the entire operation in business.

Ruggles's years of service to the cause had led him to this place. His personal life and work life were now so intertwined that he operated out of his own house, a place where mobs had torched his business and criminals had tried to kidnap him. Yet he refused to take a lower profile and welcomed through his doors fugitives and Black people under threat of abduction. His bravery and perseverance brought him admiration from nearly all quarters in the movement, from evangelicals who saw God's will working through him, to radicals who wanted to disrupt slave commerce by any means necessary.

So it wasn't surprising that on January 16, 1837, when the Committee of Vigilance held its anniversary meeting at the Third Free Presbyterian Church, in the audience were Arthur and Lewis Tappan. Despite Ruggles's allegiance to Garrison, the brothers still fully supported his endeavors. Arthur was especially taken by the accomplishments of the committee and the gut-wrenching stories Ruggles presented. One speaker, John Reymond, a Baptist pastor, told how he had been arrested and imprisoned on a writ from a now-dead Virginia slaveholder. As a condition of his release, he had been forced to leave his home—"*banished from my native State!*" Then Ruggles presented the family of a man named Peter John Lee, who had been abducted, leaving his wife and two young children without a husband and father. As they stood before the crowd, many in the audience wept at this "most appalling spectacle of the fiendish spirit of American slavery."

Ruggles was one of the few radicals the Tappans admired without reservation, and it was easy to see why—he was a fighter. While so much in the world of abolition depended on slow, incremental progress, Ruggles and the Committee did something few others had tried: putting immediate abolition into practice. His group didn't merely protest injustice. It patrolled the streets, it boarded the ships, it disrupted the criminal gangs, and it exposed the politicians and cops and judges who profited from the illicit trade in Black people. In short, it forced the issue and made abolition a vital, living thing, instead of something to be attacked without consequence. The Committee of Vigilance did not believe in martyrdom.

Still, although Ruggles was certainly not interested in being a martyr, he doubtless sacrificed for the cause. He had few close friends with whom he could share his private feelings and fears, and he had no wife or close family in the city. He was often alone in his labors, struggling with finances because of the money he channeled to the Committee and perpetually trying to manage the expenses. He was beleaguered with bowel and other health ailments, and he was losing his eyesight—unusual for a man of twenty-seven years, and almost certainly due to the grinding stresses of his work. But still he persisted and coped with a lengthening list of court cases, public appearances, and organizing work . . . and articles to write for his old friend Samuel Cornish.

For months, Cornish and Ruggles had been publicizing the efforts of the Committee of Vigilance in the pages of Cornish's latest newspaper, the *Colored American*. In return, Ruggles not only helped pay Cornish's salary as the editor of the new publication, but he lobbied the state legislature to allow the paper's agents to canvass the entire state for financial support. The Tappans and Gerrit Smith also helped fund the creation of the paper, and its field agents distributed hundreds of copies in hopes of attracting subscribers, with pledges of $5 to $10 annually to support the venture.

Cornish had several goals for his newspaper:

- Establish a press organ written by and for African Americans with a broad reach, giving them a voice that could speak directly not just to the obvious evil of slavery, but to the more insidious forms of racial prejudice and inequality that were legion throughout the North.
- Champion petition drives to the New York legislature to secure the right to vote for all Black men, free of property restrictions, and to ensure fugitive slaves would receive fair jury trials instead of summary judgments by proslavery officials.
- Preach moral reform and exhort readers not to take vacations or waste money; to avoid Negro pews or other segregation in church, at restaurants, and in other public places; and to work tirelessly for self-education and self-improvement.
- Demand that the needs of the Black community not be open to negotiation, and address them through newspapers like

his own: "Colored men must . . . establish and maintain the
PRESS, and through it speak out in THUNDER TONES,
until the nation repent and render to every man that which
is just and equal."

With the *Colored American* as his press organ, Ruggles announced
case after case of men and women arrested on the thinnest of pretenses
and subjected to trumped-up prosecution. He called out officials like
Richard Riker and Tobias Boudinot, who had tried to kidnap him,
and shamed them for their actions. He detailed the abduction of Black
children, giving their identifying characteristics and the circumstances
behind their disappearances. And he provided detailed advice to African
Americans about which people to avoid, what methods the kidnappers
used, and the places where they used them. He summarized his findings
in the committee's first annual report, filling no less than sixty-four
pages with stories of unfair trials, abductions, executions, and other outrages against Black people—not just in New York City, but throughout
the nation—with special attention to those in the North who aided the
slave catchers and profited by their actions.

One recent case showed how the system worked: city police had
arrested a free Black man, George Jones, on a charge of assault. Given
no time to mount a proper defense, Jones appeared in court to find himself confronted by someone who claimed to be his "master," and several
dubious witnesses testified that he had been enslaved until he escaped. It
was a mess of a case, clouded by the witnesses being notorious criminals,
but Riker pronounced Jones guilty, "and in the space of three hours from
his first arrest, he was in chains on his way to the South."

How many George Joneses had Ruggles seen in the last year? How
many average working men and women had been taken on a whim and
whisked off to a life in captivity? They were far too many to count. While
he had made a difference for a few hundred of them, many more had been
stripped of their liberty and sent to a world of plantation terror. Ruggles
felt restless over the situation, that the Committee of Vigilance or any

other abolitionist group could only do so much in the service of freedom while America was still in the grip of the slaveholders' power.

In the face of such outrages, Ruggles came to reject pacifism. His literary mentors like David Walker and Maria Stewart had done the same thing, even though most abolitionists—and nearly all white activists—detested violence of any kind. But Ruggles knew self-defense was the key to the survival of Black people, and he announced his perspective in the widely read, non-abolitionist paper the *New York Sun*:

> My depressed countrymen, we are all liable; your wives and children are at the mercy of merciless kidnappers. We have no protection in law, because the legislators withhold justice . . . where such outrages are committed, peace and justice cannot dwell. While we are subject to be thus inhumanely practised upon, no man is safe; we must look to our own safety and protection from kidnappers; remembering that "self-defence is the first law of nature."

Ruggles and the committee then passed a resolution that made clear the need for solutions beyond the law: "That while we the people of color, are deprived of that *bulwark of personal freedom*, a trial by jury, it is in vain to look for justice in the courts of law, especially where every advantage is given to slaveholders and kidnappers by the law and practice of those courts."

The resolution, along with Ruggles's other statements, had an effect. African Americans became acutely aware of just how many kidnappers lurked in their midst, and they resolved to do something about it. That moment came in April 1837, when authorities arrested a New Yorker named William Dixon on suspicion of being a fugitive slave. In court, evidence showed that he had been recently employed in New York and Boston, and a cartman, a barber, and a veterinarian all swore to his residency. But Richard Riker and his courtroom associates refused to let Dixon go and held him without bond, threatening to provide a rapid trial and conviction that would send him into Southern captivity. Ruggles quickly publicized the Dixon case and announced that the concept of "innocent until proven guilty" had been turned on its head—because, as *The Liberator* put it, "every colored man is presumed to be a slave, unless he can prove his freedom!"

The reaction was swift. Hustling Dixon out of the courthouse and into a park, a team of sheriff's deputies were met with a surprise: a crowd of a thousand Black New Yorkers had gathered to set him free. They set upon the deputies and tore Dixon away from them, and a riot broke out between the squad of white policemen and the Black people determined to protect him. At huge risk to their own safety, they provided an avenue for Dixon to escape. He ran through the crowd and out of the park, but the deputies tracked him down and took him back into custody. Then the crowd pushed back the officers once more and recaptured him, and a white lawyer ripped the coat off one deputy to hold him at bay. Soon a greater mass of officers arrived and pulled Dixon away from the crowd for the last time, and they arrested both him and the lawyer.

The major papers were shocked at the violence, though not all were surprised by it. The *Evening Post* remarked that "The fashion of mobbing which has been set by the whites, is now taken up by the colored race." Others used vicious stereotypes to describe "a strapping negro wench" and a "dapper looking buck negro" as the instigators. Another even imagined a fanciful chase down Broadway, with Dixon pursued by a theater actor on horseback until he was recaptured in a coal cellar, after which he was beaten with clubs by the police—the one detail from the story likely to be true.

Some of the most damning criticism came from an unlikely source. This editorial called the mayhem a disgrace and denounced "illiterate people" and "ignorant mobs" that "can do no good, but much harm." For any people "congregated together under circumstance of great excitement lose self-government, and become mere subjects of passion." Samuel Cornish, in the *Colored American*, had made it plain: he still refused to accept violence, even to fight a travesty of the law. Other Black and white abolitionists echoed his view and fell back on their traditional perspective that violence, even in self-defense, was abhorrent.

But David Ruggles could not agree. Along with a rising tide of new young Black abolitionists, he had moved beyond pacifism, even if it put him at odds with old friends like Cornish and the Tappans. It seemed quite clear to him: from the abductions of innocent people to the mob terror in major cities, the way to counter violence was not to accept it, but to meet it head-on, whether by emancipating captives on a slave ship or freeing an innocent man from a corrupt legal system. Ruggles rejected the advice of the *Evening Post*, which he had heard in the rhetoric of more than a few of his colleagues: "If blacks have any friends, they will counsel them to demean themselves peacefully." Ruggles would not be demeaned, even if it cost him his friends.

The Dixon case and others like it would stay in the news for months, and the strain only increased between Ruggles and his allies over the proper steps to fight injustice. Making the divisions even worse was the Panic of 1837, which damaged the finances of countless Americans but hit the abolitionist movement especially hard. Cornish found it difficult to secure operating funds for the *Colored American*, Ruggles had to scramble to raise money for court fees and other costs, and the pace of kidnapping increased to its highest level yet. New Yorkers' desperation for cash, a national credit squeeze, the high price of cotton, and the opening of the Texas slave market made man-stealing an even more lucrative business and lured many whites, and a few Black informants, into the illicit trade in human liberty.

The Panic had a national impact and spread quickly in every direction. Thousands of businesses of every size shuttered within weeks or even days. Southern merchants were reduced to only paying five cents or less on every dollar of their debts to New York creditors. Numerous banks and trading houses collapsed on Wall Street, and the failures continued to mount until "nearly every one has become infected in a degree with the panic." *Niles' Weekly Register* summed up the gloomy state of affairs as a disaster without compare, a growing depression, in which "there are many honest and worthy individuals who are irretrievably ruined."

Among them were two brothers who operated a silk shop on Pearl Street, men who had funded philanthropic endeavors for years and rebuilt their business after the devastating fires of 1835. Their firm, Arthur Tappan and Company, had finally succumbed to its creditors and was no longer solvent. To the shock of abolitionists everywhere, the company collapsed with more than a million dollars in debt.

★ ELEVEN ★

HEART BURNINGS

Arthur Tappan's financial house had collapsed around him, and he had to figure out how to rebuild it. He worked to negotiate terms with his creditors, scraped together cash to pay off the banks that called in their debt, reduced his inventories of unsold goods, and cut off most of the funding he gave to abolitionists. He even moved into a boarding-house to save money.

With the economy falling into a depression, Arthur faced a financial hole that few businessmen had ever escaped from. He couldn't ask for help from his colleagues in the movement—most of them ministers who had little spare cash, or Garrison, who had never had any to begin with—and the federal government took no responsibility for bailing out private businesses or facing up to the mess it had created. Andrew Jackson had safely left office by the time the crisis hit, leaving his successor, Martin Van Buren, with the responsibility of cleaning it up, or taking the blame.

Lewis couldn't believe the debt Arthur had incurred. He may have thought he understood how Arthur ran the business, but he had no idea just how leveraged the company was. How long had they been operating on borrowed time? Lewis wondered whether he could even stay with the company after the calamity. He thought of going in a new direction.

Perhaps he could devote his life to the antislavery cause, or hit the road as a field agent to do the Lord's work. Weld had done it. Thirty-nine seminarians were on the cusp of doing it. Why shouldn't he join them? He had spoken in public. Exhorted crowds to crush human bondage. Spoken at Chatham Street Chapel, and roused his listeners to righteous indignation. He even implored schoolchildren to "pray God to *break the rod of the oppressor and let the oppressed go free!*" But then he paused.

Could he really imagine the perils of such a life? What it might be like to be pummeled with rocks like Weld, or tied in ropes and led to the gallows like Garrison, or see his son beaten and his family ambushed like James Forten? When Lewis's house was attacked in the New York riots, he at least had the wherewithal to flee the city for Poughkeepsie. Now he was a party to a failed business, low on cash, and the object of Southern bounties. Even if he did become an evangelist, how easy it would be to kidnap him on the road and send him to Georgia for a speedy execution! Indeed, James Birney prevailed upon him to abandon the idea. The road was no place for a once-rich man. Better to stay in New York and try to rebuild the Tappan fortune. And in any case, the Anti-Slavery Society now had those thirty-nine men—and two women—who were far better equipped to deal with mobs than he was.

—⁂—

The two women, Angelina Grimké and her sister Sarah, had attended Theodore Weld's training in November. They were there as observers and expected great things from Weld the teacher. Angelina had heard how he had transformed Ohio with his silver tongue, had enflamed the countryside with the fire of abolition and faced furious resistance, becoming known as "the most mobbed man in America." She expected to see a heroic figure, a statesman with a noble bearing. Instead, she saw a humble chap in weather-beaten clothing—"John the Baptist attire"—and found him . . . underwhelming.

"I wondered whether he was really as great as I had heard," Angelina wrote. But she stayed to listen to a two-hour stem-winder in which Weld summoned all his fire—decrying, denouncing, inspiring—all of it making for a "moral and intellectual feast." She couldn't have been more impressed. She took in most of the lectures and asked questions and made arguments and did all the sharp and insightful things field agents were expected to do, and she felt free to speak out in a way she never could in a Quaker meetinghouse. Garrison introduced her to Weld after the speech, and she immediately saw how this "man raised up by God" could do wonders for the movement. But then again, so could she.

The expectations had been great ever since her *Appeal to the Christian Women of the South* had made her a pariah in her home region and a celebrity among Northern abolitionists. Though she had spent months working with the Philadelphia Female Anti-Slavery Society, promoting the free produce movement, and helping the petition campaign, she was now mainly known as the Southerner who stuck it in the eye of the South. The woman who had fired up readers of *The Liberator* with her call to martyrdom—"Yes! LET IT COME"—and had brilliantly dissected racism and injustice with her *Appeal*. Her fans couldn't wait for her lecture tour.

Sarah Grimké had committed to joining her, with a pamphlet of her own to boost her profile. In the *Epistle to the Clergy of the Southern States*, Sarah told any Southern ministers who bothered to read it that they were unrepentant sinners abusing the Good Book to justify their own cruelty and debasement. She accused them of launching a "REIGN OF TERROR" to cover up the horrors of slavery and quoted Ezekiel to remind them of the power of divine judgment: "The soul that sinneth it shall die." What made her writing especially shocking was that she was a woman publicly condemning an entire class of men—clerics who considered themselves pious, even holy. It was an almost unheard of transgression against social norms, and one that increased her fame in the North almost to the level of her sister's.

At forty-four, Sarah was thirteen years older than Angelina, but she had been the trailblazer in recent years: first to reject slavery, first to leave the South, first to join the Society of Friends, first to be rebuked by them. The church elders found her antislavery activities improper, even threatening, and let her know it. In one recent meeting in Philadelphia, after Sarah had finished speaking, one of them interrupted her—"Perhaps the Friend may be satisfied now"—the equivalent of telling her to shut up. She would not soon forget the insult, or all the obstacles the hierarchy had put in her path. The disrespect drove her determination.

In tandem the sisters planned to hold a series of "parlor talks" in the homes of upstanding New York women—or that was the idea, at least. Once word got out, there was so much demand to hear them speak that even the largest parlor could not accommodate all the guests. So the Grimkés rearranged their plans and decided to appear in a Baptist church before an all-female audience. Gerrit Smith tried to talk them out of it. By appearing in such a public venue, they would violate social norms against women stepping out of their sphere, and how would that look? Could they endure the controversy?

Weld rebutted Smith's objection. He'd been advising the sisters since November and helping them prepare for the lecture tour, and they trusted his judgment. He told them to stand fast. They must swallow any fear, counter dissent, and face down mobs if they must. God had called them to their mission. After Weld's pep talk, Angelina wrote, "I felt no more fear. We went to the meeting at three o'clock and found about three hundred women there." They gave these women a lecture they would not forget.

The Bible had condemned slavery, they said—*look it up!* The slave-holders and colonizers had sinned against God, against morality and human decency, and their iniquity had infected the North as well. How many had been passive and indifferent against the suffering of the slave, against the burdens laid upon their Black brothers and sisters? And what would they in the audience do to change things? Could they sit quietly for a day longer while so many writhed under the lash and grieved from injustice, or felt torment under the reign of the mob? No good Christian woman could accept such a state of affairs, and neither should they. Never should they.

Angelina and Sarah held the crowd rapt for nearly two hours. They brought the verve and color of their writing to their speeches, made detailed arguments, answered questions, and agreed to hold a second lecture to follow the first. It was said to be the first time American women had addressed other American women in a public assembly outside of a Quaker meetinghouse. But, of course, Maria Stewart had done the same thing six years earlier.

Black women like Stewart had been first to break down the barriers, using similar biblical condemnations of slavery and warnings of divine retribution, speaking to large audiences and drawing waves of criticism. Stewart had been so vigorously attacked, even by abolitionists, that the backlash forced her to withdraw from public life. Now the Grimkés were attempting the same thing on a wider scale, with hopes that the backlash wouldn't silence them too.

The American Anti-Slavery Society supported the tour in hopes that nothing the Grimkés said would deviate from the mainstream of Tappan-approved abolitionism. Maria Stewart's criticisms of men and demands for women's equality—unwise. Garrison's call to revolution and attacks on ministers—unacceptable. David Ruggles's justification for violence in self-defense—unimaginable. But even though the Grimkés kept their distance from the radicals in the winter of 1837, their words were still transformative. They spoke to one overflowing crowd after another, drawing hundreds of souls eager to sign up to be members of the Anti-Slavery Society to fight injustice however they could. And they told them the most critical need *right now* was for them to enlist in the campaign to gather signatures against slavery, in the ongoing effort to bury congressmen under mountains of paper.

By the second session of the 24th Congress, the mass of petitions had overwhelmed Washington. Legislators found their desks crammed so full of papers sent by irate constituents that some erupted in anger— especially if those legislators were from the South. Said one observer, "The Southern hotspurs are almost ready to dance with rage at the attack, as they called it, upon their peculiar domestic institutions." Sarah Forten and other organizers in Boston and Philadelphia, along with agents of the American Anti-Slavery Society, arranged the composition and circulation of the papers, with each petitioner amassing nearly three hundred signatures. Angelina claimed the canvassing was even more important than the signatures themselves, for it spread the message of antislavery across the North.

In New York, Theodore Weld, John Whittier, and Henry Stanton labored constantly to manage their petition effort, with Weld sleeping in a garret and eating vegetarian food like an ascetic monk. Samuel Cornish did double duty, advocating for signatures in *Colored American* while working with David Ruggles to push the state legislature to guarantee fugitives the right to a jury trial and to give all Black men the right to vote. Whittier cheered news of the national campaign's success, saying there were "petitions enough to break all the tables in the Capitol." The *New York American* said the mass of paper would be enough "to erect a pyramid that shall vie with the proudest on the plains of Egypt as a great moral monument to the expressed will of a free people." In the end the petitions filled a congressional storage room, 20 by 30 by 14 feet, to the ceiling.

But that was all they did, for the reassembled Congress refused to read them. Legislators passed the gag law for another session and decided that the petitions on slavery would "be laid on the table, and no further action whatever shall be had thereon." In the Senate, where petitions were routinely ignored, John Calhoun followed up on the gag law in the House by driving the passage of resolutions that insisted Congress would defend slavery from those trying to imperil it. Yet such actions only encouraged more petitioners to gather more signatures, forcing Congress to take more unpopular steps to ignore the interests of its constituents and stanch debate on the most important issue in the nation.

John Quincy Adams refused to accept this state of affairs and did whatever he could to get the documents read in the House. On one occasion, he held up a petition and openly violated the gag rule, reading off fragments of text about liberty and relieving "the wrongs of the African," only to be shouted down by angry Southerners. Then he paraphrased, discussed some of the finer points of the petitions . . . slowly . . . drawing out . . . explosive charges . . . against the South. More rage erupted, more calls to order, more denunciations. And Adams picked up again, humbly alluding to sin and moral turpitude, while the reaction grew all the more frantic and ridiculous. Adams soon became the one politician in Congress abolitionists could depend on to carry their message and drive the other side crazy. As one observer noted, Adams "consults with no one, takes the advice of no one, and holds himself accountable to no one but the nation."

The same, in fact, could have been said for William Lloyd Garrison, who during the fiasco of the gag law was celebrating a victory in Massachusetts. There, he had convinced the state legislature to guarantee the right to public petition and to hear any entreaties from constituents, regardless of subject matter, even "for the removal of a great social, moral and political evil." Surprisingly, the vote had been overwhelming: 378–16 in one house, and 33–0 in the other. Garrison wrote to George Benson with excitement, "It is the most extraordinary change in political action, on a moral subject, in the annals of legislation."

As winter turned into spring, this feeling of extraordinary change spread beyond the petition campaign. The Grimkés realized they were making history on their tour, had broken barriers in the North while transforming themselves for the better. Sarah enjoyed the experience greatly, at last feeling free to speak in a public forum without being shamed or insulted. Of her newly strengthened beliefs in Christian abolition, she wrote, "They have given a new spring to my existence, and shed over my whole being sweet and hallowed enjoyments." For Angelina the tour not only bolstered her confidence; it encouraged her to take more risks than ever. At the Spring Street Presbyterian Church, she even spoke from the pulpit, where women were usually forbidden, and created a stir that her allies and enemies would not soon forget.

The proslavery press was aghast: how dare she speak from the throne of God's house! Colonizers were particularly incensed, and with each new speech of the Grimkés, they launched new insults, calling them "fanatical women," destroyers of the republic, female maniacs who had bellowed scandal in hallowed halls. Some said Angelina should be called "Devilina" for her infernal behavior. Others accused them of being loose women, or demons in human form, their long gray Quaker gowns and bonnets concealing untold wickedness. Some men didn't stop at berating them in print but attended their lectures to harangue them in person. On one occasion, a member of the Colonization Society showed up at Angelina's lecture to rebut her arguments point by point. A lively debate ensued, after which the man withdrew. Angelina wrote, "He gave up so much that I could not see what he had to stand on when we left him."

These were good enemies to have. They added to the momentum and made glaring the contrast between their message and that of their opponents. For even if they endured a torrent of insults, or a volley of lies and accusations, it could only inspire sympathy. This was Weld's view at least. He had lived through day after day of indignities in his travels, yet still he had thrived. Only his voice had been damaged, and that had been of his own volition.

Weld committed to the success of the Grimkés in the public arena. He defended them against their enemies and made sport of the charges of their adversaries. He even joined them on the tour to offer moral support should they need it. He and the sisters exchanged thoughts and strategies, probed the weaknesses of each other's arguments, teased each other over their foibles, and grew comfortable in each other's presence. Angelina admired Weld and took to heart what he said: persecution couldn't crush the movement, but might ensure its victory. She had told Garrison this before the Boston riot, to welcome the possibility of martyrdom. Now she and Sarah had their chance, too, if not to become the target of a mob then at least to show how Christian soldiers could bear up under the weight of public controversy. Let it come.

The sisters continued their tour, speaking to audiences in New Jersey, still a slave state, and in upstate New York towns like Poughkeepsie, where they received a warm welcome in a Black church, and Peterboro, where they stayed at Gerrit Smith's country estate. Angelina found herself full of enthusiasm—"I love the work. I count myself greatly favored in being called to it."—and she and Sarah were confident enough about what they had accomplished that they decided to venture back to Philadelphia.

Angelina knew many Quaker women supported them. She saw them at their lectures and alluded to the beliefs they shared, from the power of the inner light to the nature of divinity. Perhaps she could make a gesture that would inspire them, that would show her resolve against the forces they faced. So the Grimkés attended a meeting of the Society of Friends in Philadelphia and took a seat on the "colored bench" alongside Sarah and Grace Douglass.

The men in the ruling committee, known as the Overseers, were furious at their transgression, and they brought charges against them for violating the rules of the meeting. But the Grimkés would not back down and defended what they had done. After all, how could the Friends talk of the inner light, the presence of God in everyone, and still assume that one person's access to the Holy Spirit was greater than another? The Overseers didn't appreciate being contradicted and asked them to resign their membership—lest they be publicly disowned. They refused to do so and challenged the church elders to expel them. And with that, they left Philadelphia to resume their mission.

Angelina did not feel comforted by departing on such terms. No hearts had been changed, no prejudices overturned. The Quakers were, in many ways, like most of the Northerners they had met, paying lip service to high-minded ideals but enforcing the most rigid segregation in practice.

In New York, the major women's abolition group, the Ladies' New York City Anti-Slavery Society, crowed about the evils of slavery yet refused to allow Black members. It was hard for her to believe such a group in America's largest city could be so far behind their counterparts in Boston and Philadelphia, and she wrote to a friend disgusted that their racism "is a canker worm among them and paralyzes every effort. They are doing *literally nothing* as a Society for the colored people."

By contrast, Angelina felt she had made an effort to encourage Black and white women to commingle as sisters, to share ideas and intimacies, and to break the racial codes that affected every part of American life. She taught Sunday school for Black youth in New York, she lectured before mixed-race audiences in Poughkeepsie, she made alliances with women of color. But still . . .

Angelina had been raised to be a slaveholder in low-country South Carolina. She had grown up in an atmosphere of comfort and privilege at the expense of Black people. And while she had since embraced a very different existence, there was a lot she did not know or understand about Black women's lives. So to better understand their conditions in the North, she and her sister wrote to a friend and asked her to describe her experience with white people. Sarah Forten did not hesitate in her response.

As a leader and manager of the Philadelphia Female Anti-Slavery Society, Sarah was a smart choice as correspondent. She came from a family of some wealth, had a classical education, and enjoyed literary and spiritual pursuits not unlike the sisters' own. But there the similarities with the Grimkés ended. Her white Quaker friends had never been held prisoner in their own house in the face of an angry white mob, or had their siblings attacked with bludgeons, or lived in fear of kidnapping or other threats. So Sarah Forten gave them a sense of what it meant to be a Black woman in a country plagued by white supremacy.

In short: she could not believe the cruelty and idiocy of racism. The idea that American society had ordered itself in this way, ignoring individual merit and valuing skin tone above all else. What gave whites the right to judge her, especially since they had no claim to be superior based on "education—birth—or worldly circumstances"? They had just one thing to hang over her head—race—and it disgusted her to think she could be regarded as inferior based on that.

She told the Grimkés she despised the taint of bigotry in a person: "I am particularly sensitive on this point, and consequently seek to avoid as much as possible from mingling with those who exist under its influence." Indeed, the prejudice against color "engendered feelings of discontent and mortification" so strong that she sometimes didn't want to leave her house or visit public spaces where whites were known to be hostile to Black people.

The Colonization Society was the worst offender, and "I despise the aim of that Institution most heartily—and have never yet met one man or woman of Color who thought better of it than I do." In fact, its members were so foolish and ignorant, "I only marvel that they are in possession of any knowledge at all." But open bigots were obvious villains. Sarah had also felt the sting of racism among abolitionists, in their patronizing attitudes and subtle insults, and in the distance they maintained from her. Still, Sarah refused to let her anger and frustration sap her energies: "I am striving to live above such heart burnings," especially at a time when there was so much work to be done.

Sarah had been reappointed as one of the managers of the Philadelphia Female Anti-Slavery Society and remained crucial to its endeavors: writing and assembling petitions to Congress, building a school for Black children, running the Anti-Slavery Sewing Circles, funding abolitionist newspapers, and crafting letters, reports, and pamphlets, among other duties. There was so much to do, and completing one batch of work just brought about another batch of it. But her group expanded along with its list of projects and quadrupled in size to eighty members.

Sarah's energy did not flag, and she took on new projects whenever she had time. In December she helped organize the society's first antislavery fair, in which needlework, pottery, artworks, and baked goods were sold to benefit the movement. John Whittier offered poems, musicians sang songs, and orators spoke ennobling words. There were tables filled with goods nestled in evergreens and flowers, and Sarah served as postmaster, mailing ceremonial letters. Garrison attended the fair and couldn't have been more impressed, for they had "in one day realized the handsome sum of five hundred and forty-two dollars!—Now that money is so scarce, this is almost equal to a thousand dollars in ordinary times."

The Philadelphians needed the money to support their next endeavor: the construction of a grand building that could host antislavery lectures, or events like the fair, or anything else that might inspire visitors to take up the cause. Here, abolitionist orators would always be welcome, instead of being barred from churches or driven out of assembly halls whose landlords feared racially mixed crowds. To begin the project, Sarah joined a committee to sell shares to build this "temple of liberty," which would be called Pennsylvania Hall. It would rise in the same stately Greek Revival style as a public legislature but would be open to all people, and not just politicians of one sex and color—the first great monument to the movement.

In support of her efforts, Sarah, in May 1837, visited New York City for the first Anti-Slavery Convention of American Women, which hosted more than a hundred delegates from ten states, drawing a third of its attendees from Philadelphia. Among them were Sarah's colleagues Grace Douglass, Sarah Douglass, and Lucretia Mott. It was said to be the largest assembly of American women in history, there was no color bar, and Black and white attendees served equally as delegates and officers.

Angelina Grimké was the chief author of the convention's major publication, the *Appeal to the Women of the Nominally Free States*, which began with Sarah's Forten's famous poem "Appeal to Woman" and an epigraph by Catharine Beecher. Sarah's poetry and her letter to the Grimkés on racism undoubtedly influenced Angelina's *Appeal*, in which she criticized white women for oppressing and subjugating Black women and demanded they take action to destroy injustice.

Sarah Grimké echoed some of the same points in her pamphlet, *An Address to the Free Colored Americans*, in which she spoke out about racial conditions in the United States and encouraged Black people to let "your righteousness exceed the righteousness of our white fellow-citizens," a basic tenet of moral reformers from Samuel May to Samuel Cornish. However, the idea wasn't without controversy.

Not everyone at this point agreed that Black Americans should inspire whites with their good conduct even if it led to martyrdom. Factions had grown within the women's societies, with white evangelicals praising self-sacrifice and Black women suspecting they would be the ones to actually bear it. The Grimkés may have written well about the abuse of African Americans, but in the end their remedy for it was the same as that of the Tappans, Garrison, and just about every other white abolitionist: endure it. As Sarah Grimké wrote, "We entreat you in the name of the Lord Jesus, to forbear any attempts violently to rescue your brethren. Such attempts can only end in disappointment; they infuriate public sentiment still more against you, and furnish your blood-thirsty adversaries with a plausible pretext to treat you with cruelty."

Tellingly, the sisters composed their work at the same time the Dixon case was rattling the world of New York abolition. David Ruggles and his New York Committee of Vigilance were now widely known to advocate the liberation of Black people held captive in any form, rejecting moral reform as a cure for racism and assuming "moral suasion" would not work. This had divided Ruggles from his white counterparts and incurred the enmity of the press. But his position only increased his popularity and made more Black New Yorkers adopt his view: "Self-defence is the first law of nature." The Grimkés could not endorse such a belief, and instead made a plea for greater self-sacrifice.

Like most of the Philadelphians, Sarah Forten had no public comment about any of this, about whether the sisters were correct or if the assertive stance of the Vigilance Committee could be justified. But a year later, she would make her position abundantly clear.

—⁂—

A month after the convention the Grimkés arrived in Boston to begin a lecture tour that took them to seventeen stops in ten towns, speaking in front of both women-only crowds and mixed, or "promiscuous," audiences that included men. They went from Roxbury to Salem to Lynn and throughout Massachusetts, speaking to eight thousand people, with Garrison promoting their lectures in *The Liberator* as they went.

Theodore Weld didn't travel with them this time, but they kept him posted on their tour by exchanging letters. He mocked those who condemned their public speaking: "Why! folks talk about women's preaching as tho' it was next to highway robbery—eyes astare and mouth agape." Angelina told him how, as she spoke in front of her listeners, "I cannot help smiling in the midst of 'rhetorical flourishes' to witness their perfect amazement at hearing a woman speak in the churches."

Angelina brought a special kind of energy to her lectures. She came armed with ideas she had gleaned from Black women like Sarah Forten, and most likely Maria Stewart, that racial injustice must be crushed in the North just like slavery in the South. She parried the attacks of the men who said she had stepped outside her sphere, she faced off against colonizers, and she defeated attempts to shut her up.

She managed a difficult balance, avoiding ideological battlefields and the war between Garrison and the ministers. She led her listeners where they had never gone, blending the language of evangelicalism with the fervor of radical change, and inspired her listeners to follow through with that change. She felt so close to the edge, so near the tipping point, where abolition might finally emerge from the fringe and transform the heart of the nation. She seemed so close to getting there . . .

But the war would find her first.

The Grimkés had been in Massachusetts for only a few weeks when the Reverend Nehemiah Adams fired off a "Pastoral Letter" that was read in countless Congregational churches on the following Sunday. In it he blasted the lectures of women like the Grimkés, saying, "Churches should not permit strangers to preach on subjects ministers don't agree with" and women had no business speaking in public. "The power of woman is in her dependence . . . But when she assumes the place and tone of a man as a public reformer, our care and protection of her seem unnecessary . . .

and her character becomes unnatural." Three more missives, notably *The Appeal of Clerical Abolitionists on Antislavery Measures*, echoed the same idea: women had no right to tell men what to do, they were better off relying on men to get what they wanted, and their social activism made them seem less like women, and therefore sinful or even sinister.

The attacks gave license to the Boston press to go after the Grimkés as never before. The *Boston Morning Post* claimed they were spinsters who had no chance at landing husbands so they had resorted to stirring up the public out of frustration. It asked, "Why are all the old hens abolitionists? Because not being able to obtain husbands they think they stand some chance for a negro, if they can only make amalgamation fashionable." Other denunciations were just as caustic. But none of the backlash shocked Angelina, who wrote to a friend, "We are willing to bear the brunt of the storm, if we can only be the means of making a breach in the wall of public opinion . . . our whole sex needs an emancipation from the thraldom of public opinion."

The Grimkés were happy to continue on their tour, not changing their message to suit their critics, just as they had always done. But then Garrison got involved.

The ministers' charges had enflamed his wrath. Their pastoral letters had closed off Congregational churches to any abolitionist activity whatsoever, and clerics even said *The Liberator* should not be read or circulated by those who considered themselves good Christians. In their eyes he was a monster. They said his accusations against the brethren smacked of heresy, his lack of church membership and strange lifestyle marked him as an outcast, and his zealotry made him a threat to the republic. His followers worshipped a false idol, and his newspaper catered to a "mobocratic" spirit—a particularly vicious jibe since Garrison had been the victim of an actual mob just two years before.

The clerical attack appalled him, but what shocked him was the lack of any defense from the American Anti-Slavery Society. He wanted them to offer their support after the condemnation, but Lewis Tappan would not allow it. Garrison fired off an angry note to Lewis, writing,

"I can only marvel at the short-sightedness of you all. My dear friend, is it a small matter that, in the very crisis of our campaign, sedition shows itself in our camp—bold and rampant sedition?"

But Lewis had had quite enough of Garrison's accusations by this point. He had warned him against using intemperate language in *The Liberator*, but the publisher did not listen. He had asked for unity within the movement—the bare minimum it needed against so many enemies—and Garrison had ignored him. He had implored him to focus on slavery and injustice, and Garrison remained forever distracted by religious squabbles and health obsessions. What more could he say to this man?

Lewis spelled it out. He told him there was no sedition. The ministers were plainly wrong in their attacks, but Garrison should stay out of the fray for once and refrain from attacking their beliefs—for in doing so, "you denounce probably a majority of the members of the American anti-slavery societies in the United States." He shouldn't attack the executive committee either for not taking a stand on the clerical controversy, for if he did, "the war will all be on one side." Instead, Lewis advised him to respond to his enemies with "a short, well-tempered, dignified, Christlike reply."

To Garrison this was nothing less than an insult.

He told George Benson the attitude of the home office "is shameful, is criminal, and is anything but magnanimous" and "our friends in New York would be glad, on the whole, to see me cashiered, or voluntarily leave the ranks." But he had no intention of doing this, or of taking Lewis's advice to emulate Christ. Because although Garrison may have felt like a messiah at times, he was certainly no Jesus.

He came out blasting in *The Liberator*. He questioned the ministers' credentials and called them hypocrites, worthless to the cause of abolition, a blight on human decency. He refused to withdraw his earlier accusations, that they were "nothing better than hirelings, in the bad sense of that term—that they are blind leaders of the blind, dumb dogs that cannot bark, spiritual popes—that they love the fleece better than the flock—that they are mighty hindrances to the march of human freedom, and to the enfranchisement of the souls of men."

It all smelled of politics, that dirty pursuit Garrison abhorred. He rejected the leadership of the ministers, the Anti-Slavery Society, Lewis Tappan, and anyone else who had crossed him. He announced he would only follow God's lead going forward—hypocrites and cowards be damned! Scripture was greater than any mortal entity, and anyone who lived by God's law could stand above human law. As he had earlier written, "I will not consult any other statute-book than THE BIBLE; and whatsoever requirement of man I believe is opposed to the spirit of the gospel, I will at all hazards disobey. Every man is bound to understand the laws of the country in which he lives, but he is not bound to obey any one of them, if it conflict with his allegiance to his Maker."

Every abolitionist in the Northeast now had to decide whether to support Garrison or abandon him in his clerical war. Arthur and Lewis Tappan could not endorse his ideas, which they called "wild" and "absurd," and their allies like Gerrit Smith and James Birney also kept their distance. Samuel Cornish, too, disapproved of the way the editor had set himself at odds with others in the movement, and he worried that African Americans would be drawn into these charged debates and be harmed by them. "There is nothing to be gained by brother contending with brother," he wrote, fearing that the same kind of warfare that had broken out between Garrison and the white clerics could be just as destructive among Black abolitionists, with far greater consequences.

This broke out into the open when Cornish wrote an article titled "Keep Cool, Brethren," urging Boston's Black ministers allied with Garrison to temper their zeal and not add to the divisions. He concluded by writing, "the trite saying, 'save me from my friends' is as applicable to the present, as to any other period of the world's history." The ministers didn't appreciate Cornish's takedown of their alliance with Garrison. They charged his "Keep Cool" article was "scorchingly hot, and inexplicably intolerant towards our colored friends in the region," and that his treatment of Black Bostonians was so rude it didn't even merit a reply. Garrison made sure to print their comments in *The Liberator*.

The whirlwind of Garrison's controversies picked up force as the pro-slavery and colonization press amplified the split in the movement and tried to sow doubt about his sanity. The Grimkés, though, resisted the urge to keep their distance from him. He had defended them from the clerical attack, joined with them in their crusades, and promoted their lecture tour in his newspaper. The sisters knew they could work with him to fight the intolerance of the clergymen and the indolence of the Tappans. But what they did not expect was that the most lacerating assault would not come from those men, but from a singularly influential woman.

Catharine Beecher had been an influence on Angelina for six years, ever since she had accepted her application to train to be a teacher at Hartford Seminary. Though the Quaker hierarchy had prevented Angelina from attending the school, ever since then the two women had corresponded and developed a respectful, if at times tenuous, relationship—despite differences over abolition. Beecher commanded a wide readership by offering strategies for women to become teachers and to manage their domestic affairs. She was respected enough that Angelina gave her the epigraph before her convention *Appeal* and considered her a friend, if not quite an ally. But she wasn't prepared for this.

In *An Essay on Slavery and Abolitionism, Addressed to Miss A. D. Grimké*, Beecher disparaged Angelina's work as an abolitionist with the same energy that her father Lyman had directed against Garrison. Openly supporting the clerical attack, she said Angelina had transgressed her role as a woman to take part in a political campaign, in service of a doctrine that promoted ideas that were "not only illogical, but false" and could lead to violence and the division of the country. Men were the proper agents of political action and social change, and women could make their opinions known privately, but to do so publicly invited only shame. "For the more intelligent a woman becomes . . . the more her taste will conform to the graceful and dignified retirement and submission it involves. An ignorant, a narrow-minded, or a stupid woman, cannot feel nor understand the rationality, the propriety, or the beauty of this relation."

Beecher's words had the effect she intended. The public mood began to shift, even among abolitionists, to question the conduct of the sisters. Angelina was stunned by the attack—Beecher had not only impugned her morals and assailed her mission; she had even gotten her name wrong on the title page (Angelina's middle name was Emily). She wrote to a friend, "Catharine's arguments are the most insidious things I ever read, and I feel it my duty to answer them; only, I know not how to find language strong enough to express my indignation at the view she takes of woman's character and duty." She found the language soon enough, and set about destroying her argument. She had joined the war.

In a series of thirteen "Letters to Catherine E. Beecher" (with the educator's first name misspelled), the Grimkés laid out the reasons why Beecher was wrong about abolition and why the need for racial justice was so pressing. They addressed Beecher's charges point by point and refuted them, giving no quarter to their onetime friend. But the twelfth letter was the boldest, titled "Human Rights Not Founded on Sex," in which Angelina said keeping women confined to their sphere had only imprisoned them:

> Woman has been taught to lean upon an arm of flesh, to sit as a doll arrayed in "gold, and pearls, and costly array," to be admired for her personal charms, and caressed and humored like a spoiled child, or converted into a mere drudge to suit the convenience of her lord and master . . . [This condition] has robbed woman of essential rights, the right to think and speak and act on all great moral questions, just as men think and speak and act; the right to share their responsibilities, perils and toils; the right to fulfil the great end of her being, as a moral, intellectual and immortal creature, and of glorifying God in her body and her spirit which are His.

It was as bold and striking an argument on the subject as anyone had made in the 1830s, and it was meant for an audience far beyond the parlor of Catharine Beecher. For Angelina had staked out a claim to women's equality that did not equivocate and did not allow for compromise.

Garrison cheered the message—it was correct, it was clear, and he endorsed it fully. He met with the Grimkés, and they bolstered each other's confidence once more, like "iron sharpeneth iron." Angelina couldn't have been more encouraged, imagining that once united, women and Black Americans could fully assert their God-given rights. She wrote to John Whittier and Theodore Weld that "the time to assert a right is the time when that right is denied. We must establish this right for if we do not, it will be impossible for us to go on with the work of Emancipation."

But she spoke into a void. Her correspondents refused to listen.

Whittier had already chastised her for tying herself to Garrison and the turmoil he had unleashed. He accused her of being distracted from the battle against slavery, and he claimed her actions would only weaken the movement, "in a selfish crusade against some paltry grievance." Weld followed Whittier's argument by charging she was dividing her energies and forgetting the racial struggle was paramount, not her own concerns.

Angelina felt belittled by the charges. Did Weld not know or understand her at all? She debated his points and he rebutted hers, until their letters became a contest of angry words. Weld felt so sure she was mistaken he became more hectoring, more insistent that she was losing her focus. In return she wrote, "I like to pay my debts, and as I received $10 worth of scolding I should be guilty of injustice did I not return the favor." Sarah added, "Angelina is so wrathy I think it will be unsafe to trust the pen in her hands."

Angelina made a damning charge: that Weld's friends on the executive committee of the American Anti-Slavery Society had abandoned her and her sister in the face of the ministers' attacks. A field agent named Henry Wright had come to their defense, and the committee promptly removed him from his station, over the sisters' objections. Angelina accused the men on the committee of deception and dishonesty, scheming to undermine her and Sarah while offering them only platitudes. It was all a lie.

The charge outraged Weld: "Why dear child? What is the matter with you? Patience! Rally yourself. Recollect your womanhood, and put on charity which is the bond of perfectness." He said her accusations against his colleagues were wrong: "Not a particle of evidence do you bring forward. Your 'proof' is merely your own construction . . . you have done the Ex. Committee *most causeless* and most *cruel* wrong." He followed up with an even more damning letter saying her charges were "ALL MOONSHINE."

Angelina didn't bother to respond to him. She couldn't believe that so many of her friends had failed to defend her—even Weld, with whom she had shared her inner thoughts and feelings. He had been a mentor and an intimate yet still had sided with the men who had disparaged her name. Their bitter argument marked the end of the chain reaction the ministers had catalyzed, one that cleaved the world of abolition as it rose to national prominence, with most of the damage being done between people who claimed to despise slavery. All the conflict and betrayal filled Angelina with sickness, literally.

She took ill in November along with her sister. While Sarah had a bad case of bronchitis, Angelina contracted typhoid fever and lay severely ill, confined to a bed in Brookline. The combination of the lightning tour of the region, the nonstop speaking and letter writing, and the stress of being pilloried from all sides, including her own—it was all too much.

But even as the Grimkés faced illness and schism, an event resounded from the far side of the country that would serve to unite, at least temporarily, all the feuding wings of the movement. In a little town in the distant state of Illinois, a mob had attacked an antislavery publisher, destroyed his press, and murdered him. It was another horrific resurgence of mob violence, but what really resonated was that this would-be martyr refused to go quietly. Instead of surrendering to his persecutors, he shot at them, meeting his death with a gun in his hand.

★ TWELVE ★

THE WORLD
UPSIDE DOWN

It was December, and Faneuil Hall hadn't seen a crowd this large and boisterous in years. It had been scarcely a month since the killing of the publisher Elijah Lovejoy in a little town called Alton, 1,200 miles west, and Bostonians were all in a stir. Like two years before, the moment seemed ripe for violence, and the state attorney general, James Austin, was ready to take advantage of it.

The crowd had not even settled in when Austin launched into his harangue. He told them Lovejoy died like a fool—that this publisher, this *zealot* had tried to preach abolition in the wrong place, on the border of a slave state. Three times he had tried to print his infamous newspaper, and three times he had failed, because his cause was infamous. Austin said Lovejoy only cared about "giving liberty to these wild beasts of the forest" and wanted to allow the enslaved to be "let loose to prowl about our streets." Luckily a band of patriots had stopped him with a proud act of defiance, just like "the patriotic Tea-Party of the Revolution."

The crowd exploded with excitement and seemed on the verge of bursting out of the Hall and prowling the streets themselves. Yet one man in the audience rose up, a man who had witnessed the near-lynching of Garrison in 1835, and he took Austin's spark to mob violence—and doused it. The young lawyer Wendell Phillips rebuked him for daring to compare the outrages of a gang of criminals who had murdered an innocent man to the heroics of the nation's founders. "Sir, for the sentiments he has uttered on soil consecrated by the prayers of Puritans and the blood of patriots, the earth should have yawned and swallowed him up!" The audience responded with cheers, forgetting that just a few minutes before it had been cheering the opposing argument.

Eventually the story came out in all its details, to be learned and memorized by generations of abolitionists: how Lovejoy had moved from gradual to immediate abolition, how he had tried twice to set up his press only to have a mob destroy it each time, how on the third attempt he and his supporters had armed themselves inside a warehouse to protect the press, and how they had fought off their assailants with a volley of fire. Lovejoy died after being hit with five shots, and the mob destroyed his press, enshrining his legend.

He was called the first martyr of the cause, even though Black people who had died in slavery and those who had been murdered by mobsters were the real first martyrs. Nonetheless, Lovejoy's death had immediate consequences, which even the Southern press understood: the spilling of his blood would inspire such sympathy that "every drop would cause a new abolition society to spring up."

Lewis Tappan acted fast. He realized Lovejoy's death had offered a prime opportunity to arouse public sympathy for the cause, so he organized a grand memorial service in the recently christened Broadway Tabernacle. This church, near the Five Points, was the perfect place to hold such an event, with December 22 marked to commemorate the murder. Resolutions by the American Anti-Slavery Society commemorated him, and *Human Rights* newspaper provided a biography and narrative of his death in a special limited edition. The society's office stationery even announced, "LOVEJOY the First MARTYR to American LIBERTY. MURDERED for asserting the FREEDOM OF THE PRESS."

Yet Lovejoy was no common martyr. He had admitted, in the days before his killing, that he stood armed to the teeth: "A loaded musket is standing at my bedside, while my two brothers, in an adjoining room, have *three others*, together with *pistols, cartridges*, etc." Some of these weapons they had fired at the mob, likely drawing first blood, in a clear demonstration of self-defense over self-sacrifice. William Lloyd Garrison was not pleased.

He granted that the murder of Lovejoy would do salutary things for the cause, but he could not stomach this resort to violence. In *The Liberator*, Garrison said the publisher should not have taken up arms. Jesus of Nazareth had let himself be nailed to the cross instead of bludgeoning his foes or trying to murder them—why hadn't Lovejoy followed his example? Sarah Grimké, too, worried that he had set a terrible precedent. She said God had given abolitionists all the tools they needed to take on slavery peacefully, and the mayhem in Illinois had only served to make abolition yet another battleground. "God will take the work of abolishing slavery out of our hands," she wrote, so "how can we expect his blessing upon our efforts, if we take carnal weapons to fight his battles? . . . How appalling the spectacle!"

African Americans didn't agree, and most allied with the Tappans' view of Lovejoy. Samuel Cornish's *Colored American* carried a front-page memorial to Lovejoy with a black border; he and David Ruggles and Theodore Wright raised a collection to help the publisher's widow; and there were mass meetings in churches, sermons in praise of the publisher, and condemnations of mob villainy.

—m—

For all this activity, though, there were larger issues facing the Black community than a white man's death in a distant US state—things like the disappearance of their voting rights in Pennsylvania. A petition campaign presented to a January constitutional convention had stripped them of their suffrage completely. In the aftermath, Robert Purvis, the brother-in-law of Sarah Forten, led a protest that culminated in the *Appeal of Forty Thousand Citizens Threatened with Disenfranchisement to the People of Pennsylvania*. In it he wrote, "When you have taken from an individual his right to vote, you have made the government, in regard to him, a mere despotism, and you have taken a step toward making it a despotism for all." But the despotism had the last word, as the legislature ignored the entreaties of Purvis and his allies and the courts rejected their lawsuits.

James Forten supported the *Appeal* and couldn't have been more disappointed, though not surprised, given the catalog of horrors he had seen in recent years against Black people in the state. His son James Jr. had been present in the gallery when the convention passed its measures, after which he and his friends were thrown out of the building, as "physical force was brutally applied in their ejectment." In response to these events, the Fortens hung mourning crepe from their house, a symbol of the death of their rights.

James's daughter Sarah seemed even less surprised than he was. She had written for years about the hypocrisies embedded in the nation's history, the struggles against prejudice and ignorance, and here they were again—facing the same idiocy with little power to stop it. Nonetheless, they would soon have a venue where people could at least speak out about it: a forum for abolition that would be known throughout the country.

It was wintertime and the shell of Pennsylvania Hall was complete, leaving only the interior appointments to be finished. The structure was one of the most impressive in downtown Philadelphia, a three-story Greek Ionic temple crowned with the motto "Virtue, Liberty and Independence." The Pennsylvania Anti-Slavery Society would be the owner of the building, but Sarah and her board of managers had done much of the legwork getting it built on schedule, to host the second annual Anti-Slavery Convention of American Women, in May.

Two thousand people donated $20 each for a share in the Hall, with Sarah and her colleagues overseeing the campaign and disbursing the funds. They needed to finish the building on time, now that the Philadelphia Female Anti-Slavery Society had grown so much in four years and required more meeting rooms, office space, and a repository for their antislavery literature. They needed it so their speakers could lecture without getting harassed or intimidated, and to manage the petition campaign, which had expanded beyond all expectation.

Legions of girls and women continued to canvass the state, with the number of signatures per petitioner increasing dramatically. The Philadelphians felt confident in their strategy, since they now had the resources to inundate every county in the state with petitions. This was true in much of the Northeast, where so many women volunteered for the cause in some cities that it was difficult to coordinate them all. The petition drive had spread from urban areas into little towns and villages, reaching people whose only positive acquaintance with antislavery might be the appearance of a young girl or woman at their doorstep. And that petitioner's pleas, her biblical and moral arguments, had made the difference in enough cases that abolition made slow headway into the heartland. The result was even more paper to send to Washington, DC, to disturb the peace and tranquility of lawmakers who preferred to maintain the status quo in their little patch of the slave empire.

The congressmen's solution to the unwanted mailings was, once again, to pass the gag law. But now Lewis Tappan and James Birney had devised a political strategy to counter it. They had started talking to Northern representatives who opposed the rule, trying to develop plans to tie the House in knots over its refusal to read the petitions. Still hobbled by the failure of his brother's business, Lewis couldn't spare any funds to execute the campaign, but what he lacked in resources he made up for in energy. Through adroit maneuvering and diplomacy, he gathered friends here and there in Congress, trying to undo the censorship regime the Southerners had created. Even if his new friends weren't quite abolitionists, they could still be useful to the cause, and like a good politician, Lewis used whatever tactics he could to win them over.

His and other abolitionists' greatest ally in Congress continued to be former president John Quincy Adams, "Old Man Eloquent," who had gotten as bold as any activist in denouncing the gag law and trying to dismantle it. On one occasion, he announced that nine women from Fredericksburg, Virginia, had presented signatures, only to be interrupted by a Southern objection to accepting the petitions of "mulatto [women] of infamous character." Adams retorted that white Southern men had made them infamous, and "there existed great resemblances in the South between the progeny of the colored people and the white men who claimed the possession of them"—accusing slaveholders of rape.

Adams refused to stop there. He expressed outrage when Southerners challenged the character of Northern women, offering detailed rebuttals that turned into filibusters that dragged on for days. He praised the heroines of the Bible and women who had taken on villainy, supported the Revolution, sacrificed their comforts for the nation, and fought battles in men's clothing. He rejected the social codes that hampered them, saying women "exhibit the most exalted virtue when they do depart from the domestic circle, and enter on the concerns of their country, of humanity, and of their God." He even said the right to petition implied the right to vote—a claim almost never uttered by a man outside of radical circles—and that denial of a civil right amounted to nothing less than injustice.

Adams's rhetorical flair made it into countless newspapers in the North, *Niles' Weekly Register*, and of course *The Liberator* and *The Emancipator*. Realizing his influence, the Philadelphians tried to get him to speak at the opening of Pennsylvania Hall. Though he declined, he sent a note praising them for driving the petition campaign forward, and for constructing such a magnificent edifice, a place where "freedom of speech in the city of [William] Penn shall no longer be AN ABSTRACTION."

Yet Adams's effect on abolition was still something of an abstraction, a promise for a future where slavery could be openly discussed in Congress, and one day regulated or outlawed. The more crucial work—more immediate than the petition campaign, more pressing than the opening of the hall—was still the protection of Black people from kidnappers and bounty hunters.

—ɯ—

By March 1838 David Ruggles and his Committee of Vigilance were involved in no fewer than 173 cases at once—an amazing number considering each case required arraignment and trial, evidence gathering, and all else needed to keep Black men, women, and children away from the cargo holds of slave ships and Southern auction blocks.

The William Dixon case was key. The riot in the park did not free him, but Ruggles never gave up on him. He fiercely pursued the case, helping the committee raise $1,000 to cover his court fees and meet his $500 bail. None of this came cheap, and Ruggles had to search through his network of New York ministers, philanthropists, and lawyers to assemble the resources. He eventually got Dixon free on bond, then gained his release due to a lack of evidence against him.

Ruggles also harbored fugitives in his home, fed and nourished them, then sent them onward with road money and names and locations of the next safe harbor—anywhere from Utica and Hartford to Vermont and Canada. Some of the fugitives might go to their new homes by ship, others by canal boat or horse, traveling by whatever means necessary.

These were heroic labors, but they came at a cost. His eyesight, never good, now faltered even more, and his bowel disorders had become painful and chronic. He was perpetually out of money, frustrating for a man who raised so much of it for others, and lived close to penury five blocks from the Five Points. He never shied from confrontation, but the conflicts had worn on him, month after month. The latest: He went to the house of a white man with a warrant. The man wouldn't accept it and shoved him over and kicked him down several flights of stairs.

Ruggles ended up with a damaged liver, but he still got the man arrested for assault. He also fought being kept off steamships and stagecoaches, confined to Negro pews and inferior seats, and made to feel second class. Usually he got thrown out or beaten up, but he kept coming back. Each time he did, he ached a little more.

He now openly preached self-defense, no matter what the fallout. At one meeting he proposed a resolution: "we cannot recommend non-resistance to persons who are denied the protection of equitable law, when their liberty is invaded and their lives endangered by avaricious kidnappers." The ministers Theodore Wright, Charles Ray, and Samuel Cornish all thought it was too much, an open rejection of nonviolence and the kind of idea they could never support. But Ruggles was no minister, and he vowed to defend himself with force and anyone he protected. The man-stealers would have to fight to get around him.

This stance should have made him a pariah to the American Anti-Slavery Society, but it didn't. Lewis Tappan still admired him for his work, even if he wasn't a pacifist. For Ruggles put in the work and raised the funds and built the bridges to all parts of the movement. This kind of radicalism matched with pragmatism could do great things for the cause, and Lewis and Gerrit Smith and their allies couldn't help but support it. They contributed to Ruggles's committee, printed his pamphlets, and gave him aid when he needed it. Lewis and Arthur also endorsed his latest effort and one of his most important, to publish the first magazine by an African American in the United States.

The inaugural issue of the *Mirror of Liberty* appeared in July 1838, and it codified everything Ruggles had fought for over the previous decade. There were political and social arguments and an essay in favor of women's rights. He wrote, "The Mirror is consecrated to the genius of liberty. It is trammeled by no sect, association or company of men; but is, in a word, a free and independent Journal." And New Yorkers could read that journal in Ruggles's new antislavery reading room, which he had designed to be a literary refuge in a city that all too often barred Black people from its libraries and lyceums.

With all his pursuits, Ruggles found his reputation growing, though the price of maintaining that reputation remained steep. The Committee of Vigilance scarcely had the resources to manage the huge volume of cases it had taken on (522 and counting), but Ruggles couldn't just turn away people in need, so the caseload expanded further. Every day he would trudge back to the docks, or to a tavern in the Five Points, or onboard a ship based on a tip he had heard about fugitives or people held captive. That tip might or might not lead anywhere. Sometimes it got him into trouble.

His latest headache was a boardinghouse owner named John Russell. Ruggles learned from a tip that he had forced three Gambians onto a slave brig to take them to New York. Ruggles posted a letter attesting to his guilt in an article for the *Colored American*, but Russell sued for libel and won a judgment of more than $600. It was a large amount to pay, especially during a national depression. But the cost wouldn't fall on Ruggles. It would come down on Samuel Cornish.

Cornish, as the paper's editor, was shocked. He couldn't come up with the money, and he didn't see why he should have to. Ruggles had never vetted the article with him. He trusted the word of his ally, just as that ally had trusted the word of the tipster. And the cost for that faith was $600. Cornish asked the Tappans to help him pay the judgment, but the Tappans were in no position to do so since they were trying to emerge from bankruptcy. Cornish demanded Ruggles pay for his mistake, but Ruggles was already in arrears and had to direct whatever money he had to the Vigilance Committee. So the two allies were set at odds, and another divide began to open within the ranks of abolition.

There would be other court cases to weigh on Ruggles, other episodes where he would be led in the wrong direction and face repercussions. But what else could he do? He and his committee had found a strategy to unlock the vise of slavery, to impede its power, and he could no sooner walk away from it than he could walk away from abolition. He could do the work better than anyone, but the cost of that work was growing every day: the stress of racism, segregation, courtroom battles, dramatic rescues, and one confrontation after another. He kept going despite his exhaustion and infirmity, giving whatever reserves of strength he had left for the cause. In body, if not in spirit, Ruggles had become an old man at age twenty-eight.

—⁂—

Angelina Grimké could testify to the pain of broken alliances, to go along with the pain of exhaustion and ill health. The last few months of 1837 had been dreadful, confined as she was to a sick bed with typhoid, with a fever that lasted a month. Sarah Grimké worried the stress of her being a social trailblazer had wounded her terribly, to the point of not even being able to read letters in bed. "I fear her nature has been so overtasked and her whole system is prostrated."

Angelina did not give up, and day by day she recovered. She forced herself to hit the lecture circuit once again at the beginning of 1838—but not as one would expect. Instead of speaking to small groups to get her stamina back, she was slated to deliver some of the most important speeches of her life.

Henry Stanton made a surprising proposal: that she address the Massachusetts state legislature in February. It was something a woman had never done before in America, and it filled her with both excitement and dread. Stanton told her a key committee chairman had approved the idea, and she agreed to it. She would speak in support of the thousands of signatures women in the Northeast had gathered and sent to legislators. The peril of a backlash loomed, of course, but she was willing to make the sacrifice. Few had ever been given such an opportunity, and "Perhaps it is best *I* should bear the responsibility *wholly* myself." But while she was preparing once more to bear a burden for the cause, she had to answer the call of a man who had been a much greater burden to her three months before.

Since the beginning of the year, she had been corresponding again with Theodore Weld, trying to impress upon him how scornfully he had treated her, especially in a notorious letter from October. "Brother, I think in some things you wronged me in *that letter never to be forgotten*," she wrote. She said she could bear the injury, despite feeling "ABIDING PAIN" at the wound. Weld was humble in response and tried to account for his offensive words, such as when he described her beliefs as "ALL MOONSHINE." After some dodging, he admitted his guilt and took responsibility for his sins. He said he could be crude and intemperate but, like a good Christian, was trying to overcome his failings, to become a better man, and to justify her esteem for him.

Then it was time for the shocker: "I know it will surprise and even amaze you, Angelina, when I say to you as I now do, that for a long time, *you have had my whole heart*."

He said he had been enamored with her since her famed letter to *The Liberator*, and detailed how his affection had developed, how it had grown until his ardor was now inexhaustible. He had suppressed his feelings to everyone he knew until this very moment—even though he had "*no expectation* and almost no *hope* that my feelings are in any degree RECIPROCATED BY YOU."

This was a lot to process for anyone about to make history, but Angelina tried to make the best of it. She told Weld she wasn't at all surprised he felt this way, and her feelings had grown for him too, though the nastiness of his autumn letters had made her question him. She allowed that her heart had grown fond of him, and that they shared so many feelings and beliefs, they were practically two halves of the same whole. She reminded him that social conditions had kept her from announcing her feelings first—"The customs of Society gave *you* privileges, *rights* which it denied to me"—whereas he was always free to express his emotions. In return, he expressed his love and ecstasy with many exclamation marks.

Angelina thus had a great deal on her mind when she came to Boston on February 21. She entered the Massachusetts State House along with the stalwart of the Boston Female Anti-Slavery Society, Maria Chapman. Though she was nervous, she tried not to display her fear before the crowd. The audience was a mix of supporters, adversaries, radicals, colonizers, and politicians and their staff. Chapman gave her a quiet benediction: "God strengthen you, my sister."

Angelina faced the men of the committee and attempted to speak three times, but each time she was interrupted by hoots and jeers from the gallery. The committee chair tried to call the proceeding to order but soon decided it would be better for her to address the crowd directly from the platform—facing the audience just as she had spoken from the pulpit in church. She rose and began her oration.

She told her listeners she stood before them as a Southerner, a repentant slaveholder, who had come to testify to the cruelty and horror of slavery, "cemented by the blood and sweat and tears of my sisters in bonds." She wished to speak on behalf of the twenty-thousand women who had put their names to the petitions now before the legislators, demanding an end to any official support for the barbarism of human bondage. She said it was women's role in this campaign that was most crucial, "and because it is a *political* subject, it has often been tauntingly said, that *women* had nothing to do with it. Are we aliens, because we are *women*?"

"I hold, Mr. Chairman, that American women have to do with this subject, not only because it is moral and religious, but because it is *political*, inasmuch as we are citizens of this republic, and as such, *our* honor, happiness, and well being, are bound up in its politics, government, and laws."

She spoke for two hours to the now-silenced crowd, and when she finished, the room exploded in applause. Many observers realized how important her speech was, how influential it could be, and even compared it to Washington's Farewell Address. Her friends in the hall were overjoyed at the success of her oration, especially Wendell Phillips, a rising speaker himself. They congratulated her and wiped away tears, struck by how she had made one of her greatest speeches before so important a body. Angelina admitted to being caught up in the moment, writing, "We Abolition Women are turning the world upside down."

The next day Angelina, accompanied by Sarah, returned to the legislature and fielded questions from the representatives about the nature and details of slavery. She recited facts and gave her testimony, feeling the energy returning after the torpor of winter. It was all happening so fast, the possibility of change, the opportunity to drive it. She planned her next steps: more speeches in the Northeast, more calls for petitioners, more support for the women's societies, more hosannas for women in politics. Then she took a trip back to Philadelphia to christen Pennsylvania Hall, and to be wed. For Weld had proposed marriage, and she had accepted.

More than a few abolitionists were surprised by the news. The matrimony would mark the uniting of the former and current most popular speakers in the movement, in a ceremony both unconventional and interdenominational. Weld welcomed the approval of his evangelical family members, who were more relieved he had found a woman to marry him than they were disturbed that the woman was a Quaker. Lewis Tappan, too, was in support of it, impressed that Weld had "great moral courage in taking as his wife so strong a woman."

Garrison, however, was not convinced the marriage would be good for his close ally Angelina. He warned that "Weld's sectarianism would bring her into bondage, unless she could succeed in emancipating *him* . . . How far will she feel it her duty to comply with his sabbatical notions, observance of forms, church-going worship, &c. I do not know." She listened politely to Garrison's concerns and dismissed them. But in the end his fears came to fruition: Because Angelina would marry outside the Quaker faith, she would be expelled from the Society of Friends.

—⁂—

There would, of course, be no sabbatical notions or churchgoing worship for Garrison. He had expanded his war against the clerics and broadened his attack to include governments in general. He announced in the January 5, 1838, edition of *The Liberator* that "Next to the overthrow of slavery, the cause of PEACE will command our attention." By peace he didn't just mean the opposite of war—he meant that government should never use coercion and force upon its citizens, nor should it keep standing armies and navies and militias. People should not vote or hold elected office, they should not sue in court, they should not strike each other, and they definitely should not murder each other!

Garrison nursed a quiet grudge against the ghost of Lovejoy, the martyr who had gone down with guns blazing. In *The Liberator* Garrison provided a forum to question whether he had acted morally and condemned the use of violence even in self-defense. He printed a letter from Lewis Tappan, who agreed that the issue of nonresistance was a crucial one for the movement, and he would "rejoice to see the arguments, for and against, on the Peace question." Tappan and Garrison agreed to support a Boston peace convention in September that would hash out the arguments in full.

It was no idle concern. In New York and Philadelphia, a new crop of abolitionists questioned whether Garrison's old plea for martyrdom and pacifism had any meaning in an America plagued with mayhem. David Ruggles had shown the tactical use of violence could at least draw publicity and fend off the agents of slavery, and Black New Yorkers lauded him for it. In Pennsylvania, the legal outrage over disenfranchisement had made many African American citizens lose whatever faith they may have had in the political system. They responded by planning their own vigilance committee, modeling it after Ruggles's group.

The cracks in the movement were the widest in Boston, where Garrison and the enemy ministers had long established their battle lines, and where Maria Chapman was marshaling her forces in support of his clerical war. In the 1837 report she wrote for the Boston Female Anti-Slavery Society, she called the clergymen of her city weak and temporizing, comparing them to proslavery men and accusing them of trying to stifle the energy of the movement and neuter it "in the torpid bosom of the church." On the title page of the report, she wrote that it included "a Sketch of the Obstacles Thrown in the Way of Emancipation by Certain Clerical Abolitionists and Advocates for the Subjection of Women." Her evangelical sisters added a disapproving disclaimer, saying "we cherish the most serious objections" to the content. In response, Chapman quit as secretary of the group and went on to agitate against them.

In New York Theodore Weld had already chosen sides between the factions, and he had been pressing the Grimkés to abandon their allegiance to Garrison over what he saw as his flirtations with anarchy. After all, only government could eradicate slavery, so the lack of government meant the persistence of slavery! Lewis Tappan felt much the same way, that if they depended on moral suasion to lead the way to emancipation, it might never happen. Angelina listened to their arguments respectfully, but she refused to disavow Garrison, her and Sarah's one reliable ally who had never wavered in his support, unlike her fiancé.

Their disagreement, however, did not thwart their wedding plans, and neither did it hamper Angelina in delivering a series of brilliant speeches at Boston's Odeon, a lecture hall and auditorium that could seat a thousand people—though two or three times that number came to hear her speak. The experience left her feeling amazed at the power she could wield over people's hearts, or at least their opinions, using only her voice. "My tongue was loosed, my spirit unfettered and lifted above all human feeling and I spoke (if I am any judge) with more power and authority than I ever did in Boston before." If there was any doubt she was now the prime attraction among abolitionists in America, it was dispelled by these lectures. She felt confident she would have the same effect over the crowd in Philadelphia when Pennsylvania Hall opened, just days after her nuptials with Weld.

Matrimony for Angelina Grimké arrived on May 14, in the parlor of a Philadelphia cottage, before a small crowd of notables—Garrison, Stanton, Lewis Tappan, John Whittier, Maria Chapman, and a passel of rebels from Lane Seminary, among thirty others. Theodore Wright gave his blessings, but no one officiated the ceremony. State law allowed the signatures of twelve witnesses to act as official approval for the wedding. Weld emerged, dapper for once, having traded in his John the Baptist attire for a sensible brown coat, while Angelina appeared in a modest beige gown. They improvised their vows, with Weld offering his unconditional love to her and abjuring the power that men had over women in wedlock, and Angelina offering to fervently and purely love him. She never said the word "obey."

No drinks were served and no reception followed, but the mood was relaxed and festive. Lucretia Mott did not attend, for fear of being expelled from the Society of Friends for the transgression of attending a marriage outside the faith, and John Whittier had to perch outside the door to keep from meeting a similar fate. One young Quaker schoolteacher named Abby Kelley did, however, put caution aside and enter the parlor. She would prove to be just as brave at the Anti-Slavery Convention of American Women, when Pennsylvania Hall finally opened its doors.

The next day, inaugural events for the Hall began with a ceremonial reading of letters and orations by various figures in the movement, before a crowd of mostly white men. The tone was high-minded and lofty, with speakers vowing to uphold righteousness and bring unity to the struggle against slavery. Garrison was there as an observer and not on the agenda to speak. But as the day dragged on, a group of Quaker women demanded he say a few words, since he had become such a figure of renown, "the man for whose head the South had offered thousands of dollars." He was happy to comply.

Without notes he stood up. Yes, he said, his enemies had proposed "putting me into a strong cage . . . and carrying me about the country as a rare monster, to be seen at certain hours, at so much a sight for adults— children half price." But he said there were larger issues to consider than his own safety. Namely, why wasn't there a single Black speaker on the agenda at this event? It couldn't be an accident, could it? "I fear this exclusion may be traced to a wicked prejudice, or to a fear of giving public offence." He charged that his colleagues were guilty of "squeamishness" and of backsliding in their commitment to abolition.

The crowd stirred nervously. This was supposed to be a day of noble words and self-congratulation, but Garrison had upended the program. He charged his listeners with cowardice, with being unwilling to commune with Black people because they were afraid of being called *amalgamators*. It was a brash and timely accusation, referring to the threats that were already littering the streets of Philadelphia.

Just outside the building, menacing handbills encouraged white citizens *"to interfere, forcibly if they must"* with the women's convention—a racially mixed gathering that would begin the next day. Garrison could not believe the men before him had shown such spinelessness in cowering to the masses, even as their wives and sisters and daughters had freely chosen to defy white public opinion. He said, "slavery will not be overthrown without excitement, a most tremendous excitement," and not until the movement "brings down upon it a shower of brickbats and rotten eggs, and is threatened with a coat of tar and feathers." This sent the proceeding into a lather of dispute, with men rising to haggle over his points. Garrison was pleased that he had ignited a firestorm almost as soon as the Hall was open.

The next day, the debate became physical on the streets outside. Dozens of men lingered around the Hall, looking for a fight. Some of them even breached the doors to shout insults and profanities at those they found inside. The number of flyers increased on the streets, too, imploring Philadelphians—both working- and middle-class white men— to show up in force to prevent sedition from taking root in their fair city.

Amid these tensions the women's convention began. After an afternoon of meetings on the ground floor, the evening gave way to speeches on the second story, where a crowd of abolitionists filled the auditorium to its capacity of three thousand people, with more turned away at the door.

They arrived at a beautiful space lit with modern gas chandeliers and decorated with blue silk panels and plush chairs, damask couches, and walnut furniture, and covered with a ceiling featuring a great carving of a sunflower, at the center of which "was a concave mirror, which at night sparkled like a diamond." The audience was Black and white, men and women, from all over the Northeast, with many Philadelphians and Bostonians, and local Quaker women clad in their gray gowns and bonnets—among them the Grimké sisters and Lucretia Mott.

Despite the tranquility inside the hall, outside it men yelled and bellowed in the streets, feeding a growing cacophony from a swarm of people that had grown to the thousands. Some of them broke into the lobby and could be heard stamping around downstairs. The din grew loud enough in the building that the first speaker had to raise his voice to be heard—not a problem since it was, once again, William Lloyd Garrison.

This time he had planned his speech, and he began by comparing himself to Martin Luther and calling his opponents "an adulterous and perverse generation—a brood of vipers—hypocrites—children of the Devil, who could not escape the damnation of hell." He castigated slaveholders, colonizers, and gradualists as liars and schemers and said he would rather see the nation fall than slavery persist. "There cannot be union where there is not equity, nor equity where there is oppression."

He had scarcely finished speaking when the mob broke inside the room.

Burly men, young toughs, and angry merchants came in hissing and jeering. They shouted out insults and catcalls and shoved whoever got in their way—including women who stepped in their path.

The men charged up through the aisles toward the platform, hoping to get their hands on Garrison and finish the job their friends had started in Boston: putting him at the end of a rope. But a swell of audience members stopped them, corralled them, kept them at bay. Garrison saw the tumult unfolding, and he compared it to "the very fiends of the pit" escaping their bonds in hell. Some of the brawnier abolitionists eventually forced them back outside, barring the door shut behind them.

But now thrown out of the building, the mob roused tempers even higher on the streets. The massive horde of people now numbered ten thousand. Maria Chapman rose to make a few remarks, but she could barely speak above the din, before—

Stones shattered the windows. Then bricks.

Chapman raised her voice but couldn't be heard. The mob was screaming, hurling projectiles, breaking the glass. The room fell silent in shock.

None of the missiles hit the delegates—not yet. Iron shutters protected the windows, just as they had at Arthur Tappan's store in the New York riots. The difference: Tappan's men also had guns for protection. The delegates had nothing but faith.

Suddenly, Angelina got up to speak. The audience before her was convulsed with fear, ready to flee the building. But she wanted them to stay put.

She asked, what did they expect? Everyone knew how they were hated and had been hunted by the mob. Would they be like a "reed shaken with the wind" and drift away?

A scream outside interrupted her, but she kept going.

The people outside, she told them, were maddened with wrath. Because racial hatred drove people to insanity—*listen, they could hear it outside!*—and only abolition could salve the wounds of slavery and injustice. She knew it intimately because she spoke as a Southerner who had witnessed the horrors of slavery and could testify to the—

More screams. Windows shattering. Rocks breaking windows.

She kept at it: "What would the breaking of every window be? What would the levelling of this Hall be?" She told them it would *not* be the victory of slavery, but its defeat. And she bade them to have courage: "What if the mob should now burst in upon us, break up our meeting and commit violence upon our persons—would this be any thing compared with what the slaves endure?"

Another tumult. The glass, the yelling.

She said Southerners knew wickedness, they knew the terrors of slavery, but had connived to keep its horrors from the outside world. She looked forward to a day when the North would never want to shame itself by supporting the South—

The smashing went on. So did Angelina.

She said her listeners must face mobs with full hearts, to battle them not with guns and stones, but with truth and virtue. The women in her audience must keep petitioning, and everyone must keep driving forward, hold their heads up, and know no fear. Don't doubt or despair. Rejoice in fulfilling God's plan!

She felt it now. The power and authority. She had made the audience stay seated, rapt and riveted, during one of the worst moments of their lives. Now they were emboldened, ready to sacrifice themselves in the face of violence, just as she had once said: "Yes! LET IT COME!"

Angelina sat down to thunderous applause, and a Quaker school-teacher replaced her. It was Abby Kelley, young and fearless, with impromptu words inspired by the moment, or by God. She said the mob clamor was "a moral whirlwind" and the crashing of windows a sign of "a moral earthquake," but they need not worry. She spoke of Lazarus as the morally dead man of the South and the North as the rich man who finds him, prepared for resurrection. Then Lucretia Mott tried to speak for a few minutes, but she stopped abruptly.

Everyone had to leave the building.

They couldn't hold out against the mob much longer. It was better to adjourn and come back the next day, to continue their work once refreshed. So they followed the model from the Boston riot: the delegates filed out, two by two, the white women's arms interlocked with the Black women's. They found a passage through the swarm of mobsters and faced their jeers and catcalls, but they were left unharmed.

The next day the women returned and held meetings and passed resolutions. They spent the afternoon in quiet diligence, trying to ignore the large mass of white men who had returned to encircle the building. Among the crowd were dock workers and other laboring men and mechanics, as well as gentlemen of property and standing. Undeterred, the women inside the Hall continued their work—until the mayor told them not to.

Mayor Jonathan Swift informed them he could not guarantee their safety for another night, in the face of the restive crowd outside. The conventioneers agreed to adjourn early, to prevent another onslaught that night. Satisfied, the mayor took the key to the building to secure it against any intrusion. The delegates quietly departed, and he went out to face the ruffians. He made a short but agreeable speech and wished them a good evening, and they cheered three times as he left the scene. Then they broke inside with axes.

As one report had it:

> Doors and windows were broken through, and with wild yells the reckless horde dashed in, plundered the Repository, scattering the books in every direction, and, mounting the stairways and entering the beautiful hall, piled combustibles on the Speaker's forum, and applied the torch to them, shrieking like demons—as they were, for some time. A moment more, and the flames roared and crackled through the building, and though it was estimated that fifteen thousand persons were present, and though the fire companies were early on the scene, not one effort was made to save the structure so recently erected, at such great cost, and consecrated to such Christian uses. In a few hours the smouldering walls alone were left.

The mob didn't stop there. They spilled out into the streets and alleys, looking for more people and things to destroy. They went in search of their next target, the house of Lucretia and James Mott. Knowing they were next on the rioters' list, the Motts sent their children away and awaited their fate in the parlor.

But the mob did not fall upon their house. At the last minute, it changed direction and set fire to several homes owned by Black citizens, as well as the Shelter for Colored Orphans, the mobsters deciding to immolate the home of Black children instead of white Quakers. Over the next few nights, scattered hoodlums assaulted and intimidated any Black Philadelphians they found and tried to ransack and destroy the First African Presbyterian Church.

Abolitionists were stunned and sickened by the latest atrocity. Garrison agreed that it was an appalling spectacle but, having escaped town before the mob had done its worst, he saw the destruction of the Hall as a useful sacrifice: "it will do incalculable good to our cause; for the wrath of man worketh out the righteousness of God." To some degree he was right. Abolitionists used the mob attack to apply moral suasion for the movement, and prints of the burning building circulated throughout the North. Wavering minds in the North turned in favor of the cause, and colonizers and proslavery apologists faced even more criticism for enabling barbarity.

And yet—

The Southern press exalted in the Hall's destruction and saw it as a victory. Their editorialists praised the mob's character and esteemed them for doing a good deed, printing the testimony of eyewitnesses who had a hand in the arson. The episode, they said, was full of "terrible majesty, beauty and delight . . . beautiful spires of flame."

No one was punished or even arrested for the crime, and the participants boasted of their actions. The Pennsylvania abolitionists who owned the building saw their investment vaporized, the Philadelphia women's society saw their efforts to establish it come to naught, and Maria Chapman faced an outbreak of what Garrison called "brain fever," reducing her to a "raving maniac" for a few months. And among all the delegates, Angelina Grimké Weld saw the worst of it.

She had faced down the attackers and inspired thousands in the Hall with her speech, people who would go on to drive the movement and make their own speeches. But the year's frenzied schedule of writing and exhortations and conflict and violence—it all came at the same cost for her as it had for Weld and Ruggles and the other men and women who pushed abolition to new heights. She retired from public life and retreated to Fort Lee, New Jersey, with Weld and her sister Sarah. While there, she found herself beset with mysterious ailments that affected her for the rest of her life. That marked the end of her public career. She would never again enflame a crowd to action, or calm its spirit against an outside threat.

Garrison seemed to be the one force in abolition that grew stronger with each attack. Having survived his near hanging in 1835, he'd become determined to fear nothing and to follow his own truth, even if it meant the demise of unity among colleagues. He still chafed over how he had been treated by clerics, and how the American Anti-Slavery Society had done nothing to defend him. Blaming them for the schism, he wrote to the executive committee the following year with a litany of accusations. He charged that Lewis Tappan had "counselled the division in our ranks" and his colleagues were "waging unceasing warfare" against him and his allies.

He no longer cared if he offended the members of that society, and he redoubled his energies for the causes dearest to him. He pushed ever harder for abolitionists to admit women to their organizations and to give them equal voting rights and opportunities for leadership. He also became more insistent that political action was vile and corrupting. In September he attended the Peace Convention, which would inaugurate the New England Non-Resistance Society. Under Garrison's influence, the society forbade the support of lawsuits, incarceration, or military service; pursuit of elected office; allegiance to any government; and any kind of violence, be it personal or political. Lydia Child saw most of the delegates as "swinging loose from any regular society" to form their own alternative community of firebrands.

Garrison said the founding of the society would someday be marked with the same reverence as the Fourth of July. The smattering of ministers present accepted some of his doctrine, but they could not accept Garrison's unyielding support for the rights of women, or that they be given full powers to lead and vote within the new organization. Also controversial: the rise of Abby Kelley, who stepped into the void of Angelina Grimké's retirement and emerged as one of the most powerful speakers for the cause, her determination steeled by her speech under threat of the Philadelphia mob. Now, she parlayed her oratory into a leadership role, gaveling meetings to order and calling ministers out of line. For the middle-aged clerics this was too much, being put in their place by a twenty-seven-year-old woman, and they began walking out. This left Garrison firmly in control of the new group, and an entire wing of the abolition movement.

Another wing of that movement, however, resisted Garrison's notions of peace and self-sacrifice. For any time a Black abolitionist had been attacked, there had been no commemorative engravings sold or martyrs glorified. Instead, he could expect his church to remain burned and his career destroyed, like Peter Williams. Or he could see his home and business under siege with no help from the police, like David Ruggles. Or he could lose his life without any investigation, like David Walker. To these men, and to the women who faced the same threats, martyrdom was not a helpful political tool. It was a sacrifice to their enemies without justice or purpose—and more and more Black citizens began to realize it.

After the demise of Pennsylvania Hall and the brutalizing of Black Philadelphia, the recently formed Vigilant Association of Philadelphia grew in membership and influence. Inspired by its counterpart in New York, the organization rescued fugitives and kept Black Pennsylvanians out of harm's way, protecting them from kidnappers and slaveholders. In July it added a women's auxiliary, the Female Vigilant Association. One of the primary drivers behind the vigilance work was Robert Purvis. One of the strongest women supporters was Sarah Forten.

Sarah opened the treasury of the Philadelphia Female Anti-Slavery Society to the Vigilant Association and organized fairs and bazaars to drum up funds. The two groups sealed their alliance, with the Anti-Slavery Society donating hundreds of dollars to help the Association board fugitives in private homes and give them clothing, lawyers, and medical attention—and a means to escape farther north. The Fortens made a commitment to the Vigilant Association for good reason: They had seen Pennsylvania Hall in flames, the building Sarah had labored to help build for more than a year. They had seen their neighbors attacked and their institutions immolated. And they had seen politicians and police fail to stop it. So nonresistance might be fine for those who could afford it, but for the Fortens it was not an option. They moved toward rescue and resistance, using their own money and labor, with no help from the authorities or from those who preached passivity in the face of pandemonium.

This had been the philosophy of David Ruggles for years now, and his influence had spread beyond Philadelphia to inspire new groups in Pittsburgh, Boston, and Albany. Black citizens led and operated most of these vigilance committees, providing more resources to help fugitives escape bondage and the unjustly accused find new homes. Yet for the original committee in New York, times were tougher. Its treasury strained to pay for all its endeavors, and Ruggles's own finances were depleted. He struggled through what he called "seasons of mental anxiety" worsened by his physical ailments.

The Russell case continued to take a toll on his reputation and on his friendship with Samuel Cornish. The close ties the men had developed now frayed in full. In the *Colored American*, Cornish accused Ruggles of mismanaging the funds of the committee and sapping it of money through his own financial bumbling—and, of course, not paying Cornish's legal fees. He said Ruggles lacked judgment and prudence and had hurt the cause of fugitives to boost his own notoriety. But Ruggles said he would not quarrel with his old friend in public, preferring to "bleed in silence."

Ruggles then became embroiled in the Darg case, in which an escaped slave allegedly took up to $8,000 from a Virginia slaveholder. Ruggles helped him find freedom, though he had no knowledge of the theft. Nonetheless, Ruggles was arrested and thrown into a cell with "four drunken, half crazy, infamous wretches" and spent three days there—with bail set at $3,000, a sum he could not hope to pay. His old allies came to the rescue: a Black man named J. W. Higgins, who operated a grocery, and the publisher of *The Emancipator*, Arthur Tappan. These days, Arthur could not spread around his money as he once did, and he struggled to unburden his business from the weight of its debts. But even with his finances weakened, Arthur still found enough money to set Ruggles at liberty. Despite all the fractures in the movement, the

Tappans continued to stand by Ruggles, and he by them. For all their work together, they owed each other nothing less.

Amid his struggles, Ruggles continued his work. In September, he was due to meet a certain Frederick Bailey. The man had come to New York seeking refuge, but found the city had few good places to hide. He had been sleeping among the barrels on the docks, until a friend directed him to meet someone who could help. Ruggles welcomed Bailey into his home on Lispenard Street and learned he was a caulker. He told him New York was infested with informants and man-stealers and said he might do better in the whaling trade of New Bedford, where Ruggles had once been a mariner, what seemed like a long time ago.

He took a liking to Bailey, harbored him for a few days in his home, and even helped him arrange a marriage with his fiancée in his living room. Bailey explored Ruggles's antislavery reading room, perused pamphlets and newspapers, and received a lecture or two from his new friend. Ruggles told him he should stay away from the bottle, fight all forms of oppression, and find allies wherever he could. The fight for abolition would be a long one.

He offered Bailey five dollars for his journey onward but, in reality, gave him much more than that—a boost in spirit, a lesson in confidence— and the man would not forget it. He later wrote of Ruggles, "This brave and devoted man suffered much from the persecutions common to all who have been prominent benefactors." Ruggles would meet him again years later, after the man had launched his own career as an abolitionist, under the name Frederick Douglass.

★ EPILOGUE ★

CRASHING UNANIMITY

The 450 friends of William Lloyd Garrison assembled in a mood of joy at train depots throughout New England on May 11, 1840. They had come from towns large and small to take a ride on the Boston and Providence Railroad, in hopes of transforming the movement to abolish slavery. Once aboard the train, they disregarded the signs that said women had to sit in one car, men in another, Black citizens in one, whites in another, and they sat wherever they pleased. Garrison couldn't be happier to see so many of his allies onboard the train—"the most untiring and zealous friends"—laughing and telling old stories, singing spirituals, and steeling themselves for the battle to come. Because once this army of acolytes reached Providence, they would board the steamship *Rhode Island* for the overnight sail to New York City, where they would attempt to take over the American Anti-Slavery Society.

The following day, more than a thousand delegates assembled at the Fourth Free Church, a cramped and stifling Presbyterian meetinghouse. The drama began quickly. To break the hierarchy that had run the organization for six years, Garrison chose the rising orator Abby Kelley as the hammer. Fresh off a winter lecture tour in which she denounced many of the same nemeses as Garrison—clerics, moderates, and gradualists— Kelley was among the most polarizing figures in the movement. Garrison insisted she be appointed to the all-male business committee.

"Doubted! Doubted!"

A volley of men's voices demanded a vote on Kelley's nomination, which Garrison was happy to provide. Aided by the mass of delegates from New England, Kelley won the vote, 571 to 451. Lewis Tappan and his colleagues on the executive committee knew they had been thwarted. Lewis resigned from the committee he had helped create and criticized Garrison for "throwing a firebrand into the anti-slavery ranks; it is contrary to the usages of civilized society." He privately called Garrison "the Massachusetts madman" and vowed there could be no compromise with such a zealot.

Later in the week, Lewis assembled three hundred clergymen and other allies on the lower level of the church to form his own group. It would be called the American and Foreign Anti-Slavery Society, and it would work with abolitionists in Britain to advance a mission more friendly to clergymen and resistant to radical change. Women would have their own auxiliary, but they would otherwise be barred from membership. With the creation of such a group, Lewis broke abolition into open schism, doing in reality what he had long accused Garrison of doing in spirit.

None of this deterred the so-called madman in the slightest. Now in control of the American Anti-Slavery Society, Garrison secured the appointment of Lucretia Mott, Maria Chapman, and Lydia Child to the executive committee, integrated the membership by race and sex, and passed resolutions against political action and violence in any form. Another proclamation announced that the Christian church in America was "the foe of freedom, humanity and pure religion." Guided by Garrison, the new leadership appointed delegates for the upcoming World Anti-Slavery Convention in London. In defiance of women's exclusion from the event, they appointed Mott as one of the representatives.

Garrison exalted in his triumph. He had waited years to secure victory over the Tappans and didn't mind gloating over it. He wrote, "We have made clean work of every thing—adopted the most thorough-going resolutions—and taken the strongest ground—with *crashing* unanimity."

Abolition quickly divided into factions. Garrison kept forming new groups, including the Friends of Universal Reform, which questioned the nature of the Sabbath and the role of ministers in the church. He attacked "revivalism, the divine interpretation of the Bible, the ordinance of Baptism, and the atoning powers of Christ" while taking an interest in heresies like spiritualism. He combined his heterodoxy with renewed condemnations of national institutions, and he denigrated the Constitution as "a covenant with death and an agreement with Hell." A decade later, he burned a copy of it in public.

Garrison and his allies did occasionally achieve tangible results, such as an 1840 petition campaign to the Massachusetts legislature that led to the formal repeal of an anti-amalgamation law. But his primary role in the coming years would involve inciting controversy through provocative words and actions—and doing so without apology. He roused passions at antislavery conventions, spoke adamantly for women's rights, and eviscerated his critics without hesitation. He had little use for those who moderated their beliefs and wrote, "An inquiring spirit is not an irreverent one. He who honestly doubts is not a dangerous member of society."

After the Garrisonian takeover, the American Anti-Slavery Society continued to splinter. A breakaway group provided the nucleus for the Liberty Party, which rejected Garrison's withdrawal from public affairs and ran James Birney in a quixotic presidential campaign in 1840, standing on a platform denouncing slavery, racial injustice, and abuses of Native peoples and Mormons, among others. In an election in which only white men could vote, Birney received less than a third of 1 percent of the national vote. He did a bit better when he ran again in 1844, attracting just over 2 percent.

Lewis Tappan saw such electoral crusades as having no more value than Garrison's rhetorical ones: neither made any tangible difference to the men and women locked in captivity in the South, or led to change in Washington, DC, the nexus of the slave empire. But as the years passed, Lewis's splinter group, the American and Foreign Anti-Slavery Society, didn't do much better. It had no compelling literature to distribute, and it failed to garner widespread support among the moderates to whom Lewis had aimed it. By the mid-1850s it foundered from a dearth of members and a lack of interest.

Lewis found more success with a high-profile legal case. It involved an enslaved crew of Mende people from Sierra Leone who mutinied against their Portuguese captors aboard the vessel *Amistad*. They demanded to return to their home in Africa, but the surviving Portuguese instead piloted the boat toward the United States, believing their case would inspire support in slavery-friendly America. The Mende were imprisoned once they arrived.

In response to their jailing in the United States, Lewis's *Amistad* Committee raised funds and promoted their cause in the mainstream press, finding lawyers to argue their case in federal court. The US Supreme Court ruled in their favor in 1841—due, in part, to a lengthy speech made in their defense by John Quincy Adams. The thirty-five men and women who had survived the ordeal returned to West Africa, and Lewis built the case into a signature victory against oppression, even though it dealt only with violations of the international slave trading ban and various treaties, not with domestic slavery or racial inequality. Nonetheless, Lewis used it as a springboard for funding Christian missions to West Africa and, in 1846, helped found the American Missionary Association with the same designs.

By this time Lewis had managed to extricate himself from his brother's failing silk business and establish a new firm for rating the credit of businesses, the Mercantile Agency. Providing a way for banks and businesses to ensure the credibility of other firms, the agency would create a new kind of business and lead the way to a successor firm, Dun & Bradstreet. It would prove to be lucrative enough that Arthur would take over as co-partner when Lewis retired from the business at the end of the decade—but it would also lead to charges of hypocrisy.

Few of the employees the firm hired were people of color, and fewer of them were hired but for the most menial labors. Echoing the feelings of many Black New Yorkers, a jeweler named Edward Clark called the brothers out publicly for not practicing what they preached about racial equality: "Wherever the colored man is connected with the houses of these gentlemen it is as the lowest drudges. If a colored man enters as a porter in the store of Mr. Tappan, does he advance him afterward according to his merits?" Lewis responded that he would hire a Black employee for a job with greater prestige, but he could find none who were qualified to his standards. As Clark might have suspected, this showed that where it counted—in their business—the Tappans could only see Black Americans as their subordinates, never as their equals.

As the Tappans rebuilt their fortune, less of their money went to the New York Committee of Vigilance and David Ruggles. The committee endured several difficult years, due to lawsuits and charges of mismanagement of funds, and Ruggles took the blame. He tried to protest that he had been the one to keep the committee in business, despite not receiving his full salary as an officer, having to pay countless expenses out of pocket, and sitting in jail for the criminal actions of slaveholders. But the other committee members no longer had faith in him and forced his resignation as secretary. He wrote a letter in his own defense, but Lewis would not publish it in *The Emancipator*, and Samuel Cornish refused to print it in the *Colored American* since, by this time, he and Ruggles had become committed enemies.

Cornish used the troubles of the committee as an opportunity to impugn the character of his former friend, calling him a liar in his newspaper, as well as a "notorious individual" and an embezzler. Cornish was still furious over having to pay the costs of the libel judgment in the

Russell case, which he put squarely on Ruggles. Eventually, Ruggles was able to publish his defense—in a new paper aligned with Garrison, the *National Anti-Slavery Standard*—and called his accusers imbeciles and traitors to the cause. As for Cornish, he was nothing less than "the Prince of Darkness." Ruggles sued the Committee of Vigilance for his back wages and rallied what colleagues he had left to defend his name and reputation.

Ruggles's finances had never been worse, and his health continued to fail. He looked forward to taking a sabbatical outside the country, but he had neither money nor benefactors to pay his way. Making matters worse, he was functionally blind and relied on an assistant to help him read and write. Even mustering the strength to fend off the slander against him proved difficult, since his *Mirror of Liberty* would soon print its final issue and he had no forum in which to publish his thoughts. In sympathy, William Whipper wrote that Ruggles had been maligned to no good end: "Let not a faithful public servant that has lost his eyesight in the cause of liberty, suffer a worse infliction by having his character assailed because he is now too poor to defend it."

Ruggles searched for all manner of cures for his maladies, from experimental and bizarre treatments to the standard medicine of the time, but none seemed to work. He wrote that he had been "bled, leeched, cupped, plastered, blistered, salivated, dosed with arsenic, nux-vomica, iodine, strychnine and other poisonous drugs," but still had nothing to show for his miseries but continuing bowel problems, bodily numbness, and near blindness. A physician gave him but a few weeks to live.

By 1842 Ruggles had no choice but to abandon New York and retreat to Northampton, Connecticut, on the advice of Lydia Child. Here he managed to recover some of his strength and explore the practice of hydrotherapy. Surprisingly, he found it had a salutary effect on his ailments. He became so impressed by its efficacy that he created his own water-cure hospital, relying on a newfound network of friends and supporters for funding. It proved successful enough that by the end of the decade (and the last few years of his short life), he had attracted a devoted clientele who came to him for therapeutic baths and other treatments. One of them was the perpetually infirm William Lloyd Garrison, who stayed at the clinic for four months.

Ruggles did not, however, retreat from abolition, and he found that many young Black abolitionists revered him, knowing how much he had accomplished for the cause. And he wasn't done yet. Even as a nearly blind man, Ruggles still fought segregation on trains and steamships, found himself thrown off public transportation more than once, and publicized such bigotry in the press. And he found an increasing number of allies to join with him in protest. Among them were Frederick Douglass and other Black men and women he had helped to safety and freedom.

By his own count Ruggles rescued six hundred people from abduction and slavery, though in practice the actual number may have been much higher, and unknowable. His success in building a model to thwart Southern slave hunters, protect Black people in court, and send them onward to Canada would create a precedent that many others would follow, in cities from Worcester and Albany to distant Cleveland and Detroit. At first, Ruggles's success in organizing resistance to slavery made him known as the most prominent ally of the "freedom seekers." He would later come to be called one of the first conductors of the Underground Railroad.

As the years passed Samuel Cornish would remain estranged from Ruggles and, indeed, from an increasing number of his colleagues in the abolition movement. Whereas Cornish, as a Presbyterian minister, had championed tradition and constancy to work toward the goal of racial equality, many abolitionists were now attacking the church for its transgressions, or fighting slaveholders in public, or using intemperate language in print. None of this was for Cornish, who simply wanted to live free from prejudice in the comfortable style he felt he deserved. So he moved his family to New Jersey.

It wasn't long before his chosen new home, Belleville, proved to be as malignant as his old one in New York City. One of his sons died in a drowning accident, and the other faced unrelenting prejudice at the religious school where Cornish sent him. As for himself, he wrote in the *Colored American* that the New Jerseyans treated him with "proscription and persecution, and assault." There seemed to be no refuge for him anywhere in the United States. Yet he refused to leave the country, as John Russwurm had done fifteen years before, having committed to do his part to address the sins of the nation and fight against injustice from the pages of his newspaper.

But even his work at the paper would prove to be short-lived, as he allowed Charles Ray to take over as editor while he stepped back from public view. He rejected the Liberty Party, partisan campaigning, and any other doomed pursuit. Gerrit Smith and others criticized him for his inaction, but he refused to submit to demands that he assume a greater public role. And in any case, he had grown wary of the entreaties of white abolitionists. He wrote that people like Lewis Tappan, James Birney, and Theodore Weld might be helpful allies, but "we should not dare to trust them. They are but men and of like passions with other good men"— meaning prone to pride and self-indulgence. If ever they achieved power, "we fear, like their predecessors, they might overlook and forget the colored man and the slave." He still joined the Tappans' organizations, like the American and Foreign Anti-Slavery Society and their missionary group, but his public appearances became less frequent, his behavior more guarded.

It was a strange, slow decline for such a consequential figure. In his earlier life, Cornish had been a trailblazer in African American journalism, published figures like David Ruggles and David Walker, founded institutions and societies, and codified the very ideas—anti-colonization, immediate abolition, Black self-empowerment—that were now essential to the movement. Yet in his older age, he became obscure outside of New York and his reputation faltered. Charles Ray marked him as a relic, calling him an "old School man . . . he stands by the old paths, but does not inquire for the new." Paradoxically, Cornish condemned others for violating tradition and the hierarchy of church and class, even though that tradition had been the cause of so much that was damaging to Black Americans, including Cornish himself.

The old prescription for equality that Cornish and almost all white abolitionists advocated for Black people—the demand for moral reform, the striving for respectability—came under withering fire by a younger generation of Black abolitionists. One of the most prominent was Peter Paul Simons, who accused Cornish of looking down his nose at working-class laborers like himself and slandering the character of those without as much money or education as he had. Simons charged that he and his colleagues had kowtowed before whites and that "blind submission" was the real cause of any degradation Black people felt. Instead of submission, "we must show ACTION! ACTION! ACTION! . . . and we will be in truth an independent people."

By the 1840s, the entire program that had animated most abolitionists in the previous decade—pacifism, moral reform, martyrdom—began to collapse within African American circles. The smashing of slavery in the South and unjust laws in the North would require a range of tactics: petitioning and working within politics, rescuing the kidnapped, helping fugitives, and using violence if needed against oppression. "Respectability" now meant fighting racism, not staying meek and mannerly. In this view, the only people who weren't respectable were those who did nothing against a corrupt and depraved system.

This divided Black and white activists further. Frederick Douglass, for one, would differ with Garrison on issues like political involvement, nonresistance, and the need for Black leadership in abolition against the old white hierarchy. (Following their dispute, the men would not speak again for decades.) Charles Remond advocated radical action to liberate slaves, even if it meant violence against their captors. He urged them "to RISE AT ONCE, en masse, and THROW OFF THEIR FETTERS." Henry Highland Garnet went further and tried to get an official resolution approved, at an 1843 Black convention, in support of the uprising of the enslaved—it failed by a single vote. Garnet later published the speech he gave at the convention, "Address to the Slaves of the United States," as the most powerful rejection yet of self-sacrifice: "It is sinful in the extreme for you to make voluntary submission . . . You had far better all die—die immediately, than live slaves, and entail your wretchedness upon your posterity . . . Let your motto be resistance! resistance! resistance!"

Garnet would become equally well-known for advocating for Black nationalism and the creation of offshore colonies run by Black people—to compete with and destroy the system of slave-grown agriculture. His ideas were controversial, but they would capture the imagination of many new activists and influence the movement to come at midcentury. In fact, Garnet's work proved to be so influential it was republished a century later, to guide a new generation of revolutionaries in the 1960s.

Yet even as the ground was shifting for abolition in the 1840s, several key figures in Philadelphia would not be there to influence it. On March 4, 1842, in his midseventies, James Forten died after experiencing months of asthma and edema. His funeral drew up to five thousand people from both the elite and the working class, and many from the nautical trade. Several weeks later a memorial took place in Philadelphia's historic "Mother Bethel" AME Church, in a ceremony that marked the end of an era.

It had been a quarter-century since the church had seen this many visitors, for the famed 1817 meeting where the Black community had rejected colonization, presided over by Forten himself. And now he lay in repose in the same building, with up to four thousand souls mourning him. Except this time, the churchgoers were both Black and white. Robert Purvis, his son-in-law, took note and said that in death, James had brought people together from throughout the city, and "Prejudice, soul-crushing, man-despising, God-hating prejudice, was victimized on the 6th of March, 1842."

But if prejudice had a temporary respite with his passing, it returned in full force in the days after. The laws restricting the suffrage of African Americans were as formidable as ever, along with other measures to stifle their liberties, and support for James's optimism about the founding ideals of the nation had died long before he did. And while his legacy in advancing abolition was unmatched in the city, it didn't take long before his in-laws began fighting over his money.

ABOVE: First AME Church, Philadelphia. Site of the first mass resistance to the colonization movement. *Library Company of Philadelphia.* BELOW: President Jackson's reaction to a failed assassination attempt. *Library of Congress.*

RIGHT: Portrait of William Lloyd Garrison at age twenty-seven. *Artist Nathaniel Jocelyn. National Portrait Gallery.* BELOW CENTER: Masthead of *The Liberator*, July 2, 1831. BOTTOM LEFT: Lewis Tappan engraving by J. C. Buttre. *New York Public Library.* BOTTOM RIGHT: Arthur Tappan and Co. store on Pearl Street, by Alexander Jackson Davis. *Museum of Modern Art.*

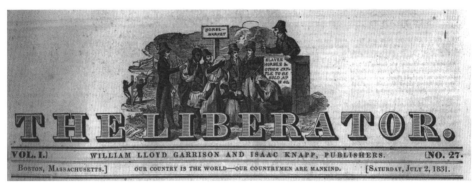

FOR LIBERIA

"NUISANCES" GOING AS "MISSIONARIES," "WITH THEIR OWN CONSENT."
Having driven colored people from school, we next DRIVE them to Liberia.
"They sent out two shiploads of vagabonds that were COERCED away as truly
as if it had been done with the cartwhip."—*R. J. Breckenridge*, 1834. "I am ac-

ABOVE: Anti-colonization image from the *American Anti-Slavery Almanac* for 1839. *Library Company of Philadelphia.* LEFT: Drawing of David Ruggles by unknown artist. *David Ruggles Center for History and Education.* BELOW: Racist cartoon against race mixing. *New York Public Library.*

ABOVE LEFT: Reverend Samuel Cornish by Francis Kearny. *Presbyterian Historical Society.* ABOVE RIGHT: Cartoon of common New York street hooligan. *Library Company of Philadelphia.* BELOW: The metaphorical "Judge Lynch" ruling from a throne of cotton over an execution. *Library Company of Philadelphia.*

ABOVE: *Five Points*, anonymous painting based on *Five Points, 1827*, lithograph by George Catlin. *Metropolitan Museum of Art*. BELOW: Chatham Street Chapel (earlier Chatham Garden Theatre). From *Our Theatres To-Day and Yesterday* by Ruth Dimmick.

Racist handbill against workplace integration. *Boston Public Library.*

RIGHT: Portrait of James Forten by unknown artist. *Historical Society of Pennsylvania.* BELOW: "Grave of the Slave" music by Francis (Frank) Johnson, based on a poem by Sarah Forten. *Free Library of Philadelphia.*

ABOVE: Portrait of Prudence Crandall by Francis Alexander. *Division of Rare and Manuscript Collections, Cornell University Library.* BELOW: Mob attack on a Black school, from the *American Anti-Slavery Almanac* for 1839. *Library Company of Philadelphia.*

COLORED SCHOOLS BROKEN UP, IN THE FREE STATES.
When schools have been established for colored scholars, the law-makers and the mob have combined to destroy them;—as at Canterbury, Ct., at Canaan, N. H., Aug. 10, 1835, at Zanesville and Brown Co., Ohio, in 1836.

LEFT: "Am I Not a Woman and a Sister?" embossing seal of American Anti-Slavery Society. *Massachusetts Historical Society.* BELOW: James Watson Webb, publisher of the *Courier and Enquirer,* ready for a duel. *Library of Congress.*

SCENE IN WASHINGTON.

I'm a small Army in Myself.
I am afraid there is not much
danger here after all."
(Colonel of Congress)

Sunday Feb. 25. 1838.

RIGHT: George Thompson, British abolitionist. *Boston Public Library.* BELOW: Post office attack during the 1835 Charleston riot. *Library Company of Philadelphia.*

DISTRICT OF COLUMBIA.

THE RESIDENCE OF 7000 SLAVES.

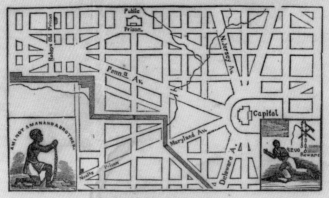

PART OF WASHINGTON CITY.

RIGHT TO INTERFERE.

ABOVE AND BELOW: Details from 1836 abolition poster
"Slave Market of America." *Library of Congress.*

PUBLIC PRISONS IN THE DISTRICT.

s for which they were built, and used by Slaveholders for the confinement of refractory
prisonment of Free Americans, seized and sold to pay their jail fees!

JAIL IN WASHINGTON,—SALE OF A FREE CITIZEN TO PAY HIS JAIL FEES!

ABOVE: Cartoon of attempted lynching of William Lloyd Garrison in 1835 Boston riot. *Library Company of Philadelphia.* BELOW: Theodore Weld, based on daguerreotype by unknown artist. *Library of Congress.*

ABOVE: Lithograph of David Ruggles and associates confronted by a slaveholder. *Library of Congress.*
BELOW: Kidnapping of a free Black man, from the *American Anti-Slavery Almanac* for 1839. *Library Company of Philadelphia.*

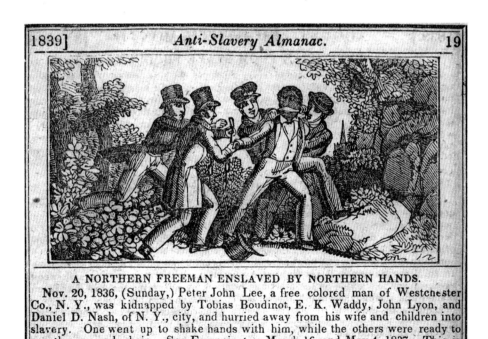

ABOVE: *View of the Great Fire of New York, 1835*, by Nicolino Calyo. *Museum of Fine Arts, Houston.* BELOW LEFT: Portrait of Sarah Grimké by unknown artist. *Massachusetts Historical Society.* BELOW RIGHT: Portrait of Angelina Grimké by unknown artist. *Massachusetts Historical Society.*

ABOVE: Andrew Jackson and friends waging war against their enemies. *Library Company of Philadelphia.* BELOW LEFT: John Calhoun, from *The Mentor* magazine. *New York Public Library.* BELOW RIGHT: Arthur Tappan in later years. *From* The Life of Arthur Tappan *by Lewis Tappan.*

ABOVE: Mob attack on Elijah Lovejoy's press office in 1837. *Library of Congress.* BELOW: Pennsylvania Hall in ruins. *From* The History of Pennsylvania Hall *by anonymous author.*

Financial records revealed debts of almost $32,000—half the value of the estate—attributed to leniency with his debtors, rigidity from his creditors, and a national depression that had damaged the solvency of his and other firms. Lawsuits soon enveloped the company, some of which would drag on for a decade. Two of them were entered by Robert Purvis, who moved on from speaking ennobling words at James's funeral to suing his sons for thousands of dollars in unpaid debts.

Despite these troubles within the Forten and Purvis families, Purvis's wife, Harriet, and sister-in-law Margaretta Forten continued to work with the Philadelphia Female Anti-Slavery Society. They and their colleagues petitioned Congress, hosted antislavery fairs, supported women's conventions, and aided the local vigilance committee. Others in the society achieved their own success. Sarah Douglass would become a pioneer for her visual artistry, medical studies, and public speaking, and she would both teach and run schools for Black girls and women. Another member, Lucretia Mott, would attend the 1840 World Anti-Slavery Convention—and be excluded from it, like other women. While there, she would meet Elizabeth Cady Stanton, recently married to Henry Stanton. Together they would form an alliance and, eight years later, help organize the Seneca Falls Convention. That event would come to be regarded as the birthplace of the modern women's rights movement, though the foundation had been laid decades before in Philadelphia and other cities.

Yet even amid these achievements for the members of the Philadelphia Female Anti-Slavery Society in the 1840s and beyond, one name was conspicuously absent.

Sarah Forten had often spoken of the "thrall" of marriage and mused about staying single, yet in early 1838 she married Joseph Purvis, the brother of Robert, a real estate investor with only a passing interest in abolition. The ceremony was neither elegant and romantic like her sister Harriet's nor a great draw for abolitionists like the Grimké-Weld nuptials. Instead, she eloped in New Jersey and was wed by a justice of the peace. She would give birth to her first child by the end of the year.

In the interim she saw the destruction of Pennsylvania Hall and the terror of the mob ravaging the Black community in her city. Joseph pressed upon her the need to relocate out of the troubled metropolis and retreat to one of his property holdings in Bensalem Township, twenty miles away. She duly resigned from the Philadelphia society, gave up her poetry and writing, and set about running a farmstead and raising children. She would have eight of them in twelve years and vanish from an active role in the movement.

In the 1850s her husband died without a will, leaving the family finances in disarray. Sarah would struggle financially and ask for loans from friends like Theodore Weld to help her stay afloat. Eventually she would get her affairs in order with the help of Margaretta, but she still kept away from Philadelphia and avoided many of the philanthropic pursuits that kept her siblings so busy. But Sarah's work from the 1830s would not be forgotten, especially by her niece Charlotte. A poet and a friend and ally of William Lloyd Garrison, Charlotte Forten would embody so much of what had made Sarah a prominent figure in her youth—artistic talent, fearlessness, ambition—and her work would be published in outlets from *The Liberator* to the *Atlantic Monthly*. After the Civil War, Charlotte would witness the end of slavery while teaching Black residents of the Sea Islands in South Carolina, then would work for the Freedmen's Aid Society, to try to make real the promise of emancipation that had seemed so distant to her aunt and grandfather many years before.

The other major legacy of Sarah Forten, which endured even as she retired from abolition, was the series of petition drives to Congress. Not only did these continue into the 1840s—to argue against DC slavery and challenge the gag rule—but the Philadelphia society and other women's groups redoubled their commitment to them. A new flood of petitions combined with high tensions between North and South led to politicians' stiffening the gag rule and writing it into regular procedure. Now, the petitions wouldn't even be received, much less laid on the table as before. This ensured the debate would only increase in intensity and make Congress look all the more intransigent and indifferent to public appeal. John Quincy Adams tried to work around the rules, and he saw his speeches printed throughout the mainstream press, often to acclaim.

Thanks to the efforts of Adams, the work of petitioners, and the growing storm of bad press, Congress finally had to relent. A combination of Northern and Southern Whigs and Northern Democrats overturned the gag rule in December 1844. It was a considerable victory for the women of Boston, Philadelphia, and elsewhere, accomplished not just through changing the minds of the public, signature by signature, but by supporting the election of a new breed of Northern politicians much more antagonistic to slavery than the old guard of complaisant men, willing to bow to the South's demands.

One of them was William Seward, who had been elected governor of New York. He oversaw the repeal of the nine-month law, which allowed Southerners to bring their captives into the state for that amount of time; ensured that any enslaved person who set foot in New York could make a case in court for his or her freedom; and refused to return fugitives from Southern states if they came to New York. All these measures had been advanced in the previous five years through petitions, lectures, and public advocacy from figures like Samuel Cornish, Charles Ray, and David Ruggles, and now they had come to fruition.

Even with these victories, though, antislavery campaigners still felt under threat. In 1842 Philadelphia secured its reputation as the most dangerous city in the North for Black citizens when a mob of working-class white men attacked their homes and churches in such a vicious frenzy that "the colored population fled in the utmost terror in every possible direction." They nearly got their hands on a key target, Robert Purvis. He avoided assault and seeing his home destroyed, but he still stood in shock at "one of the most ferocious and bloody-spirited mobs that ever cursed a Christian community . . . Every thing around me is as dark as the grave . . . And the bloody *Will* is in the heart of the community to destroy us." He and Harriet soon followed the lead of her sister Sarah and moved out of Philadelphia, to a farmstead where they felt somewhat safer from the ravages of mobs. They also built a special room in the house to accommodate fugitives from slavery.

Another pair who retreated from urban living were Theodore and Angelina Grimké Weld, along with Sarah Grimké. They moved from Fort Lee, New Jersey, to buy a fifty-acre farm in Belleville (the same town in which Samuel Cornish had been assaulted), where they lived in an old stone and clapboard house in a rustic setting.

Angelina bore three children within five years. She and Sarah dealt with the domestic labors, while Weld went to New York several times a week to work for the American Anti-Slavery Society. His modest salary was their chief source of income, at a time when the depression was still pummeling the economy and good jobs were scarce. While Angelina came into a $5,000 inheritance after her mother's death, she lost it when her investment broker went bankrupt. That inheritance would be the last financial tie to her family in South Carolina.

Weld traveled to Washington at the height of the gag law controversy to supply research to John Quincy Adams on slavery. He knew where to find the damning evidence because he and Angelina and Sarah had been researching conditions for African Americans in the South for several years. Drawing on publications from Charlotte to New Orleans, Charleston to Vicksburg, they amassed some twenty thousand sources to create an antislavery volume that would illustrate the horrors of human bondage by using the Southerners' own words. It would be called *American Slavery as It Is: Testimony of a Thousand Witnesses*.

A later historian called it "the most crushing indictment of any institution ever written." In the book's two hundred pages, the Grimkés and Weld presented firsthand accounts, news articles, advertisements, and other sources—arranged in chapters about labor, punishment, the abuse of women, and other topics—to give readers a detailed view of human bondage and the almost unimaginable cruelty of it. To Weld's commentary on these subjects Angelina added her own accounts, with thinly veiled portraits of family members and neighbors who had been responsible for some of the outrages. When the book was published, the

South censored it, the Northern press mocked it, and politicians tried to ignore it, but it still managed to sell a hundred thousand copies, a stunning number for the time. All proceeds went to the American Anti-Slavery Society. The authors did not identify themselves and refused any royalties.

The book's readership spread through word of mouth alone, finding an audience not only among abolitionists but among those whose families were indifferent to or even supportive of slavery. The greatest effect would be on the twenty-year-old sister of Catharine Beecher, Angelina's former friend turned nemesis. The book would so profoundly influence her, and inform her understanding of slavery, that she claimed to have slept with it under her pillow. A dozen years later she would write her own portrait of the South. When published it would be the only abolitionist volume to outsell *American Slavery as It Is* and would irreversibly turn Northern public opinion against slavery—*Uncle Tom's Cabin*, by Harriet Beecher Stowe.

Angelina was encouraged by the success of *American Slavery as It Is* but found that life in rural New Jersey was far from a country idyll. She relied on Sarah and Weld to help her through the difficult pregnancies and labor she had to endure, including a miscarriage, to go along with the mysterious ailments that continued to plague her. Amid all this she also faced criticism from women like Lydia Child, who saw her withdrawal from public life as a disservice to the movement, and from activists who couldn't believe that such a galvanizing figure could just disappear into obscurity. One wrote, "The Grimkés, I think, are extinct."

But Angelina and Sarah were hardly dormant on their farm. They regularly hosted visitors active in antislavery and remained attuned to the growth of the movement, learning of its shifts in ideology and embrace of more confrontational tactics. They turned away from denominational religion and practiced their own brand of Christian faith, while moving past Garrison's notions of moral suasion and martyrdom. By the mid-1850s, Angelina had come to see that human bondage was a greater sin against God than even murder, and she wrote to Garrison in *The Liberator*, "We are compelled to choose between two evils, and all that we can do is to take the *least*, and baptize liberty in blood, if it must be so." It was a stark change from her attitude of nearly twenty years before, when she wrote her first letter to the newspaper, in praise of martyrdom . . . before seeing what that sacrifice might look like in person.

If Angelina had largely withdrawn from public view by the early 1840s, her husband Weld tried to stay engaged—visiting Washington to assist the small but growing antislavery faction and establish contact with politicians of all stripes, even those who disagreed with him. He was a regular presence at the so-called Abolition House, a boarding house at the foot of the US Capitol where both pro- and antislavery politicians lodged, and friendships were made and new alliances formed, to promote abolition in a city hostile to it. Weld had come a long way since being the target of rocks and bricks on the stump in Ohio and New York a decade before, and he now hobnobbed with Representative Adams and other figures to encourage federal legislators to address the issues raised by petitioners. They almost always failed but, nonetheless, gained a few more allies with each session of Congress until, by the end of the decade, abolition had become a growing minority faction in the legislature.

Weld played a role in converting several of the major antislavery politicians of the next generation to the cause. An agent he had trained, part of "The Seventy," helped convince Thaddeus Stevens to reject accommodation with the South. This would have a sizable impact two decades later, when the Pennsylvania Whig turned Republican helped secure congressional passage of the Thirteenth and Fourteenth Amendments to the US Constitution, respectively abolishing slavery and establishing citizenship for freedmen.

Long before that time, though, Weld retreated from an active role in the movement, even as his young seminarians among The Seventy fanned out across the country to raise the banner of antislavery, using fiery oratory and methodical organizing to convince people, one by one, to join the cause. They weren't alone in their countryside activism, either, as girls and women continued to advocate for the movement in door-to-door campaigns, and African Americans drove vigilance committees and the Underground Railroad to protect Black people and secure their freedom.

The ultimate effect of advancing the cause into the heartland, as Weld had predicted, was to slowly change the minds of a significant number of Northerners—if not always to turn them into abolitionists, then at least to open their eyes to the horror of plantation slavery. It would be this audience that would provide the core readership for *Uncle Tom's Cabin* and other works that debunked the Southern argument for human bondage. Some of them would go further and stand up for the movement in the face of proslavery newspapers and politicians who had formerly whipped up mobs to silence such activists before they ever had a chance to speak.

The greatest fears of press barons like James Watson Webb were then realized, as abolition became "the Hydra" that he had warned his readers about. But while Webb had once decried the influence of prominent men like Garrison and the Tappans, the new "monster" comprised the brothers, sisters, sons, and daughters of those who had been converted to the cause, and could speak of it cogently and eloquently, thanks to their training. This mass of neighborhood activists would be harder to demonize, harder to mock and caricature, and harder to beat with bricks and stones. They were not mysterious, unfamiliar threats to the American way of life; they were friends and relatives making their argument face to face, person to person—and even their most committed opponents discovered it was much more difficult to abuse them without considerable backlash. Thus, throughout the 1840s, mob violence against abolitionists declined as the movement became a familiar part of the Northern polity, while demagogues soon found another target for their abuse: immigrants.

However, even though abolition had survived the onslaught of violence, it did not heal its schism or become unified after the tumult of the 1830s. The growing number of converts instead chose from a wide variety of antislavery groups to join, from the most conservative evangelicals who saw fighting human bondage as a step toward moral perfection, to radical figures who wanted to raze the corrupt foundation of American society through revolution and social upheaval. Some abolitionists thought Weld might be the person to unite all the disparate factions once again, but he had no such illusions. In a letter to Lewis Tappan, he wrote, "All hopes of fusing into one the main divisions of the anti-slavery host seemed to me utterly vain . . . Deep, irreconcilable, personal animosities and repulsions, added to diverse other considerations made such a cooperation impossible." Later generations of historians would be left to ponder whether the schism gave strength to the movement, by making it locally adaptable and resilient, or hampered its efforts to convert the majority of Northerners to the cause until deep into the Civil War.

By that time, Weld had come to see another of his predictions come to pass—that the focus of antislavery would not be confined to the major cities of the Northeast, but would expand along the western frontier. While Lewis had once criticized him for splitting wood and grubbing up stumps in the Ohio outback, Weld had, nonetheless, seeded the ground for abolition in a place formerly hostile to it and inspired many others to follow his example, pushing farther and farther west. From Weld's base in Ohio, new generations of antislavery men and women spread into states like Illinois, where the publisher Elijah Lovejoy met his end and the small-town lawyer Abraham Lincoln would rise to fame; and Iowa, where African American businessman Alexander Clark would assist fugitive slaves on the Underground Railroad and later fight segregation in federal court; and Kansas, where John Brown would lead an insurrection that would help push the nation into war over slavery.

Many abolitionists found their home on the frontier, settling farms and towns to establish bases of antislavery and pressing elected governments to resist slaveholders' attempts to write oppression into law. The challenges could be daunting, as Southern politicians pushed for legislation to bring enslavement to the Great Plains, and abolitionists resorted to organized protest or guerrilla battles to stop it. The result would be years of irregular, sometimes lethal, combat in Bleeding Kansas and other contested territories, with figures like Brown using violence not only in self-defense but in preemptive strikes against their opponents.

It was a measure of how far abolition had traveled from the days when Garrison counseled peace and martyrdom against a bloodthirsty foe. Now, as Angelina Grimké understood, many antislavery men and women would choose the lesser of the evils, giving their sanction to violence to stop the far greater evil of slavery. Catharine Beecher's own brother, Henry Ward Beecher, would even give his name to the "Beecher's Bibles" that frontier abolitionists held as their prized possessions—not holy books, but rifles. Indeed, if the Constitution had been written in blood, as Garrison had said, his successors would shed their own blood to rewrite it.

None of this surprised Weld as he settled down into retirement. Even two decades before the outbreak of war, he had predicted the dissolution of the nation over slavery, knowing a mighty convulsion would surely "hurl these two systems of labor and of living into mortal conflict. The end must come." He lived through that bloody conflict in his senior years and saw the end of slavery and the nation as he knew it, and the rise of another nation in the generation that followed. Just before the turn of the twentieth century, Weld died at ninety-one years of age—once the most mobbed man in America, and one of the last survivors of the republic of violence.

NOTES

INTRODUCTION

p. ix   "Three thousand souls packed into the church"—David Brion Davis, *The Problem of Slavery in the Age of Emancipation* (New York: Alfred A. Knopf, 2014), 173.

p. ix   "Some of these colonizers said free African Americans could not benefit"— Benjamin Quarles, *Black Abolitionists* (New York: Da Capo Press, 1969), 5–7.

p. x   "Henry Clay's claim that Black people were 'a dangerous and useless part'"—"Resolutions Passed by the Colored Inhabitants of Philadelphia," January 1817, quoted in *First Annual Report of the Board of Managers of the New-England Anti-Slavery Society* (Boston: Garrison and Knapp, 1833), 36.

p. x   "We never will separate ourselves voluntarily from the slave population"— "Resolutions Passed by the Colored Inhabitants of Philadelphia," 36.

p. x   "The whole continent seems to be agitated"—Letter from James Forten to Paul Cuffe, January 25, 1817, quoted in Wilson Moses, ed., *Classic Black Nationalism: From the American Revolution to Marcus Garvey* (New York: New York University Press, 1996), 50.

p. xi   "It would take until 1829 for a major white ally"—*The Letters of William Lloyd Garrison*, Vol. 1, *I Will Be Heard! 1822–1835*, ed. Walter M. Merrill (Cambridge, MA: Harvard University Press, 1971), 75.

p. xi   "a riot broke out at the White House when a crowd of up to twenty thousand people"—Margaret Bayard Smith, *Forty Years of Washington*

Society: Portrayed by the Family Letters of Mrs. Samuel Harrison Smith (London: T. Fisher Unwin 1906), 295–296.

p. xi   "he was '*literally* nearly pressed to death'"—Smith, *Forty Years of Washington Society*, 295.

p. xi   "Street crime spiked throughout the country"—Roger Lane, "Criminal Violence in America: The First Hundred Years," *Annals of the American Academy of Political and Social Science* 423 (1976): 12.

p. xi   "The annual consumption of spirits in 1830"—W. J. Rorabaugh, *The Alcoholic Republic: An American Tradition* (New York: Oxford University Press, 1979), 8–9.

p. xi   "men battled with pistols, shotguns and even bowie knives"—Lane, "Criminal Violence," 6.

p. xii "President Jackson carried around bullets in his body"—Abigail Zuger, "A President's Doctors Are Finally Exonerated," *New York Times*, August 11, 1999.

p. xii "wishing he could hang him 'as high as Haman'"—Herman Von Holst, *John C. Calhoun* (Boston: Houghton, Mifflin and Co., 1883), 104.

p. xii "Jackson beat the man so severely with his cane"—Jennifer Latson, "How Divine Providence—and a Heavy Stick—Saved a President's Life," *Time*, January 20, 2015, https://time.com/3676512/andrew-jackson-assassination-attempt.

p. xii "There is even now something of an ill omen amongst us"—Abraham Lincoln, "The Perpetuation of Our Political Institutions," Address before the Young Men's Lyceum, Springfield, IL, January 27, 1838.

p. xii "more than fifty major incidents in two years alone"—David Grimsted, "Rioting in Its Jacksonian Setting," *American Historical Review* 77, no. 2 (1972): 362–364.

p. xii "more than one thousand people died in riots"—Grimsted, "Rioting in Its Jacksonian Setting," 364.

p. xiii "he deployed federal troops to quell the violence" to "made sure to ask the rioters if there was 'anything he could do'"—Michael Shiner, *The Diary of Michael Shiner Relating to the History of the Washington Navy Yard, 1813–1869*, Library of Congress Manuscript, mm82094458, 60–73.

p. xiii "A wave of German and Irish Catholic immigrants"—Edward Pessen, "We Are All Jeffersonians, We Are All Jacksonians: Or a Pox on Stultifying Periodizations," *Journal of the Early Republic* 1, no.1 (1981): 5.

p. xiv "The more radical in temperament, like John Humphrey Noyes"—Walter M. Merrill, *Against Wind and Tide: A Biography of William Lloyd Garrison* (Cambridge, MA: Harvard University Press, 1963), 133.

p. xiv "It had been built into the US Constitution"—David Waldstreicher, "How the Constitution Was Indeed Pro-Slavery," *The Atlantic*, September 19, 2015, https://www.theatlantic.com/politics/archive/2015/09/how-the-constitution-was-indeed-pro-slavery/406288; Gordon Lloyd and Jenny S.

Martinez, "The Slave Trade Clause," National Constitution Center,
https://constitutioncenter.org/interactive-constitution/interpretation
/article-i/clauses/761.

p. xiv   "New York was the nation's chief port for cotton exports"—Bertram Wyatt-
Brown, *Lewis Tappan and the Evangelical War against Slavery* (Cleveland:
Case Western Reserve University Press, 1969), 104.

p. xiv   "exporting anywhere from $76 to $131 million annually"—Leslie M.
Harris, *In the Shadow of Slavery: African Americans in New York City,
1626–1863* (Chicago: University of Chicago Press, 2004), 190.

p. xiv   "Thousands of northern merchants, manufacturers and others"—"Hints on
Anti-Abolition Mobs," *Anti-Slavery Record* 2, no. 7 (July 1836): 2.

p. xv   "Southern planters felt comfortable enough in the North"—Dorothy B.
Porter, "David Ruggles, An Apostle of Human Rights," *Journal of Negro
History* 28, no. 1 (1943): 34–35.

p. xv   "a time when large Northern states were beginning to outlaw human
bondage"—Leo H. Hirsch Jr., "The Slave in New York," *Journal of Negro
History* 16, no. 4 (1931): 395–396; Richard S. Newman, *The Transformation
of American Abolitionism: Fighting Slavery in the Early Republic* (Chapel Hill:
University of North Carolina Press, 2002), 24, 72.

p. xv   "many whites in the region still romanticized the South"—Lorman Ratner,
Powder Keg: Northern Opposition to the Anti-Slavery Movement, 1831–1840
(New York: Basic Books, 1968), 42–43.

p. xv   "T. D. Rice became one of the most popular figures"—Ratner, *Powder Keg*,
22–23.

p. xv   "The most important manifesto came of this early movement"—David
Walker, *The Appeal in Four Articles . . .* (Boston: David Walker, 1830),
14–18, 45, 56.

p. xv   "Jefferson, who had promised freedom to all in the Declaration of
Independence then denied it to African Americans"—Thomas Jefferson,
Notes on the State of Virginia (orig. pub. London: John Stockdale, 1787; repr.,
Richmond, VA: J. W. Randolph, 1853), 149–157.

p. xvi   "slaveholding politicians like Henry Clay"—Henry Clay, Speech at the
Organization of the American Colonization Society, in *The Papers of
Henry Clay*, Vol. 2, ed. James H. Hopkins and Mary W. M. Hargreaves
(Louisville: University of Kentucky Press, 1961), 264.

p. xvi   "Copies circulated through the mail and aboard ships among the free and
enslaved"—Paul Goodman, *Of One Blood: Abolitionism and the Origins of
Racial Equality* (Berkeley: University of California Press, 1998), 31.

p. xvi   "Leading politicians of the region demanded the book be suppressed"—
Timothy P. McCarthy, "'To Plead Our Own Cause': Black Print Culture
and the Origins of American Abolitionism," in *Prophets of Protest:
Reconsidering the History of American Abolitionism*, ed. Timothy Patrick
McCarthy and John Stauffer (New York: W. W. Norton, 2006), 144.

p. xvi   "calling it the 'diabolical Boston pamphlet'"—Quarles, *Black Abolitionists*, 16–17.

p. xvi   "They want us for their slaves, and think nothing of murdering us"—Walker, *Appeal*, 29–30.

p. xvi   "one of the most remarkable products of the age"—Wendell Phillips Garrison and Francis Jackson Garrison, *William Lloyd Garrison: The Story of His Life Told by His Children*, Vol. 1, *1805–1835* (New York: Century Co., 1885), 231.

p. xvii   "The mixing or blending of different things"—Noah Webster, "Amalgamation," in *An American Dictionary of the English Language* (New York: S. Converse, 1828), http://webstersdictionary1828.com/Dictionary/Amalgamation.

p. xvii   "when applied to race, it became one of the most loaded words in the English language"—Harris, *In the Shadow of Slavery*, 191–192.

p. xvii   "which colonizers called 'a principle of repulsion' that was 'utterly abhorrent'"—Patrick Rael, *Black Identity and Black Protest in the Antebellum North* (Chapel Hill: University of North Carolina Press, 2002), 169.

p. xvii   "He routinely worked in the movement with African Americans"—Newman, *Transformation*, 114–115.

p. xviii "Turner and a force of up to sixty other slaves took up arms"—John W. Cromwell, "The Aftermath of Nat Turner's Insurrection," *Journal of Negro History* 5, no. 2 (1920): 210–212.

p. xviii "The media amplified these accusations"—Leonard L. Richards, *Gentlemen of Property and Standing: Anti-Abolition Mobs in Jacksonian America* (London: Oxford University Press, 1970), 31–33.

CHAPTER ONE: ROLL, LAVA TIDE

p. 1   "$5,000 for the capture of the infamous blackguard"—*The Liberator*, December 17, 1831.

p. 1   "conspiracy to seize my body by legal writs on false pretenses"—Letter from William Lloyd Garrison to Harriet Minot, April 22, 1833, quoted in Merrill, *The Letters of William Lloyd Garrison*,Vol. 1, 223–224.

p. 2   "At last he made it to an artist's garret in New Haven"—Garrison and Garrison, *Story of His Life*, Vol. 1, 342–343.

p. 2   "He found himself indicted by grand juries"—Gilbert Hobbs Barnes, *The Anti-Slavery Impulse: 1830–1844* (orig. pub. New York: American Historical Association, 1933; repr., Harcourt, Brace & World, 1964), 51.

p. 2   "At present he is a marked man"—Harriet Martineau, *The Martyr Age of the United States* (Boston: Weeks, Jordan & Co., 1839), 7.

p. 2   "I WILL BE HEARD!"—William Lloyd Garrison, *The Liberator*, January 1, 1831.

p. 2   "Southern resentment had reached a level of hysteria"—Barnes, *Anti-Slavery Impulse*, 51.

p. 3 "Garrison had already experienced enough tumult for an entire life"—
Manisha Sinha, *The Slave's Cause: A History of Abolition* (New Haven, CT:
Yale University Press, 2016), 215.

p. 3 "The ostensible reason for the speaking tour was to raise money"—Letter
from William Lloyd Garrison to Harriet Minot, April 9, 1833, quoted in
Merrill, *The Letters of William Lloyd Garrison*, Vol. 1, 218.

p. 3 "the narrow boundaries of a selfish patriotism"—Garrison and Garrison,
The Story of His Life, Vol. 1, 369.

p. 4 "They called Andrew Jackson a tyrant"—Peter O'Connor, "The
Inextinguishable Struggle between North and South: American
Sectionalism in the British Mind, 1832–1863" (Thesis, University of
Northumbria, 2014), 139.

p. 4 "giving an open, deliberate and base denial"—William Lloyd Garrison,
Address to the World Anti-Slavery Convention, London, July 12, 1833,
quoted in *The Liberator*, November 9, 1833.

p. 4 "the nation slept 'upon the brink of a volcano which is in full operation'"—
William Lloyd Garrison, *The Liberator*, November 9, 1833.

p. 5 "only after five years and at the cost of awarding twenty million pounds"—
An Act for the Abolition of Slavery Throughout the British Colonies,
August 28, 1833, The Mid-Victorian Royal Navy, Legislation on the Slave
Trade, https://www.pdavis.nl/Legis_07.htm.

p. 5 "unsurpassed in the annals of villainy"—*The Liberator*, July 13, 1833.

p. 5 "pygmean dimensions"—Garrison and Garrison, *The Story of His Life*,
Vol. 1, 357–358.

p. 6 "the Colonization Society is becoming more and more abhorrent"—*The
Liberator*, October 20, 1832.

p. 6 "the ACS advocated for their removal due to the inability of white
people"—Goodman, *Of One Blood*, 20.

p. 6 "he wrote lacerating letters to him, challenged him to debates"—Merrill,
Against Wind and Tide, 70–71; Garrison and Garrison, *The Story of His Life*,
Vol. 1, 353.

p. 7 "a protest against the ACS that he later had printed in *The Liberator*"—*The
Liberator*, October 12, 1833.

p. 7 "he enjoyed his time in the company of giants"—Garrison and Garrison,
The Story of His Life, Vol. 1, 351, 355, 361–362.

p. 7 "Why, my dear sir, I thought you were a black man"—Garrison and
Garrison, *The Story of His Life*, Vol. 1, 351.

p. 7 "Baptist minister Nathaniel Paul, had been in Europe for a full year"—
Davis, *Problem of Slavery*, 296–298.

p. 8 "abundantly prosper you and your mission"—Letter from William Lloyd
Garrison to Nathaniel Paul, August 17, 1833, quoted in Merrill, *The Letters
of William Lloyd Garrison*, Vol. 1, 262.

p. 8 "He later asked Paul for £40"—Merrill, *Against Wind and Tide*, 72.

p. 8   "Black abolitionists in America had already funded a good portion"—
        Charles H. Wesley, "The Negroes of New York in the Emancipation
        Movement," *Journal of Negro History* 24, no. 1 (1939): 77; also Wesley,
        "The Negro in the Organization of Abolition," *Phylon* 2, no. 3 (1941):
        224–225.

p. 8   "Garrison's arguments against colonization had been developed by Black
        Americans"—Mary Kelley, "'Talents Committed to Your Care': Reading
        and Writing Radical Abolitionism in Antebellum America," *New England
        Quarterly* 88, no. 1 (2015): 46.

p. 8   "They attacked it from the pulpit and in public gatherings"—Sandra
        Sandiford Young, "John Brown Russwurm's Dilemma: Citizenship or
        Emigration?" in McCarthy and Stauffer, *Prophets of Protest*, 100–101; also
        Introduction, McCarthy and Stauffer, *Prophets of Protest*, xviii.

p. 8   "He claimed that funding for the scheme would be as inexhaustible"—
        Davis, *Problem of Slavery*, 187.

p. 9   "envisioned colonization societies 'in every State, county and town'"—
        William Lloyd Garrison, Address at Park Street Church (Boston,
        Massachusetts, July 4, 1829), 10.

p. 9   "he met William Watkins, a Black writer, teacher, and minister"—
        Goodman, *Of One Blood*, 41.

p. 9   "trampled beneath their own feet their own solemn and heaven attested
        declaration"—Ronald Osborn, "William Lloyd Garrison and the United
        States Constitution: The Political Evolution of an American Radical,"
        Journal of Law and Religion 24, no.1 (2008–2009): 70.

p. 9   "a compact by which we have enabled [slaveholders] already to plunder"—
        "The Great Crisis," *The Liberator*, December 29, 1832.

p. 10   "They named organizations after him"—Quarles, *Black Abolitionists*, 105.

p. 10   "Garrison's newspaper barely managed to stay in business in the 1830s"—
        Garrison and Garrison, *The Story of His Life*, Vol. 1, 431–433; Newman,
        Transformation, 115.

p. 10   "a FAITHFUL REPRESENTATIVE OF OUR sentiments and
        interests"—Newman, *Transformation of American Abolitionism*, 105–106.

p. 10   "The success of my mission seems to have driven [my enemies] to the verge
        of madness"—*The Liberator*, October 12, 1833.

p. 10   "in America he had been forced to occupy the segregated 'Negro pew' in
        church"—*The United States, 1830–1846*, Vol. 3, *The Black Abolitionist Papers*,
        ed. C. Peter Ripley (Chapel Hill: University of North Carolina Press,
        1991), 38–39.

p. 11   "It was the idea that slavery and racism were immoral"—Tunde Adeleke,
        "Afro-Americans and Moral Suasion: The Debate in the 1830s," *Journal of
        Negro History* 83, no. 2 (1998): 128–129.

p. 11   "the flames of a thousand burning villages fearfully reddening the wide
        heavens"—Letter from William Lloyd Garrison to Harriott Plummer,

March 4, 1833, quoted in Merrill, *The Letters of William Lloyd Garrison*, Vol. 1, 206–207.

p. 11   "No matter how they persecuted him"—Letter from William Lloyd Garrison to Harriott Plummer, March 4, 1833, quoted in Merrill, *The Letters of William Lloyd Garrison*, Vol. 1, 206–207; *The Liberator*, October 11, 1833.

p. 12   "Elliott Cresson, too, tried to enact his revenge"—Garrison and Garrison, *The Story of His Life*, Vol. 1, 380.

p. 12   "caned, kicked, beat, or spat at rival editors"—James l. Crouthamel, "James Watson Webb: Mercantile Editor," *New York History* 41, no. 4 (1960): 401.

p. 13   "nothing less than the most powerful newspaper in America"—Edwin G. Burrows and Mike Wallace, *Gotham: A History of New York City to 1898* (New York: Oxford University Press, 1998), 440.

p. 13   "shall we, by promptly and fearlessly crushing this many-headed Hydra"—Garrison and Garrison, *The Story of His Life*, Vol. 1, 381; Wyatt-Brown, *Lewis Tappan*, 105.

p. 13   "Arthur had known Garrison since 1830"—Lewis Tappan, *Life of Arthur Tappan* (New York: Hurd and Houghton, 1870), 163, 171; Samuel J. May, *Some Recollections of Our Antislavery Conflict* (Boston: Fields, Osgood & Co., 1869), 16–17.

p. 13   "Garrison left Maryland for Boston soon after"—Garrison and Garrison, *The Story of His Life*, Vol. 1, 196.

p. 14   "in their economics and their attitudes, the Tappans were much more traditional than he"—Barnes, *Anti-Slavery Impulse*, 19–23; Wyatt-Brown, *Lewis Tappan*, 102.

p. 14   "They allowed no haggling in their business"—John Strausbaugh, *City of Sedition: The History of New York City During the Civil War* (New York: Twelve/Hachette, 2016), 24.

p. 14   "They propped up the Society for the Encouragement of Faithful Domestic Servants"—Harris, *In the Shadow of Slavery*, 175–176, 183–184, 190–191; Barnes, *Anti-Slavery Impulse*, 23–25.

p. 15   "they had tried to create a manual labor school for African American workers"—James Brewer Stewart, "The Emergence of Racial Modernity and the Rise of the White North, 1790–1840," *Journal of the Early Republic* 18, no. 2 (1998): 203–204; Lewis Tappan, *Life of Arthur Tappan*, 145–152.

p. 15   "instead supported political conventions of Black citizens"—Wyatt-Brown, *Lewis Tappan*, 102–103.

p. 15   "That enterprising group sent its agents into the field"—Merrill, *Against Wind and Tide*, 57–59; Roman J. Zorn, "The New England Anti-Slavery Society: Pioneer Abolition Organization," *Journal of Negro History* 42, no. 3 (1957): 171–172.

p. 16   "the flyer was addressed 'To all persons from the South'"—J. T. Headley, *The Great Riots of New York, 1712 to 1873* (New York: E. B. Treat, 1873), 82.

p. 16   "Other threats were more direct"—Wyatt-Brown, *Lewis Tappan*, 104.

p. 16   "Countless planters visited the city and brought their slaves"—Porter,
         "Apostle of Human Rights," 34–35.

p. 16   "Webb's *Courier and Enquirer* spoke to both groups"—Crouthamel, "James
         Watson Webb," 402–403.

p. 17   "a genuine, drunken, infuriated mob of blackguards of every species"—*The
         Liberator*, October 3, 1833.

p. 17   "Some vowed to ship Garrison in a box to Georgia"—Garrison and
         Garrison, *The Story of His Life*, Vol. 1, 383–384.

p. 17   "Others carried bowie knives and pistols"—John Neal, *Wandering
         Recollections of a Somewhat Busy Life* (Boston: Roberts Brothers, 1869), 402.

p. 17   "They didn't realize one of the heads of the Hydra was marching alongside
         them"—*The Liberator*, October 12, 1833.

p. 17   "Not only did Arthur Tappan operate a silk shop on Pearl Street"—Lewis
         Tappan, *Life of Arthur Tappan*, 61, 275.

p. 17   "some of them purchased the stockings"—Strausbaugh, *City of Sedition*, 24.

p. 17   "Ten thousand dollars for Arthur Tappan!"—Tappan, *Life of Arthur Tappan*,
         170.

p. 17   "Let us rout them!"—Tappan, *Life of Arthur Tappan*, 170.

p. 18   "he had helped fund the construction"—Wyatt-Brown, *Lewis Tappan*, 105.

p. 18   "the building meant for his preaching was no better"—Wyatt-Brown, *Lewis
         Tappan*, 71.

p. 19   "Soon there were two thousand of them in the street"—Headley, *Great
         Riots of New York*, 82–83; Tappan, *Life of Arthur Tappan*, 170–71.

p. 19   "They hunted around for the silk merchant and his brother"—Wyatt-
         Brown, *Lewis Tappan*, 105–107.

p. 19   "The Declaration says all men are created equal"—Harris, *In the Shadow of
         Slavery*, 194–195; Tappan, *Life of Arthur Tappan*, 171–172.

p. 20   "GREAT PUBLIC MEETING. THE AGITATORS DEFEATED!"—*Courier and
         Enquirer* (New York), October 3, 1833.

p. 20   "the New York Anti-Slavery Society had, in fact, organized"—*Courier and
         Enquirer* (New York), October 3, 1833.

CHAPTER TWO: WEAPONS OF LIGHT AND TRUTH

p. 22   "whites dominated the population and Black people could be kidnapped
         and sold as fugitive slaves"—R. J. M. Blackett, "Freedom, or the Martyr's
         Grave: Black Pittsburgh's Aid to the Fugitive Slave," in *African Americans
         in Pennsylvania: Shifting Historical Perspectives*, ed. Joe Trotter and Eric
         Ledell Smith (University Park: Penn State University Press, 1994), 149.

p. 22   "As the general agent for *The Emancipator*, he had been traveling through
         these hinterlands"—Graham Russell Gao Hodges, *David Ruggles: A
         Radical Black Abolitionist and the Underground Railroad in New York City*
         (Chapel Hill: University of North Carolina Press, 2010), 56.

p. 22 ""two ladies, two gentlemen, a two leg[g]ed animal and myself"—David Ruggles, *The "Extinguisher" Extinguished, or David M. Reese, M.D. "Used Up"* (New York: D. Ruggles, 1834), 45.

p. 22 "Madmen! Fanatics! Disorganizers! Amalgamaters!"—David Ruggles, *Extinguisher*, 45.

p. 23 "I kept my seat; he of course [grunted] and left the room"—David Ruggles, *Extinguisher*, 46.

p. 23 "Ruggles saw the hypocrisy of it from his home in the Five Points"—Hodges, *Radical Black Abolitionist*, 44, 57.

p. 23 "I do not wish it, nor does any colored man or woman of my acquaintance"—Ruggles, *Extinguisher*, 12.

p. 24 "it is this horror of amalgamation"—Ruggles, *Extinguisher*, 46.

p. 24 "speaking in Black churches and assembly halls"—Porter, "Apostle of Human Rights," 27–28.

p. 24 "long double-breasted jacket, white pants, stovepipe hat, a cravat, and thick eyeglasses"—Hodges, *Radical Black Abolitionist*, 138.

p. 24 "or as he called it, 'the daughter of slavery'"—Ruggles, *Extinguisher*, 18n.

p. 24 "So while the ACS was running out of money"—Stewart, "Emergence of Racial Modernity," 194.

p. 25 "liquor, just like slavery, bore the fruit of 'licentiousness, misery, and death'"—Ruggles, *Extinguisher*, 10–11.

p. 25 "Yet all their complaints did little to help them pay off a deficit of $46,000"—Zorn, "New England Anti-Slavery Society," 172.

p. 25 "Boston is now fairly redeemed from the thraldom of colonization corruption"—Letter from William Lloyd Garrison to George W. Benson, March 13, 1834, quoted in Merrill, *The Letters of William Lloyd Garrison*, Vol. 1, 294.

p. 25 "Rev. Henry Ludlow planned a mock 'funeral of colonization'"—*The Liberator*, May 17, 1834.

p. 25 "to mob us and our friends with clubs, stones, brick-bats, &c."—Ruggles, *Extinguisher*, 18.

p. 25 "to every coloured American, 'a moral Upas tree'," Ruggles, *Extinguisher*, 40.

p. 25 "He'd been a mariner working out of New Bedford"—Hodges, *Radical Black Abolitionist*, 29.

p. 26 "the 'butter merchant' who provided goods for a fair price"—Porter, "Apostle of Human Rights," 27.

p. 26 "He'd seen his business fail after an intruder broke in and stole $280"—Hodges, *Radical Black Abolitionist*, 46.

p. 26 "Black people were routinely segregated: made to sit in distant pews in church"—Linda K. Kerber, "Abolitionists and Amalgamators: The New York City Race Riots of 1834," *New York History* 48, no.1 (1967): 28; Tappan, *Life of Arthur Tappan*, 191–192.

p. 26   "with his hands like claws tore both clothes, buttons and skin"—*The Emancipator*, January 28, 1834.

p. 27   "thanks be to Him who said 'let there be light,'"—Ruggles, *Extinguisher*, 18n.

p. 27   "He was beginning to question the idea of moral suasion"—Hodges, *Radical Black Abolitionist*, 4.

p. 27   "Ruggles took the literary defiance of David Walker"—Hodges, *Radical Black Abolitionist*, 9.

p. 27   "The pleas of crying soft and sparing never answered the purpose of a reform"—*Emancipator*, February 3, 1835.

p. 28   "But they got along well with David Ruggles and worked with him regularly"—Hodges, *Radical Black Abolitionist*, 7, 62.

p. 28   "slander always accompanied an unpopular cause"—Wyatt-Brown, *Lewis Tappan*, 127.

p. 28   "So Arthur hatched a plan to distribute 7,600 copies of *The Emancipator*"—Wyatt-Brown, *Lewis Tappan*, 103.

p. 28   "Sinful as slavery is, it is not more so than a plan of emancipation"—Ratner, *Powder Keg*, 97.

p. 29   "'revilers and false witnesses' and 'a corrupt priesthood'"—William L. van Deburg, "William Lloyd Garrison and the 'Pro-Slavery Priesthood': The Changing Beliefs of An Evangelical Reformer, 1830–1840," *Journal of the American Academy of Religion* 43, no. 2 (1975): 231.

p. 29   "If you will give up your fanatical notions"—Garrison and Garrison, *The Story of His Life*, Vol. 1, 215.

p. 29   "since then relations with him had only soured"—Ratner, *Powder Keg*, 99, 126n.

p. 29   "Beecher had even tried to pry the Tappans away"—J. Earl Thompson Jr., "Lyman Beecher's Long Road to Conservative Abolitionism," *Church History* 42, no. 1 (1973): 102.

p. 29   "it drove 'decent people' out of the movement"—Wyatt-Brown, *Lewis Tappan*, 127–128.

p. 29   "whether his 'holy indignation' is always as holy"—Henry Mayer, *All on Fire: William Lloyd Garrison and the Abolition of Slavery* (New York: St. Martin's Press, 1998), 194.

p. 29   "Lewis realized they needed to create an even broader organization"—Wyatt-Brown, *Lewis Tappan*, 109.

p. 30   "fanatics, amalgamationists, disorganizers, disturbers of the peace"—May, *Some Recollections*, 83.

p. 30   "Upon arriving in the hall, sixty members from ten states"—Merrill, *Against Wind and Tide*, 77–78.

p. 30   "it embraced integration in both its membership and leadership"—David E. Swift, *Black Prophets of Justice: Activist Clergy Before the Civil War* (Baton Rouge: Louisiana State University Press, 1989), 64–65.

p. 30   "they were almost always denied membership in white-run organizations"—Newman, *Transformation*, 2, 5, 6, 83, 88.

p. 31   "Garrison also became the author of the Declaration of Sentiments"—Newman, *Transformation*, 80.

p. 31   "we have printed beyond our means"—Letter from William Lloyd Garrison to John B. Vashon, November 5, 1833, quoted in Merrill, *The Letters of William Lloyd Garrison*, Vol. 1, 267–268.

p. 31   "'TWO MILLIONS of our people' shackled against their will"—William Lloyd Garrison, *Declaration of the American Anti-Slavery Convention*, December 1833.

p. 31   "overthrow the most execrable system of slavery"—Garrison, *Declaration*.

p. 31   "the newly formed society agreed to purchase a supply of Garrison's publications"—Barnes, *Anti-Slavery Impulse*, 57.

p. 32   "J. R. Tyson, belittled 'new fangled' ideas of immediate abolition"—Paul J. Polgar, *Standard Bearers of Equality: America's First Abolition Movement* (Chapel Hill: University of North Carolina Press, 2019), 320.

p. 32   "prejudice dwelt in his little heart"—*The Rights of All*, October 9 and 16, 1829.

p. 32   "After all, how could men like Key assume that whites"—*Freedom's Journal*, March 30, 1827; *The Rights of All*, July 17, 1829.

p. 32   "But that uncertainty also gave Cornish pause"—*The Rights of All*, July 17, 1829.

p. 32   "Cornish liked Ruggles and admired how this young man"—Hodges, *Radical Black Abolitionist*, 37, 44.

p. 33   "Cornish had learned theology in Philadelphia from the founder"—Kenneth J. Ross, "We Speak for Ourselves: What Samuel Cornish Learned from John Gloucester," Presbyterian Historical Society, February 20, 2019, https://www.history.pcusa.org/blog/2019/02/we-speak-ourselves-what-samuel-cornish-learned-john-gloucester.

p. 33   "Cornish's work was successful, as he pushed hard for church leaders"—Hodges, *Radical Black Abolitionist*, 38; Swift, *Black Prophets*, 22–23.

p. 33   "His ministry soon owed $10,000"—Swift, *Black Prophets*, 23.

p. 34   "We wish to plead our own cause"—*Freedom's Journal*, March 16, 1827.

p. 34   "Cornish published the work of various writers"—McCarthy, "To Plead Our Own Cause," 118.

p. 34   "undermined public faith in the 'wise and philanthropic men'"—*Georgetown Columbian and Daily Advertiser*, May 29, 1827.

p. 34   "Russwurm came out in favor of colonization"—John Russwurm, "A Candid Acknowledgment of Error," *Freedom's Journal*, February 16, 1829.

p. 35   "But it stood sapped of momentum by Russwurm's decision"—Swift, *Black Prophets*, 41.

p. 35   "They had all been managers of the American Bible Society"—Tappan, *Life of Arthur Tappan*, 194.

p. 35 "He warned them not to smoke in the streets or dress too fancily"—
Freedom's Journal, July 13, 1827.

p. 35 "'Nothing serves more to keep us in our present degraded condition'"—
Freedom's Journal, June 29, 1827.

p. 36 "they had difficulty visiting cultural institutions"—Dorothy B. Porter, "The
Organized Educational Activities of Negro Literary Societies, 1828–1846,"
Journal of Negro Education 5, no. 4 (1936): 565.

p. 36 "Cornish, Wright, and the Tappans proposed raising $10,000"—Porter,
"Negro Literary Societies," 557–558, 565–566.

p. 36 "Arthur Tappan, as treasurer, paid his salary"—Swift, *Black Prophets*, 59.

p. 36 "within a year it was hosting scientific lectures that drew up to five hundred
people"—Porter, "Negro Literary Societies," 567.

p. 36 "this mixture was enough to create an uproar in the house of the Lord"—
Tappan, *Life of Arthur Tappan*, 194.

p. 37 "how white must the complexion of the Saviour be"—Tappan, *Life of Arthur
Tappan*, 195.

p. 37 "He had already blistered abolitionists for impeding the work of
colonizers"—*Courier and Enquirer*, June 23, 1834.

p. 37 "attacking him for supposedly saying 'the Saviour of mankind is a negro'"—
Richards, *Gentlemen of Property and Standing*, 121.

p. 37 "claiming he had divorced his wife to marry a Black woman"—Paul A.
Gilje, *The Road to Mobocracy: Popular Disorder in New York City, 1763–1834*
(Chapel Hill: University of North Carolina Press, 1987), 163; *Courier and
Enquirer*, June 23, 1834.

p. 38 "A voter didn't have to register in advance"—Headley, *Great Riots of New
York*, 68–69.

p. 38 "Black men could try to vote if they had $250 in property"—Harris, *In the
Shadow of Slavery*, 118.

p. 38 "He now vilified the Democratic Party at every turn"—Crouthamel, "James
Watson Webb," 413.

p. 38 "When Webb published a damning article in the *Courier and Enquirer*"—
Gilje, *Road to Mobocracy*, 138.

p. 38 "The Whigs hoisted the U.S. flag and built a boat called the
Constitution"—Burrows and Wallace, *Gotham*, 574; Headley, *Great Riots of
New York*, 69–70.

p. 39 "Webb quickly recruited 300 volunteers as his own private army"—Robert
William July, *The Essential New Yorker, Gulian Crommelin Verplanck*
(Durham, NC: Duke University Press, 1951), 191–192.

p. 39 "twenty Whigs 'stretched bleeding and maimed on the floor'"—Headley,
Great Riots of New York, 71–72.

p. 39 "howling and screaming in a savage manner"—*The Liberator*, April 12,
1834.

p. 39   "The Democrats assailed the rolling Constitution"—Carl E. Prince, "The Great 'Riot Year': Jacksonian Democracy and Patterns of Violence in 1834," *Journal of the Early Republic* 5, no. 1 (1985): 12.

p. 39   "the crowd savaged 15 of his watchmen"—Gilje, *Road to Mobocracy*, 139.

p. 40   "The US Navy dispatched Marines, infantry, and squadrons of cavalry"— Headley, *Great Riots of New York*, 76.

p. 40   "He had earlier claimed credit for inventing the insult 'King Andrew'"— July, *Essential New Yorker*, 187.

p. 40   "he invented a new insult for them: 'amalgamists'"—Kerber, "Abolitionists and Amalgamators," 30.

p. 40   "no white person would consent to marry a negro"—E. S. Abdy, *Journal of a Residence and Tour in the United States of North America, from April, 1833, to October, 1834*, Vol. 3 (London: John Murray, 1835), 127.

p. 40   "entered into a conspiracy against the human species"—Richards, *Gentlemen of Property and Standing*, 115.

p. 41   "A silly cry of 'amalgamation' had exasperated the public mind"—Abdy, *Journal of a Residence*, 117.

p. 41   "throwing all manner of filth upon abolitionists"—*The Liberator*, May 24, 1834; Letter from William Lloyd Garrison to Samuel May, July 23, 1834, quoted in Merrill, *The Letters of William Lloyd Garrison*, Vol. 1, 381.

p. 41   "So Garrison ran Webb's editorial . . . on the front page of his May 31 edition"—*The Liberator*, May 31, 1834.

p. 41   "Webb accused abolitionists of laying the foundation for war"—*Courier and Enquirer*, quoted in *The Liberator*, May 31, 1834.

p. 42   "went ahead with the 'funeral of colonization'"—*The Liberator*, May 17, 1834.

p. 42   "Lewis also helped organize an anti-slavery week in May"—Wyatt-Brown, *Lewis Tappan*, 115.

p. 42   "There is a point beyond which the patience and endurance of the public"— *Courier and Enquirer*, quoted in *The Liberator*, May 31, 1834.

p. 43   "Let us not deceive ourselves. Although our cause is certainly advancing"— Letter from William Lloyd Garrison to George Benson, June 16, 1834, quoted in Merrill, *The Letters of William Lloyd Garrison*, Vol. 1, 365.

CHAPTER THREE: THE OTHER CONFEDERACY

p. 45   "they also requested that the customary 'From A. Tappan and Co.'"— Vivian Simmons Lane, "The Tappan Brothers," *Negro History Bulletin* 6, no. 8 (1943): 172.

p. 45   "found himself mired in red ink from speculating in cotton and woolen mills"—Wyatt-Brown, *Lewis Tappan*, 23–24, 32.

p. 45   "Lewis would invest half his salary back into the business"—Wyatt-Brown, *Lewis Tappan* , 32, 42.

p. 45   "Arthur supposedly never said a profane word in his life"—Lane, "Tappan Brothers," 171.

p. 45   "Christian spy cells to watch tavern-keepers and other dispensers of pleasure"—Wyatt-Brown, *Lewis Tappan*, 66–68.

p. 46   "other ministers in the American Anti-Slavery Society, who saw it as 'scandalous and disheartening'"—*New-York Evangelist*, July 12, 1834.

p. 46   "Black and white parishioners singing hymns together and sitting side by side"—Donald Williams, *Prudence Crandall's Legacy: The Fight for Equality in the 1830s, Dred Scott, and Brown v. Board of Education* (Middletown, CT: Wesleyan University Press, 2016), 178.

p. 46   "the publisher whom Garrison called a 'murderous hypocrite'"—Letter from William Lloyd Garrison to Samuel May, July 23, 1834, quoted in Merrill, *The Letters of William Lloyd Garrison*, Vol. 1, 382.

p. 46   "Stone let his readers know abolitionists would gather"—Richards, *Gentlemen of Property and Standing*, 115–116.

p. 46   "The friends of the union and of the South are requested to attend"— Handbill of July 1834, quoted in *The Liberator*, July 12, 1834.

p. 47   "When smitten as with fire from heaven, the captive's chain shall sink in dust"—John Greenleaf Whittier, "Hymn," in *The Poetical Works of John Greenleaf Whittier*, ed. W. Garrett Horder (New York: Henry Frowde, 1904), 292.

p. 47   "a solemn address was offered to the Throne of Grace"—Tappan, *Life of Arthur Tappan*, 204.

p. 47   "hundreds of anti-abolitionists infiltrated the chapel"—Swift, *Black Prophets*, 67.

p. 47   "A group of city watchmen soon arrived and chased the blustering men out of the chapel"—Richards, *Gentlemen of Property and Standing*, 116.

p. 47   "They went on to attack a group of Black people in a nearby city park"—*The Emancipator*, July 8 and 15, 1834.

p. 48   "known for renditions of Handel's *Messiah*"—Delmer D. Rogers, "Public Music Performances in New York City from 1800 to 1850," *Inter-American Yearbook of Musical Research* 6 (1970): 8–10.

p. 48   "finding the house occupied by colored people"—Lewis Tappan quoted in the *Journal of Commerce*, reprinted in *The Liberator*, July 12, 1834.

p. 48   "But that didn't stop him and a group of fifteen other musicians"—John Lossing, *History of New York City: Embracing an Outline Sketch of Events from 1609 to 1830, and a Full Account of Its Development from 1830 to 1884*, Vol. 1 (New York: Perine, 1884), 331–332; Richards, *Gentlemen of Property and Standing*, 117.

p. 48   "so the Sacred Music Society men attacked them"—Headley, *Great Riots of New York*, 84.

p. 48 "passersby poured in from the Five Points, clambering up to the balconies"—Wyatt-Brown, *Lewis Tappan*, 117; Lewis Tappan quoted in *Journal of Commerce*, reprinted in *The Liberator*, July 12, 1834.

p. 48 "The white citizens present were there with no disposition to disturb the blacks"—*Courier and Enquirer*, July 8, 1834.

p. 49 "with canes loaded with leaden bullets on the head, [and] knocked some down and injured others severely"—*Commercial Advertiser*, July 10, 1834, quoted in *Niles' Weekly Register*, July 19, 1834.

p. 49 "The Colonization men have let loose a Legion of fiends"—*The Liberator*, July 19, 1834.

p. 49 "In the name of the country, in the name of heaven"—*Courier and Enquirer*, July 8, 1834.

p. 49 "*The Liberator* reported that proslavery businessmen in town had ordered their employees"—*The Liberator*, August 2, 1834.

p. 49 "The crowd grew larger as he left the Five Points, becoming more and more vocal"—Headley, *Great Riots of New York*, 84.

p. 49 "a tremendous noise [with] mingled groans, hisses and execrations"—Wyatt-Brown, *Lewis Tappan*, 117.

p. 50 "we caution the colored people of this city against it"—*Courier and Enquirer*, July 9, 1834.

p. 50 "Others 'struck up a Jim Crow chorus' in the style of T. D. 'Daddy' Rice"—Burrows and Wallace, *Gotham*, 557.

p. 50 "damn the Yankees, they are a damn set of jack-asses, and fit to be gulled"—Richards, *Gentlemen of Property and Standing*, 116.

p. 50 "When the character of our country is assailed by foreigners"—*New York Sun*, quoted in Thomas A. Bogar, *Thomas Hamblin and the Bowery Theatre: The New York Reign of "Blood and Thunder" Melodramas* (London: Palgrave Macmillan, 2018), 124.

p. 50 "But Farren had already fled the city in terror"—Bogar, *Thomas Hamblin and the Bowery Theatre*, 123–124.

p. 51 "claiming the crowd had been pacified by the theater manager"—*New York Sun*, July 11, 1834.

p. 51 "men wielding clubs and bricks smashed open the doors"—Headley, *Great Riots of New York*, 86.

p. 51 "The rioters set a great bonfire to the furniture pile"—*The Memorial History of the City of New-York, from Its First Settlement to the Year 1892*, Vol. 3, ed. James Grant Wilson, (New York: New-York History Co., 342).

p. 51 "men of excellent standing, among whom were sundry members of churches"—*The Liberator*, July 19, 1834.

p. 51 "two gangs—the Battenders and Huge Paws—with merchants and wealthier men watching"—Wyatt-Brown, *Lewis Tappan*, 118; Headley, *Great Riots of New York*, 87.

p. 52   "'Away to Arthur Tappan's!' they chanted in July"—*Commercial Advertiser*, July 10, 1834, quoted in *Niles' Weekly Register*, July 19, 1834.

p. 52   "he funded the causes synonymous with antislavery"—Tappan, *Life of Arthur Tappan*, 143, 146–148.

p. 52   "The mayor refused to protect the building from the attackers"—Lane, "Tappan Brothers," 171.

p. 52   "handled them so roughly that they were compelled to take refuge in flight"—Headley, *Great Riots of New York*, 90.

p. 52   "shattered the windows on the lower level and tried to break down the front door"—Tappan, *Life of Arthur Tappan*, 284.

p. 52   "Break open the doors if you dare!"—Lossing, *History of New York City*, 337.

p. 52   "Arthur Tappan was nominally a pacifist"—Tappan, *Life of Arthur Tappan*, 222.

p. 53   "The oldest clerks were put on guard"—Tappan, *Life of Arthur Tappan*, 284.

p. 53   "Moneyed men were exceedingly frightened"—Tappan, *Life of Arthur Tappan*, 223.

p. 53   "They worked in a broad array of occupations"—Gilje, *Road to Mobocracy*, 164.

p. 54   "The armed men communicated across wards and neighborhoods"—Richards, *Gentlemen of Property and Standing*, 119.

p. 54   "when the men blocked off entire streets with chained carts and wagons"—Lossing, *History of New York City*, 337; Richards, *Gentlemen of Property and Standing*, 119.

p. 54   "into this beleaguered neighborhood came two to three thousand men"—Tappan, *Life of Arthur Tappan*, 213–215.

p. 54   "The mob spread news around the neighborhood"—Gilje, *Road to Mobocracy*, 166.

p. 55   "their homes faced vandalism, robbery, and incineration"—Kerber, "Abolitionists and Amalgamators," 33; Richards, *Gentlemen of Property and Standing*, 120.

p. 55   "Rioters also demolished the African School on Orange Street"—*The Liberator*, July 19, 1834.

p. 55   "Whenever a colored person appeared, it was signal of combat, fight and riot"—*The Liberator*, July 19, 1834.

p. 55   "A coat of tar and feathers might be of service to this man"—*Bunker Hill Aurora*, quoted in *The Liberator*, August 8, 1834.

p. 55   "a small group of watchmen took a volley of rocks"—Headley, *Great Riots of New York*, 91.

p. 55   "The attackers smashed the windows, shouting racial slurs"—Richards, *Gentlemen of Property and Standing*, 121; Tappan, *Life of Arthur Tappan*, 211–213.

p. 55   "This time they penetrated the building, demolished the pulpit and pews"—*The Liberator*, July 19, 1834.

p. 55 "They threw paving stones into the parlor, sliced up the carpets"—Stephen Rachman, Introduction to *The Hasheesh Eater: Being Passages from the Life of a Pythagorean* by Fitz Hugh Ludlow (New York: Harper and Bros., 1857), xii.

p. 55 "He was New York's first Black Episcopal priest"—Swift, *Black Prophets*, 69.

p. 56 "It is next to impossible to describe the scene"—*Commercial Advertiser*, July 12, 1834.

p. 56 "For two hours, uninterrupted, they savaged the church"—Kerber, "Abolitionists and Amalgamators," 33.

p. 56 "The mobsters also descended upon three other Black-owned homes"— *Commercial Advertiser*, July 12, 1834.

p. 56 "Only when the violence spread into more 'respectable' districts"—Swift, *Black Prophets*, 66–67.

p. 56 "when he heard a rumor that the masses of working-class men"—Tappan, *Life of Arthur Tappan*, 212; Wyatt-Brown, *Lewis Tappan*, 119.

p. 56 "however repugnant to the good sense of the community"—Proclamation by Cornelius W. Lawrence, mayor of the city of New York, July 11, 1834.

p. 57 "Mayor Lawrence called up the 27th Regiment of the National Guard"— Headley, *Great Riots of New York*, 92–95.

p. 57 "Three cheers for James Watson Webb, of the Courier!"—Abdy, *Journal of a Residence*, 120.

p. 57 "the *Newspapers*; especially Webb, with his Courier, and Stone"—*The Liberator*, July 19, 1834.

p. 57 "If any man ever deserved to be sent to the Penitentiary or State Prison"— Letter from William Lloyd Garrison to Samuel May, July 23, 1834, quoted in Merrill, *The Letters of William Lloyd Garrison*, Vol. 1, 383.

p. 57 "the other confederacy [that] includes those who have instigated the riots"—*The Liberator*, July 19, 1834.

p. 57 "deeply injured abolitionists was . . . *now*, while their lives"—*The Liberator*, July 19, August 2, 1834.

p. 58 "In the days after, the mere sight of a Black man at a church in Newark"— *The Liberator*, July 19, 1834.

p. 58 "Other disorders in the house of God erupted in New Britain, Connecticut"—David Grimsted, *American Mobbing, 1828–1861: Toward Civil War* (New York: Oxford University Press, 1998), 36.

p. 58 "doctrines which outrage public feelings, they have no right to demand"— *Courier and Enquirer*, July 11, 1834.

p. 58 "'wicked and absurd doctrines' that he loathed"—*Courier and Enquirer*, July 14, 1834.

p. 58 "we have styled them 'Colonization riots'"—*New-York Sentinel*, quoted in *The Liberator*, July 26, 1834.

p. 58   "It is ridiculous to talk about respect for the laws"—*Journal of Commerce*, quoted in *The Liberator*, July 26, 1834.

p. 58   "enjoying a pristine landscape where 'the perfume of the flowers is wafted upon every breeze'"—Letter from William Lloyd Garrison to George Benson, July 10, 1834, quoted in Merrill, *The Letters of William Lloyd Garrison*, Vol. 1, 374.

p. 58   "even though his house was only a short distance from Arthur Tappan's"—Hodges, *Radical Black Abolitionist*, 67.

p. 59   "Samuel Cornish escaped the violence, lacking a congregation"—Swift, *Black Prophets*, 66, 69.

p. 59   "Let me advise you to resign, at once, your connexion"—Letter from Benjamin Onderdonk to Peter Williams Jr., July 12, 1834, quoted in *The Liberator*, July 19, 1834.

p. 59   "it is a most difficult matter to avoid extremes on subjects of great public excitement"—Letter from Peter Williams Jr. to "the Citizens of New-York," July 14, 1834, quoted in *The Liberator*, July 19, 1834.

p. 60   "sometimes ventured out to support philanthropic causes"—Swift, *Black Prophets*, 117.

p. 60   "NON-RESISTANCE!—PATIENCE!!—FORBEARANCE!!!"—Editorial from *The Emancipator*, reprinted in *The Liberator*, July 19, 1834.

p. 60   "silent anti-slavery preacher to the crowds who will flock to see it"—Wyatt-Brown, *Lewis Tappan*, 118.

p. 60   "shove[d] a man out doors who came into his office"—Editorial from the *Boston Daily Advocate*, reprinted in *The Liberator*, August 2, 1834.

p. 61   "indict Dr. Cox, Mr. Tappan, and their associates as PUBLIC NUISANCES"—*The American*, quoted in Tappan, *Life of Arthur Tappan*, 219.

p. 61   "they disavowed 'any desire to promote or encourage intermarriages'"—*The American*, quoted in Tappan, *Life of Arthur Tappan* , 215.

p. 61   "they defended themselves, 'as patriots, as Christians, as friends of the Union'"—Letter from Arthur Tappan et al. to Mayor Cornelius W. Lawrence, quoted in *The Liberator*, July 26, 1834.

p. 61   "Foreign critics, especially British abolitionists, called it outrageous"—Kerber, "Abolitionists and Amalgamators," 35; Abdy, *Journal of a Residence*, 123–124.

p. 62   "with instructions to send it right back where it came from, with no reply"—Kerber, "Abolitionists and Amalgamators," 36.

CHAPTER FOUR: TRIED AS BY FIRE

p. 63   "that good and decent people protesting slavery"—Letter from William Lloyd Garrison to Helen Benson, July 15, 1834, quoted in Merrill, *The Letters of William Lloyd Garrison*, Vol. 1, 375.

p. 63   "O, but love is a naughty thing! How it becomes a part of our person"—
          Letter from William Lloyd Garrison to Helen Benson, July 21, 1834,
          quoted in Merrill, *The Letters of William Lloyd Garrison*, Vol. 1, 379.

p. 64   "such momentous consequences to a large portion of our countrymen"—
          Letter from William Lloyd Garrison to Samuel May, July 28, 1834, quoted
          in Merrill, *The Letters of William Lloyd Garrison*, Vol. 1, 384.

p. 64   "Once word got out, the townsfolk became furious"—May, *Some
          Recollections*, 42.

p. 64   "all true friends of the cause—must make this a common concern"—Letter
          from William Lloyd Garrison to George Benson, March 8, 1833, quoted in
          Merrill, *The Letters of William Lloyd Garrison*, Vol. 1, 212.

p. 64   "She visited him in Boston to get his advice on the next steps"—Letter
          from Prudence Crandall to *The Brooklyn Advertiser*, May 7, 1833.

p. 64   "She agreed and soon received assistance from Black ministers"—Donald
          E. Williams, *Prudence Crandall's Legacy: The Fight for Equality in the 1830s,
          Dred Scott, and Brown v. Board of Education* (Middletown, CT: Wesleyan
          University Press, 2014), 183.

p. 64   "He was happy to act as an adviser and to suggest pupils"—Julie Winch, *A
          Gentleman of Color: The Life of James Forten* (New York: Oxford University
          Press, 2002), 248.

p. 64   "the white folk in town heaped insults upon her and threatened her"—May,
          Some Recollections, 42–43.

p. 64   "threw manure down her well and spread rumors"—Zorn, "New England
          Anti-Slavery Society," 167.

p. 64   "they put pressure on the town druggist and doctor to refuse her medical
          care"—Miriam R. Small and Edwin W. Small, "Prudence Crandall,
          Champion of Negro Education," *New England Quarterly* 17, no. 4 (1944):
          524–525.

p. 64   "they barred her from attending church; they attacked her house"—Merrill,
          The Letters of William Lloyd Garrison, Vol. 1, 213n.

p. 64   "they slit the throat of a cat and hung it over her schoolhouse door as a
          warning"—Williams, *Prudence Crandall's Legacy*, 189.

p. 65   "The colored people never can rise from their menial condition in our
          country"—May, *Some Recollections*, 47.

p. 65   "He cajoled the Connecticut legislature into passing a 'Black Law'"—Small
          and Small, "Prudence Crandall," 517–518.

p. 65   "Savage Barbarity! Miss Crandall Imprisoned!!!"—*The Liberator*, July 6,
          1833.

p. 65   "Local abolitionists feted her and painted her portrait"—*The Liberator*,
          April 12, 1834.

p. 65   "They showered her with praise, and she received letters of support"—Small
          and Small, "Prudence Crandall," 525–526.

p. 65   "harassed, insulted, even arrested and threatened with whipping"—Small and Small, "Prudence Crandall," 517.

p. 66   "Allowing Crandall to lodge in jail overnight (though her bond could have been paid)"—Small and Small, "Prudence Crandall," 519–520.

p. 66   "the Court of Errors finally produced a ruling, on July 22"—G. Smith Wormley, "Prudence Crandall," *Journal of Negro History* 8, no. 1 (1923): 78–79.

p. 66   "It would be a perversion of terms and the well-known rule of construction"—Wormley, "Prudence Crandall," 78–79.

p. 66   "one of the first books by an American woman to argue for immediate abolition"—Lydia Maria Child, *An Appeal in Favor of That Class of Americans Called Africans* (Boston: Allen and Ticknor, 1833).

p. 66   "He often paired the column with an image of an enslaved woman praying in chains"—Mary Kelley, "'Talents Committed to Your Care': Reading and Writing Radical Abolitionism in Antebellum America" *New England Quarterly* 88, no. 1 (2015): 53.

p. 67   "Poor slave! Shall we sorrow that death was thy friend"—Sarah Forten, "The Grave of the Slave," in *The Liberator*, January 22, 1831.

p. 67   "One book of the era warned Black girls with 'purity of mind and strict moral worth'"—*Sketches of the Higher Classes of Colored Society in Philadelphia* (Philadelphia: Merrihew and Thompson, 1841), 50.

p. 67   "In their home, they enjoyed the comforts of genteel living"—Winch, *Gentleman of Color*, 285.

p. 68   "She recited her poetry at family gatherings, among literature clubs"—Gay Gibson Cima, *Performing Anti-Slavery: Activist Women on Antebellum Stages* (Cambridge, UK: Cambridge University Press, 2014), 72

p. 68   "We never travel far from home and seldom go into public places"—Letter from Sarah Forten to Angelina Grimké, April 15, 1837, in Gilbert Barnes and Dwight Dumond, eds. *Letters of Theodore Dwight Weld, Angelina Grimké Weld, and Sarah Grimké*, Vol. 1 (New York: D. Appleton–Century Co., 1934), 379.

p. 68   "Sarah's ancestry was wide-ranging—African, Dutch, and Native American"—Julie Winch, "Sarah Forten's Anti-Slavery Networks," in *Women's Rights and Transatlantic Antislavery in the Era of Emancipation*, eds. Kathryn Kish Sklar and James B. Stewart (New Haven, CT: Yale University Press, 2007), 144; Cima, *Performing Anti-Slavery*, 73.

p. 68   "She'd been involved in literary circles and lyceum lectures for years"—Todd S. Gernes, "Poetic Justice: Sarah Forten, Eliza Earle, and the Paradox of Intellectual Property," *New England Quarterly* 71, no. 2 (1998): 231.

p. 68   "Guests appeared like the founder of the African Methodist Episcopal Church"—Janice Sumler-Lewis, "The Forten-Purvis Women of Philadelphia and the American Anti-Slavery Crusade," *Journal of Negro History* 66, no. 4 (1981–1982): 282.

p. 68   "John Greenleaf Whittier honored her and her siblings"—Gernes, "Poetic Justice," 240.

p. 68   "I never rise to address a colored audience, without feeling ashamed of my own color"—William Lloyd Garrison, *An Address, Delivered Before the Free People of Color, in Philadelphia, New-York, and Other Cities, During the Month of June, 1831* (Boston: Stephen Foster, 1831), 3.

p. 69   "I am astonished that any man should be so prejudiced against his fellow man"—James Forten, letter to *The Liberator*, January 22, 1831.

p. 69   "commending him, as he sailed to Britain, as 'the Champion of the slave'"—Sarah Forten, "To the Hibernia," *The Liberator*, May 25, 1833.

p. 69   "Can the name of 'MY COUNTRY'—the deeds which we sing"—Sarah Forten, "My Country," *The Liberator*, January 4, 1834.

p. 70   "James remembered how, as a child, he had stood near the Pennsylvania state house"—Winch, "Sarah Forten's Anti-Slavery Networks," 144.

p. 70   "His captors gave him the opportunity to return with them to Britain"— Julie Winch, "Onward, Onward, Is Indeed the Watchword: James Forten's Reflections on Revolution and Liberty," in *Prophets of Protest*, eds. McCarthy and Stauffer, 82–83.

p. 70   "It cannot be that the authors of our Constitution intended to exclude us"— James Forten, *Letters from a Man of Colour, on a Late Bill Before the Senate of Pennsylvania*, letter 2 (Philadelphia: James Forten, 1813).

p. 71   "he was willing to help Cuffe find Black individuals"—Winch, *Gentleman of Color*, 185–187, 193; Davis, *Problem of Slavery*, 171–173.

p. 71   "to separate the blacks from the whites is as impossible"—James Forten, letter to *The Liberator*, January 22, 1831.

p. 71   "its object was to 'get rid of the free people of colour'"—*Freedom's Journal*, June 8, 1827.

p. 71   "Philadelphia had witnessed its most recent race riot in November 1829"—J. Thomas Scharf and Thompson Westcott, *History of Philadelphia, 1609–1884*, Vol. 1 (Philadelphia: L. H. Everts & Co., 1884), 624; Theodore Hershberg, "Free Blacks in Antebellum Philadelphia: A Study of Ex-Slaves, Freeborn, and Socioeconomic Decline," *Journal of Social History* 5, no. 2 (1971–1972): 185.

p. 72   "The colonizers did nothing to stop this kind of violence"—Stewart, "Emergence of Racial Modernity," 193–195.

p. 72   "the largest minority community in any Northern city, reaching fifteen thousand in 1830"—Emma Jones Lapsansky, "'Since They Got Those Separate Churches': Afro-Americans and Racism in Jacksonian Philadelphia," *American Quarterly* 32, no. 1 (1980): 57.

p. 72   "The latest outrage was House Bill 446, which would create a color bar"— Rogers, "David Walker and the Political Power," 217; Winch, *Gentleman of Color*, 285.

p. 72   "he submitted a statement to the state senate"—James Forten, *Letters from a Man of Colour, on a Late Bill Before the Senate of Pennsylvania*, Letter I

(Philadelphia: James Forten, 1813); Melvin L. Rogers, "David Walker and the Political Power of the Appeal," *Political Theory* 43, no. 2 (2015): 217.

p. 72   "Why are [the state's] borders to be surrounded by a wall of iron"—James Forten, William Whipper, and Robert Purvis, "To the Honourable the Senate and the House of Representatives of the Commonwealth of Pennsylvania," printed in *The Liberator*, April 14, 1832.

p. 73   "Mankind are becoming more enlightened"—James Forten in *The Liberator*, January 22, 1831.

p. 73   "I am wholly indebted to the Abolition cause"—Letter from Sarah Forten to Angelina Grimké, April 15, 1837, quoted in Barnes and Dumond, *Weld-Grimké Letters*, Vol. 1, 379.

p. 73   "twenty-one women, including Sarah Forten, assembled in the schoolroom"—Sumler-Lewis, "Forten-Purvis Women," 283.

p. 74   "her mother, Charlotte, and her sisters Harriet and Margaretta were among the founders"—Beth A. Salerno, *Sister Societies: Women's Antislavery Organizations in Antebellum America* (DeKalb: Northern Illinois University Press, 2005), 32; Sumler-Lewis, "Forten-Purvis Women," 283.

p. 74   "operating a well-regarded liberal arts academy for Black students"—V. P. Franklin, "'They Rose and Fell Together': African American Educators and Community Leadership, 1795–1954," *Journal of Education* 172, no. 3 (1990): 44.

p. 74   "Lucretia Mott, a 'Hicksite' reformer and minister who questioned the elders"—Anna Davis Hallowell, *James and Lucretia Mott, Life and Letters*, ed. Anna D. Hallowell (Boston: Houghton, Mifflin, 1884), 122–124.

p. 74   "right principles are stronger than great names"—Hallowell, *James and Lucretia Mott*, 113–116.

p. 74   "opened her home up to Black women like the Fortens"—Salerno, *Sister Societies*, 32.

p. 75   "We deem it our duty, as professing Christians, to manifest our abhorrence"—Constitution of the Philadelphia Female Anti-Slavery Society, in *The Liberator*, August 19, 1834.

p. 75   "They called their work frivolous and mocked them"—Perry, *Lift Up Thy Voice*, 125.

p. 75   "claiming they 'should not debase themselves by engaging in public work'"—William E. Cain, Introduction, *William Lloyd Garrison and the Fight Against Slavery: Selections from the Liberator* (New York: St. Martin's Press, 1995), 28.

p. 75   "seeing women's groups as a potent force in the movement"—Newman, *Transformation*, 139.

p. 75   "the Philadelphia society bought subscriptions to both *The Liberator* and *The Emancipator*"—Ira V. Brown, "Cradle of Feminism: The Philadelphia Female Anti-Slavery Society, 1833–1840," *Pennsylvania Magazine of History and Biography* 102, no. 2 (1978): 149.

p. 75 "it made his paper core reading material for activist women"—Newman, *Transformation*, 7.

p. 76 "Lydia Child wrote that abolitionists 'have not the slightest wish to do violence'"—Lydia Maria Child, ed., *The Oasis* (Boston: Benjamin Bacon, 1834), ix.

p. 76 "No doubt but there has always existed the same amount of prejudice"— Letter from Sarah Forten to Angelina Grimké, April 15, 1837, quoted in Barnes and Dumond, *Weld-Grimké Letters*, Vol. 1, 379.

p. 76 "The Colonization Society had many women supporters"—Salerno, *Sister Societies*, 14–15.

p. 77 "Oh, woman, woman, in thy brightest hour"—Sarah Forten, "An Appeal to Woman," *The Liberator*, April 1, 1834.

p. 77 "The poem became a great success and would be used as an ode"—Winch, *Gentleman of Color*, 268, 426n.

p. 77 "coming from men who felt Sarah had been too strident"—James Scott, "Reply to Ada," *The Liberator*, February 22, 1834.

p. 78 "Stewart was an African American widow who had, in 1831"—Marilyn Richardson, *Maria W. Stewart: America's First Black Woman Political Writer, Essays and Speeches* (Bloomington: Indiana University Press, 1987), 10–11.

p. 78 "How long shall the fair daughters of Africa be compelled"—Maria Stewart, *Religion and the Pure Principles of Morality, The Sure Foundation on Which We Must Build*, reprinted in *The Liberator*, October 8, 1831.

p. 78 "She soon stepped outside the world of print"—Dorothy Sterling, ed. *We Are Your Sisters: Black Women in the Nineteenth Century* (New York: W. W. Norton, 1984), 154.

p. 78 "encouraged them to defend one another from injustice"—Christina Henderson, "Sympathetic Violence: Maria Stewart's Antebellum Vision of African American Resistance," *MELUS* 38, no. 4 (2013): 52.

p. 78 "fairer sisters, whose hands are never soiled, whose nerves are never strained"— Maria Stewart, Lecture at Franklin Hall, Boston, September 21, 1832.

p. 79 "Have the sons of Africa no soul? Have they no ambitious desires?"—Maria Stewart, Address at African Masonic Hall, Boston, February 27, 1833.

p. 79 "an apocalyptic vision of divine punishment against America"— Richardson, *Maria W. Stewart*, 26.

p. 79 "they will spread horror and devastation around"—Stewart, Address at African Masonic Hall.

p. 79 "White critics and Black ministers condemned Stewart"—Richardson, *Maria W. Stewart*, 26–27.

p. 79 "I find it is no use for me, as an individual, to try to make myself useful"— Maria Stewart, Farewell Address to Her Friends in the City of Boston, September 21, 1833.

p. 79 "that elusive boundary that separated women's 'sphere of influence'"— Historical Society of Pennsylvania, "Our Sphere of Influence: Women

Activists and the Philadelphia Female Anti-Slavery Society," Exploring
Diversity in Pennsylvania History Series, www.hsp.org

p. 79   "the *Pennsylvania Inquirer*, in July 1834, warned abolitionists not to
call a meeting"—*Pennsylvania Inquirer*, July 14, 1834; Elliott Drago,
"Neither Northern nor Southern: The Politics of Slavery and Freedom in
Philadelphia, 1820–1847" (PhD diss., Temple University, 2017) 163–165.

p. 80   "certain arrangements . . . to get up a MOB in this city"—Benjamin Lundy,
The Genius of Universal Emancipation, July 1834.

p. 80   "hundreds of petitions circulated to the legislature"—Winch, *Gentleman of
Color*, 287.

p. 80   "They carried names like the Rats, the Bouncers, and the Blood Tubs"—
John Runcie, "'Hunting the Nigs' in Philadelphia: The Race Riot of August
1834," *Pennsylvania History: A Journal of Mid-Atlantic Studies* 39, no. 2
(1972): 191.

p. 80   "after a day's work, 'were turned loose upon the street at night'"—Runcie,
"The Race Riot of August 1834," 206.

p. 80   "Many sported bowie knives or pistols or dirks"—Runcie, "The Race Riot
of August 1834," 188.

p. 80   "The firemen put up obstacles"—John C. McWilliams, "'Men of Colour':
Race, Riots, and Black Firefighters' Struggle for Equality from the AFA to
the Valiants," *Journal of Social History* 41, no. 1 (2007): 107–109.

p. 80   "Cartoons circulating in print viciously parodied the small number"—
Lapsansky, "Separate Churches," 65.

p. 80   "dressy blacks and dandy coloured beaux and belles"—John Fanning
Watson, *Annals of Philadelphia* (Philadelphia, E. L. Carey and A. Hart,
1830), 479.

p. 81   "Along with a townhouse, they owned a country estate and a carriage"—
Watson, *Annals of Philadelphia*, 63.

p. 81   "he coveted to wed his daughter to a whiter species"—Abraham
Ritter, *Philadelphia and Her Merchants, as Constituted 50 to 70 Years Ago*
(Philadelphia: Abraham Ritter, 1860), 46–47.

p. 81   "a brash and noisy carnival near the diverse neighborhood of
Moyamensing"—Drago, "Neither Northern nor Southern," 167.

p. 81   "They formed a group of up to sixty men wearing similar outfits"—Abdy,
Journal of a Residence, 320.

p. 81   "They had the names of 'Yorkers' they were after"—Drago, "Neither
Northern nor Southern," 167.

p. 82   "They spotted a fifteen-year-old Black boy out on an errand"—Abdy,
Journal of a Residence, 320.

p. 82   "An eyewitness heard them talking, saying they would scatter for now"—
Runcie, "The Race Riot of August 1834," 191–192.

p. 82   "The city sent out armed men, including a horse patrol"—Abdy, *Journal of a
Residence*, 321.

p. 82   "The constables arrested some men lurking right outside their home"—
Drago, "Neither Northern nor Southern," 167–168.

CHAPTER FIVE: THE INCUBUS

p. 83   "some of them found themselves in jail, held on a bond of $300 each"—
Abdy, *Journal of a Residence*, 320.

p. 84   "They stewed over Saturday, fumed on Sunday"—Runcie, "The Race Riot
of August 1834," 190.

p. 84   "Five hundred of them descended on the Flying Horses"—Runcie,
"The Race Riot of August 1834," 190; Drago, "Neither Northern nor
Southern," 168; Ellis Paxson Oberholtzer, *Philadelphia; A History of
the City and Its People, A Record of 225 Years*, Vol. 2 (Philadelphia: J. S.
Clarke, 1912), 382.

p. 84   "The authorities usually ignored the area"—Runcie, "The Race Riot of
August 1834," 203–204.

p. 84   "The only thing in their way was a group of constables, night watchmen,
and sheriff's deputies"—Drago, "Neither Northern nor Southern," 168.

p. 84   "The lawmen guarded the streets near the southern border of
Philadelphia"—*Niles Weekly Register*, August 23, 1834, 435–436.

p. 84   "the number of lawmen on patrol diminished as the number of rioters
expanded"—Drago, "Neither Northern nor Southern," 168.

p. 85   "The mobsters flooded into Moyamensing and found house after house"—
Niles Weekly Register, August 23, 1834, 435–436.

p. 85   "They stole silverware, watches, and pocketbooks"—Runcie, "The Race
Riot of August 1834," 194; Lapsansky, "Separate Churches," 64.

p. 85   "Some ended up in the woods and clearings outside town"—*Niles Weekly
Register*, August 23, 1834, 435–436.

p. 85   "Stories later described the people left behind: a dead child left beside its
bed"—*Niles Weekly Register*, August 23, 1834, 435–436.

p. 85   "The authorities arrested only twenty or so hoodlums"—*Philadelphia
Gazette*, August 15, 1834.

p. 85   "the streets were 'covered with feathers torn from beds'"—*Philadelphia
Inquirer*, August 15, 1834.

p. 85   "In his own house, Mayor Swift sheltered a dozen Black people fleeing the
mob"—*Pennsylvanian*, August 15, 1834; Abdy, *Journal of a Residence*, 321,
325–328.

p. 86   "Their little property is totally lost, and many were driven from their
dwellings"—*Pennsylvanian*, August 16, 1834.

p. 86   "So he assembled a posse comitatus and swore them into service"—
Pennsylvanian, August 16, 1834; Runcie, "The Race Riot of August 1834,"
190.

p. 86   "They drifted into other parts of the city and found new targets"—
Pennsylvanian, August 16, 1834; Lapsansky, "Separate Churches," 64.

p. 86 "They also damaged the First African Presbyterian Church"—Drago, "Neither Northern nor Southern," 170.

p. 86 "A group of sixty Black men, part of the Benezet Society brotherhood"—Drago, "Neither Northern nor Southern," 175.

p. 87 "Only ten men ever appeared in court"—Runcie, "The Race Riot of August 1834," 208.

p. 87 "The community had been one of the most established in the Northeast"—Lapsansky, "Separate Churches," 60–64.

p. 87 "James Forten received death threats"—Winch, *Gentleman of Color*, 290.

p. 87 "An observer explained that 'a man of wealth and great respectability'"—Abdy, *Journal of a Residence*, 324.

p. 87 "Reports came out of men of 'high and honorable office' threatening police officers"—*Philadelphia Inquirer*, August 18, 1834.

p. 88 "The Pennsylvania Abolition Society created its own report"—*Report of the Committee Appointed to Ascertain the Cause and Particulars of the Late Riot*, Pennsylvania Abolition Society Papers, Historical Society of Pennsylvania, 1834.

p. 88 "Jackson himself worried that the 'spirit of mob-law is becoming too common'"—Letter from Andrew Jackson to Amos Kendall, August 9, 1835, quoted in John Spencer Bassett, ed. *Correspondence of Andrew Jackson*, Vol. 5 (Washington, DC: Carnegie Institution, 1931), 360.

p. 88 "He suspected a secret plan by the aristocratic class"—Robert Remini, *Andrew Jackson: The Course of American Democracy, 1833–1845*, Vol. 3 (Baltimore: Johns Hopkins University Press, 1984), 344.

p. 89 "Black people and abolitionists were still the main focus of their attacks"—Richards, *Gentlemen of Property and Standing*, 15–16.

p. 89 "beyond them were Democratic and Whig poll workers"—Richards, *Gentlemen of Property and Standing*, 12–15; Michael Feldberg, *The Turbulent Era: Riot and Disorder in Jacksonian America* (New York: Oxford University Press, 1980), 54–72.

p. 89 "The state of society is awful. Brute force has superseded the law"—*Niles' Weekly Register*, August 8, 1835, 393.

p. 89 "He saw the press and the Colonization Society as the most culpable"—*The Liberator*, August 23, 1834.

p. 89 "If we are to be hunted as wild beasts, by a ferocious mob"—*The Liberator*, August 23, 1834.

p. 89 "he advertised his wares in *The Liberator* under 'ANTI-SLAVERY BOOK STORE'"—David Ruggles, advertisement in *The Liberator*, August 30, 1834.

p. 90 "hosted a circulating library of works on slavery and colonization"—*The Liberator*, July 14, 1834.

p. 90 "Among the books he had on offer were several by Maria Stewart"—Hodges, *Radical Black Abolitionist*, 60–61.

p. 90   "Ruggles was especially taken with Stewart's attempt to change the
         minds"—Hodges, *Radical Black Abolitionist*, 81–83.

p. 90   "not an evangelical church north of the Ohio and the Pennsylvania line
         would own"—David Ruggles, *Abrogation of the Seventh Commandment, by
         the American Churches* (New York: David Ruggles, 1835), 20.

p. 90   "the editors of the most filthy prints in the country"—Ruggles,
         Extinguisher, 18; Ruggles, *The Liberator*, August 30, 1834.

p. 90   "Reese called Garrison's Declaration of Sentiments 'sophistical, dangerous,
         and Anti-American'"—David Reese, *A Brief Review of the First Annual
         Report of the American Anti-Slavery Society* (New York: Howe & Bates,
         1834), 38–40.

p. 90   "revised the history of the July riots"—David Reese, *A Brief Review of the
         First Annual Report of the American Anti-Slavery Society*, 41–42.

p. 91   "He claimed the doctor was 'choking the truth'"—David Ruggles, *The
         "Extinguisher" Extinguished! Or David M. Reese, M.D. "Used Up"* (New
         York: David Ruggles, 1834), 7.

p. 91   "castigated Reese for claiming that whites were superior to Blacks"—
         Ruggles, *Extinguisher*, 12, 22–24, 32–33.

p. 91   "the agents of slaveholders operated freely in the North"—Russel M. Nye,
         Fettered Freedom: Civil Liberties and the Slavery Controversy, 1830–1860
         (East Lansing: Michigan State University Press, 1963), 258–259.

p. 91   "The kidnappers known as 'black-birders' were especially ruthless"—Bella
         Gross, "Life and Times of Theodore S. Wright, 1797–1847," *Negro History
         Bulletin* 3, no. 9 (1940): 135.

p. 92   "he discovered new outrages perpetrated by 'kidnapping clubs'"—Hodges,
         Radical Black Abolitionist, 88.

p. 92   "groups like the Manumission Society and Pennsylvania Abolition
         Society"—Newman, *Transformation*, 5, 18–19, 25, 66.

p. 92   "Vigilance committees drew up mobs to attack people who spoke out about
         slavery"—Nye, *Fettered Freedom*, 177–178.

p. 93   "These men can be silenced in but one way—*Terror—death*"—Drew Gilpin
         Faust, *James Henry Hammond and the Old South: A Design for Mastery* (Baton
         Rouge, LA: LSU Press, 1985), 161.

p. 93   "as a reward to be paid for the delivery of Arthur Tappan"—*Richmond
         Enquirer*, quoted in *Niles' Weekly Register*, August 22, 1835, 440.

p. 93   "anyone who circulated such material 'is justly worthy'"—Clinton,
         Mississippi, Public Resolution, quoted in Horace Greeley, *The American
         Conflict: A History of the Great Rebellion in the United States of America,
         1860–65*, Vol. 1 (Hartford, CT: O. D. Case & Co., 1866), 128n7.

p. 93   "The cry of the whole South should be death"—*Augusta Chronicle*, quoted in
         Greeley, *American Conflict*, 128n8.

p. 93   "We again warn the Fanatics of the north"—*Richmond Enquirer*, quoted in
         The Liberator, December 6, 1834.

p. 93   "The bounty that hung over his head was worth $5,000"—Ruth Barrett, "Abolitionist Literature and the Mails in Jackson's Time" (thesis, University of Omaha, 1950), 38.

p. 94   "One man found with copies of *The Liberator* faced a mob"—Henrietta Buckmaster, *Let My People Go: The Story of the Underground Railroad and the Growth of the Abolition Movement* (New York: Harper and Bros., 1941), 65.

p. 94   "Our joy will spring from fountains of affection"—Letter from William Lloyd Garrison to Helen Garrison, August 23, 1834, quoted in Merrill, *The Letters of William Lloyd Garrison*, Vol. 1, 404.

p. 94   "It is somewhat difficult to decide who are most hated"—Letter from William Lloyd Garrison to Helen Garrison, August 23, 1834, quoted in Merrill, *The Letters of William Lloyd Garrison*, Vol. 1, 405.

p. 95   "a team of men with weighted clubs and iron bars smashed panes of glass"—*The Liberator*, September 20, 1834.

p. 95   "I have never before felt so sensible of the uncalled for, cruel persecution"—*The Liberator*, September 20, 1834.

p. 95   "While her school no longer existed, five different libel suits against him did"—Garrison and Garrison, *The Story of His Life*, 391.

p. 95   "Shame, shame, shame to those men who had no more honor"—*The Liberator*, March 23, 1833.

p. 95   "She married, sold her house, and left Canterbury"—Small and Small, "Prudence Crandall," 526–527.

p. 96   "distinguished philanthropist and most eloquent orator arrived in the ship Champlain"—*The Liberator*, September 27, 1834.

p. 96   "Thompson had shared a dais with him to preach against injustice"—Garrison and Garrison, *The Story of His Life*, Vol. 1, 351, 357.

p. 96   "helped him taunt colonizers and expose them to ridicule"—Merrill, *Against Wind and Tide*, 70.

p. 96   "his work in America would be as substantial as Marquis de Lafayette's"—Garrison and Garrison, *The Story of His Life*, Vol. 1, 434–435.

p. 96   "Thompson had 'the identical mission of the Son of God'"—William Lloyd Garrison, Introduction, *Lectures of George Thompson, History of His Connection with the Anti-Slavery Cause in England* (Boston: Isaac Knapp, 1836), xviii.

p. 97   "received gifts for Prudence Crandall's school"—C. Duncan Rice, "The Anti-Slavery Mission of George Thompson to the United States, 1834–1835," *Journal of American Studies* 2, no. 1 (1968): 20–21.

p. 97   "the Glasgow Ladies' Emancipation Society sponsored his trip"—William Caleb McDaniel, "Our Country Is the World: Radical American Abolitionists Abroad" (PhD diss., Johns Hopkins University, 2006), 47.

p. 97   "numerous lodgers held a meeting, and notified the landlord"—*Niles' Weekly Register*, September 27, 1834.

p. 97   "the guests had passed resolutions against him"—Rice, "Anti-Slavery Mission," 21.

p. 97   "They claimed the British abolitionist had come to undermine American society"—*The Liberator*, September 27, 1834.

p. 97   "We of the south are prepared to give him a *warm reception*"—*Richmond Enquirer*, quoted in *The Liberator*, December 6, 1834.

p. 98   "Well may the enemies of liberty tremble"—*The Liberator*, September 27, 1834.

p. 98   "Many English critics printed caustic reviews"—Lorman Ratner, "Northern Concern for Social Order as Cause for Rejecting Anti-Slavery, 1831–1840," *The Historian* 28, no.1 (1965): 11–13.

p. 98   "their support for slavery was 'inconsistent with the law of God'"—Harriet Martineau, *Autobiography*, Vol. 1 (Boston: James R. Osgood, 1877), 351, 362.

p. 98   "He said Thompson 'would undoubtedly stir up the bile'"—William Lloyd Garrison, Introduction, *Lectures of George Thompson*, xii.

p. 99   "The financial health of *The Liberator* had once again declined precipitously"—Garrison and Garrison, *The Story of His Life*, Vol. 1, 433–434.

p. 99   "he solicited donations to keep *The Liberator* in business"—Letter from George Thompson to Robert Purvis, November 10, 1834, Boston Public Library, Anti-Slavery Collection, Digital Commonwealth, www.digitalcommonwealth.org.

p. 99   "There are few things which would pain me more than the downfall of The Liberator"—Letter from George Thompson to Robert Purvis, November 10, 1834, Boston Public Library, Anti-Slavery Collection, Digital Commonwealth, www.digitalcommonwealth.org.

p. 99   "In Portland he lectured in an 'Abyssinian church'"—Letter from George Thompson to William Lloyd Garrison, October 28, 1834, quoted in *Letters and Addresses by George Thompson During His Mission in the United States* (Boston: Isaac Knapp, 1837), 12–13.

p. 99   "on the grounds 'that I was regarded as a foreign emissary'"—Letter from George Thompson to William Lloyd Garrison, October 28, 1834, quoted in *Letters and Addresses by George Thompson During His Mission in the United States* (Boston: Isaac Knapp, 1837), 13–14.

p. 100   "the *silly women* who squandered their money for his support"—*Boston Centinel*, quoted in Garrison, Introduction, *Lectures of George Thompson*, xxi.

p. 100   "Webb's *Courier and Enquirer* attacked the 'Glasgow seamstresses'"—*Courier and Enquirer*, quoted in Garrison, Introduction, *Lectures of George Thompson*, xxi–xxii.

p. 100   "Thompson had embezzled eighty pounds from his employer"—Rice, "Anti-Slavery Mission," 26.

p. 100   "the lecture was interrupted by hideous noises from certain brutes and reptiles"—*The Liberator*, December 6, 1834.

p. 100   "who posted a notice to the 'freeborn sons of America'"—Lowell, Handbill, Massachusetts, December 2, 1834, quoted in *The Liberator*, December 6, 1834.

p. 101   "this deadly missile was hurled with tremendous force at his head"—*The Liberator*, December 6, 1834.

p. 101   "the non-payment of our numerous subscribers"—Letter from William Lloyd Garrison to George Benson, January 12, 1835, quoted in Merrill, *The Letters of William Lloyd Garrison*, Vol. 1, 435.

p. 101   "He faced $2,000 in unpaid subscriptions"—Letter from George Thompson to Robert Purvis, November 10, 1834.

p. 101   "Garrison wasted no time in thrashing the group in print"—*The Liberator*, March 14, 1835.

p. 101   "later he labeled it an 'ANTI-GARRISON SOCIETY'"—*The Liberator*, July 4, 1835.

p. 102   "An observer saw that they 'hate Garrison more than they detest slavery'"—*The Liberator*, May 30 and June 27, 1835.

p. 102   "severe and denunciatory language with which he often assails his opponents"—*Boston Recorder*, quoted in *The Liberator*, January 31, 1835.

p. 103   "Some writhed and gnashed upon us; some sneered; some ridiculed"—Letter from William Lloyd Garrison to Helen Garrison, March 19, 1835, quoted in Merrill, *The Letters of William Lloyd Garrison*, Vol. 1, 468.

p. 103   "the American people have no fear of God before their eyes"—Letter from William Lloyd Garrison to Helen Garrison, March 19, 1835, quoted in Merrill, *The Letters of William Lloyd Garrison*, Vol. 1, 468.

CHAPTER SIX: THE TORCH OF DISAFFECTIONS

p. 104   "The Jackson men had begun the fracas by attacking a tavern owned by the Whigs"—*Philadelphia Gazette*, October 15, 1834.

p. 105   "lecturing to a crowd of . . . three thousand in Bethel Church"—Mayer, *All on Fire*, 194; Letter from William Lloyd Garrison to Helen Garrison, March 19, 1835, quoted in Merrill, *The Letters of William Lloyd Garrison*, Vol. 1, 469.

p. 105   "He pleads with Christians of every name, to arouse from their lethargy"—Letter from Arnold Buffum to William Lloyd Garrison, March 4, 1835, quoted in *Letters and Addresses by George Thompson*, 46.

p. 105   "one of the most remarkable women I ever saw"—Letter from William Lloyd Garrison to Helen Garrison, March 19, 1835, quoted in Merrill, *The Letters of William Lloyd Garrison*, Vol. 1, 468.

p. 106   "his eloquence surpasses any thing ever before heard"—Letter from Sarah Forten to Elizabeth Whittier, March 23, 1835, quoted in Sterling, *We Are Your Sisters*, 121–122.

p. 106   "the alarm was excessive—and the meeting adjourned in great confusion"— Letter from Sarah Forten to Elizabeth Whittier, March 23, 1835, quoted in Sterling, *We Are Your Sisters*, 121–122; Letter from Arnold Buffum to William Lloyd Garrison, March 4, 1835, quoted in *Letters and Addresses by George Thompson*, 46.

p. 106   "He felt humbled to be the object of such acclaim"—Brown, "Cradle of Feminism," 150; Winch, "Sarah Forten's Anti-Slavery Networks," 152.

p. 106   "he told Garrison that if he could have chosen the place of his birth"— Garrison, Introduction, *Lectures of George Thompson*, xx.

p. 106   "Robert Purvis had recently returned from Britain"—Brown, "Cradle of Feminism," 149.

p. 106   "Sarah Forten communicated with British abolitionists"—Winch, "Sarah Forten's Anti-Slavery Networks," 150, 152.

p. 107   "Female Societies probably did more for the abolition of slavery"—*Second Annual Report of the American Anti-Slavery Society* (New York: William Dorr, 1835), 88.

p. 107   "They had already built a school for Black children"—Brown, "Cradle of Feminism," 149–150.

p. 107   "Mott had circulated a petition against slavery that she sent to Congress"— Patrick H. Breen, "The Female Antislavery Petition Campaign of 1831–32," *Virginia Magazine of History and Biography* 110 No, 3 (2002): 377, 397.

p. 107   "a representative from New York had presented the names of eight hundred women"—Garrison and Garrison, *The Story of His Life*, vol.1, 482.

p. 108   "these zealots 'were ready to light the torch of disaffections'"—Henry Clay, February 16, 1835, quoted in *Register of Debates in Congress*, Vol. 11 (Washington, DC: Gales and Seaton, 1835), 1397.

p. 108   "all that delicacy and maternal tenderness"—Barnes, *Anti-Slavery Impulse*, 140.

p. 108   "the admonition of the apostle Paul"—1 Corinthians 14:34–35, Bible, New International Version (Grand Rapids, MI: Zondervan, 1984).

p. 108   "Sarah and the other Philadelphians worked out a plan in concert with women's groups"—Newman, *Transformation*, 147; Brown, "Cradle of Feminism," 150.

p. 108   "She would be one of the principals"—Minutes of the Philadelphia Female Anti-Slavery Society, June 13, 1835, in Friends of Freedom Collection, Historical Society of Pennsylvania.

p. 108   "preparing documents to send to Congress for the September opening"— Newman, *Transformation*, 148.

p. 109   "The latest tumult began with a story of an enslaved man who had attacked his owner"—*The Liberator*, July 25, 1835.

p. 109   "One man tried to hide in his chimney"—*Philadelphia Gazette*, July 14, 1835.

p. 109   "the firefighters battled in the streets for hours over their hose and apparatus"—*Philadelphia Gazette*, July 14, 1835.

p. 109   "Some of the Black people inside fought back, armed with axes or guns"—*Philadelphia Inquirer,* July 15, 1835.

p. 109   "Those attacked raced across rooftops to escape"—*U.S. Gazette,* July 15, 1835.

p. 110   "cold-blooded, incendiary, *smoothly* ruffian, and *hypocritically* cruel"—*The Liberator,* July 25, 1835.

p. 110   "promoted the idea of Black men improving their lot"—Stewart, "Emergence of Racial Modernity," 197.

p. 110   "Garrison, too, felt that a commitment to pacifism, temperance, and piety"—Stewart, "Emergence of Racial Modernity," 188; Garrison and Garrison, *The Story of His Life,* vo1. 1, 255.

p. 110   "Moral reformers derided such behavior as a distraction from their goal"—Stewart, "Emergence of Racial Modernity," 191.

p. 111   "James Forten's allies Robert Purvis and William Whipper the prime advocates"—Harris, *In the Shadow of Slavery,* 184.

p. 111   "Whipper helped create the American Moral Reform Society"—Ripley, *Black Abolitionist Papers,* 146.

p. 111   "he saw as rooted in 'the depravity of our morals'"—William Whipper, Alfred Niger, and Augustus Price, *Minutes of the Fifth Annual Convention for the Improvement of the Free People of Colour in the United States* (Philadelphia: William P. Gibbons, 1835), 25.

p. 111   "We are unable to conceive of any better method"—Whipper, Niger, and Price, *Minutes of the Fifth Annual Convention,* 29.

p. 111   "we do most cordially hope that a moral fabric may be reared"—Whipper, Niger, and Price, *Minutes of the Fifth Annual Convention,* 31.

p. 112   "vague, wild, indefinite and confused in their views"—*Colored American,* August 26, 1837, quoted in Harris, *In the Shadow of Slavery,* 184.

p. 113   "Lewis called it 'AN ANTI-GARRISON SOCIETY'"—*The Liberator,* January 31, 1835.

p. 113   "He disavowed the American Union in a meeting of the Anti-Slavery Society"—Letter from William Lloyd Garrison to Helen Garrison, March 6, 1835, quoted in Merrill, *The Letters of William Lloyd Garrison,* Vol. 1, 465; Wyatt-Brown, *Lewis Tappan,* 140.

p. 113   "hundreds of new antislavery groups had formed"—*Second Annual Report of the American Anti-Slavery Society,* 83–87.

p. 114   "for an economical cost, they could flood the South with pamphlets and newspapers"—Mayer, *All on Fire,* 193.

p. 114   "So he took over as the chairman of publications"—Wyatt-Brown, *Lewis Tappan,* 143.

p. 114   "A monthly *Emancipator* with more uncompromising rhetoric" to "almost as if Garrison had written them"—Bertram Wyatt-Brown, "The Abolitionists' Postal Campaign of 1835," *Journal of Negro History* 50, no. 4 (1965): 228–230.

p. 114   "Lewis set a goal of raising $30,000 to fund the publications"—Wyatt-Brown, "The Abolitionists' Postal Campaign of 1835," 228.

p. 114   "to send them to every corner of the United States, but especially the South"—Mayer, *All on Fire*, 193.

p. 114   "politicians, ministers, businessmen, and other key figures"—Susan Wyly-Jones, "The 1835 Anti-Abolition Meetings in the South: A New Look at the Controversy over the Abolition Postal Campaign," *Civil War History* 47, no. 4 (2001): 290–291.

p. 114   "he employed cheap steam-press printing and the national network"—Wyatt-Brown, *Lewis Tappan*, 145; Wyly-Jones, "1835 Anti-Abolition Meetings," 300.

p. 114   "The Society sent off more than a million pieces of mail for the four publications"—W. Sherman Savage, *The Controversy over the Distribution of Abolition Literature, 1830–1860* (Washington, DC: Association for the Study of Negro Life and History, 1938), 13.

p. 115   "The publications were visually striking"—Savage, *The Controversy over the Distribution of Abolition Literature*, 10.

p. 115   "describing Black women freezing to death rather than submit to whipping"—"Cases of Cruelty," *Anti-Slavery Record* 1, no. 6 (1835): 64–65.

p. 115   "focusing on the physical and emotional toll of human bondage for Black women"—George Bourne, *Picture of Slavery in the United States of America* (Middletown, CT: Edwin Hunt, 1834), 88, 91–95, 109–110.

p. 115   "one vast brothel, in which multiform incests, polygamy, adultery, and other uncleannesses"—George Bourne, *Slavery Illustrated in Its Effects upon Woman and Domestic Society* (Boston: Isaac Knapp, 1837), 27.

p. 115   "The Tappans' associate David Ruggles had said much the same thing"—Ruggles, *Abrogation of the Seventh Commandment*, 1.

p. 115   "drove the point that violations of the body weren't just a by-product of slavery"—Child, *An Appeal in Favor*, 19–23.

p. 115   "slavery produces amalgamation at the most rapid rate possible"—"Amalgamation," *Anti-Slavery Record* 1, no. 1 (1835): 7–8.

p. 116   "the *Norfolk Herald* announced that thirty copies of *Human Rights*"—*Norfolk Herald*, quoted in Wyly-Jones, "The 1835 Anti-Abolition Meetings," 294.

p. 116   "excite sedition among the colored population of the south"—*Norfolk Herald*, quoted in *Niles' Weekly Register*, August 8, 1835.

p. 116   "the *Charleston Mercury* enflamed the anger of its readers"—*Charleston Mercury*, July 30, 1835.

p. 116   "The *Charleston Southern Patriot* went further, demanding the suppression"—*Charleston Southern Patriot*, quoted in *Niles' Weekly Register*, August 8, 1835, 402–403.

p. 116   "The steamship *Columbia* arrived in Charleston"—Wyatt-Brown, "Abolitionists' Postal Campaign," 230.

p. 116   "They broke in through a window and carried off all the mail they could grab"—*Charleston Courier*, quoted in *The Liberator*, August 15, 1835.

p. 116   "The next day the white townsfolk held a meeting"—Horace Greeley, *The American Conflict: A History of the Great Rebellion in the United States of America, 1860–65* (Chicago: O. D. Case & Co., 1866), 128–129.

p. 116   "It was a festive affair, with a balloon ascending"—*The Liberator*, August 15, 1835.

p. 117   "claiming they 'would be likely to produce incalculable evil'"—*The Liberator*, August 15, 1835.

p. 117   "A former governor and four other men formed a committee"—Remini, *Andrew Jackson*, 259.

p. 117   "We owe an obligation to the laws, but we owe a higher one"—Buckmaster, *Let My People Go*, 85.

p. 117   "reports appeared in the Southern press"—Savage, *The Controversy*, 14.

p. 117   "that secret subversives had penetrated the South and littered it"—Wyly-Jones, "1835 Anti-Abolition Meetings," 300–301.

p. 117   "Vigilance committees formed to suppress the mail"—Wyly-Jones, "1835 Anti-Abolition Meetings," 303.

p. 117   "Those suspected of sympathizing with abolition were publicly defamed"—Jennifer Rose Mercieca, "The Culture of Honor: How Slaveholders Responded to the Abolitionist Mail Crisis of 1835," *Rhetoric and Public Affairs* 10, no. 1 (2007): 65–66.

p. 117   "A committee found a man in Nashville, Amos Dresser"—*Niles' Weekly Register*, August 22, 1835, 440–441.

p. 117   "Torchlight parades and protest meetings erupted with demagogues"—Wyatt-Brown, "Abolitionists' Postal Campaign," 230–231.

p. 117   "Several white people found guilty of 'association with Negroes'"—Buckmaster, *Let My People Go*, 85.

p. 118   "They launched into diatribes"—Wyly-Jones, "1835 Anti-Abolition Meetings," 296–298.

p. 118   "a crime of so deep a dye, in comparison with which murder"—*National Intelligencer*, quoted in *Niles' Weekly Register*, August 8, 1835, 402.

p. 118   "hiring an assassin to go to Georgia to murder the governor"—*The Liberator*, August 28, 1835.

p. 118   "one from a Norfolk rally that promised $50,000"—Wyatt-Brown, "Abolitionists' Postal Campaign," 231.

p. 118   "A state grand jury indicted the entire membership"—Wyatt-Brown, "Abolitionists' Postal Campaign," 235.

p. 118   "Rumors of a pilot boat from Savannah waiting"—Lewis Tappan, *Life of Arthur Tappan*, 245.

p. 118   "like the times of the French Revolution"—Wyatt-Brown, *Lewis Tappan*, 153.

p. 118   "with all its kindred horrors of rape, sack, and slaughter" to "Keep a look out, Arthur"—*Courier and Enquirer*, September 1, September 5, and October 1, 1835.

p. 119   "Southern businessmen took action to boycott Arthur Tappan and Company"—Wyatt-Brown, "Abolitionists' Postal Campaign," 234.

p. 119   "You demand that I shall cease my anti-slavery labors"—Lewis Tappan, *Life of Arthur Tappan*, 269.

p. 119   "We will persevere, come life or death"—*Niles' Weekly Register*, September 12, 1835, 20–21.

p. 119   "the storm of mostly negative publicity provided Arthur Tappan and Company"—Wyatt-Brown, "Abolitionists' Postal Campaign," 232; *The Liberator*, November 21, 1835.

p. 119   "sold dozens of goods that advertised the cause"—Wyatt-Brown, *Lewis Tappan*, 155; *The Liberator*, November 21, 1835.

p. 119   "It had already expanded its membership with chapters throughout the United States"—*Second Annual Report of the American Anti-Slavery Society*, 37–38, 83–87.

p. 120   "the great slavemart of the American continent"—American Anti-Slavery Society Executive Committee, *Address to the Public*, September 8, 1835, quoted in Lewis Tappan, *Life of Arthur Tappan*, 246–247.

p. 120   "the days of our republic are numbered"—American Anti-Slavery Society Executive Committee, *Address to the Public*, 247.

p. 120   "Postmaster General Kendall took advantage of the outrage in the white South"—Grimsted, *American Mobbing*, 23.

p. 120   "So Gouvernor, to aid in 'preserving the public peace'"—*Niles' Weekly Register*, August 15, 1835; Mercieca, "Culture of Honor," 60.

p. 121   "the people are to be governed by the law just so long as it pleases them"—Philip Hone, *The Diary of Philip Hone, 1828–1851*, ed. Bayard Tuckerman, Vol. 1 (New York: Dodd, Mead and Co., 1889), 155–156.

p. 121   "Even William Stone's fearsomely proslavery *Commercial Advertiser*"—Grimsted, *American Mobbing*, 24.

p. 121   "record the names of recipients 'and have them exposed thro the publik journals'"—Letter from Andrew Jackson to Amos Kendall, August 9, 1835, in Bassett, *Correspondence of Jackson*, 360–361.

p. 121   "they ought to be made to atone for this wicked attempt"—Letter from Andrew Jackson to Amos Kendall, August 9, 1835, in Bassett, *Correspondence of Jackson*, 360.

p. 121   "the Anti-Slavery Society sent out its mail from other cities"—Mercieca, "Culture of Honor," 61.

p. 122   "There are some features in Southern slavery which are humanity itself"—Amos Kendall, *Autobiography of Amos Kendall*, ed. William Stickney (New York: Lee, Shepard and Dillingham, 1872), 502.

p. 122   "in December, issued a report claiming that the federal government"—
          Report of the Postmaster General to the President of the United States,
          December 1, 1835, *The Congressional Globe*, 24th Congress, First Session
          (Washington, DC: Blair and Rives, 1836), Appendix, 9.

p. 122   "prohibit, under severe penalties, the circulation in the southern States"—
          Message from Andrew Jackson to US House of Representatives and US
          Senate, December 8, 1835, *The Congressional Globe*, 24th Congress, First
          Session, 10.

p. 122   "known for crafting elaborate defenses of white supremacy and slavery
          (calling it a 'positive good')"—John Calhoun, Speech on the Reception of
          Abolition Petitions, February 1837, in *Speeches of John C. Calhoun* (New
          York: Harper & Brothers, 1843), 225.

CHAPTER SEVEN: LAYING ON VIOLENT HANDS

p. 123   *"Niles' Weekly Register* reported so many riots and insurrections"—*Niles'
          Weekly Register*, August 22, 1835, 439–442.

p. 123   "It started after police arrested Reuben Crandall"—David Grimsted,
          "Rioting in Its Jacksonian Setting," *American Historical Review* 77, no. 2
          (1972): 377.

p. 124   "district attorney Francis Scott Key ordered his arrest"—Jefferson Morley,
          "The 'Snow Riot,'" *Washington Post*, February 6, 2005.

p. 124   "A riot against Black Washington ensued"—Mary Beth Corrigan, "The
          Ties That Bind: The Pursuit of Community and Freedom among Slaves and
          Free Blacks in the District of Columbia, 1800–1860," in Howard Gillette
          Jr., ed. *Southern City, National Ambition: The Growth of Early Washington,
          D.C.: 1800–1860* (Washington, DC: George Washington University
          Center for Washington Area Studies, 1995), 79–80.

p. 124   "anything he could do for them in an honorable way"—Michael Shiner,
          *The Diary of Michael Shiner Relating to the History of the Washington Navy
          Yard, 1813–1869*, Library of Congress MSS 20:957, 63, Naval History and
          Heritage Command library, www.history.navy.mil/our-collections.html.

p. 124   "the progress of Misrule in the City of Washington"—*The Liberator*,
          August 29, 1835.

p. 124   "Garrison placed his New England Anti-Slavery Society under the
          umbrella"—Zorn, "New England Anti-Slavery Society," 176.

p. 124   "inspired the creation of forty-seven local branches in ten states"——Zorn,
          "New England Anti-Slavery Society," 172.

p. 125   "How wise, how benevolent, how invaluable"—Letter from William Lloyd
          Garrison to George Benson, September 4, 1835, quoted in Merrill, *The
          Letters of William Lloyd Garrison*, Vol. 1, 494.

p. 125   "he also wrote of Sodom and Gomorrah"—Letter from William Lloyd
          Garrison to George Benson, September 4, 1835, quoted in Merrill, *The
          Letters of William Lloyd Garrison*, Vol. 1, 494.

p. 125   "I have just received a letter written evidently by a friendly hand"—Letter
          from William Lloyd Garrison to George Benson, September 4, 1835,
          quoted in Merrill, *The Letters of William Lloyd Garrison*, Vol. 1, 495.

p. 125   "in Concord he faced flying rocks and eggs"—Richards, *Gentlemen of
          Property and Standing*, 64.

p. 125   "probably escaped under the protection of a petticoat"—*Niles' Weekly
          Register*, August 22, 1835, 439.

p. 125   "John Greenleaf Whittier encountered an angry crowd"—Richards,
          Gentlemen of Property and Standing, 64.

p. 125   "During the last six months of his stay here"—May, *Some Recollections*, 122.

p. 126   "He described his friend in almost saintly terms"—Letter from William
          Lloyd Garrison to George Benson, September 4, 1835, quoted in Merrill,
          The Letters of William Lloyd Garrison, Vol. 1, 495.

p. 126   "many of the rabble were foreigners of the *lowest* grade"—*The Liberator*,
          December 6, 1834.

p. 126   "He also made claims about American religion that his listeners found
          jolting"—Letter from George Thompson to *Christian Advocate and Journal*,
          May 20, 1835.

p. 127   "he attacked the faculty as well as students to incite a debate"—*New York
          Journal of Commerce*, July 13, 1835.

p. 127   "The *Commercial Advertiser* even reported a rumor"—Richards, *Gentlemen of
          Property and Standing*, 65.

p. 127   "Even more ill-advised was Thompson's attack on a Baptist minister"—
          Thomas F. Harwood, "British Evangelical Abolitionism and American
          Churches in the 1830's," *Journal of Southern History* 28, no. 3 (1962): 290.

p. 127   "But he had also received a warning from a Southern colonizer"—Rice,
          "Anti-Slavery Mission," 25.

p. 127   "Cox withdrew out of caution"—George Thompson and Frederick
          Chesson, "Scrap Books Compiled by Thompson and Chesson," Vol. 1,
          1835, clip from *Reformer* newspaper (Birmingham, UK), www.loc.gov
          /item/2013659691.

p. 127   "by slavery's 'torpedo power a man has been struck dumb'"—*Second Annual
          Report of the American Anti-Slavery Society*, 21–22.

p. 127   "an outbreak of hissing and stamping"—*New York Baptist Register*, from
          Thompson and Chesson, "Scrap Books" [unnumbered].

p. 127   "Expressions of much dissatisfaction were now heard"—*Second Annual
          Report of the American Anti-Slavery Society*, 22–23.

p. 127   "Critics seized on this 'tiger-like malice' in Thompson's character"—Letter
          from R. Reed to *The Liberator*, in *Discussions on American Slavery Between
          George Thompson and Robert J. Breckenridge*, ed. William Lloyd Garrison
          (Boston: Isaac Knapp, 1836), 93.

p. 127   "he defended his conduct in *The Liberator*"—*The Liberator*, September 5,
          1835.

p. 128   "he quietly removed the offensive oratory from the meeting"—Rice, "Anti-Slavery Mission," 25.

p. 128   "In New Hampshire Samuel Noyes deeded land for a school for Black youth"—Sinha, *Slave's Cause*, 231.

p. 128   "the most hideous outcries, yells, from a crowd of men"—May, *Some Recollections*, 152–153.

p. 128   "May's appearances met with violence and bloodthirsty demands"—May, *Some Recollections*, 155.

p. 128   "Faneuil Hall . . . hosted some 1,500 people"—May, *Some Recollections*, 151–152.

p. 128   "He praised the country's founders who had also been slaveholders"—*Niles' Weekly Register*, September 5, 1835, 10–11.

p. 129   "All men are invited to join in this holy crusade"—*Niles' Weekly Register*, September 5, 1835, 11.

p. 129   "It is the language of the heart—simple, but strong"—*Niles' Weekly Register*, September 5, 1835, 1.

p. 129   "'pollution and disgrace' for the meeting, the 'COFFIN OF LIBERTY'"—*The Liberator*, August 29, 1835.

p. 129   "we had better not attempt to lecture"—Letter from William Lloyd Garrison to Henry Benson, September 12, 1835, quoted in Merrill, *The Letters of William Lloyd Garrison*, Vol. 1, 526.

p. 129   "That some of us will be assassinated or abducted, seems more than probable"—Letter from William Lloyd Garrison to George Benson, September 12, 1835, quoted in Merrill, *The Letters of William Lloyd Garrison*, Vol. 1, 527.

p. 130   "Religious prosecution always begins with *mobs*"—Letter from Angelina Grimké to William Lloyd Garrison, quoted in *The Liberator*, September 19, 1835.

p. 130   "Yes! LET IT COME"—Letter from Angelina Grimké to William Lloyd Garrison, quoted in *The Liberator*, September 19, 1835.

p. 130   "soul-thrilling epistle . . . with a spirit worthy of the best days of martyrdom"—Letter from William Lloyd Garrison to George Benson, September 12, 1835, quoted in Merrill, *The Letters of William Lloyd Garrison*, Vol. 1, 527.

p. 130   "a nine-foot-high gallows cut from maple wood and draped in seaweed"—Mayer, *All on Fire*, 199; Merrill, *Against Wind and Tide*, 102.

p. 130   "pray, be very careful all of you, especially about venturing out at night"—Letter from William Lloyd Garrison to Henry Benson, September 15, 1835, quoted in Merrill, *The Letters of William Lloyd Garrison*, Vol. 1, 528.

p. 131   "setting the template for the strategy now undertaken by other women's groups"—Newman, *Transformation*, 147; Daniel Carpenter and Colin D. Moore, "When Canvassers Became Activists: Antislavery Petitioning and the Political Mobilization of American Women," *American Political Science Review* 108, no. 3 (2014): 482, 492.

p. 131   "Mr. Garrison is regarded as a brother by every one of us"—*Right and Wrong in Boston: Report of the Boston Female Anti-Slavery Society; With a Concise Statement of Events Previous and Subsequent to the Annual Meeting of 1835* (Boston: Boston Female Anti-Slavery Society, 1836), 38.

p. 131   "warned Thompson that he wouldn't be able to hide under ladies' petticoats"—Mayer, *All on Fire*, 200.

p. 131   "said they belonged in 'their proper sphere—the domestic fireside'"— *Commercial Gazette*, October 15, 1835.

p. 131   "THOMPSON—THE ABOLITIONIST. That infamous foreign scoundrel THOMPSON"—Handbill quoted in *Niles' Weekly Register*, October 31, 1835, 145.

p. 132   "You will be killed as sure as fate, if you show your heads at that hall"— *Right and Wrong in Boston*, 29.

p. 132   "The greater the opposition to a right action"—*Right and Wrong in Boston*, 22.

p. 132   "The mayor blithely responded, 'You give us a great deal of trouble'"—*Right and Wrong in Boston*, 29.

p. 132   "this crowd was thick with 'a great multitude of neatly dressed young men'"—Theodore M. Hammett, "Two Mobs of Jacksonian Boston: Ideology and Interest," *Journal of American History* 62, no. 4 (1976): 846.

p. 132   "The merchants connected by business with the South"—Samuel Sewall, *A Memoir*, ed. Nina Moore Tiffany (New York: Houghton, Mifflin, 1898), 52.

p. 132   "they did find abolition tracts and pamphlets that looked suspicious"—*Niles' Weekly Register*, October 31, 1835, 145.

p. 133   "He asked Chapman's group if he should offer an address"—*Right and Wrong in Boston*, 30.

p. 133   "the peculiar dress of his hair and beard has given offence to many"—May, *Some Recollections*, 66.

p. 133   "He dressed like a tramp"—Henry Stanton, *Random Recollections* (New York: Harpers & Brothers, 1887), 71.

p. 133   "a boot from the hallway kicked open the lower panel"—Merrill, *Against Wind and Tide*, 105.

p. 133   "if it was necessary to die in that cause, [we] might as well die there and then"—Theodore Lyman, "Account by Mayor Lyman," in *Papers Relating to the Garrison Mob*, ed. T. Lyman (Cambridge, MA: Welch, Bigelow, and Co., 1870), 17.

p. 133   "personal friends are the instigators of this mob"—*Right and Wrong in Boston*, 33.

p. 134   "the Boston Female Anti-Slavery Society left Anti-Slavery Hall"—Sewall, *Memoir*, 46; *Niles' Weekly Register*, October 31, 1835, 145.

p. 134 "These men are fathers; they have daughters just coming forward into womanhood"—*Right and Wrong in Boston*, 28–30.

p. 134 "we could only find relief and composure under this shock"—*Right and Wrong in Boston*, 38.

p. 134 "Thompson! Thompson! Garrison! Where is Thompson? Where is Garrison?"—*Niles' Weekly Register*, October 31, 1835, 145.

p. 134 "Mayor Lyman knew Garrison was inside, having briefly spoken to him"—Lyman, "Account by Mayor Lyman," 19.

p. 134 "Samuel Sewall had been scouting around the building"—Sewall, *Memoir*, 47.

p. 134 "He seemed more agitated than I had ever seen him"—Sewall, *Memoir*, 47.

p. 135 "We must have Garrison! Out with him! Lynch him!"—Merrill, *Against Wind and Tide*, 106.

p. 135 "The window was twenty-five feet above the ground"—*Niles' Weekly Register*, October 31, 1835, 145–146.

p. 135 "A young abolitionist named Campbell helped him"—Mayer, *All on Fire*, 204.

p. 135 "but at least one newspaper report said he was 'convulsed with terror'"—*Niles' Weekly Register*, October 31, 1835, 145–146.

p. 135 "They belonged to Daniel and Buff Cooley"—Mayer, *All on Fire*, 204–205.

p. 136 "One of them whipped out a club and nearly brained Garrison with it"—Sewall, *Memoir*, 49–50.

p. 136 "Don't hurt him! He's an American!"—Merrill, *Against Wind and Tide*, 107.

p. 136 "They are going to hang him; for God's sake, save him!"—Lyman, "Account by Mayor Lyman," 21.

p. 136 "He found a spare coat, hat, and pants for him to wear"—Garrison and Garrison, *The Story of His Life*, Vol. 2, 24; *The Liberator*, November 7, 1835.

p. 136 "he would have the sheriff issue a warrant for Garrison's arrest"—Mayer, *All on Fire*, 205.

p. 136 "Garrison agreed as long as the jail stint wouldn't result in a fine"—Lyman, "Account by Mayor Lyman," 23.

p. 136 "Garrison hurried down the steps of City Hall protected by two lines"—Ellis Ames, quoted in *Proceedings of the Massachusetts Historical Society*, Vol. 8 (Boston: Massachusetts Historical Society, 1881), 341–342.

p. 137 "Samuel Sewall saw the coach wedged in"—Sewall, *Memoir*, 51.

p. 137 "Men grabbed at the wheels, tried to open the doors"—Merrill, *Against Wind and Tide*, 107; Garrison and Garrison, *The Story of His Life*, Vol. 2, 26–27.

p. 137 "Garrison seemed to bound from the carriage to the jail door with a single leap"—Lyman, "Account by Mayor Lyman," 23.

p. 137 "Sewall visited him and found him to be in lively spirits, overjoyed to be alive"—Sewall, *Memoir*, 51.

p. 137 "a good conscience and a cheerful mind"—*The Liberator*, November 7, 1835.

p. 137   "He protested this show of bad faith by the authorities"—Mayer, *All on Fire*, 206.

p. 137   "Garrison agreed, and departed for Brooklyn"—Merrill, *Against Wind and Tide*, 111.

p. 137   "almost every press organ tore into him and other abolitionists"— Hammett, "Two Mobs," 865.

p. 137   "expressed their decisive reprobation, of the outrageous perseverance of fanatics"—*Boston Centinel*, quoted in *Niles' Weekly Register*, October 31, 1835, 146.

p. 138   "a meeting of gentlemen of property and standing from all parts of the city"—*Boston Gazette*, quoted in *Niles' Weekly Register*, October 31, 1835, 146.

p. 138   "WHO ARE THE AUTHORS OF THIS RIOT?"—*The Liberator*, October 31, 1835.

p. 138   "I felt perfectly calm, nay very happy"—*The Liberator*, November 7, 1835.

p. 138   "Confine me as a prisoner—but bind me not as a slave"—*The Liberator*, November 7, 1835.

p. 139   "the hue and cry of 'persecution' raised in their favor!"—*Courier and Enquirer*, quoted in *The Liberator*, November 7, 1835.

p. 139   "sales of *The Liberator* increased markedly"—Merrill, *Against Wind and Tide*, 111; McDaniel, "Our Country Is the World," 48.

p. 139   "my life was sought. I believe many were prepared to take it"—Garrison and Garrison, *The Story of His Life*, Vol. 2, 58–59.

p. 139   "My heart swells with sorrow, my cheeks burn with indignation"—Letter from William Lloyd Garrison to Helen Garrison, November 9, 1835, quoted in Merrill, *The Letters of William Lloyd Garrison*, Vol. 1, 551.

p. 139   "Thompson bid his farewell to Garrison"—Letter from George Thompson to William Lloyd Garrison, November 27, 1835, quoted in *Letters and Addresses by George Thompson*, 117–118.

p. 140   "especially against the emissaries from foreign parts"—Message from Andrew Jackson to US House of Representatives and US Senate, December 8, 1835, in *The Congressional Globe*, 24th Congress, First Session, 10.

p. 140   "Cincinnati, for example, remained notorious for its brutal 1829 race riots"—Sinha, *Slave's Cause*, 207.

p. 140   "Weld spoke of God's wrath upon slaveholders"—Perry, *Lift Up Thy Voice*, 134–135.

p. 141   "he had led a series of debates over slavery and colonization"—Robert Abzug, *Passionate Liberator: Theodore Dwight Weld and the Dilemma of Reform* (New York: Oxford University Press, 1980), 89–94; Perry, *Lift Up Thy Voice*, 101–105.

p. 141   "Arthur Tappan sent financial assistance to help the students in their protest"—Barnes, *Anti-Slavery Impulse*, 74–77.

p. 141   "promoted an alternative school for them in Cincinnati"—Merrill, *Against Wind and Tide*, 120.

p. 141　"he went from one village to another in the Ohio countryside"—Perry, *Lift Up Thy Voice*, 133–134.

p. 141　"for a few days I had frequent turns of dizziness"—Letter from Theodore Weld to Elizur Wright, March 2, 1835, quoted in *The Liberator*, April 4, 1835.

p. 141　"a sizable crowd assembled 'with tin horns, sleigh bells, drums, etc.'"— Letter from Theodore Weld to Elizur Wright, October 6, 1835, quoted in Barnes and Dumond, *Weld-Grimké Letters*, Vol. 1, 237.

p. 142　"By persisting through the initial violence and insults"—Barnes, *Anti-Slavery Impulse*, 81–83.

p. 142　"Weld was convinced it worked best in the rural heartland"—Perry, *Lift Up Thy Voice*, 135.

p. 143　"most decidedly and unanimously in favor of your coming to New York"— Letter from Elizur Wright to Theodore Weld, November 5, 1835, quoted in Barnes and Dumond, *Weld-Grimké Letters*, Vol. 1, 241.

p. 143　"the favorite of several western colleges that the Tappans funded"—Barnes, *Anti-Slavery Impulse*, 38.

p. 143　"one of the vice presidents of the American Anti-Slavery Society, Rev. Beriah Green"—*Second Annual Report of the American Anti-Slavery Society*, 25.

p. 143　"see the face, and grasp the hand, and hear the voice"—Letter from Beriah Green to Theodore Weld, September 21, 1835, quoted in Barnes and Dumond, *Weld-Grimké Letters*, Vol. 1, 233–234.

p. 144　"warning of 'disorderly fanatics' who would 'degrade the city'"—*Albany Argus*, quoted in *Niles' Weekly Register*, October 31, 1835, 146.

p. 144　"Colonizers had already taken aim at Green"—Sinha, *Slave's Cause*, 233; Richards, *Gentlemen of Property and Standing*, 86.

p. 144　"James Watson Webb joined the denunciation"—Richards, *Gentlemen of Property and Standing*, 87.

p. 144　"it would be better to have Utica razed to its foundations"—May, *Some Recollections*, 164.

p. 144　"an opposing meeting of 'respectable mechanics' came out in favor"—Sinha, *Slave's Cause*, 233.

p. 144　"they successfully got the Common Council to revoke its permission"— May, *Some Recollections*, 164.

p. 144　"A city alderman tried to keep them from entering the building"—*Niles' Weekly Register*, October 31, 1835, 162.

p. 145　"Open the way! Break down the doors! Damn the fanatics! Knock them down!"—*The Enemies of the Constitution Discovered . . . The Dispersion of the State Anti-Slavery Convention by the Agitators* (New York: Leavitt, Lord & Co., 1835), 82.

p. 145　"a 'Committee of 25'—leading a horde of angry whites—burst into the church"—May, *Some Recollections*, 165.

p. 145   "They belched forth blasphemies and foamed like the troubled sea"—*Niles'* *Weekly Register*, October 31, 1835, 163.

p. 145   "The Beardsley mob was in high spirits from the grog shops"—May, *Some Recollections*, 166.

p. 145   "Give us Tappan! Hustle them out of the house!"—*Enemies of the Constitution*, 84.

p. 145   "manhandled the presiding minister, Oliver Wetmore"—May, *Some Recollections*, 167.

p. 145   "by destroying the offices of the one newspaper in town"—Richards, *Gentlemen of Property and Standing*, 91–92.

p. 146   "He had always refused them, until he witnessed the violence"—May, *Some Recollections*, 168–169.

p. 146   "It is not to be disguised, that a war has broken out"—Gerrit Smith, quoted in *Enemies of the Constitution*, 164.

p. 146   "At his estate, the New York State Anti-Slavery Society came into being"— *Niles' Weekly Register*, October 31, 1835, 163.

CHAPTER EIGHT: TROJAN WARS

p. 147   "Among the delegates chased out of Utica was David Ruggles"—*Proceedings of the New York Anti-Slavery Convention, Held at Utica, October 21 . . .* (Utica, NY: Standard & Democrat, 1835), 45.

p. 147   "Ruggles met dozens of new contacts to help him broaden his network"— Hodges, *Radical Black Abolitionist*, 86, 92–93.

p. 148   "Take Notice!—There is an incendiary depot at the corner"—Handbill quoted in *The Liberator*, September 26, 1835.

p. 148   "a herald of light and truth—and a balm for the lacerated bodies"—*The Liberator*, September 26, 1835.

p. 149   "Ruggles accused several Black New Yorkers by name"—Hodges, *Radical Black Abolitionist*, 88.

p. 149   "At the inaugural meeting—held by the 'Friends of Human Rights'"— Porter, "Apostle of Human Rights," 31–32.

p. 149   "the committee vowed to protect the rights of Black people"—*First Annual Report of the New York Committee of Vigilance* (New York: Committee of Vigilance, 1837), 3.

p. 149   "The *New York Express* fretted over the possibility of the committee"— Harris, *In the Shadow of Slavery*, 213.

p. 149   "up to a hundred men and women made up an Effective Committee"— Harris, *In the Shadow of Slavery*, 211.

p. 150   "Most notable were minister Theodore Wright"—Swift, *Black Prophets*, 78.

p. 150   "Why do the white people hate us so?"—*Colored American*, March 18, 1837.

p. 151   "STRONGHOLD of an unholy prejudice against color"—*Colored American*, March 11, 1837.

p. 151   "Cornish would soon become essential to the Committee of Vigilance"—
          Swift, *Black Prophets*, 104.

p. 151   "He received encouragement from Lewis Tappan"—Ripley, *Black
          Abolitionist Papers*, 179n.

p. 151   "it is the privilege and should be esteemed the duty of every abolitionist"—
          Hodges, *Radical Black Abolitionist*, 126.

p. 151   "he said it had a separate purpose from the American Anti-Slavery
          Society"—*First Committee of Vigilance Report*, 12.

p. 151   "the Committee of Vigilance was mostly run by Black people"—Harris, *In
          the Shadow of Slavery*, 210; Hodges, *Radical Black Abolitionist*, 120.

p. 152   "women's rights are as sacred as men's rights"—David Ruggles, quoted in
          Ripley, *Black Abolitionist Papers*, 176n.

p. 152   "The people served by the Committee included a wide swath"—Porter,
          "Apostle of Human Rights," 36–38; *First Committee of Vigilance Report*,
          13–16.

p. 152   "He literally went to the doors of white employers"—Quarles, *Black
          Abolitionists*, 151–152; Porter, "Apostle of Human Rights," 33.

p. 152   "let us in every case of oppression and wrong"—*First Committee of Vigilance
          Report*, 13.

p. 152   "Among his greatest foes was the city recorder, Richard Riker"—Hodges,
          Radical Black Abolitionist, 87.

p. 153   "sent them into captivity in lieu of a fair trial"—Porter, "Apostle of Human
          Rights," 35–36.

p. 153   "pouncing on an innocent person and dragging him"—Hodges, *Radical
          Black Abolitionist*, 94.

p. 153   "Let a remedy be prescribed to protect us from slavery"—David Ruggles,
          New York Sun, quoted in *The Liberator*, August 6, 1836.

p. 153   "he learned that the slave ship *Brillante* had docked in the harbor"—David
          Ruggles, *New York American*, January 4, 1836.

p. 153   "Ruggles alerted the *New York Evening Post* to the presence of the slave
          ship"—Hodges, *Radical Black Abolitionist*, 97.

p. 153   "Ruggles followed it up by getting the *New York Sun* to publish a disturbing
          account"—David Ruggles, *New York Sun*, quoted in *First Committee of
          Vigilance Report*, 35.

p. 154   "He said the Black people on board were 'bona fide seamen'"—*New York
          Journal of Commerce*, quoted in *First Committee of Vigilance Report*, 36.

p. 154   "Ruggles saw as a 'moral and political cancer'"—David Ruggles, *New York
          American*, January 4, 1836.

p. 154   "no bringing in, no holding, and no selling"—*First Committee of Vigilance
          Report*, 38.

p. 154   "Ruggles's deposition was rejected on technical grounds"—*First Committee
          of Vigilance Report*, 43.

p. 154 "on future voyages, follow the same inhuman traffic with perfect impunity"—*First Committee of Vigilance Report*, 46.

p. 154 "On Christmas Eve, a handful of Black New Yorkers took action"—Hodges, *Radical Black Abolitionist*, 97.

p. 154 "The press responded with indignation"—David Ruggles, *New York American*, January 4, 1836.

p. 154 "A few days later, they paid a visit to Ruggles" to "others of his clan made a rush up to my room like hungry dogs"—David Ruggles, *New York American*, January 4, 1836.

p. 155 "I would soon have put an end to his existence: he would never interfere with Brazilians again"—*First Committee of Vigilance Report*, 75.

p. 155 "we have got him now, he shall have no quarters"—*First Committee of Vigilance Report*, 76.

p. 156 "Now, I thank Heaven that I am still permitted to live"—David Ruggles, *New York American*, January 4, 1836.

p. 156 "the Tappans and the rest of the executive committee"—Wyatt-Brown, *Lewis Tappan*, 168.

p. 156 "he condemned the 'unconstitutional and wicked' designs"—Message from Andrew Jackson to Congress, December 8, 1835.

p. 157 "flames had already engulfed structures on both sides of their granite building"—Tappan, *Life of Arthur Tappan*, 273.

p. 157 "City authorities did all they could to protect the businesses there"—"The Great New York Fire of 1835 and the Marketing of Disaster," New-York Historical Society, blog.nyhistory.org/the-great-new-york-fire-of-1835-and-the-marketing-of-disaster; George Sheldon, *The Story of the Volunteer Fire Department of the City of New York* (New York: Harper & Brothers, 1882), 194.

p. 157 "As Lewis and his crew hauled products out of the business"—Wyatt-Brown, *Lewis Tappan*, 168.

p. 158 "The Tappans and the volunteers saved two-thirds of the stock"—Wyatt-Brown, *Lewis Tappan*, 169.

p. 158 "Other merchants lost much more, up to $20 million"—"The Great New York Fire of 1835," New-York Historical Society.

p. 158 "a detachment of US Marines and sailors secured the streets against looting"—*An Account of the Conflagration of the Principal Part of the First Ward of the City of New York* (New York: C. Foster, 1836), 7.

p. 158 "describing the ruin of 'our largest shipping and wholesale dry goods merchants'"—*Courier and Enquirer*, December 17, 1835.

p. 158 "Arthur announced that he and his business were financially strong"—Wyatt-Brown, *Lewis Tappan*, 168.

p. 158 "new and commodious warehouse, No. 25 Beaver-street"—Tappan, *Life of Arthur Tappan*, 276.

p. 158   "the Tappans couldn't get fully reimbursed for their losses"—Wyatt-Brown,
          Lewis Tappan, 168–169.

p. 159   "In a Christmastime letter Weld warned Lewis of 'The terrors of God!'"—
          Letter from Theodore Weld to Lewis Tappan, December 22, 1835, quoted
          in Barnes and Dumond, *Weld-Grimké Letters*, Vol. 1, 247.

p. 159   "He didn't want to build himself up as a hero or be celebrated"—Letter
          from Elizur Wright to Theodore Weld, May 26, 1835, quoted in Barnes
          and Dumond, *Weld-Grimké Letters*, Vol. 1, 221.

p. 159   "I am a *Backwoodsman untamed*"—Abzug, *Passionate Liberator*, 146.

p. 160   "Lewis lashed out in frustration and scolded Weld over his methods"—
          Abzug, *Passionate Liberator*, 140–141.

p. 160   "Really, after so long a time I must forsooth solemnly avow my
          principles"—Letter from Theodore Weld to Lewis Tappan, March 9, 1836,
          quoted in Barnes and Dumond, *Weld-Grimké Letters*, Vol. 1, 270–274.

p. 160   "all for the sake of his own '*blustering bravado defiance*'"—Letter from
          Theodore Weld to Lewis Tappan, March 9, 1836, quoted in Barnes and
          Dumond, *Weld-Grimké Letters*, Vol. 1, 273.

p. 160   "If I ate in the City it was at *their* tables"—Letter from Theodore Weld
          to Lewis Tappan, March 9, 1836, quoted in Barnes and Dumond, *Weld-
          Grimké Letters*, Vol. 1, 273.

p. 160   "He demanded that more be done to aid Black people"—Abzug, *Passionate
          Liberator*, 143–144.

p. 161   "He condemned the 'stateliness and Pomp and Circumstance'"—Letter
          from Theodore Weld to Lewis Tappan, April 5, 1836, quoted in Barnes and
          Dumond, *Weld-Grimké Letters*, Vol. 1, 286.

p. 161   "a man like Weld thinks the center of the world is where he acts"—Letter
          from Lewis Tappan to Charles Grandison Finney, March 22, 1832, quoted
          in Barnes and Dumond, *Weld-Grimké Letters*, Vol. 1, 68n.

p. 161   "By early 1836 they had prevailed upon Weld to finish his Ohio mission"—
          Perry, *Lift Up Thy Voice*, 136.

p. 162   "Churches competed for the honor of entertaining him"—Barnes, *Anti-
          Slavery Impulse*, 84.

p. 162   "Weld boldly chose to deliver sixteen lectures there"—John Myers, "The
          Beginnings of Anti-Slavery Agencies in New York State, 1833–1836,"
          Proceedings of the New York State Historical Association 60 (1962): 171.

p. 162   "the crowds now overflowed for his oratory"—John Myers, "The Beginnings
          of Anti-Slavery Agencies in New York State, 1833–1836," *Proceedings of the
          New York State Historical Association* 60 (1962): 171.

p. 163   "speaking to rapt crowds and inspiring up to nine hundred people" to "440
          locals had signed the constitution of a new antislavery society"—John
          Myers, "The Beginnings of Anti-Slavery Agencies in New York State,
          1833–1836," *Proceedings of the New York State Historical Association* 60
          (1962): 173–174.

p. 163   "our Cause is *work*, *work*, boneing down to it"—Letter from Theodore Weld to Lewis Tappan, April 5, 1836, quoted in Barnes and Dumond, *Weld-Grimké Letters*, Vol. 1, 289.

p. 163   "The fate of Arthur Tappan and Company had grown bleaker by the month"—Wyatt-Brown, *Lewis Tappan*, 174.

p. 164   "He talked him into loaning the firm $150,000"—Wyatt-Brown, *Lewis Tappan*, 174.

p. 164   "Proslavery legislators and merchants had spread rumors"—Perry, *Lift Up Thy Voice*, 138–139.

p. 165   "The Mayor and the City officers were with a few exceptions totally inefficient"—Letter from Theodore Weld to Ray Potter, June 11, 1836, quoted in Barnes and Dumond, *Weld-Grimké Letters*, Vol. 1, 309.

p. 165   "Several thousand people swarmed around him, hurling stones"—Myers, "Beginnings of Anti-Slavery Agencies," 175.

p. 165   "He wrote defiant letters in which he said he would sacrifice himself"—Letter from Theodore Weld to Ray Potter, June 11, 1836, quoted in Barnes and Dumond, *Weld-Grimké Letters*, Vol. 1, 310.

p. 166   "Wright wrote to Weld to let him know that Troy was much less critical"—Letter from Elizur Wright to Theodore Weld, May 19, 1836, quoted in Barnes and Dumond, *Weld-Grimké Letters*, Vol. 1, 304–305; Abzug, *Passionate Liberator*, 147.

p. 166   "Simeon Jocelyn and the Rhode Island Anti-Slavery Society separately wrote letters"—Letters from Simeon Jocelyn and the Rhode Island Anti-Slavery Society to Theodore Weld, May 29, 1836, quoted in Barnes and Dumond, *Weld-Grimké Letters*, Vol. 1, 305–306.

p. 166   "it was 'very unfortunate' that Weld wouldn't be heading to Rhode Island"—Letter from William Lloyd Garrison to William Chace, June 11, 1836, quoted in Merrill, *The Letters of William Lloyd Garrison*, Vol. 2, 123–124.

p. 166   "he tried to speak and get a hearing before the public"—Myers, "Beginnings of Anti-Slavery Agencies," 175–176.

p. 166   "not a day passed during which he was not stoned"—Myers, "Beginnings of Anti-Slavery Agencies," 176.

p. 167   "Others saw him as 'permanently shaken' by the Troy experience"—Perry, *Lift Up Thy Voice*, 139.

p. 167   "he was forced to stop public speaking lest he lose his voice altogether"—Merrill, *Against Wind and Tide*, 123.

p. 167   "He would step away from the lecture circuit and instead train field agents"—Perry, *Lift Up Thy Voice*, 140; Abzug, *Passionate Liberator*, 150.

p. 167   "he would get to work tracking down legislation about the slave trade"—Wyatt-Brown, *Lewis Tappan*, 170–171.

CHAPTER NINE: THE WHOLE ARMOR OF GOD

p. 168 "You are called fanatics. Well, what if you are?"—James Forten, Address to Philadelphia Female Anti-Slavery Society, April 14, 1836, quoted in Ripley, *Black Abolitionist Papers*, 161.

p. 169 "Vengeance is mine, and I will repay"——James Forten, Address to Philadelphia Female Anti-Slavery Society, April 14, 1836, quoted in Ripley, *Black Abolitionist Papers*, 161.

p. 169 "James implored them not to 'surrender your pure and unsullied principles'"—James Forten, Address to Philadelphia Female Anti-Slavery Society, April 14, 1836, quoted in Ripley, *Black Abolitionist Papers*, 156.

p. 169 "Andrew Jackson had demanded Congress prohibit 'under severe penalties'"—Remini, *Andrew Jackson*, 261.

p. 170 "the desperate struggle has commenced between *freedom* and *despotism*"—James Forten, Address to PFASS, quoted in Ripley, *Black Abolitionist Papers*, 156.

p. 170 "County officials passed laws against them, grand juries indicted them in absentia"—Savage, *The Controversy*, 37–38.

p. 170 "Public meetings in places like Portsmouth, New Haven, and Bangor"—Savage, *The Controversy*, 33, 50.

p. 170 "we were endeavoring to excite the slaves to insurrection"—Letter from William Lloyd Garrison to Isaac Knapp, June 22, 1836, quoted in Merrill, *The Letters of William Lloyd Garrison*, Vol. 2, 132.

p. 170 "the South 'wants the Northern States to PUNISH their incendiary citizens'"—*Richmond Whig*, quoted in *The Liberator*, October 8, 1836.

p. 171 "John Calhoun, newly appointed as the head of a select Senate committee"—Clement Eaton, "Censorship of the Southern Mails," *American Historical Review* 48, no. 2 (1943): 270.

p. 171 "he claimed radical zealots had mounted a warlike campaign against the South"—Clement Eaton, "Censorship of the Southern Mails," *American Historical Review* 48, no. 2 (1943): 271.

p. 171 "convulsions that would devastate the country"—John Calhoun, Report from the Senate Select Committee, "The Adoption of Efficient Measures to Prevent the Circulation of Incendiary Abolition Petitions Through the Mail," February 4, 1836, in *Speeches of John C. Calhoun, Delivered in the Congress of the United States to the Present Time* (New York: Harper and Brothers, 1843), 196.

p. 171 "by its passage the evil would be cured"—John Calhoun, in *Congressional Globe*, 24th Congress, First Session, 348.

p. 171 "his bill would make the federal government the enforcer of local censorship laws"—Savage, *The Controversy*, 79; *Congressional Globe*, 24th Congress, First Session, 165.

p. 171 "this censorship would set a precedent to crush the movement by law"—*The Liberator*, October 8, 1836.

p. 172 "Martin Van Buren finally broke the tie as vice president"—Thomas Hart Benton, *Thirty Years' View, or A History of the Working of the American Government for Thirty Years, from 1820 to 1850* (New York: Appleton and Co., 1858), 587.

p. 172 "The recent scenes in Congress are a specimen of the evil times we live in"—James Forten, Address to PFASS, quoted in Ripley, *Black Abolitionist Papers*, 158.

p. 172 "Sarah Forten had been working for months to help draft and circulate petitions"—Sumler-Lewis, "Forten-Purvis Women," 284.

p. 173 "Oh! I know I should love that girl—wonder if I shall ever see her"— Winch, *Gentleman of Color*, 268–269.

p. 173 "Let us know no rest till we have done our utmost to convince the mind"— Boston Female Anti-Slavery Society, *Address to the Women of Massachusetts*, July 13, 1836.

p. 173 "We shall never, therefore, be intimidated by the threats of the violent"— *Right and Wrong in Boston*, 79.

p. 173 "She took his hand and escorted him through the gauntlet"—Sarah Gertrude Pomeroy, *Little-Known Sisters of Well-Known Men* (Boston: Dana Estes, 1912), 124–125.

p. 173 "moral courage and devotion to the cause of the oppressed colored American"—*The Liberator*, November 28, 1835.

p. 174 "as the enemies of our cause will have room to accuse him of cowardice"— Winch, *Gentleman of Color*, 269.

p. 174 "It said the prisons in the nation's capital that held slaves"—Pennsylvania Female Anti-Slavery Society, *Address to the Women of Pennsylvania* (Philadelphia: Merrihew and Gunn, 1836), 3–4.

p. 174 "the centre of our American republic is now a slave market"— Pennsylvania Female Anti-Slavery Society, *Address to the Women of Pennsylvania*, 3.

p. 175 "Let *us* then go up, year after year, and year after year"—Pennsylvania Female Anti-Slavery Society, *Address to the Women of Pennsylvania*, 7.

p. 175 "the American Anti-Slavery Society, which also relied on women petitioners"—Barnes, *Anti-Slavery Impulse*, 134–140.

p. 175 "stores, banks, and barber shops . . . at hustings, at church fairs"—Barnes, *Anti-Slavery Impulse*, 136–137.

p. 175 "A later report from a women's antislavery convention called the job 'weary work'"—*Circular of the Anti-Slavery Convention of American Women*, in *Proceedings of the Third Anti-Slavery Convention of American Women* (Philadelphia: Merrihew and Thompson, 1839), 26–27.

p. 175 "we may also overthrow the injurious prejudices"—Anne Weston, *National Enquirer*, July 8, 1837.

p. 176 "In a few cases, girls as young as eleven went out into the field"—Carpenter and Moore, "When Canvassers Became Activists," 494.

p. 176   "Among these adolescents was the obscure sixteen-year-old daughter"—Ida
         Husted Harper, *The Life and Work of Susan B. Anthony*, Vol. 1 (Indianapolis:
         Bowen-Merrill, 1899), 20–23; Barnes, *Anti-Slavery Impulse*, 143.

p. 176   "No matter what their age, the petitioners had to memorize a script"—
         Carpenter and Moore, "When Canvassers Became Activists," 481,
         488–489.

p. 176   "They said such actions 'fill us with horror'"—*The Fathers and Rulers Petition
         Form*, in Barnes and Dumond, *Weld-Grimké Letters*, Vol. 1, 175; Susan
         Zaeske, "'The South Arose as One Man': Gender and Sectionalism in
         Antislavery Petition Debates, 1835–1845," *Rhetoric and Public Affairs* 12,
         no. 3 (2009): 348.

p. 177   "McKean thought the campaign might incite such a baleful reaction"—
         Brown, "Cradle of Feminism," 152.

p. 177   "They called the women 'old maids' whose chatter was only good"—James
         Garland, *Register of Debates*, 24th Congress, 1st Session (December 23,
         1835), 2064.

p. 177   "hoydenish women, effeminate men, and uppity blacks"—Sinha, *Slave's
         Cause*, 278.

p. 177   "woman is to be made the instrument of destroying our political
         paradise"—John Tyler, "Speech of Governor Tyler at the Gloucester
         Meeting," in *African Repository and Colonial Journal*, Vol. 11 (Washington,
         DC: James Dunn, 1835), 310.

p. 177   "Woman in the parlor, woman in her proper sphere"—Francis Granger,
         Register of Debates, 24th Congress, 1st Session (December 22, 1835), 2032.

p. 177   "might even appear 'obtrusive, indecorous, and unwise'"—Catharine
         Beecher, *Essay on Slavery and Abolitionism* (Philadelphia: Henry Perkins,
         1837), 103.

p. 178   "now suffered from a 'scrofulous affection' throughout his body"—Garrison
         and Garrison, *The Story of His Life*, Vol. 2, 83.

p. 178   "a leg wound that put him in constant pain"—Letter from William Lloyd
         Garrison to Henry Benson, August 21, 1836, quoted in Merrill, *The Letters
         of William Lloyd Garrison*, Vol. 2, 165.

p. 178   "catarrh in the head almost entirely destroying the sense of smell"—Letter
         from William Lloyd Garrison to Helen Garrison, May 21, 1836, quoted in
         Merrill, *The Letters of William Lloyd Garrison*, Vol. 2, 101.

p. 178   "Some called her 'the new light of the movement'"—Perry, *Lift Up Thy
         Voice*, 114–115.

p. 179   "The Grimkés were upper crust in the low country"—Goodman, *Of One
         Blood*, 179–183.

p. 179   "Once she departed Charleston, she never saw the city or her mother
         again"—Ellen Todras, *Angelina Grimké: Voice of Abolition* (North Haven,
         CT: Linnet Books, 1999), 34.

p. 179   "Sarah and Angelina disputed these practices"—Gerda Lerner, *The Grimké Sisters from South Carolina: Pioneers for Women's Rights and Abolition* (orig. pub. New York: Houghton Mifflin, 1967; repr., Chapel Hill: University of North Carolina Press, 2004), 91.

p. 179   "they met Black women leaders of the group who gave them a much wider perspective"—Todras, *Voice of Abolition*, 58.

p. 179   "Galvanizing them further was the spring 1835 visit of George Thompson"—Lerner, *Grimké Sisters*, 83.

p. 180   "He and other church elders demanded she retract her statement"— Angelina Grimké, *Walking by Faith: The Diary of Angelina Grimké, 1828– 1835*, ed. Charles Wilbanks (Columbia: University of South Carolina Press, 2003), 212.

p. 180   "the extreme pain of extravagant praise to be held up as a saint"—Grimké, *Walking by Faith*, 212.

p. 180   "The negative reaction among church elders put her at a distance from other Quakers"—Perry, *Lift Up Thy Voice*, 128.

p. 180   "it was an hour that went pleasantly, profitably, rapidly"—Letter from William Lloyd Garrison to Helen Garrison, May 21, 1836, quoted in Merrill, *The Letters of William Lloyd Garrison*, Vol. 2, 102.

p. 181   "Southern politicians and the press became ever more offended by them"— Scott R. Meinke, "Slavery, Partisanship, and Procedure in the U.S. House: The Gag Rule, 1836–1845," *Legislative Studies Quarterly* 32, no. 1 (2007): 35.

p. 181   "subvert the institutions of the South"—James Hammond, *Register of Debates*, 24th Congress, 1st Session (February 1, 1836), 2450.

p. 181   "While in previous years, Americans had submitted petitions"—Barnes, *Anti-Slavery Impulse*, 112–114.

p. 181   "bosom of society heave with new and violent emotions"—William Preston, *The Congressional Globe*, 24th Congress, First Session (March 1, 1836), 221.

p. 182   "direct violation of the constitution of the United States"—John Quincy Adams, *Journal of the House of Representatives of the United States*, 24th Congress, First Session (May 27, 1836) (Washington, DC: Blair and Rives, 1836), Appendix, 1410.

p. 182   "Charles Pinckney, from South Carolina, worked out a compromise"—John M. McFaul, "Expediency vs. Morality: Jacksonian Politics and Slavery," *Journal of American History* 62, no. 1 (1975): 32.

p. 182   "threaten to bring the citizens of the different states into collision"— "Slavery in the District of Columbia," Report to the House of Representatives, 24th Congress, First Session (May 18, 1836) Reports of Committees, Vol. 3, report 691, 3.

p. 182   "the gag law became a source of controversy"—Meinke, "Slavery, Partisanship, and Procedure," 36.

p. 182   "more women joined the antislavery societies to canvass for the cause"—Carpenter and Moore, "When Canvassers Became Activists," 494.

p. 183   "farewell, a long farewell to our freedom"—William Leggett, "The Abolitionists," *Evening Post*, August 8, 1835.

p. 183   "Committee hearings broke down into shouting matches"—Jane Pease and William Pease, *Bound with Them in Chains: A Biographical History of the Antislavery Movement* (Westport, CN: Greenwood Press, 1972), 290–291.

p. 183   "The Constitution secures to us the freedom of speech"—Samuel May, *Proceedings of the New England Anti-Slavery Convention, May 24–26, 1836* (Boston: Isaac Knapp, 1836), 52.

p. 183   "attempts to silence them had faltered in one Northern state after another"—Garrison and Garrison, *The Story of His Life*, Vol. 2, 75–77.

p. 183   "Garrison recited a roll call of failed attempts to muzzle his friends and allies"—Letter from William Lloyd Garrison to Isaac Knapp, June 22, 1836, quoted in Merrill, *The Letters of William Lloyd Garrison*, Vol. 2, 133.

p. 183   "John Calhoun's censorship bill failed in the Senate by six votes"—*The Congressional Globe*, 24th Congress, First Session (June 8, 1836), 539.

p. 184   "no honorable, or high-minded, or reputable man"—Letter from William Seward to Thurlow Weed, quoted in Frederick Seward, *William H. Seward: An Autobiography* (New York: Derby and Miller, 1891), 293.

p. 184   "both houses of Congress passed a bill reorganizing the post office"—*Niles' Weekly Register*, August 6, 1836, 381.

p. 184   "Andrew Jackson may have signed the bill, but he refused to enforce it"—Remini, *Andrew Jackson*, 261–262.

p. 184   "Oh that it could be rained down into every parlor in our land"—Katherine DuPre Lumpkin, *The Emancipation of Angelina Grimké* (Chapel Hill: University of North Carolina Press, 1974), 90.

p. 184   "I know you do not make the laws"—Angelina Grimké, "Appeal to the Christian Women of the South," *Anti-Slavery Examiner* 1, no. 2 (1836): 16.

p. 185   "Are you willing to enslave *your* children?"—Grimké, "Appeal to the Christian Women," 13.

p. 185   "the white public stood 'dreadfully afraid of Amalgamation'"—Grimké, "Appeal to the Christian Women," 30.

p. 185   "If a law commands me to *sin, I will break it*"—Grimké, "Appeal to the Christian Women," 20.

p. 185   "when some copies did arrive in Charleston, the townsfolk burned them"—Perry, *Lift Up Thy Voice*, 133.

p. 186   "Have not *women* stood up in all the dignity and strength of moral courage"—Grimké, "Appeal to the Christian Women," 21.

p. 186   "an admirable work . . . full of holy zeal—powerful reasoning"—Letter
          from Sarah Forten to Elizabeth Whittier, September 10, 1836, quoted in
          Winch, *Gentleman of Color*, 269.

CHAPTER TEN: STAGGER THEM GREATLY

p. 188   "he found himself in a place called Hollidaysburg"—Letter from Theodore
          Weld to Lewis Tappan, October 10, 1836, quoted in Barnes and Dumond,
          Weld-Grimké Letters, 342.

p. 189   "He had to find a collection of young men in training for the ministry"—
          Barnes, *Anti-Slavery Impulse*, 104–105; Merrill, *Against Wind and Tide*, 123.

p. 189   "He traveled through the backcountry with Henry Stanton and John
          Whittier"—Abzug, *Passionate Liberator*, 150.

p. 189   "Elizabeth Whitter watched him in action in Boston"—Abzug, *Passionate
          Liberator*,151.

p. 189   "to *stagger them greatly* in their new notions"—Letter from James Thome to
          Theodore Weld, September 9, 1836, quoted in Barnes and Dumond, *Weld-
          Grimké Letters*, Vol. 1, 340.

p. 190   "The Lord sent confusion into their councils and discomfiture into their
          ranks"—Letter from Theodore Weld to Lewis Tappan, October 10, 1836,
          quoted in Barnes and Dumond, *Weld-Grimké Letters*, Vol. 1, 344.

p. 190   "Most of them are entirely out of money and cannot get to their fields of
          labor"—Letter from Theodore Weld to Lewis Tappan, October 24, 1836,
          quoted in Barnes and Dumond, *Weld-Grimké Letters*, Vol. 1, 345.

p. 190   "The Wall Street fever is terrible, and has siezed [*sic*] some of our
          committee"—Letter from Elizur Wright to Theodore Weld, November 4,
          1836, quoted in Barnes and Dumond, *Weld-Grimké Letters*, Vol. 1, 346.

p. 190   "*drive* on until you hear from us"—Letter from Elizur Wright to Theodore
          Weld, November 4, 1836, quoted in Barnes and Dumond, *Weld-Grimké
          Letters*, Vol. 1, 346.

p. 191   "It seems Finney had begun separating Black and white students"—Abzug,
          Passionate Liberator, 155–156.

p. 191   "doing the same in church services at Chatham Street Chapel"—Wyatt-
          Brown, *Lewis Tappan*, 177–178; Charles Cole Jr., "The Free Church
          Movement in New York City," *New York History* 34, no. 3 (1953): 295.

p. 191   "James Birney, who published a pro-colonization newspaper called *African
          Repository*"—Barnes, *Anti-Slavery Impulse*, 69.

p. 191   "It became the official paper of the Ohio Anti-Slavery Society"—Savage,
          The Controversy, 94; Levi Coffin, *Reminiscences of Levi Coffin, The Reputed
          President of the Underground Railroad* (Cincinnati: Robert Clarke, 1880), 524.

p. 191   "Over the summer, a mob broke into a building housing his news office"—
          Coffin, *Reminiscences*, 525; Nye, *Fettered Freedom*, 130–132; Savage, *The
          Controversy*, 97.

p. 191   "Afterward the rioters went hunting for Birney"—*Niles' Weekly Register*, August 13, 1836, 398.

p. 192   "the recent outrages were caused by the establishment of the abolition press"—*Niles' Weekly Register*, August 13, 1836, 398.

p. 192   "bloodthirsty men—mayor and chief men at their head"—Letter from William Allen et al. to Theodore Weld, August 9, 1836, quoted in Barnes and Dumond, *Weld-Grimké Letters*, Vol. 1, 324.

p. 192   "Weld wrote to them, imploring them to keep their distance"—Sinha, *Slave's Cause*, 236.

p. 192   "the guest speakers included Charles Stuart"—Barnes, *Anti-Slavery Impulse*, 105; Letter from William Lloyd Garrison to Henry Benson, December 3, 1836, quoted in Merrill, *The Letters of William Lloyd Garrison*, Vol. 2, 187.

p. 192   "He told them about the evils of slavery"—Letter from William Lloyd Garrison to Henry Benson, December 3, 1836, quoted in Merrill, *The Letters of William Lloyd Garrison*, Vol. 2, 187.

p. 193   "Weld oversaw most of the thrice-daily sessions"—Abzug, *Passionate Liberator*, 152.

p. 193   "Weld was the central luminary, around which they all revolved"—Letter from William Lloyd Garrison to Henry Benson, December 3, 1836, quoted in Merrill, *The Letters of William Lloyd Garrison*, Vol. 2, 187.

p. 193   "He was the master spirit, the principal speaker in that assembly"—Letter from Sarah Grimké to Mary Grimké, July 15, 1839, quoted in Barnes, *Anti-Slavery Impulse*, 251n.

p. 193   "It would be the last time he ever spoke at length in a public forum"— Abzug, *Passionate Liberator*, 152.

p. 193   "How can you stand *fourteen such* lectures as you give in succession?"— Letter from Elizur Wright to Theodore Weld, March 16, 1835, quoted in Barnes and Dumond, *Weld-Grimké Letters*, Vol. 1, 210.

p. 193   "To support them, Lewis would have to collect funds from state affiliates"— Wyatt-Brown, *Lewis Tappan*, 171.

p. 194   "Earlier in the year, he and Arthur had constructed a new building"— Tappan, *Life of Arthur Tappan*, 277.

p. 194   "Conditions had become so volatile in the financial world"—Remini, *Andrew Jackson*, 427.

p. 194   "the Tappans found it hard to borrow money"—Tappan, *Life of Arthur Tappan*, 279–280.

p. 194   "They tried to secure a second loan from Nicholas Biddle"—Wyatt-Brown, *Lewis Tappan*, 174.

p. 194   "The most recent report of the Anti-Slavery Society spelled it out"—*Third Annual Report of the American Anti-Slavery Society* (New York: William Dorr, 1836), 48–67.

p. 195 "Never did the church give evidence of more fearful corruption"—*Third Annual Report of the American Anti-Slavery Society* (New York: William Dorr, 1836), 67.

p. 195 "Among them, prejudice had made a resurgence"—Swift, *Black Prophets*, 75; Wyatt-Brown, *Lewis Tappan*, 178–179.

p. 195 "Lewis moved to have the Reverend Theodore Wright make a keynote address"—Letter from Lewis Tappan to Theodore Weld, March 15, 1836, quoted in Barnes and Dumond, *Weld-Grimké Letters*, Vol. 1, 276–277.

p. 195 "if ever there is a split in our ranks it will arise from collision on this point"—Diary of Lewis Tappan, April 6, 1836, in Lewis Tappan Papers, Library of Congress, mm75042317.

p. 196 "he proclaimed the Sabbath as 'the great sun of the moral world'"—Lyman Beecher, quoted in *The Liberator*, July 23, 1836.

p. 196 "He reminded readers of the seventeenth-century Puritans"—Lyman Beecher, quoted in *The Liberator*, July 23, 1836.

p. 196 "They called Garrison a menace to the nation"—Garrison and Garrison, *The Story of His Life*, Vol. 2, 112–113.

p. 196 "Yet Garrison would not relent in his criticism"—*The Liberator*, August 6, 1836.

p. 196 "the publisher had been the source of 'animosity and contention among brethren'"—*The Liberator*, September 2, 1836.

p. 196 "He didn't stop there: He paid Garrison's way to New York"—Wyatt-Brown, *Lewis Tappan*, 186.

p. 197 "we harmoniously agreed to differ'"—Letter from William Lloyd Garrison to Henry Benson, December 3, 1836, quoted in Merrill, *The Letters of William Lloyd Garrison*, Vol. 2, 188.

p. 197 "Garrison realized how easily he could become 'a great stumbling block'"—Letter from William Lloyd Garrison to Henry Benson, December 3, 1836, quoted in Merrill, *The Letters of William Lloyd Garrison*, Vol. 2, 188; Garrison and Garrison, *The Story of His Life*, Vol. 2, 114–117.

p. 197 "But here was someone who defied the truth of Exodus"—William Birney, *James G. Birney and His Times* (New York: D. Appleton, 1890), 296; Wyatt-Brown, *Lewis Tappan*, 185.

p. 197 "Garrison had blasted the Constitution"—Letter from William Lloyd Garrison to Thomas Shipley, December 17, 1835, quoted in Merrill, *The Letters of William Lloyd Garrison*, Vol. 1, 584.

p. 197 "I am conscious that a mighty sectarian conspiracy is forming to crush me"—Letter from William Lloyd Garrison to Samuel May, September 23, 1836, quoted in Merrill, *The Letters of William Lloyd Garrison*, Vol. 2, 178.

p. 197 "He dabbled in 'Thompsonian medicine'"—Mayer, *All on Fire*, 272.

p. 197 "He even explored Sylvester Graham's health regimen"—Mayer, *All on Fire*, 272; Abzug, *Passionate Liberator*, 158.

p. 198 "I have not been very well. There is something wrong about my system"—
Letter from William Lloyd Garrison to Henry Benson, November 4, 1836,
quoted in Merrill, *The Letters of William Lloyd Garrison*, Vol. 2, 182.

p. 198 "But the worst part of all was that Lewis actually liked him"—Wyatt-
Brown, *Lewis Tappan*, 185–186.

p. 198 "before an audience 'completely electrified'"—*The Liberator*, December 24, 1836.

p. 198 "The American press universally cried, 'away with them'"—*The Liberator*,
December 24, 1836.

p. 199 "His Committee of Vigilance was now a year old"—*First Annual Report of
the New York Committee of Vigilance*, 84.

p. 199 "The group took on one new case a day"—Hodges, *Radical Black
Abolitionist*, 90.

p. 199 "with one thousand members and associates acting as the grassroots
power"—Proceedings of the Meeting of the New York Vigilance
Committee, November 21, 1836, in Ripley, *Black Abolitionist Papers*, 172.

p. 199 "His personal life and work life were now so intertwined"—Hodges,
Radical Black Abolitionist, 109.

p. 200 "on January 16, 1837, when the Committee of Vigilance held its anniversary
meeting"—Tappan, *Life of Arthur Tappan*, 181–182.

p. 200 "One speaker, John Reymond, a Baptist pastor, told how he had been
arrested"—*First Annual Report of the New York Committee of Vigilance*, 82.

p. 200 "most appalling spectacle of the fiendish spirit of American slavery"—*First
Annual Report of the New York Committee of Vigilance*, 82.

p. 200 "He had few close friends with whom he could share his private feelings"—
Hodges, *Radical Black Abolitionist*, 110.

p. 201 "Ruggles not only helped pay Cornish's salary as the editor of the new
publication"—Swift, *Black Prophets*, 78; Hodges, *Radical Black Abolitionist*,
103; Quarles, *Black Abolitionists*, 95, 109.

p. 201 "The Tappans and Gerrit Smith also helped fund the creation of the
paper"—Ripley, *Black Abolitionist Papers*, 217n2; Pease and Pease, *Bound
with Them in Chains*, 148.

p. 201 "with pledges of $5 to $10 annually to support the venture"—Quarles, *Black
Abolitionists*, 87.

p. 201 "Establish a press organ written by and for African Americans"—*Colored
American*, March 4, 1837.

p. 201 "Champion petition drives to the New York legislature"—Quarles, *Black
Abolitionists*, 171; *Colored American*, April 29, July 15, December 16, 1837.

p. 201 "Preach moral reform and exhort readers not to take vacations or waste
money"—*Colored American*, March 4, 1837.

p. 202 "Colored men must . . . establish and maintain the PRESS"—*Colored
American*, March 4, 1837.

p. 202 "He called out officials like Richard Riker and Tobias Boudinot"—Hodges,
Radical Black Abolitionist, 104, 109, 127.

p. 202   "He summarized his findings in the committee's first annual report"—*First Annual Report of the New York Committee of Vigilance*, 17–80.

p. 202   "One recent case showed how the system worked"—*First Annual Report of the New York Committee of Vigilance*, 54.

p. 202   "Riker pronounced Jones guilty, 'and in the space of three hours'"—*First Annual Report of the New York Committee of Vigilance*, 54.

p. 203   "My depressed countrymen, we are all liable"—David Ruggles in *New York Sun*, quoted in *The Liberator*, August 6, 1836.

p. 203   "That while we the people of color, are deprived of that *bulwark of personal freedom*"—Ripley, *Black Abolitionist Papers*, 171; *The Emancipator*, October 6, 1836.

p. 203   "evidence showed that he had been recently employed in New York and Boston"—*The Liberator*, April 21, 1837.

p. 204   "every colored man is presumed to be a slave, unless he can prove his freedom!"—*The Liberator*, April 21, 1837.

p. 204   "a team of sheriff's deputies were met with a surprise"—*Niles' Weekly Register*, April 22, 1837, 117.

p. 204   "Then the crowd pushed back the officers once more"—*New Era*, quoted in *The Liberator*, April 21, 1837.

p. 204   "The fashion of mobbing which has been set by the whites"—*Evening Post*, quoted in *The Liberator*, April 21, 1837.

p. 204   "Others used vicious stereotypes to describe 'a strapping negro wench'"—*Evening Post*, quoted in *The Liberator*, April 21, 1837.

p. 204   "This editorial called the mayhem a disgrace and denounced 'illiterate people'"—*Colored American*, April 15–29, 1837.

p. 205   "If blacks have any friends, they will counsel them to demean themselves peacefully"—*Evening Post*, quoted in *The Liberator*, April 21, 1837.

p. 205   "the Panic of 1837, which damaged the finances of countless Americans"—Hodges, *Radical Black Abolitionist*, 104.

p. 205   "Southern merchants were reduced to only paying five cents or less on every dollar"—*New York Transcript*, April 6, 1837.

p. 205   "nearly every one has become infected in a degree with the panic"—*Bicknell's Reporter*, April 10, 1837.

p. 206   "there are many honest and worthy individuals who are irretrievably ruined"—*Niles' Weekly Register*, April 15, 1837, 100.

p. 206   "Their firm, Arthur Tappan and Company, had finally succumbed to its creditors"—Tappan, *Life of Arthur Tappan*, 279–282; Wyatt-Brown, *Lewis Tappan*, 174.

CHAPTER ELEVEN: HEART BURNINGS

p. 207   "He worked to negotiate terms with his creditors"—Tappan, *Life of Arthur Tappan*, 176, 282, 294–296.

p. 208   "he had no idea just how leveraged the company was"—Wyatt-Brown, *Lewis Tappan*, 175.

p. 208   "pray God to *break the rod of the oppressor and let the oppressed go free!*"— Lewis Tappan quoted in *Slave's Friend* 2, no. 5 (November 17, 1836).

p. 208   "James Birney prevailed upon him to abandon the idea"—Diary of Lewis Tappan, May 22–23, 1837, in Lewis Tappan Papers, Library of Congress, mm75042317.

p. 209   "John the Baptist attire"—Abzug, *Passionate Liberator*, 124.

p. 209   "I wondered whether he was really as great as I had heard"—Lerner, *Grimké Sisters*, 103.

p. 209   "Yes! LET IT COME"—Angelina Grimké, *The Liberator*, September 19, 1835.

p. 209   "She accused them of launching a 'REIGN OF TERROR'"—Sarah Grimké, *An Epistle to the Clergy of the Southern States*, December 1836, reprinted in Sarah and Angelina Grimké, *On Slavery and Abolitionism* (New York: Penguin, 2014), 26.

p. 209   "The soul that sinneth it shall die"—Sarah Grimké, *An Epistle to the Clergy of the Southern States*, December 1836, reprinted in Sarah and Angelina Grimké, *On Slavery and Abolitionism* (New York: Penguin, 2014), 28.

p. 210   "Perhaps the Friend may be satisfied now"—Letter from Sarah Grimké to Theodore Weld, March 10, 1837, quoted in Barnes and Dumond, *Weld-Grimké Letters*, Vol. 1, 373.

p. 210   "So the Grimkés rearranged their plans and decided to appear in a Baptist church"—Lerner, *Grimké Sisters*, 116.

p. 210   "I felt no more fear. We went to the meeting at three o'clock"—Catherine Birney, *The Grimké Sisters: Sarah and Angelina Grimké, The First American Women Advocates of Abolition and Women's Rights* (Boston: Lee & Shepard, 1885), 163–164.

p. 210   "They gave these women a lecture they would not forget"—Perry, *Lift Up Thy Voice*, 147–148, 150–151.

p. 211   "It was said to be the first time American women had addressed"—Birney, *Sarah and Angelina Grimké*, 163–164.

p. 211   "They spoke to one overflowing crowd after another"—Perry, *Lift Up Thy Voice*, 147.

p. 212   "The Southern hotspurs are almost ready to dance with rage at the attack"—*The Emancipator*, January 19, 1837.

p. 212   "with each petitioner amassing nearly three hundred signatures"— Carpenter and Moore, "When Canvassers Became Activists," 494.

p. 212   "Angelina claimed the canvassing was even more important"—Angelina Grimké, *Appeal to the Women of the Nominally Free States* (Boston: Isaac Knapp, 1838), 59–60.

p. 212   "Weld sleeping in a garret and eating vegetarian food like an ascetic monk"—Letter from Theodore Weld to Angelina Grimké, April 15, 1838, quoted in Barnes and Dumond, *Weld-Grimké Letters*, Vol. 2, 634–635.

p. 212   "Samuel Cornish did double duty, advocating for signatures"—Swift, *Black Prophets*, 83.

p. 212   "petitions enough to break all the tables in the Capitol"—Letter from John Whittier to Mary Caldwell, August 8, 1837, quoted in *Whittier Correspondence from the Oak Knoll Collections, 1830–1892*, Vol. 2, ed. John Albree (Salem, MA: Essex Book & Print Club, 1910), 53.

p. 212   "to erect a pyramid that shall vie with the proudest on the plains of Egypt"—*New York American*, quoted in *The Liberator*, February 16, 1838.

p. 212   "petitions on slavery would 'be laid on the table'"—"Abolition Report," May 26, 1836, 24th Congress, 1st Session, quoted in *Register of Debates in Congress*, Vol. 12 (Washington, DC: Gales and Seaton, 1836), 4052.

p. 212   "John Calhoun followed up on the gag law in the House by driving the passage"—Wyly-Jones, "1835 Anti-Abolition Meetings," 308.

p. 213   "Yet such actions only encouraged more petitioners"—Carpenter and Moore, "When Canvassers Became Activists," 483.

p. 213   "he held up a petition and openly violated the gag rule"—*Congressional Globe*, January 23, 1837, 24th Congress, Second Session, 19; Barnes, *Anti-Slavery Impulse*, 123.

p. 213   "Adams 'consults with no one, takes the advice of no one'"—Joshua Giddings, quoted in Walter Buell, *Joshua R. Giddings: A Sketch* (Cleveland: William W. Williams, 1882), 79.

p. 213   "for the removal of a great social, moral and political evil"—Garrison and Garrison, *The Story of His Life*, Vol. 2, 128.

p. 213   "It is the most extraordinary change in political action"—Letter from William Lloyd Garrison to George Benson, April 3, 1837, quoted in Merrill, *The Letters of William Lloyd Garrison*, Vol. 2, 252.

p. 214   "They have given a new spring to my existence"—Letter from Angelina and Sarah Grimké to Jane Smith, January 1837, quoted in Birney, *Sarah and Angelina Grimké*, 165.

p. 214   "they launched new insults, calling them 'fanatical women'"—Letter from Sarah Grimké to Sarah Douglass, February 22, 1837, in Weld-Grimké Family Papers, William L. Clements Library, University of Michigan; Lerner, *Grimké Sisters*, 121.

p. 214   "Others accused them of being loose women"—Sinha, *Slave's Cause*, 279–280.

p. 214   "He gave up so much that I could not see what he had to stand on when we left him"—Birney, *Sarah and Angelina Grimké*, 164.

p. 214   "Weld committed to the success of the Grimkés in the public arena"—Todras, *Voice of Abolition*, 85, 90–91.

p. 215   "The sisters continued their tour, speaking to audiences in New Jersey"—Lerner, *Grimké Sisters*, 120.

p. 215   "I love the work. I count myself greatly favored in being called to it"—
          Letter from Angelina Grimké to Jane Smith, January 20, 1837, quoted in
          Todras, *Voice of Abolition*, 69.

p. 215   "She saw them at their lectures and alluded to the beliefs they shared"—
          Birney, *Sarah and Angelina Grimké*, 163.

p. 215   "So the Grimkés attended a meeting of the Society of Friends"—Lerner,
          Grimké Sisters, 121.

p. 216   "their racism 'is a canker worm among them'"—Lumpkin, *The
          Emancipation*, 104.

p. 216   "She taught Sunday school for Black youth in New York"—Birney, *Sarah
          and Angelina Grimké*, 167–168; Goodman, *Of One Blood*, 186.

p. 216   "she and her sister wrote to a friend and asked her to describe her
          experience"—Ripley, *Black Abolitionist Papers*, 221.

p. 217   "no claim to be superior based on 'education—birth—or worldly
          circumstances'"—Letter from Sarah Forten to Angelina Grimké, April 15,
          1837, quoted in Ripley, *Black Abolitionist Papers*, 221–222.

p. 217   "I am particularly sensitive on this point"—Letter from Sarah Forten to
          Angelina Grimké, April 15, 1837, quoted in Ripley, *Black Abolitionist
          Papers*, 221.

p. 217   "I despise the aim of that Institution most heartily" to "I am striving to
          live above such heart burnings"—Letter from Sarah Forten to Angelina
          Grimké, April 15, 1837, quoted in Ripley, *Black Abolitionist Papers*,
          221–223.

p. 217   "But her group expanded along with its list of projects"—Gernes, "Poetic
          Justice," 244.

p. 217   "In December she helped organize the society's first antislavery fair"—
          Letter from Sarah Forten to Elizabeth Whittier, December 25, 1836,
          quoted in Ripley, *Black Abolitionist Papers*, 201; Third Annual Report of the
          Pennsylvania Female Anti-Slavery Society, reprinted in *National Enquirer*,
          January 1, 1837.

p. 218   "in one day realized the handsome sum of five hundred and forty-two
          dollars!"—Letter from William Lloyd Garrison to Sarah Benson,
          December 24, 1836, quoted in Merrill, *The Letters of William Lloyd
          Garrison*, Vol. 2, 194.

p. 218   "the construction of a grand building that could host antislavery lectures"—
          Sumler-Lewis, "Forten-Purvis Women," 284.

p. 218   "Sarah joined a committee to sell shares to build this 'temple of liberty'"—
          Gernes, "Poetic Justice," 244.

p. 218   "hosted more than a hundred delegates from ten states"—Quarles, *Black
          Abolitionists*, 27; Brown, "Cradle of Feminism," 155–156.

p. 218   "she criticized white women for oppressing and subjugating Black
          women"—Angelina Grimké, *An Appeal to the Women of the Nominally Free
          States* (Boston: Isaac Knapp, 1837), 19–24.

p. 218   "she spoke out about racial conditions in the United States"—Sarah Grimké, *An Address to the Free Colored Americans* (New York: William Dorr, 1837), 11–12.

p. 219   "We entreat you in the name of the Lord Jesus, to forbear any attempts"— Grimké, *An Address to the Free Colored Americans*, 29.

p. 219   "to begin a lecture tour that took them to seventeen stops in ten towns"— Mayer, *All on Fire*, 233.

p. 220   "Garrison promoting their lectures in *The Liberator* as they went"—*The Liberator*, June 16, 1837.

p. 220   "Why! folks talk about women's preaching"—Letter from Theodore Weld to Angelina and Sarah Grimké, July 22, 1837, quoted in Barnes and Dumond, *Weld-Grimké Letters*, Vol. 1, 412.

p. 220   "I cannot help smiling in the midst of 'rhetorical flourishes'"—Letter from Angelina Grimké to Theodore Weld, August 12, 1837, quoted in Barnes and Dumond, *Weld-Grimké Letters*, Vol. 1, 414.

p. 220   "The power of woman is in her dependence"—Nehemiah Adams, Pastoral Letter, quoted in *Right and Wrong in Boston: Annual Report of the Boston Female Anti-Slavery Society* (Boston: Isaac Knapp, 1837), 47–48.

p. 221   "women had no right to tell men what to do"—Pastoral Letter from the General Association of Massachusetts to the Churches Under Their Care, quoted in *The Liberator*, August 11, 1837; *The Appeal of Clerical Abolitionists on Antislavery Measures*, quoted in *The Liberator—Extra*, August 19, 1837.

p. 221   "Why are all the old hens abolitionists?"—*Boston Morning Post*, quoted in *New Hampshire Patriot*, August 15, 1837.

p. 221   "We are willing to bear the brunt of the storm"—Letter from Angelina Grimké to Jane Smith, July 25, 1837, quoted in K. K. Sklar, *Women's Rights Emerges Within the Antislavery Movement, 1830–1870* (New York: St. Martin's Press, 2000), 117.

p. 221   "Their pastoral letters had closed off Congregational churches"—*The Appeal of Clerical Abolitionists on Antislavery Measures*, quoted in *The Liberator— Extra*, August 19, 1837.

p. 221   "His followers worshipped a false idol"—Mayer, *All on Fire*, 235.

p. 222   "I can only marvel at the short-sightedness of you all"—Letter from William Lloyd Garrison to Lewis Tappan, September 13, 1837, in Merrill, *The Letters of William Lloyd Garrison*, Vol. 2, 299.

p. 222   "He had warned him against using intemperate language"—Letter from Lewis Tappan to William Lloyd Garrison, September 21, 1837, quoted in Garrison and Garrison, *The Story of His Life*, Vol. 2, 165.

p. 222   "you denounce probably a majority of the members"—Letter from Lewis Tappan to William Lloyd Garrison, September 21, 1837, quoted in Garrison and Garrison, *The Story of His Life*, Vol. 2, 165.

p. 222   "a short, well-tempered, dignified, Christlike reply"—Letter from Lewis Tappan to William Lloyd Garrison, quoted in letter from Garrison to

George Benson, September 23, 1837, quoted in Merrill, *The Letters of William Lloyd Garrison*, Vol. 2, 306.

p. 222 "is shameful, is criminal, and is anything but magnanimous"—Letter from Garrison to George Benson, September 16, 1837, in Merrill, *The Letters of William Lloyd Garrison*, Vol. 2, 303.

p. 222 "nothing better than hirelings, in the bad sense of that term"—*The Liberator*, August 18, 1837.

p. 223 "I will not consult any other statute-book than THE BIBLE"—*The Liberator*, July 4, 1835.

p. 223 "Arthur and Lewis Tappan could not endorse his ideas"—Perry, *Lift Up Thy Voice*, 170; Merton Lynn Dillon, *The Abolitionists: The Growth of a Dissenting Minority* (DeKalb: Northern Illinois University Press, 1974), 114–116.

p. 223 "There is nothing to be gained by brother contending with brother"—*Colored American*, October 7, 1837.

p. 223 "fearing that the same kind of warfare that had broken out"—*Colored American*, October 7, 1837; Donald M. Jacobs, "William Lloyd Garrison's Liberator and Boston's Blacks, 1830–1865," *New England Quarterly* 44, no. 2 (1971): 264.

p. 223 "the trite saying, 'save me from my friends'"—*Colored American*, October 7 and 14, 1837.

p. 223 "They charged his 'Keep Cool' article was 'scorchingly hot'"—*The Liberator*, October 20, 1837.

p. 224 "Catharine Beecher had been an influence on Angelina for six years"—Todras, *Voice of Abolition*, 41.

p. 224 "a doctrine that promoted ideas that were 'not only illogical, but false'"—Catharine Beecher, *An Essay on Slavery and Abolitionism, Addressed to Miss A. D. Grimké* (Philadelphia: Henry Perkins, 1837), 10.

p. 224 "For the more intelligent a woman becomes . . . the more her taste will conform"—Catharine Beecher, *An Essay on Slavery and Abolitionism, Addressed to Miss A. D. Grimké* (Philadelphia: Henry Perkins, 1837), 107–108.

p. 225 "Catharine's arguments are the most insidious things I ever read"—Letter from Angelina Grimké to Jane Smith, quoted in Birney, *Sarah and Angelina Grimké*, 198.

p. 225 "Woman has been taught to lean upon an arm of flesh"—"Human Rights Not Founded on Sex," Letter from Angelina Grimké to Catherine Beecher, October 2, 1837, reprinted in *Letters to Catherine E. Beecher, in Reply to an Essay on Slavery and Abolitionism* (Boston: Isaac Knapp, 1838), 115–116.

p. 226 "they bolstered each other's confidence once more, like 'iron sharpeneth iron'"—Letter from Angelina and Sarah Grimké to Henry Wright, August 27, 1837, quoted in Barnes and Dumond, *Weld-Grimké Letters*, Vol. 1, 438.

p. 226 "the time to assert a right is the time when that right is denied"—Letter from Angelina Grimké to John Whittier and Theodore Weld, August 20, 1837, quoted in Barnes and Dumond, *Weld-Grimké Letters*, Vol. 1, 428.

p. 226   "He accused her of being distracted from the battle against slavery"—Letter from John Whittier to Angelina Grimké, August 14, 1837, quoted in Barnes and Dumond, *Weld-Grimké Letters*, Vol. 1, 424.

p. 226   "Weld followed Whittier's argument by charging she was dividing her energies"—Letter from Theodore Weld to Angelina Grimké, August 15, 1837, quoted in Barnes and Dumond, *Weld-Grimké Letters*, Vol. 1, 425–427.

p. 226   "I like to pay my debts, and as I received $10 worth of scolding"—Letter from Angelina Grimké to Theodore Weld, September 20, 1837, quoted in Barnes and Dumond, *Weld-Grimké Letters*, Vol. 1, 450.

p. 226   "Weld's friends on the executive committee . . . had abandoned her"— Letter from Theodore Weld to Angelina Grimké, October 10, 1837, quoted in Barnes and Dumond, *Weld-Grimké Letters*, Vol. 1, 457–458.

p. 227   "Why dear child? What is the matter with you?"—Letter from Theodore Weld to Angelina Grimké, October 10, 1837, quoted in Barnes and Dumond, *Weld-Grimké Letters*, Vol. 1, 457.

p. 227   "Not a particle of evidence do you bring forward"—Letter from Theodore Weld to Angelina Grimké, October 10, 1837, quoted in Barnes and Dumond, *Weld-Grimké Letters*, Vol. 1, 458–459.

p. 227   "He followed up with an even more damning letter"—Letter from Theodore Weld to Angelina Grimké, October 16, 1837, quoted in Barnes and Dumond, *Weld-Grimké Letters*, Vol. 1, 465.

p. 227   "She took ill in November along with her sister"—Perry, *Lift Up Thy Voice*, 159.

p. 227   "a mob had attacked an antislavery publisher"—John Demos, "The Antislavery Movement and the Problem of Violent 'Means,'" *New England Quarterly* 37, no. 4 (1964): 507.

CHAPTER TWELVE: THE WORLD UPSIDE DOWN

p. 228   "the state attorney general, James Austin, was ready to take advantage of it"—May, *Some Recollections*, 227–228.

p. 228   "giving liberty to these wild beasts of the forest"—May, *Some Recollections*, 227.

p. 229   "Sir, for the sentiments he has uttered on soil consecrated"—May, *Some Recollections*, 228.

p. 229   "how Lovejoy had moved from gradual to immediate abolition"—Feldberg, *Turbulent Era*, 47–49; Ken Ellingwood, *First to Fall: Elijah Lovejoy's Fight for a Free Press in the Age of Slavery* (New York: Pegasus, 2021), 2.

p. 229   "every drop would cause a new abolition society to spring up"—Savage, *The Controversy*, 107.

p. 229   "he organized a grand memorial service"—Wyatt-Brown, *Lewis Tappan*, 158–159; New-York Historical Society Museum & Library, "Guide to the Broadway Tabernacle Church and Society Papers," dlib.nyu.edu/ findingaids/html/nyhs/broadwaytabernacle.

p. 229   "with December 22 marked to commemorate the murder"—Tappan, *Life of Arthur Tappan*, 290–291.

p. 229   "Resolutions by the American Anti-Slavery Society commemorated him"—*The Liberator*, December 1, 1837; Demos, "Antislavery Movement," 508–509.

p. 230   "LOVEJOY the First MARTYR to American LIBERTY"—Tappan, *Life of Arthur Tappan*, 159; Samuel May, *The Emancipator*, February 8, 1838; "Lovejoy the First Martyr to American Liberty . . ." [engraving], New York Public Library Digital Collections, Schomburg Center for Research in Black Culture, Manuscripts, Archives and Rare Books Division, digitalcollections.nypl.org.

p. 230   "A loaded musket is standing at my bedside"—Joseph C. and Owen Lovejoy, *Memoir of the Reverend Elijah P. Lovejoy* (New York: John S. Taylor, 1838), 258.

p. 230   "He granted the murder of Lovejoy would do salutary things"—Merrill, *Against Wind and Tide*, 142.

p. 230   "Garrison said the publisher should not have taken up arms"—*The Liberator*, August 2, 1834.

p. 230   "God will take the work of abolishing slavery out of our hands"—Letter from Sarah Grimké to Sarah Douglass, November 23, 1837, quoted in Sarah and Angelina Grimké, *The Public Years of Sarah and Angelina Grimké*, ed. Larry Ceplair (New York: Columbia University Press, 1989), 297.

p. 230   "Samuel Cornish's *Colored American* carried a front-page memoriam"—Quarles, *Black Abolitionists*, 40.

p. 230   "he and David Ruggles and Theodore Wright raised a collection"—*Colored American*, November 25 and December 9, 1837; Harris, *In the Shadow of Slavery*, 214.

p. 230   "there were mass meetings in churches"—Quarles, *Black Abolitionists*, 40.

p. 230   "A petition campaign presented to a January constitutional convention"—Sinha, *Slave's Cause*, 316–317.

p. 231   "when you have taken from an individual his right to vote"—Robert Purvis et al., *Appeal of Forty Thousand Citizens, Threatened with Disfranchisement, to the People of Pennsylvania* (Philadelphia: Merrihew and Gunn, 1838), 2.

p. 231   "physical force was brutally applied in their ejectment"—*The Pennsylvanian*, January 22, 1838; Winch, *Gentleman of Color*, 298.

p. 231   "the Fortens hung mourning crepe from their house"—Winch, *Gentleman of Color*, 301.

p. 231   "crowned with the motto 'Virtue, Liberty and Independence'"—*History of Pennsylvania Hall* (Philadelphia: Merrihew and Gunn, 1838), 3.

p. 231   "Sarah and her board of managers had done much of the legwork"—*Fourth Annual Report of the Philadelphia Female Anti-Slavery Society* (Philadelphia: Merrihew and Gunn, 1838), 5, 14, 16.

p. 231   "Two thousand people donated $20 each"—*Fourth Annual Report of the Philadelphia Female Anti-Slavery Society*, 12; Winch, *Gentleman of Color*, 302.

p. 232   "Legions of girls and women continued to canvass the state"—*Fourth Annual Report of the Philadelphia Female Anti-Slavery Society*, 6–7.

p. 232   "They had started talking to Northern representatives"—Barnes, *Anti-Slavery Impulse*, 148.

p. 233   "mulatto [women] of infamous character" to "there existed great resemblances in the South between the progeny"—"The Right of Petition: The Gag Law" in *Great Debates in American History*, ed. Marion Mills Miller, Vol. 4 (New York: Current Literature Pub. Co., 1913), 119–120.

p. 233   "offering detailed rebuttals that turned into filibusters that dragged on for days"—Zaeske, "'The South Arose,'" 359.

p. 233   "exhibit the most exalted virtue when they do depart from the domestic circle"—John Quincy Adams, *Speech of John Quincy Adams of Massachusetts, Upon the Right of the People, Men and Women, to Petition . . .* (Washington, DC: Gales and Seaton, 1838), 68.

p. 233   "He even said the right to petition implied the right to vote"—John Quincy Adams, *Upon the Right of the People*, 76–77; Zaeske, "'The South Arose,'" 362.

p. 233   "freedom of speech in the city of [William] Penn"—*History of Pennsylvania Hall*, 12.

p. 234   "David Ruggles and his Committee of Vigilance were involved in no fewer than 173 cases"—*The Emancipator*, March 1, 1838.

p. 234   "helping the committee raise $1,000 to cover his court fees and meet his $500 bail"—*Colored American*, July 8, 1837.

p. 234   "Ruggles also harbored fugitives in his home"—Hodges, *Radical Black Abolitionist*, 124–126.

p. 234   "His eyesight, never good, now faltered even more"—Hodges, *Radical Black Abolitionist*, 113.

p. 234   "Ruggles ended up with a damaged liver"—Hodges, *Radical Black Abolitionist*, 128; *New York Sun*, August 28, 1838.

p. 235   "we cannot recommend non-resistance to persons"—John and Lois Horton, *In Hope of Liberty: Culture, Community and Protest among Northern Free Blacks, 1700–1860* (New York: Oxford University Press, 1998), 239.

p. 235   "The Mirror is consecrated to the genius of liberty"—David Ruggles, *Mirror of Liberty*, quoted in *The Liberator*, July 27, 1838.

p. 235   "New Yorkers could read that journal in Ruggles's new antislavery reading room"—Ellen Gruber Garvey, "Nineteenth-Century Abolitionists and the Databases They Created," *Legacy* 27, no. 2 (2010): 361–362.

p. 235   "The Committee of Vigilance scarcely had the resources"—Hodges, *Radical Black Abolitionist*, 123.

p. 236   "Ruggles learned from a tip that he had forced three Gambians"—Porter, "Apostle of Human Rights," 40.

p. 236   "He couldn't come up with the money"—Porter, "Apostle of Human Rights," 40–41; Harris, *In the Shadow of Slavery*, 214.

p. 237   "I fear her nature has been so overtasked"—Sarah Grimké, quoted in Carol Berkin, *Civil War Wives: The Lives and Times of Angelina Grimké Weld, Varina Howell Davis and Julia Dent Grant* (New York: Vintage, 2010), 57.

p. 237   "Henry Stanton made a surprising proposal"—Birney, *Sarah and Angelina Grimké*, 227.

p. 237   "Perhaps it is best *I* should bear the responsibility *wholly* myself"—Birney, *Sarah and Angelina Grimké*, 228.

p. 237   "Brother, I think in some things you wronged me in *that letter*"—Letter from Angelina Grimké to Theodore Weld, January 21, 1838, quoted in Barnes and Dumond, *Weld-Grimké Letters*, Vol. 2, 520–525.

p. 238   "I know it will surprise and even amaze you"—Letter from Theodore Weld to Angelina Grimké, February 8, 1838, quoted in Barnes and Dumond, *Weld-Grimké Letters*, Vol. 2, 532–536.

p. 238   "*no expectation* and almost no *hope*"—Letter from Theodore Weld to Angelina Grimké, February 8, 1838, quoted in Barnes and Dumond, *Weld-Grimké Letters*, Vol. 2, 532–536.

p. 238   "She allowed that her heart had grown fond of him"—Letter from Angelina Grimké to Theodore Weld, February 11, 1838, quoted in Barnes and Dumond, *Weld-Grimké Letters*, Vol. 2, 536–538.

p. 238   "The customs of Society gave *you* privileges"—Letter from Angelina Grimké to Theodore Weld, February 11, 1838, quoted in Barnes and Dumond, *Weld-Grimké Letters*, Vol. 2, 536–538.

p. 238   "he expressed his love and ecstasy with many exclamation marks"—Letter from Theodore Weld to Angelina Grimké, February 16, 1838, quoted in Barnes and Dumond, *Weld-Grimké Letters*, Vol. 2, 554–555.

p. 238   "She entered the Massachusetts State House"—Perry, *Lift Up Thy Voice*, 163–164.

p. 238   "God strengthen you, my sister"—Lumpkin, *The Emancipation*, 137.

p. 239   "cemented by the blood and sweat and tears of my sisters in bonds"— Angelina Grimké, Address to the Massachusetts Legislature, February 21, 1838, reprinted in Sarah and Angelina Grimké, *On Slavery and Abolitionism* (New York: Penguin, 2014), 331.

p. 239   "because it is a *political* subject, it has often been tauntingly said"—Angelina Grimké, Address to the Massachusetts Legislature, February 21, 1838, reprinted in Sarah and Angelina Grimké, *On Slavery and Abolitionism* (New York: Penguin, 2014), 330.

p. 239   "I hold, Mr. Chairman, that American women have to do with this subject"—Angelina Grimké, Address to the Massachusetts Legislature,

February 21, 1838, reprinted in Sarah and Angelina Grimké, *On Slavery and Abolitionism* (New York: Penguin, 2014), 331.

p. 239 "Many observers realized how important her speech was"—Perry, *Lift Up Thy Voice*, 165.

p. 239 "We Abolition Women are turning the world upside down"—Lerner, *Grimké Sisters*, 12.

p. 240 "Weld welcomed the approval of his evangelical family members"—Abzug, *Passionate Liberator*, 197–198.

p. 240 "great moral courage in taking as his wife so strong a woman"—Letter from Angelina Grimké to Theodore Weld, April 29, 1838, quoted in Barnes and Dumond, *Weld-Grimké Letters*, Vol. 2, 647.

p. 240 "Weld's sectarianism would bring her into bondage"—Letter from William Lloyd Garrison to Helen Garrison, May 12, 1838, quoted in Merrill, *The Letters of William Lloyd Garrison*, Vol. 2, 359.

p. 240 "Next to the overthrow of slavery, the cause of PEACE"—*The Liberator*, January 5, 1838.

p. 240 "he meant that government should never use coercion and force upon its citizens"—Merrill, *Against Wind and Tide*, 145.

p. 241 "rejoice to see the arguments, for and against, on the Peace question"—*The Liberator*, January 5, 1838.

p. 241 "They responded by planning their own vigilance committee"—Joseph A. Boromé, et al., "The Vigilant Committee of Philadelphia," *Pennsylvania Magazine of History and Biography* 92, no. 3 (1968): 320.

p. 241 "accusing them of trying to stifle the energy"—*Right and Wrong in Boston: Annual Report of the Boston Female Anti-Slavery Society* (Boston: Isaac Knapp, 1837), 70.

p. 241 "we cherish the most serious objections"—*Right and Wrong in Boston*, 3.

p. 241 "Chapman quit as secretary of the group"—Jean Fagan Yellin, *The Abolitionist Sisterhood: Women's Political Culture in Antebellum America* (Ithaca, NY: Cornell University Press, 1994), 55.

p. 242 "Theodore Weld had already chosen sides between the factions"—Perry, *Lift Up Thy Voice*, 170–171.

p. 242 "neither did it hamper Angelina in delivering a series of brilliant speeches"—Todras, *Voice of Abolition*, 100.

p. 242 "My tongue was loosed, my spirit unfettered"—Todras, *Voice of Abolition*, 100.

p. 242 "Matrimony for Angelina Grimké arrived on May 14"—Lerner, *Grimké Sisters*, 242; Mayer, *All on Fire*, 244; Perry, *Lift Up Thy Voice*, 172.

p. 243 "the man for whose head the South had offered thousands of dollars"—*History of Pennsylvania Hall*, 70.

p. 243 "his enemies had proposed 'putting me into a strong cage'"—*History of Pennsylvania Hall*, 70–71.

p. 244 "menacing handbills encouraged white citizens 'to interfere, forcibly if they must'"—*History of Pennsylvania Hall*, 136–137.

p. 244   "a crowd of abolitionists filled the auditorium"—Mayer, *All on Fire*, 245.

p. 244   "covered with a ceiling featuring a great carving of a sunflower"—*History of Pennsylvania Hall*, 3.

p. 245   "an adulterous and perverse generation"—*History of Pennsylvania Hall*, 117.

p. 245   "They shouted out insults and catcalls and shoved whoever got in their way"—Perry, *Lift Up Thy Voice*, 174.

p. 245   "compared it to 'the very fiends of the pit'"—Letter from William Lloyd Garrison to Sarah Benson, May 19, 1838, quoted in Merrill, *The Letters of William Lloyd Garrison*, Vol. 2, 363.

p. 245   "the mob roused tempers even higher on the streets"—*Niles' Weekly Register*, May 26, 1838, 195.

p. 246   "Would they be like a 'reed shaken with the wind'"—*History of Pennsylvania Hall*, 123–124.

p. 246   "What would the breaking of every window be?"—*History of Pennsylvania Hall*, 123–124.

p. 247   "She said the mob clamor was 'a moral whirlwind'"—*History of Pennsylvania Hall*, 126.

p. 247   "They couldn't hold out against the mob much longer"—*The Liberator*, June 1, 1838; *Niles' Weekly Register*, May 26, 1838, 195.

p. 247   "The next day the women returned and held meetings"—*The Liberator*, June 1, 1838

p. 247   "Mayor Jonathan Swift informed them he could not guarantee their safety"—Birney, *Sarah and Angelina Grimké*, 241.

p. 247   "Then they broke inside with axes"—Letter from William Lloyd Garrison to Sarah Benson, May 19, 1838, quoted in Merrill, *The Letters of William Lloyd Garrison*, Vol. 2, 363.

p. 248   "Doors and windows were broken through"—Birney, *Sarah and Angelina Grimké*, 241.

p. 248   "They spilled out into the streets and alleys"—*Niles' Weekly Register*, May 26, 1838, 195.

p. 248   "the Motts sent their children away and awaited their fate in the parlor"—Hallowell, *James and Lucretia Mott*, 128.

p. 248   "it changed direction and set fire to several homes owned by Black citizens"—*History of Pennsylvania Hall*, 140; Martineau, *Martyr Age*, 73.

p. 248   "it will do incalculable good to our cause"—Letter from William Lloyd Garrison to Sarah Benson, May 19, 1838, quoted in Merrill, *The Letters of William Lloyd Garrison*, Vol. 2, 363.

p. 249   "The Southern press exalted in the Hall's destruction"—*History of Pennsylvania Hall*, 167–170.

p. 249   "Maria Chapman faced an outbreak of what Garrison called 'brain fever'"—Letter from William Lloyd Garrison to George Benson, May 25, 1838, quoted in Merrill, *The Letters of William Lloyd Garrison*, Vol. 2, 366.

p. 249   "She retired from public life and retreated to Fort Lee, New Jersey"—
          Birney, *Sarah and Angelina Grimké*, 241–242; Perry, *Lift Up Thy Voice*, 177.

p. 249   "she found herself beset with mysterious ailments"—Theodore Weld, *In
          Memory, Angelina Grimké Weld* (Boston: George Ellis, 1880), 43; Lerner,
          Grimké Sisters, 203–204.

p. 250   "he charged that Lewis Tappan had 'counselled the division in our
          ranks'"—Letter from William Lloyd Garrison to the Executive Committee
          of the American Anti-Slavery Society, December 6, 1839, quoted in
          Merrill, *The Letters of William Lloyd Garrison*, Vol. 2, 544–545.

p. 250   "He pushed ever harder for abolitionists to admit women to their
          organizations"—Merrill, *Against Wind and Tide*, 150–153.

p. 250   "He also became more insistent that political action was vile and
          corrupting"—Garrison and Garrison, *The Story of His Life*, Vol. 2, 273.

p. 250   "the society forbade the support of lawsuits"—Constitution of New England
          Non-Resistance Society, quoted in *The Liberator*, September 28, 1838.

p. 250   "swinging loose from any regular society"—Mayer, *All on Fire*, 250.

p. 250   "the founding of the society would someday be marked with the same
          reverence"—*The Liberator*, September 28, 1838.

p. 250   "she parlayed her oratory into a leadership role"—Mayer, *All on Fire*, 250.

p. 251   "the recently formed Vigilant Association of Philadelphia grew in
          membership"—Boromé, "Vigilant Committee of Philadelphia," 322–323.

p. 251   "Sarah opened the treasury of the Philadelphia Female Anti-Slavery
          Society"—Sumler-Lewis, "Forten-Purvis Women," 284.

p. 251   "to help the Association board fugitives in private homes"—Boromé,
          "Vigilant Committee of Philadelphia," 324–325.

p. 252   "He struggled through what he called 'seasons of mental anxiety'"—
          Hodges, *Radical Black Abolitionist*, 145.

p. 252   "Cornish accused Ruggles of mismanaging the funds"—*Colored American*,
          January 26, 1839.

p.252   "He said Ruggles lacked judgment and prudence"—Harris, *In the Shadow of
          Slavery*, 214.

p. 252   "But Ruggles said he would not quarrel"—*Colored American*, February 23
          and May 18, 1839.

p. 252   "Ruggles then became embroiled in the Darg case"—Hodges, *Radical Black
          Abolitionist*, 135–136; Porter, "Apostle of Human Rights," 41.

p. 252   "The man had come to New York seeking refuge"—Frederick Douglass, *My
          Bondage and My Freedom* (New York: Miller, Orton & Co., 1857), 340–341.

p. 253   "This brave and devoted man suffered much"—Douglass, *My Bondage and
          My Freedom*, 341.

EPILOGUE: CRASHING UNANIMITY

p. 255   "The 450 friends of William Lloyd Garrison assembled in a mood of joy"—
          Merrill, *Against Wind and Tide*, 158; Mayer, *All on Fire*, 278–279.

p. 255   "Once aboard the train, they disregarded the signs"—Mayer, *All on Fire*, 278–279.

p. 255   "the most untiring and zealous friends"—*The Liberator*, May 15, 1840.

p. 256   "more than a thousand delegates assembled at the Fourth Free Church"—Garrison and Garrison, *Story of His Life*, Vol. 2, 348.

p. 256   "Kelley was among the most polarizing figures in the movement"—Letter from Anne Weston to Maria Chapman, May 30, 1840, quoted in Yellin, *Abolitionist Sisterhood*, 244.

p. 256   "Doubted! Doubted"—Mayer, *All on Fire*, 283.

p. 256   "Kelley won the vote, 571 to 451"—*The Liberator*, May 22, 1840; Tappan, *Life of Arthur Tappan*, 303.

p. 256   "Lewis resigned from the committee"—*The Liberator*, May 15, May 22, 1840; Garrison and Garrison, *Story of His Life*, Vol. 2, 349.

p. 256   "throwing a firebrand into the anti-slavery ranks"—Garrison and Garrison, *Story of His Life*, Vol. 2, 349.

p. 256   "He privately called Garrison 'the Massachusetts madman'"—Ford Risley, *Abolition and the Press: The Moral Struggle against Slavery* (Evanston, IL: Northwestern University Press, 2008), 84.

p. 256   "Lewis assembled three hundred clergymen"—*American and Foreign Anti-Slavery Reporter*, June–July 1840, quoted in Wyatt-Brown, *Lewis Tappan*, 198.

p. 256   "Garrison secured the appointment of Lucretia Mott"—Garrison and Garrison, *Story of His Life*, Vol. 2, 349; *The Liberator*, May 15, 1840.

p. 257   "the foe of freedom, humanity and pure religion"—*The Liberator*, May 15, 1840

p. 257   "We have made clean work of every thing"—Letter from William Lloyd Garrison to Helen Garrison, May 15, 1840, quoted in Merrill, *The Letters of William Lloyd Garrison*, Vol. 2, 611.

p. 257   "he attacked 'revivalism, the divine interpretation of the Bible'"—van Deburg, "Pro-Slavery Priesthood," 235.

p. 257   "a covenant with death and an agreement with Hell"—Resolution of the Massachusetts Anti-Slavery Society, January 27, 1843; *The Liberator*, July 7, 1854.

p. 257   "as an 1840 petition campaign to the Massachusetts legislature"—Newman, *Transformation*, 121.

p. 257   "An inquiring spirit is not an irreverent one"—*The Liberator*, August 8, 1851.

p. 258   "Lewis Tappan saw such electoral crusades as having no more value"—Wyatt-Brown, *Lewis Tappan*, 198.

p. 258   "It had no compelling literature to distribute"—Wyatt-Brown, *Lewis Tappan*, 198–200; Ripley, *Black Abolitionist Papers*, 335–336n4.

p. 258   "Lewis found more success with a high-profile legal case"—Sinha, *Slave's Cause*, 406–411.

p. 258   "Lewis used it as a springboard for funding Christian missions"—Sinha, *Slave's Cause*, 406–411; Lawrence Friedman, "Confidence and Pertinacity in Evangelical Abolitionism: Lewis Tappan's Circle," *American Quarterly* 31, no. 1 (1979): 84–86.

p. 258   "Lewis had managed to extricate himself"—Wyatt-Brown, *Lewis Tappan*, 228–232.

p. 259   "Wherever the colored man is connected with the houses"—Harris, *In the Shadow of Slavery*, 227.

p. 259   "He tried to protest that he had been the one to keep the committee in business"—Porter, "Apostle of Human Rights," 41–42.

p. 259   "He wrote a letter in his own defense, but Lewis would not publish it"—Hodges, *Radical Black Abolitionist*, 149–150.

p. 259   "calling him a liar in his newspaper"—*Colored American*, September 7, 1839.

p. 260   "Ruggles was able to publish his defense"—*National Anti-Slavery Standard*, August 20, 1840.

p. 260   "Ruggles's finances had never been worse"—Porter, "Apostle of Human Rights," 44.

p. 260   "Let not a faithful public servant that has lost his eyesight"—*National Reformer*, November 11, 1839.

p. 260   "bled, leeched, cupped, plastered, blistered"—David Ruggles, "Dr. Ruggles's Hydropathic Experience," quoted in "Sympathetic Diagnosis of Disease," *Buchanan's Journal of Man* 1 (1849): 36.

p. 260   "Here he managed to recover some of his strength"—*The Liberator*, December 21, 1849.

p. 261   "One of them was the perpetually infirm William Lloyd Garrison"—Hodges, *Radical Black Abolitionist*, 189–190.

p. 261   "Ruggles still fought segregation on trains and steamships"—*The Liberator*, July 6, July 9, 1841; *The National Anti-Slavery Standard*, July 15, July 29, 1841.

p. 261   "Ruggles rescued six hundred people from abduction"—Ripley, *Black Abolitionist Papers*, 175–176, n5.

p. 261   "His success in building a model to thwart Southern slave hunters"—Jane Pease and William Pease, *They Who Would Be Free: Blacks' Search for Freedom, 1830–1861* (New York: Atheneum, 1974), 207–212.

p. 261   "It wasn't long before his chosen new home, Belleville"—Pease and Pease, *Bound with Them in Chains*, 154.

p. 262   "proscription and persecution, and assault"—*Colored American*, May 18, 1839.

p. 262   "He rejected the Liberty Party, partisan campaigning"—Pease and Pease, *Bound with Them in Chains*, 156–157.

p. 262   "we should not dare to trust them"—*Colored American*, August 31, 1839.

p. 262   "he stands by the old paths, but does not inquire for the new"—*Colored American*, November 9, 1839.

p. 263   "Peter Paul Simons, who accused Cornish of looking down his nose"—Harris, *In the Shadow of Slavery*, 202–206.

p. 263 "we must show ACTION! ACTION! ACTION!"—*Colored American*, June 1, 1839.

p. 263 "'Respectability' now meant fighting racism"—Stewart, "Emergence of Racial Modernity," 212.

p. 263 "Frederick Douglass, for one, would differ with Garrison"—Rael, *Black Identity*, 204–205.

p. 263 "He urged them 'to RISE AT ONCE'"—Charles Lenox Remond, quoted in *The Liberator*, July 9, 1847.

p. 263 "It is sinful in the extreme for you to make voluntary submission"—Henry Highland Garnet, "Address to the Slaves of the United States," National Convention of Colored Citizens, Buffalo, New York, August 16, 1843, published in Garnet, *Walker's Appeal, with a Brief Sketch of His Life* (New York: J. H. Tobitt, 1848), 89–96.

p. 264 "James Forten died after experiencing months of asthma and edema"—Winch, *Gentleman of Color*, 326–329.

p. 264 "Prejudice, soul-crushing, man-despising, God-hating prejudice"—Robert Purvis, *Remarks on the Life and Character of James Forten* (Philadelphia: Merrihew and Thompson, 1842), 1.

p. 265 "Financial records revealed debts of almost $32,000"—Winch, *Gentleman of Color*, 333–337.

p. 265 "They and their colleagues petitioned Congress"—Sumler-Lewis, "Forten-Purvis Women," 282–285.

p. 265 "Lucretia Mott, would attend the 1840 World Anti-Slavery Convention"—Douglas H. Maynard, "The World's Anti-Slavery Convention of 1840," *The Mississippi Valley Historical Review* 47, no. 3 (1960): 452, 456, 460.

p. 265 "Sarah Forten had often spoken of the 'thrall' of marriage"—Winch, "Sarah Forten's Anti-Slavery Networks," 153–154.

p. 265 "in early 1838 she married Joseph Purvis"—Winch, "Sarah Forten's Anti-Slavery Networks," 153–154.

p. 266 "In the 1850s her husband died without a will"—Winch, *Gentleman of Color*, 364–365.

p. 266 "her work would be published in outlets"—Sumler-Lewis, "Forten-Purvis Women," 286–287.

p. 266 "A new flood of petitions combined with high tensions"—Meinke, "Slavery, Partisanship, and Procedure," 37–38.

p. 267 "John Quincy Adams tried to work around the rules"—Meinke, "Slavery, Partisanship, and Procedure," 36.

p. 267 "He oversaw the repeal of the nine-month law"—Quarles, *Black Abolitionists*, 183.

p. 267 "the colored population fled in the utmost terror in every possible direction"—*Niles' National Register*, August 6, 1842, 356.

p. 267 "one of the most ferocious and bloody-spirited mobs"—Letter from Robert Purvis to Henry Wright, August 22, 1840, quoted in Margaret Hope

Bacon, *But One Race: The Life of Robert Purvis* (Albany: State University of New York Press, 2007), 99.

p. 268 "They moved from Fort Lee, New Jersey"—Perry, *Lift Up Thy Voice*, 188.

p. 268 "She and Sarah dealt with the domestic labors"—Todras, *Voice of Abolition*, 109–111.

p. 268 "Angelina came into a $5,000 inheritance after her mother's recent death"—Todras, *Voice of Abolition*, 109–111.

p. 268 "Weld traveled to Washington at the height of the gag law controversy"—Barnes, *Anti-Slavery Impulse*, 183–187.

p. 268 "they amassed some twenty thousand sources"—Birney, *Sarah and Angelina Grimké*, 258–259.

p. 268 "the most crushing indictment of any institution ever written"—Dwight Lowell Dumond, *Antislavery, The Crusade for Freedom in America* (Ann Arbor: University of Michigan Press, 1961), 249.

p. 268 "the Grimkés and Weld presented firsthand accounts"—Theodore and Angelina Grimké Weld and Sarah Grimké, *American Slavery as It Is: Testimony of a Thousand Witnesses* (New York: American Anti-Slavery Society, 1839), v–vi.

p. 269 "The book would so profoundly influence her"—Garvey, "Nineteenth-Century Abolitionists," 357.

p. 269 "she also faced criticism from women like Lydia Child"—Perry, *Lift Up Thy Voice*, 182.

p. 269 "The Grimkés, I think, are extinct"—Letter from Deborah Weston to Anne Weston, May 3, 1839, Anti-Slavery Collection, Boston Public Library.

p. 269 "They turned away from denominational religion"—Todras, *Voice of Abolition*, 124.

p. 269 "We are compelled to choose between two evils"—Angelina Grimké Weld, *The Liberator*, July 7, 1854.

p. 270 "He was a regular presence at the so-called Abolition House"—Barnes, *Anti-Slavery Impulse*, 182, 193.

p. 270 "An agent he had trained, part of 'The Seventy'"—Barnes, *Anti-Slavery Impulse*, 196.

p. 271 "throughout the 1840s, mob violence against abolitionists declined"—Ratner, *Powder Keg*, 139–140; Richards, *Gentlemen of Property and Standing*, 156–165.

p. 272 "All hopes of fusing into one the main divisions of the anti-slavery host"—Letter from Theodore Weld to Lewis Tappan, February 3, 1843, quoted in Barnes, *Anti-Slavery Impulse*, 194.

p. 272 "by making it locally adaptable and resilient"—Quarles, *Black Abolitionists*, 54.

p. 273 "a mighty convulsion would surely 'hurl these two systems of labor'"—Letter from Theodore Weld to James Birney, January 22, 1842, in Dwight Lowell Dumond, ed. *Letters of James Gillespie Birney, 1831–1857*, Vol. 2 (New York: D. Appleton–Century, 1938), 663.

BIBLIOGRAPHY

PRIMARY SOURCES

Abdy, E. S. *Journal of a Residence and Tour in the United States of North America, from April, 1833, to October, 1834,* Vol. 3. London: John Murray, 1835.

Abolition Report, May 26, 1836, 24th Congress, 1st Session.

An Account of the Conflagration of the Principal Part of the First Ward of the City of New York. New York: C. Foster, 1836.

An Act for the Abolition of Slavery throughout the British Colonies, August 28, 1833, The Mid-Victorian Royal Navy, Legislation on the Slave Trade, https://www.pdavis.nl/Legis_07.htm.

Adams, John Quincy. *Speech of John Quincy Adams of Massachusetts, Upon the Right of the People, Men and Women, to Petition . . .* Washington, DC: Gales and Seaton, 1838.

African Repository and Colonial Journal, Vol. 11. Washington, DC: James Dunn, 1835.

American Anti-Slavery Society Executive Committee, Address to the Public, September 8, 1835.

Andrews, E. A. *Slavery and the Domestic Slave Trade in the United States.* Boston: Light & Stearns, 1836.

The Appeal of Clerical Abolitionists on Antislavery Measures, August 19, 1837.

Beecher, Catharine. *An Essay on Slavery and Abolitionism, Addressed to Miss A. D. Grimké.* Philadelphia: Henry Perkins, 1837.

Benton, Thomas Hart. *Thirty Years' View, or A History of the Working of the American Government for Thirty Years, from 1820 to 1850.* New York: Appleton and Co., 1858.

Birney, Catherine. *The Grimké Sisters: Sarah and Angelina Grimké, The First American Women Advocates of Abolition and Women's Rights.* Boston: Lee & Shepard, 1885.

Birney, James G. *Letters of James Gillespie Birney, 1831–1857,* Vol. 2, edited by Dwight Lowell. Dumond. New York: D. Appleton–Century, 1938.

Birney, William. *James G. Birney and His Times.* New York: D. Appleton, 1890.

Boston Female Anti-Slavery Society, Address to the Women of Massachusetts, July 13, 1836.

Boston Female Anti-Slavery Society. *Right and Wrong in Boston: Second Annual Report of the Boston Female Anti-Slavery Society.* Boston: Boston Female Anti-Slavery Society, 1836.

Boston Female Anti-Slavery Society. *Right and Wrong in Boston: Third Annual Report of the Boston Female Anti-Slavery Society.* Boston: Boston Female Anti-Slavery Society, 1836.

Boston Female Anti-Slavery Society. *Right and Wrong in Boston: Fourth Annual Report of the Boston Female Anti-Slavery Society.* Boston: Isaac Knapp, 1837.

Bourne, George. *Picture of Slavery in the United States of America.* Middletown, CT: Edwin Hunt, 1834.

Bourne, George. *Slavery Illustrated in Its Effects upon Woman and Domestic Society.* Boston: Isaac Knapp, 1837.

Buell, Walter. *Joshua R. Giddings: A Sketch.* Cleveland: William W. Williams, 1882.

Calhoun, John. Report from the Senate Select Committee, "The Adoption of Efficient Measures to Prevent the Circulation of Incendiary Abolition Petitions Through the Mail," February 4, 1836.

Calhoun, John. *Speeches of John C. Calhoun, Delivered in the Congress of the United States to the Present Time.* New York: Harper and Brothers, 1843.

Chapman, Maria Weston. *Right and Wrong in Massachusetts.* Boston: Dow & Jackson's Anti-Slavery Press, 1839.

Child, Lydia Maria. *Anti-Slavery Catechism.* Newburyport, MA: Charles Whipple, 1836.

Child, Lydia Maria. *An Appeal in Favor of That Class of Americans Called Africans.* Boston: Allen and Ticknor, 1833.

Child, Lydia Maria. *Letters of Lydia Maria Child.* Boston: Houghton, Mifflin and Co., 1883.

Child, Lydia Maria, ed. *The Oasis.* Boston: Benjamin Bacon, 1834.

Clay, Henry. *The Papers of Henry Clay,* Vol. 2, edited by James H. Hopkins and Mary W. M. Hargreaves. Louisville: University of Kentucky Press, 1961.

Coffin, Levi. *Reminiscences of Levi Coffin, The Reputed President of the Underground Railroad.* Cincinnati: Robert Clarke, 1880.

The Colonizationist and Journal of Freedom. Boston: Geo. W. Light, 1834.

Constitution of the American Anti-Slavery Society. December 6, 1833.

Constitution of the New England Non-Resistance Society. September 28, 1838.

Constitution of the Philadelphia Female Anti-Slavery Society. 1834.

Cornish, Samuel, and Theodore Wright. *The Colonization Scheme Considered, in Its Rejection by the Colored People . . .* Newark, NJ: Aaron Guest, 1840.

Crime of the Abolitionists: Speech of Gerrit Smith in the Meeting of the New York Anti-Slavery Society, Held in Peterboro: October 22d 1835. New York, 1862.

Declaration of Sentiments and Constitution of the American Anti-Slavery Society. New York: American Anti-Slavery Society. 1835.

Diary of Lewis Tappan, in Lewis Tappan Papers. Library of Congress, mm75042317.

Douglass, Frederick. *My Bondage and My Freedom.* New York: Miller, Orton & Co., 1857.

Douglass, Frederick. *Narrative of the Life of Frederick Douglass, an American Slave.* Dublin: Webb and Chapman, 1845.

Edinburgh Emancipation Society. *A Voice to the United States of America from the Metropolis of Scotland.* Edinburgh: William Oliphant and Son, 1836.

The Enemies of the Constitution Discovered... The Dispersion of the State Anti-Slavery Convention by the Agitators. New York: Leavitt, Lord & Co., 1835.

Exposition of the Proceedings of John P. Darg, Henry W. Merritt, and Others in Relation to the Robbery of Darg... New York: Isaac T. Hopper, 1840.

Fifth Annual Report of the Philadelphia Female Anti-Slavery Society. Philadelphia: Merrihew and Thompson, 1839.

First Annual Report of the American Anti-Slavery Society. New York: American Anti-Slavery Society, 1834.

First Annual Report of the Board of Managers of the New-England Anti-Slavery Society. Boston: Garrison and Knapp, 1833.

First Annual Report of the New York Committee of Vigilance. New York: Committee of Vigilance, 1837.

Forten, James. *Address Delivered Before the Ladies' Anti-Slavery Society of Philadelphia*, April 14, 1836. Philadelphia: Merrihew and Gunn, 1836.

Forten, James. *Letters from a Man of Colour, on a Late Bill Before the Senate of Pennsylvania*. Philadelphia: James Forten, 1813.

Forten, James, William Whipper, and Robert Purvis. "To the Honourable the Senate and the House of Representatives of the Commonwealth of Pennsylvania." April 1832.

Forten, Sarah. Poems: "An Appeal to Woman," "The Grave of the Slave," "To the Hibernia," "My Country" [published variously in *The Liberator*].

Fourth Annual Report of the Philadelphia Female Anti-Slavery Society. Philadelphia: Merrihew and Gunn, 1838.

Garnet, Henry Highland. "Address to the Slaves of the United States." National Convention of Colored Citizens, Buffalo, New York, August 16, 1843.

Garnet, Henry Highland. *Walker's Appeal, with a Brief Sketch of His Life*. New York: J. H. Tobitt, 1848.

Garrison, Wendell Phillips, and Francis Jackson Garrison. *William Lloyd Garrison, 1805–1879: The Story of His Life Told by His Children: Volume 1, 1805–1835*. New York: Century Co., 1885.

Garrison, Wendell Phillips, and Francis Jackson Garrison. *William Lloyd Garrison, 1805–1879: The Story of His Life Told by His Children: Volume 2, 1835–1840*. New York: Century Co., 1885.

Garrison, William Lloyd. Address at Park Street Church. Boston, Massachusetts, July 4, 1829.

Garrison, William Lloyd. *An Address, Delivered Before the Free People of Color, in Philadelphia, New-York, and Other Cities, During the Month of June, 1831*. Boston: Stephen Foster, 1831.

Garrison, William Lloyd. Address to the World Anti-Slavery Convention, London, July 12, 1833.

Garrison, William Lloyd, ed. *Discussions on American Slavery Between George Thompson and Robert J. Breckenridge*. Boston: Isaac Knapp, 1836.

Garrison, William Lloyd. *The Letters of William Lloyd Garrison, Volume 1, I Will Be Heard! 1822–1835*, edited by Walter M. Merrill. Cambridge, MA: Harvard University Press, 1971.

Garrison, William Lloyd. *The Letters of William Lloyd Garrison, Volume 2, A House Dividing Against Itself, 1836–1840*, edited by Walter M. Merrill. Cambridge, MA: Harvard University Press, 1971.

Garrison, William Lloyd. *Thoughts on African Colonization*. Boston: Garrison and Knapp, 1832.

Greeley, Horace. *The American Conflict: A History of the Great Rebellion in the United States of America, 1860–65*, Vol. 1. Hartford, CT: O. D. Case & Co., 1866.

Greene, Asa. *A Glance at Old New York . . .* New York: A. Greene, 1837.

Grimké, Angelina. Address to the Legislative Committee of the Massachusetts Legislature, February 21, 1838.

Grimké, Angelina. "Appeal to the Christian Women of the South." *Anti-Slavery Examiner* 1, no. 2 (1836).

Grimké, Angelina. *Appeal to the Women of the Nominally Free States.* Boston: Isaac Knapp, 1838.

Grimké, Angelina. *Letters to Catherine E. Beecher, in Reply to an Essay on Slavery and Abolitionism.* Boston: Isaac Knapp, 1838.

Grimké, Angelina. *Walking by Faith: The Diary of Angelina Grimké, 1828–1835,* edited by Charles Wilbanks. Columbia: University of South Carolina Press, 2003.

Grimké, Sarah. *An Address to the Free Colored Americans.* New York: William Dorr, 1837.

Grimké, Sarah. An Epistle to the Clergy of the Southern States, December 1836.

Grimké, Sarah, and Angelina Grimké. *On Slavery and Abolitionism.* New York: Penguin, 2014.

Grimké, Sarah, and Angelina Grimké. *The Public Years of Sarah and Angelina Grimké,* edited by Larry Ceplair. New York: Columbia University Press, 1989.

Guide to the Broadway Tabernacle Church and Society Papers. New-York Historical Society Museum & Library. dlib.nyu.edu/findingaids/html/nyhs/broadwaytabernacle.

Hallowell, Anna Davis, ed. *James and Lucretia Mott, Life and Letters.* Boston: Houghton, Mifflin, 1884.

Harper, Ida Husted. *The Life and Work of Susan B. Anthony,* Vol. 1. Indianapolis: Bowen-Merrill, 1899.

Headley, J. T. *The Great Riots of New York, 1712 to 1873.* New York: E. B. Treat, 1873.

"Hints on Anti-Abolition Mobs." *Anti-Slavery Record* 2, no. 7 (1836): 1–4.

History of Pennsylvania Hall. Philadelphia: Merrihew and Gunn, 1838.

Hone, Philip. *The Diary of Philip Hone, 1828–1851,* Vol. 1, edited by Bayard Tuckerman. New York: Dodd, Mead and Co., 1889.

Jackson, Andrew. *Correspondence of Andrew Jackson,* Vol. 5, edited by John Spencer Bassett. Washington, DC: Carnegie Institution, 1931.

Jackson, Andrew. Message to US House of Representatives and US Senate, December 8, 1835.

Jefferson, Thomas. *Notes on the State of Virginia.* London: John Stockdale, 1787. Reprinted Richmond, VA: J. W. Randolph, 1853.

Johnson, Oliver. *William Lloyd Garrison and His Times.* Boston: Houghton, Mifflin and Company, 1885.

Journal of the House of Representatives of the United States. 24th Congress, First Session. Washington, DC: Blair and Rives, 1836.

Kendall, Amos. *Autobiography of Amos Kendall,* edited by William Stickney. New York: Lee, Shepard and Dillingham, 1872.

Lawrence, Cornelius W. Proclamation by the Mayor of the City of New-York, July 11, 1834.

Lincoln, Abraham. "The Perpetuation of Our Political Institutions," Address before the Young Men's Lyceum, Springfield, IL, January 27, 1838.

Lossing, Benson John. *History of New York City: Embracing an Outline Sketch of Events from 1609 to 1830, and a Full Account of Its Development from 1830 to 1884,* Vol. 1. New York: Perine, 1884.

Lovejoy, Joseph C., and Owen Lovejoy. *Memoir of the Reverend Elijah P. Lovejoy.* New York: John S. Taylor, 1838.

Ludlow, Fitz Hugh. *The Hasheesh Eater: Being Passages from the Life of a Pythagorean.* New York: Harper and Bros., 1857.

Lyman, Theodore, ed. *Papers Relating to the Garrison Mob.* Cambridge, MA: Welch, Bigelow, and Co., 1870.

Martineau, Harriet. *Autobiography,* Vol. 1. Boston: James R. Osgood, 1877.

Martineau, Harriet. *The Martyr Age of the United States.* Boston: Weeks, Jordan & Co., 1839.

Martineau, Harriet. *Retrospect of Western Travel,* vols. 1–2. New York: Harper & Brothers, 1838.

Martineau, Harriet. *Society in America,* vols. 1–2. New York: Saunders and Otley, 1837.

May, Samuel J. *Some Recollections of Our Antislavery Conflict.* Boston: Fields, Osgood & Co., 1869.

Minutes and Proceedings of the First Annual Convention of the People of Colour. Philadelphia: People of Colour Convention, 1831.

Minutes and Proceedings of the First Annual Meeting of the American Moral Reform Society. Philadelphia: Merrihew and Gunn, 1837.

Minutes of the Philadelphia Female Anti-Slavery Society, Friends of Freedom Collection, Historical Society of Pennsylvania.

Neal, John. *Wandering Recollections of a Somewhat Busy Life.* Boston: Roberts Brothers, 1869.

Nell, William, et al. "Letters of Negroes, Largely Personal and Private [Part 6]." *Journal of Negro History* 11, no. 1 (1926): 186–214.

New York Public Library Digital Collections, Schomburg Center for Research in Black Culture, Manuscripts, Archives and Rare Books Division, digitalcollections.nypl.org.

Parton, James, et al. *Sketches of Men of Progress.* New York: New York and Hartford Publishing, 1871.

Pastoral Letter from the General Association of Massachusetts to the Churches Under Their Care, August 11, 1837.

Pennsylvania Abolition Society. *The Present State and Condition of the Free People of Color in the City of Philadelphia and Adjoining Districts.* Philadelphia: Merrihew and Gunn, 1838.

Philadelphia Female Anti-Slavery Society. *Address to the Women of Pennsylvania.* Philadelphia: Merrihew and Gunn, 1836.

Porter, Dorothy, ed. *Early Negro Writing, 1760–1837.* Boston: Beacon Press, 1971.

Proceedings of the Anti-Slavery Convention of American Women, Held in New York City. New York: W. S. Dorr, 1837.

Proceedings of the Anti-Slavery Convention of American Women, Held in Philadelphia, May 15th, 16th, 17th and 18th, 1838. Philadelphia: Merrihew and Gunn, 1838.

Proceedings of the Anti-Slavery Meeting Held in Stacy Hall, Boston, on the Twentieth Anniversary of the Mob of October 21, 1835. Boston: R. F. Wallcut, 1855.

Proceedings of the Massachusetts Historical Society, Vol. 8. Boston: Massachusetts Historical Society, 1881.

Proceedings of the Meeting of the New York Vigilance Committee, November 21, 1836.

Proceedings of the New England Anti-Slavery Convention, May 24–26, 1836. Boston: Isaac Knapp, 1836.

Proceedings of the New York Anti-Slavery Convention, Held at Utica, October 21 . . . Utica, NY: Standard & Democrat, 1835.

Proceedings of the Third Anti-Slavery Convention of American Women. Philadelphia: Merrihew and Thompson, 1839.

Purvis, Robert, et al. *Appeal of Forty Thousand Citizens, Threatened with Disfranchisement, to the People of Pennsylvania*. Philadelphia: Merrihew and Gunn, 1838.

Purvis, Robert. *Remarks on the Life and Character of James Forten*. Philadelphia: Merrihew and Thompson, 1842.

Ray, Charlotte Augusta Burrough. *Sketch of the Life of the Rev. Charles B. Ray*. New York: J. J. Little, 1887.

Reese, David. *A Brief Review of the First Annual Report of the American Anti-Slavery Society*. New York: Howe & Bates, 1834.

Register of Debates in Congress, vols. 11–12. Washington, DC: Gales and Seaton, 1835–1836.

Report of a Delegate to the Anti-Slavery Convention of American Women. Boston: Isaac Knapp, 1838.

Report of the Committee Appointed to Ascertain the Cause and Particulars of the Late Riot, Pennsylvania Abolition Society Papers, Historical Society of Pennsylvania, 1834.

Report of the Postmaster General to the President of the United States. December 1, 1835. Washington, DC: Blair and Rives, 1836.

Resolution of the Massachusetts Anti-Slavery Society, January 27, 1843.

Resolutions Passed by the Colored Inhabitants of Philadelphia, January 1817.

"The Right of Petition: The Gag Law." In *Great Debates in American History*, edited by Marion Mills Miller, Vol. 4. New York: Current Literature Pub. Co., 1913.

Ripley, C. Peter, ed. *The Black Abolitionist Papers*, Vol. 3, *The United States, 1830–1846*. Chapel Hill: University of North Carolina Press, 1991.

Ritter, Abraham. *Philadelphia and Her Merchants, as Constituted 50 to 70 Years Ago*. Philadelphia: Abraham Ritter, 1860.

Ruggles, David. *Abrogation of the Seventh Commandment, by the American Churches*. New York: David Ruggles, 1835.

Ruggles, David. "Dr. Ruggles's Hydropathic Experience." In "Sympathetic Diagnosis of Disease." *Buchanan's Journal of Man* 1, no. 1 (1849): 32–37.

Ruggles, David. *The "Extinguisher" Extinguished, or David M. Reese, M.D. "Used Up."* New York: D. Ruggles, 1834.

Scharf, J. Thomas, and Thompson Westcott. *History of Philadelphia, 1609–1884*, Vol. 1. Philadelphia: L. H. Everts & Co., 1884.

Second Annual Report of the American Anti-Slavery Society. New York: William Dorr, 1835.

Sewall, Samuel. *A Memoir*, edited by Nina Moore Tiffany. New York: Houghton, Mifflin, 1898.

Seward, Frederick. *William H. Seward: An Autobiography*. New York: Derby and Miller, 1891.

Sheldon, George. *The Story of the Volunteer Fire Department of the City of New York*. New York: Harper & Brothers, 1882.

Shiner, Michael. The Diary of Michael Shiner Relating to the History of the Washington Navy Yard, 1813–1869. Library of Congress, MSS 20:957. www.history.navy.mil/our-collections.html.

"Slavery in the District of Columbia." Report to the House of Representatives, 24th Congress, First Session, Reports of Committees, Vol. 3, report 691. May 18, 1836.

Smith, Margaret Bayard. *Forty Years of Washington Society: Portrayed by the Family Letters of Mrs. Samuel Harrison Smith*. London: T. Fisher Unwin, 1906.

Sprogle, Howard. *The Philadelphia Police, Past and Present*. Philadelphia, 1887.

Stanton, Henry. *Random Recollections*. New York: Harpers & Brothers, 1887.

Stewart, Maria. Address at African Masonic Hall, Boston, February 27, 1833.

Stewart, Maria. Farewell Address to Her Friends in the City of Boston, September 21, 1833.

Stewart, Maria. Lecture at Franklin Hall, Boston, September 21, 1832.

Stewart, Maria. *Maria W. Stewart: America's First Black Woman Political Writer, Essays and Speeches*, edited by Marilyn Richardson. Bloomington: Indiana University Press, 1987.

Stewart, Maria. *Productions of Mrs. Maria W. Stewart, presented to the First African Baptist Church & Society, of the City of Boston*. Boston: Friends of Freedom and Virtue, 1835.

Stewart, Maria. *Religion and the Pure Principles of Morality, The Sure Foundation on Which We Must Build*. Boston: Isaac Knapp, 1831.

Tappan, Lewis. *Life of Arthur Tappan*. New York: Hurd and Houghton, 1870.

Third Annual Report of the American Anti-Slavery Society. New York: William Dorr, 1836.

Third Annual Report of the Philadelphia Female Anti-Slavery Society. In *The Liberator*, January 1, 1837.

Thompson, George. *Lectures of George Thompson, History of His Connection with the Anti-Slavery Cause in England*. Boston: Isaac Knapp, 1836.

Thompson, George. *Letters and Addresses by George Thompson During His Mission in the United States*. Boston: Isaac Knapp, 1837.

Thompson, George, and Frederick Chesson. "Scrap Books Compiled by Thompson and Chesson," Vol. 1. www.loc.gov/item/2013659691.

Von Holst, Herman. *John C. Calhoun*. Boston: Houghton, Mifflin and Co., 1883.

Walker, David. *The Appeal in Four Articles . . .* Boston: David Walker, 1830.

Watson, John Fanning. *Annals of Philadelphia*. Philadelphia: E. L. Carey and A. Hart, 1830.

Webster, Noah. *An American Dictionary of the English Language*. New York: S. Converse, 1828.

Weld, Theodore. *The Bible Against Slavery. An Inquiry into the Patriarchal and Mosaic Systems on the Subject of Human Rights*. New York: American Anti-Slavery Society, 1838.

Weld, Theodore. *In Memory, Angelina Grimké Weld*. Boston: George Ellis, 1880.

Weld, Theodore, Angelina Grimké Weld, and Sarah Grimké. *American Slavery as It Is: Testimony of a Thousand Witnesses*. New York: American Anti-Slavery Society, 1839.

Weld, Theodore, Angelina Grimké Weld, and Sarah Grimké. *Letters of Theodore Dwight Weld, Angelina Grimké Weld, and Sarah Grimké*, edited by Gilbert Barnes and Dwight Dumond, Vols. 1–2. New York: D. Appleton–Century Co., 1934.

Weld-Grimké Family Papers, William L. Clements Library, University of Michigan.

Whipper, William, Alfred Niger, and Augustus Price. *Minutes of the Fifth Annual Convention for the Improvement of the Free People of Colour in the United States*. Philadelphia: William P. Gibbons, 1835.

Whittier, John Greenleaf. *The Poetical Works of John Greenleaf Whittier*, edited by W. Garrett Horder. New York: Henry Frowde, 1904.

Whittier, John Greenleaf. *Whittier Correspondence from the Oak Knoll Collections, 1830–1892*, Vol. 2, edited by John Albree. Salem, MA: Essex Book & Print Club, 1910.

Williams, Peter, Jr. Letter to the Citizens of New-York, July 14, 1834.

Willson, Joseph. *Sketches of the Higher Classes of Colored Society in Philadelphia*. Philadelphia: Merrihew and Thompson, 1841.

Wilson, James Grant, ed. *The Memorial History of the City of New-York, from Its First Settlement to the Year 1892*, Vol. 3. New York: New-York History Co., 1893.

Wright, Theodore. *A Pastoral Letter, Addressed to the Colored Presbyterian Church, in the City of New York, June 20th, 1832.* New York, 1832.

SECONDARY SOURCES

Abzug, Robert. "The Influence of Garrisonian Abolitionists' Fears of Slave Violence on the Antislavery Argument, 1829–40." *Journal of Negro History* 55, no. 1 (1970): 15–26.

Abzug, Robert. *Passionate Liberator: Theodore Dwight Weld and the Dilemma of Reform.* New York: Oxford University Press, 1980.

Adeleke, Tunde. "Afro-Americans and Moral Suasion: The Debate in the 1830s." *Journal of Negro History* 83, no. 2 (1998): 127–142.

Bacon, Jacqueline. "The History of Freedom's Journal: A Study in Empowerment and Community." *Journal of African American History* 88, no. 1 (2003): 1–20.

Bacon, Margaret Hope. *But One Race: The Life of Robert Purvis.* Albany: State University of New York Press, 2007.

Bacon, Margaret Hope. "New Light on Sarah Mapps Douglass and Her Reconciliation with Friends." *Quaker History* (2001): 28–49.

Barnes, Gilbert Hobbs. *The Anti-Slavery Impulse: 1830–1844.* New York: American Historical Association, 1933.

Barrett, Ruth. "Abolitionist Literature and the Mails in Jackson's Time." Thesis, University of Omaha, 1950.

Belasco, Susan. "Harriet Martineau's Black Hero and the American Antislavery Movement." *Nineteenth-Century Literature* 5, no. 2 (2000): 157–194.

Berkin, Carol. *Civil War Wives: The Lives and Times of Angelina Grimké Weld, Varina Howell Davis & Julia Dent Grant.* New York: Vintage, 2010.

Bogar, Thomas A. *Thomas Hamblin and the Bowery Theatre: The New York Reign of "Blood and Thunder" Melodramas.* London: Palgrave Macmillan, 2018.

Boromé, Joseph A., Jacob C. White, Robert B. Ayres, and J. M. McKim. "The Vigilant Committee of Philadelphia." *Pennsylvania Magazine of History and Biography* 92, no. 3 (1968): 320–351.

Brathwaite, Jamila Shabazz. "The Black Vigilance Movement in Nineteenth Century New York City." Thesis, City College of the City University of New York, 2011.

Breen, Patrick H. "The Female Antislavery Petition Campaign of 1831–32." *Virginia Magazine of History and Biography* 110, no. 3 (2002): 377–398.

Brown, Ira V. "Cradle of Feminism: The Philadelphia Female Anti-Slavery Society, 1833–1840." *Pennsylvania Magazine of History and Biography* 102, no. 2 (1978): 143–166.

Buckmaster, Henrietta. *Let My People Go: The Story of the Underground Railroad and the Growth of the Abolition Movement.* New York: Harper and Bros., 1941.

Burrows, Edwin G., and Mike Wallace, *Gotham: A History of New York City to 1898.* New York: Oxford University Press, 1998.

Cain, William E., ed. *William Lloyd Garrison and the Fight against Slavery: Selections from* The Liberator. New York: St. Martin's Press, 1995.

Carpenter, Daniel, and Colin D. Moore. "When Canvassers Became Activists: Antislavery Petitioning and the Political Mobilization of American Women." *American Political Science Review* 108, no. 3 (2014): 479–498.

Cima, Gay Gibson. *Performing Anti-Slavery: Activist Women on Antebellum Stages.* Cambridge, UK: Cambridge University Press, 2014.

Cole, Charles, Jr. "The Free Church Movement in New York City." *New York History* 34, no. 3 (1953): 284–297.

Cromwell, John W. "The Aftermath of Nat Turner's Insurrection." *Journal of Negro History* 5, no. 2 (1920): 208–234.

Cromwell, Otelia. *Lucretia Mott.* Cambridge, MA: Harvard University Press, 1958.

Crouthamel, James L. "James Watson Webb: Mercantile Editor." *New York History* 41, no. 4 (1960): 400–422.

Davis, David Brion. *The Problem of Slavery in the Age of Emancipation.* New York: Alfred A. Knopf, 2014.

Demos, John. "The Antislavery Movement and the Problem of Violent 'Means.'" *New England Quarterly* 37, no. 4 (1964): 501–526.

Dillon, Merton Lynn. *The Abolitionists: The Growth of a Dissenting Minority.* DeKalb: Northern Illinois University Press, 1974.

Drago, Elliott. "Neither Northern nor Southern: The Politics of Slavery and Freedom in Philadelphia, 1820–1847." PhD diss., Temple University, 2017.

Dumond, Dwight Lowell. *Antislavery: The Crusade for Freedom in America.* Ann Arbor: University of Michigan Press, 1961.

Eaton, Clement. "Censorship of the Southern Mails." *American Historical Review* 48, no. 2 (1943): 266–280.

Ellingwood, Ken. *First to Fall: Elijah Lovejoy's Fight for a Free Press in the Age of Slavery.* New York: Pegasus, 2021.

Faust, Drew Gilpin. *James Henry Hammond and the Old South: A Design for Mastery.* Baton Rouge, LA: LSU Press, 1985.

Feldberg, Michael. *The Turbulent Era: Riot and Disorder in Jacksonian America.* New York: Oxford University Press, 1980.

Forbes, Ella. "African-American Resistance to Colonization." *Journal of Black Studies* 21, no. 2 (1990): 210–223.

Franklin, John Hope. *From Slavery to Freedom: A History of African Americans.* New York: Knopf, 1947.

Franklin, V. P. "'They Rose and Fell Together': African American Educators and Community Leadership, 1795–1954." *Journal of Education* 172, no. 3 (1990): 39–64.

Friedman, Lawrence. "Confidence and Pertinacity in Evangelical Abolitionism: Lewis Tappan's Circle." *American Quarterly* 31, no. 1 (1979): 81–106.

Garvey, Ellen Gruber. "Nineteenth-Century Abolitionists and the Databases They Created." *Legacy* 27, no. 2 (2010): 357–366.

Gernes, Todd S. "Poetic Justice: Sarah Forten, Eliza Earle, and the Paradox of Intellectual Property." *New England Quarterly* 71, no. 2 (1998): 229–265.

Gilje, Paul. *Rioting in America.* Bloomington: Indiana University Press, 1996.

Gilje, Paul. *The Road to Mobocracy: Popular Disorder in New York City, 1763–1834.* Chapel Hill: University of North Carolina Press, 1987.

Gillette, Howard, Jr., ed., *Southern City, National Ambition: The Growth of Early Washington, D.C.: 1800–1860*. Washington, DC: George Washington University Center for Washington Area Studies, 1995.

Goddu, Teresa. "Anti-Slavery's Panoramic Perspective." *MELUS* 39, no. 2 (2014): 12–41.

Goodman, Paul. *Of One Blood: Abolitionism and the Origins of Racial Equality*. Berkeley: University of California Press, 1998.

"The Great New York Fire of 1835 and the Marketing of Disaster." New-York Historical Society, blog.nyhistory.org/the-great-new-york-fire-of-1835-and-the-marketing-of-disaster.

Grimsted, David. *American Mobbing, 1828–1861: Toward Civil War*. New York: Oxford University Press, 1998.

Grimsted, David. "Rioting in Its Jacksonian Setting." *American Historical Review* 77, no. 2 (1972): 361–397.

Gross, Bella. "Life and Times of Theodore S. Wright, 1797–1847." *Negro History Bulletin* 3, no. 9 (1940): 133–138.

Grubbs, Patrick. "Riots (1830s and 1840s)." Encyclopedia of Greater Philadelphia. philadelphianencyclopedia.org.

Hammett, Theodore M. "Two Mobs of Jacksonian Boston: Ideology and Interest." *Journal of American History* 62, no. 4 (1976): 845–868.

Harris, Leslie M. *In the Shadow of Slavery: African Americans in New York City, 1626–1863*. Chicago: University of Chicago Press, 2004.

Harwood, Thomas F. "British Evangelical Abolitionism and American Churches in the 1830's." *Journal of Southern History* 28, no. 3 (1962): 287–306.

Henderson, Christina. "Sympathetic Violence: Maria Stewart's Antebellum Vision of African American Resistance." *MELUS* 3, no. 4 (2013): 52–75.

Henig, Gerald. "The Jacksonian Attitude toward Abolitionism in the 1830's." *Tennessee Historical Quarterly* 28, no. 1 (1969): 42–56.

Hershberg, Theodore. "Free Blacks in Antebellum Philadelphia: A Study of Ex-Slaves, Freeborn, and Socioeconomic Decline." *Journal of Social History* 5, no. 2 (1971–1972): 183–209.

Hirsch, Leo, Jr. "The Free Negro in New York." *Journal of Negro History* 16, no. 4 (1931): 415–453.

Hirsch, Leo, Jr. "The Slave in New York." *Journal of Negro History* 16, no. 4 (1931): 383–414.

Historical Society of Pennsylvania. "Our Sphere of Influence: Women Activists and the Philadelphia Female Anti-Slavery Society." Exploring Diversity in Pennsylvania History Series, www.hsp.org.

Hodges, Graham Russell Gao. *David Ruggles: A Radical Black Abolitionist and the Underground Railroad in New York City*. Chapel Hill: University of North Carolina Press, 2010.

Horton, John, and Lois Horton. *In Hope of Liberty: Culture, Community and Protest among Northern Free Blacks, 1700–1860*. New York: Oxford University Press, 1998.

Jacobs, Donald M. "William Lloyd Garrison's Liberator and Boston's Blacks, 1830–1865." *New England Quarterly* 44, no. 2 (1971): 259–277.

Jeffrey, Julie Roy. "The Liberty Women of Boston: Evangelicalism and Antislavery Politics." *New England Quarterly* 85, no. 1 (2012): 38–77.

July, Robert William. *The Essential New Yorker, Gulian Crommelin Verplanck*. Durham, NC: Duke University Press, 1951.

Kelley, Mary. "'Talents Committed to Your Care': Reading and Writing Radical Abolitionism in Antebellum America." *New England Quarterly* 88, no. 1 (2015): 37–72.

Kerber, Linda K. "Abolitionists and Amalgamators: The New York City Race Riots of 1834." *New York History* 48, no. 1 (1967): 28–39.

Lane, Roger. "Criminal Violence in America: The First Hundred Years." *Annals of the American Academy of Political and Social Science* 423 (1976): 1–13.

Lane, Vivian Simmons. "The Tappan Brothers." *Negro History Bulletin* 6, no. 8 (1943): 171–172.

Lapsansky, Emma Jones. "'Since They Got Those Separate Churches': Afro-Americans and Racism in Jacksonian Philadelphia." *American Quarterly* 32, no. 1 (1980): 54–78.

Lasser, Carol. "Voyeuristic Abolitionism: Sex, Gender, and the Transformation of Antislavery Rhetoric." *Journal of the Early Republic* 28, no. 1 (2008): 83–114.

Lerner, Gerda. *The Grimké Sisters from South Carolina: Pioneers for Women's Rights and Abolition.* New York: Houghton Mifflin, 1967.

Lloyd, Gordon, and Jenny S. Martinez. "The Slave Trade Clause." National Constitution Center, constitutioncenter.org.

Loveland, Anne. "Evangelicalism and 'Immediate Emancipation' in American Antislavery Thought." *Journal of Southern History* 32, no. 2 (1966): 172–188.

Lumpkin, Katherine DuPre. *The Emancipation of Angelina Grimké.* Chapel Hill: University of North Carolina Press, 1974.

Mayer, Henry. *All on Fire: William Lloyd Garrison and the Abolition of Slavery.* New York: St. Martin's Press, 1998.

Maynard, Douglas H. "The World's Anti-Slavery Convention of 1840." *Mississippi Valley Historical Review* 47, no. 3 (1960): 452–471.

McCarthy, Timothy Patrick, and John Stauffer, eds. *Prophets of Protest: Reconsidering the History of American Abolitionism.* New York: W. W. Norton, 2006.

McDaniel, William Caleb. "The Bonds and Boundaries of Antislavery." *Journal of the Civil War Era* 4, no. 1 (2014): 84–105.

McDaniel, William Caleb. "Our Country Is the World: Radical American Abolitionists Abroad." PhD diss., Johns Hopkins University, 2006.

McFaul, John M. "Expediency vs. Morality: Jacksonian Politics and Slavery." *Journal of American History* 62, no. 1 (1975): 24–39.

McWilliams, John C. "'Men of Colour': Race, Riots, and Black Firefighters' Struggle for Equality from the AFA to the Valiants." *Journal of Social History* 41, no. 1 (2007): 105–125.

Meinke, Scott R. "Slavery, Partisanship, and Procedure in the U.S. House: The Gag Rule, 1836–1845." *Legislative Studies Quarterly* 32, no. 1 (2007): 33–57.

Mercieca, Jennifer Rose. "The Culture of Honor: How Slaveholders Responded to the Abolitionist Mail Crisis of 1835." *Rhetoric and Public Affairs* 10, no. 1 (2007): 51–76.

Merrill, Walter M. *Against Wind and Tide: A Biography of William Lloyd Garrison.* Cambridge, MA: Harvard University Press, 1963.

Milne, Claudia. "On the Grounds of the Fresh Water Pond: The Free-Black Community at Five Points, 1810–1834." *International Journal of Historical Archaeology* 6, no. 2 (2002): 127–142.

Moore, Moses, Jr. "Revisiting the Legacy of Black Presbyterians." *Journal of Presbyterian History* 84, no. 1 (2006): 37–44.

Moses, Wilson, ed. *Classic Black Nationalism: From the American Revolution to Marcus Garvey.* New York: New York University Press, 1996.

Moulton, Amber. "Closing the 'Floodgate of Impurity': Moral Reform, Antislavery, and Interracial Marriage in Antebellum Massachusetts." *Journal of the Civil War Era* 3, no. 1 (2013): 2–34.

Myers, John. "The Beginnings of Anti-Slavery Agencies in New York State, 1833–1836." *Proceedings of the New York State Historical Association* 60 (1962): 149–181.

Myers, John. "The Early Antislavery Agency System in Pennsylvania." *Pennsylvania History* 31, no. 1 (1964): 62–86.

Nash, Gary. *Forging Freedom: The Formation of Philadelphia's Black Community, 1720–1840.* Cambridge, MA: Harvard University Press, 1988.

Newman, Richard S. *The Transformation of American Abolitionism: Fighting Slavery in the Early Republic.* Chapel Hill: University of North Carolina Press, 2002.

Nye, Russel M. *Fettered Freedom: Civil Liberties and the Slavery Controversy, 1830–1860.* East Lansing: Michigan State University Press, 1963.

Oberholtzer, Ellis Paxson. *Philadelphia: A History of the City and Its People, a Record of 225 Years,* Vol. 2. Philadelphia: J. S. Clarke, 1912.

O'Connor, Peter. "The Inextinguishable Struggle between North and South: American Sectionalism in the British Mind, 1832–1863." Thesis, University of Northumbria, 2014.

Osborn, Ronald. "William Lloyd Garrison and the United States Constitution: The Political Evolution of an American Radical." *Journal of Law and Religion* 24, no. 1 (2008–2009): 65–88.

Pease, Jane, and William Pease. *Bound with Them in Chains: A Biographical History of the Antislavery Movement.* Westport, CT: Greenwood Press, 1972.

Pease, Jane, and William Pease. *They Who Would Be Free: Blacks' Search for Freedom, 1830–1861.* New York: Atheneum, 1974.

Perry, Mark. *Lift Up Thy Voice: The Grimké Family's Journey from Slaveholders to Civil Rights Leaders.* New York: Viking Penguin, 2001.

Pessen, Edward. "We Are All Jeffersonians, We Are All Jacksonians: Or a Pox on Stultifying Periodizations." *Journal of the Early Republic* 1, no. 1 (1981): 1–26.

Pierson, Michael D. "'Slavery Cannot Be Covered Up with Broadcloth or a Bandanna': The Evolution of White Abolitionist Attacks on the 'Patriarchal Institution.'" *Journal of the Early Republic* 25, no. 3 (2005): 383–415.

Polgar, Paul J. *Standard Bearers of Equality: America's First Abolition Movement.* Chapel Hill: University of North Carolina Press, 2019.

Pomeroy, Sarah Gertrude. *Little-Known Sisters of Well-Known Men.* Boston: Dana Estes, 1912.

Porter, Dorothy B. "David Ruggles, An Apostle of Human Rights." *Journal of Negro History* 28, no. 1 (1943): 23–50.

Porter, Dorothy B. "The Organized Educational Activities of Negro Literary Societies, 1828–1846." *Journal of Negro Education* 5, no. 4 (1936): 555–576.

Prince, Carl E. "The Great 'Riot Year': Jacksonian Democracy and Patterns of Violence in 1834." *Journal of the Early Republic* 5, no. 1 (1985): 1–19.

Quarles, Benjamin. *Black Abolitionists.* New York: Da Capo Press, 1969.

Rael, Patrick. *Black Identity and Black Protest in the Antebellum North.* Chapel Hill: University of North Carolina Press, 2002.

Ratner, Lorman. "Northern Concern for Social Order as Cause for Rejecting Anti-Slavery, 1831–1840." *The Historian* 28, no. 1 (1965): 1–18.

Ratner, Lorman. *Powder Keg: Northern Opposition to the Anti-Slavery Movement, 1831–1840*. New York: Basic Books, 1968.

Remini, Robert. *Andrew Jackson: The Course of American Democracy, 1833–1845*, Vol. 3. Baltimore: Johns Hopkins University Press, 1984.

Rice, C. Duncan. "The Anti-Slavery Mission of George Thompson to the United States, 1834–1835." *Journal of American Studies* 2, no. 1 (1968): 13–31.

Richards, Leonard L. *Gentlemen of Property and Standing: Anti-Abolition Mobs in Jacksonian America*. London: Oxford University Press, 1970.

Risley, Ford. *Abolition and the Press: The Moral Struggle Against Slavery*. Evanston, IL: Northwestern University Press, 2008.

Rogers, Delmer D. "Public Music Performances in New York City from 1800 to 1850." *Inter-American Yearbook of Musical Research* 6 (1970): 5–50.

Rogers, Melvin L. "David Walker and the Political Power of the Appeal." *Political Theory* 43, no. 2 (2015): 208–233.

Rorabaugh, W. J. *The Alcoholic Republic: An American Tradition*. New York: Oxford University Press, 1979.

Ross, Kenneth J. "We Speak for Ourselves: What Samuel Cornish Learned from John Gloucester," Presbyterian Historical Society, February 20, 2019, https://www.history.pcusa.org/blog/2019/02/we-speak-ourselves-what-samuel-cornish-learned-john-gloucester.

Runcie, John. "'Hunting the Nigs' in Philadelphia: The Race Riot of August 1834." *Pennsylvania History: A Journal of Mid-Atlantic Studies* 39, no. 2 (1972): 187–218.

Salerno, Beth A. *Sister Societies: Women's Antislavery Organizations in Antebellum America*. DeKalb: Northern Illinois University Press, 2005.

Savage, W. Sherman. *The Controversy over the Distribution of Abolition Literature, 1830–1860*. Washington, DC: Association for the Study of Negro Life and History, 1938.

Sinha, Manisha. *The Slave's Cause: A History of Abolition*. New Haven, CT: Yale University Press, 2016.

Sklar, K. K. *Women's Rights Emerges Within the Antislavery Movement, 1830–1870*. New York: St. Martin's Press, 2000.

Small, Miriam R., and Edwin W. Small. "Prudence Crandall, Champion of Negro Education." *New England Quarterly* 17, no. 4 (1944): 506–529.

Sterling, Dorothy. *Ahead of Her Time: Abby Kelley and the Politics of Antislavery*. New York: W. W. Norton and Co., 1991.

Sterling, Dorothy, ed. *We Are Your Sisters: Black Women in the Nineteenth Century*. New York: W. W. Norton, 1984.

Stewart, James Brewer. "The Emergence of Racial Modernity and the Rise of the White North, 1790–1840." *Journal of the Early Republic* 18, no. 2 (1998): 181–217.

Strausbaugh, John. *City of Sedition: The History of New York City during the Civil War*. New York: Twelve/Hachette, 2016.

Sumler-Lewis, Janice. "The Forten-Purvis Women of Philadelphia and the American Anti-Slavery Crusade." *Journal of Negro History* 66, no. 4 (1981–1982): 281–288.

Sumler-Lewis, Janice. "The Fortens of Philadelphia: An Afro-American Family and Nineteenth-Century Reform." PhD diss., Georgetown University, 1978.

Swift, David E. *Black Prophets of Justice: Activist Clergy before the Civil War*. Baton Rouge: Louisiana State University Press, 1989.

Thompson, J. Earl, Jr. "Lyman Beecher's Long Road to Conservative Abolitionism." *Church History* 42, no. 1 (1973): 89–109.

Todras, Ellen. *Angelina Grimké: Voice of Abolition*. North Haven, CT: Linnet Books, 1999.

Trendel, Robert. "The Expurgation of Antislavery Materials by American Presses." *Journal of Negro History* 58, no. 3 (1973): 271–290.

Trotter, Joe, and Eric Ledell Smith, eds. *African Americans in Pennsylvania: Shifting Historical Perspectives*. University Park, PA: Penn State University Press, 1994.

van Deburg, William L. "William Lloyd Garrison and the 'Pro-Slavery Priesthood': The Changing Beliefs of An Evangelical Reformer, 1830–1840." *Journal of the American Academy of Religion* 43, no. 2 (1975): 224–237.

Vetter, Lisa Pace. "Harriet Martineau on the Theory and Practice of Democracy in America." *Political Theory* 36, no. 3 (2008): 424–455.

Wesley, Charles H. "The Negro in the Organization of Abolition." *Phylon* 2, no. 3 (1941): 223–235.

Wesley, Charles H. "The Negroes of New York in the Emancipation Movement." *Journal of Negro History* 24, no. 1 (1939): 65–103.

White, Barbara. *The Beecher Sisters*. New Haven, CT: Yale University Press, 2003.

White House Historical Association. "Slavery in the President's Neighborhood." whitehousehistory.org.

Williams, Donald E. *Prudence Crandall's Legacy: The Fight for Equality in the 1830s, Dred Scott, and Brown v. Board of Education*. Middletown, CT: Wesleyan University Press, 2014.

Winch, Julie. *A Gentleman of Color: The Life of James Forten*. New York: Oxford University Press, 2002.

Winch, Julie. "Sarah Forten's Anti-Slavery Networks." In *Women's Rights and Transatlantic Antislavery in the Era of Emancipation*, edited by Kathryn Kish Sklar and James B. Stewart, 143–157. New Haven, CT: Yale University Press, 2007.

Woodson, Carter. *A History of the Negro Church*. Washington, DC: Associated Publishers, 1921.

Wormley, G. Smith. "Prudence Crandall." *Journal of Negro History* 8, no. 1 (1923): 72–80.

Wyatt-Brown, Bertram. "The Abolitionists' Postal Campaign of 1835." *Journal of Negro History* 50, no. 4 (1965): 227–238.

Wyatt-Brown, Bertram. *Lewis Tappan and the Evangelical War against Slavery*. Cleveland: Case Western Reserve University Press, 1969.

Wyly-Jones, Susan. "The 1835 Anti-Abolition Meetings in the South: A New Look at the Controversy over the Abolition Postal Campaign." *Civil War History* 47, no. 4 (2001): 289–309.

Yee, Shirley. *Black Women Abolitionists: A Study in Activism, 1828–1860*. Knoxville: University of Tennessee Press, 1992.

Yellin, Jean Fagan. *The Abolitionist Sisterhood: Women's Political Culture in Antebellum America*. Ithaca, NY: Cornell University Press, 1994.

Zaeske, Susan. "'The South Arose as One Man': Gender and Sectionalism in Antislavery Petition Debates, 1835–1845." *Rhetoric and Public Affairs* 12, no. 3 (2009): 341–368.

Zorn, Roman J. "The New England Anti-Slavery Society: Pioneer Abolition Organization."
 Journal of Negro History 42, no. 3 (1957): 157–176.

NEWSPAPERS

American and Foreign Anti-Slavery Reporter
American Anti-Slavery Almanac
The Anti-Slavery Record
Augusta Chronicle
Bicknell's Reporter
Boston Centinel
Boston Daily Advocate
Boston Morning Post
Boston Recorder
Brooklyn Advertiser
Charleston Courier
Charleston Mercury
Charleston Southern Patriot
Christian Advocate and Journal
Colored American
Commercial Advertiser (New York)
Commercial Gazette (Boston)
Courier and Enquirer (New York)
The Emancipator
Evening Post (New York)
Freedom's Journal
The Genius of Universal Emancipation
Georgetown Columbian and Daily Advertiser
Human Rights
Journal of Commerce
The Liberator
Mirror of Liberty
National Anti-Slavery Standard
National Enquirer
National Intelligencer
National Reformer
New England Magazine
New Hampshire Patriot
New York American
New York Baptist Register
New-York Evangelist
New York Herald
New-York Sentinel
New York Sun
New York Transcript

Niles' Weekly Register
Norfolk Herald
Pennsylvania Inquirer
The Pennsylvanian
Philadelphia Gazette
Philadelphia Inquirer
Quarterly Anti-Slavery Magazine
The Reformer
Richmond Enquirer
The Rights of All
The Slave's Friend
U.S. Gazette
Washington Globe
Weekly Advocate

INDEX

4/22